NATION *AT* PLAY

Contemporary Asia in the World

Contemporary Asia in the World
David C. Kang and Victor D. Cha, Editors

This series aims to address a gap in the public-policy and scholarly discussion of Asia. It seeks to promote books and studies that are on the cutting edge of their disciplines or promote multi-disciplinary or interdisciplinary research but are also accessible to a wider readership. The editors seek to showcase the best scholarly and public-policy arguments on Asia from any field, including politics, history, economics, and cultural studies.

NATION AT PLAY

A HISTORY OF SPORT IN INDIA

RONOJOY SEN

COLUMBIA UNIVERSITY PRESS   New York

COLUMBIA UNIVERSITY PRESS

PUBLISHERS SINCE 1893

NEW YORK   CHICHESTER, WEST SUSSEX

CUP.COLUMBIA.EDU

Library of Congress Cataloging-in-Publication Data

Sen, Ronojoy.

Nation at play : a history of sport in India / Ronojoy Sen.

pages   cm

Includes bibliographical references and index.

ISBN 978-0-231-16490-0 (cloth : alk. paper) — ISBN 978-0-231-53993-7 (electronic)

1. Sports—India—History.   2. Sports—Social aspects—India.

3. India—Social life and customs.   I. Title.

GV653.S46   2015

796.0954—dc23   2015020972

Columbia University Press books are printed on permanent and durable acid-free paper.

This book is printed on paper with recycled content.

Printed in the United States of America

c 10 9 8 7 6 5 4 3 2 1

References to websites (URLs) were accurate at the time of writing. Neither the author
nor Columbia University Press is responsible for URLs that may have expired or changed
since the manuscript was prepared.

For Rousseau (my son, not the philosopher),
who is obsessed with cricket but has also begun to appreciate other sports.

CONTENTS

ACKNOWLEDGMENTS

THIS BOOK HAS BEEN A LONG TIME IN THE MAKING, GESTATING IN my head for several months before I actually put finger to keyboard. The opportunity to write it came when I began a fellowship at the Institute of South Asian Studies (ISAS) at the National University of Singapore (NUS). The illegitimacy of sport in the hard-nosed world of politics and policy, which I'm supposed to specialize in, meant that much of the research and writing for the book was done after office hours, in the evenings, late at night, and over weekends. This also meant that very little of the book was presented in public. The exception was the section on Mohammedan Sporting, which I presented at a conference on Islam in South Asia at the ISAS and has appeared in an edited volume.

Writing a book is, of course, not a solitary endeavor. In Singapore, Robin Jeffrey, who is most catholic when it comes to following sports, was an exceptionally encouraging interlocutor. He not only discussed my research and read parts of this book but also put me on to several fruitful leads. Others at NUS, John Harriss in particular, read and commented on parts of the book. I am thankful to the ISAS and the Asia Research Institute (ARI) and their directors, Tan Tai Yong and Prasenjit Duara, respectively, for providing a congenial work environment.

Among my friends and colleagues, special thanks are due to Abheek Barman, Avijit Ghosh, Niladri Mazumder, Aakar Patel, Tushita Patel, Archishman Chakraborty (Bambi), Subodh Varma, Saikat Ray, Moyukh Chatterjee, Sandeeep Ray (Shandy), Michiel Baas, Boria Majnmdar, Nalin Mehta, and Arun Thiruvengadam. Over the years, Niladri and I have watched several sports events together, on television and, on many occasions, at Eden Gardens. Avijit was my companion during a visit to Mumbai's (Bombay's) Azad Maidan and gave me access to his many writings on sports in the *Telegraph* and *Pioneer* from the pre-Internet era. Kausik Bandyopadhyay was unstinting in his support for the project and provided me with valuable material in Bengali, as did Dwaipayan Bhattacharya. Souvik Naha helped me with research in New Delhi. (Field) hockey enthusiasts K. Arumugam and P. K. Mohan kindly passed on research materials. Without the help of Krishnendu Bandyopadhyay, I would not have been able to get some of the images used in the book. Thanks to Saunak Sen for sending me material from San Francisco on Gobor Guha. I benefited greatly from chats with Ashis Nandy, Ramachandra Guha, and Rupak Saha. My teachers and mentors, Lloyd and Susanne Rudolph, encouraged this project. Their amazing breadth of scholarship covers a fascinating aspect of the story of sports in India: polo in Rajasthan. I would like to thank as well my teachers at Presidency College for sparking an abiding interest in history, which stood me in good stead while researching this book. Let me also record my thanks to the two anonymous reviewers of my manuscript.

This book would not have been complete without conversations with some of India's finest sportspersons. I consider myself blessed that I was able to interview Leslie Claudius (who died while the book was being written), Ahmed Khan, Chuni Goswami, Gurbux Singh, Ramanathan Krishnan, and Arumainayagam. The book is a tribute to them and the many sportspersons and administrators who feature in the following pages. The morning spent with Ibomcha Singh in Imphal was an eye-opener. Among the more intriguing locations that I visited was a small museum dedicated to the Bengali wrestler Gobor Guha in Goabagan Lane, not far from where my parents-in-law, Asutosh and Mitali Law, used to stay (and my mother-in-law still does) in north Kolkata (Calcutta). My father-in-law, who unexpectedly passed away shortly after I'd finished writing the book, was a fount of information about north Kolkata. He would have been extremely happy to see the book in print.

I wish to thank the staff at the NUS libraries for their research support. My thanks to the staff of the Nehru Memorial Museum Library, the British Library, the MCC library at Lord's, the Melbourne Cricket Club library, the *Times of India* library in Delhi, the Ananda Bazar Patrika library, the National Library in Kolkata, and the Bangiya Sahitya Parishad library. I am especially grateful to Shakti Roy, Mahesh Rangarajan, Adam Chadwick, and Trevor Ruddell. My appreciation goes to the International Olympic Committee for awarding me a fellowship to conduct research at the Olympic Museum in Lausanne, Switzerland. My thanks, too, to Anne Routon, Leslie Kriesel, and Whitney Johnson of Columbia University Press for patiently shepherding the book. I am grateful to Margaret B. Yamashita for doing an excellent job of editing the manuscript.

I have tried my hand at various sports, but without any success whatsoever. Two locations were central to my sports endeavors: the tiny park in our housing complex in Kolkata where my brother Sujoy and I grew up and where my parents, Sumitro and Manjusri Sen, still live; and the grounds of St. Xavier's School in Kolkata where I studied from age five to sixteen. My romance with sports is inextricably tied to these two locales and the many friends with whom I spent hours playing games.

Finally, as always, my deepest gratitude goes to Debakshi for tolerating the odd hours and weekends spent on a subject of marginal importance to her. This book was written while our son Rousseau (aka Souryaditya) grew rapidly from childhood to early adolescence. He has been an enthusiastic companion in watching numerous sports events, in both stadiums and our living room. He was perplexed by how long it took me to complete the book, but one day perhaps he'll understand why.

Finally, a note on names: the Indian government changed the name Bombay to Mumbai in 1996 and Calcutta to Kolkata in 2001. But because so many of the organizations, clubs, teams, and the like have either Bombay or Calcutta in their official title, I usually have used the older versions of these names.

In addition, I should assure American readers that in India, hockey refers to field hockey, not ice hockey, and of course, football in India (and the rest of the world) is what Americans call soccer.

NATION *AT* PLAY

INTRODUCTION

A FEW YEARS BEFORE LARGE PARTS OF INDIA ROSE UP IN
rebellion against British rule in 1857, Horatio Smith wrote in the *Calcutta
Review* of the Indian that he and the rest of his countrymen were most familiar with:

> The most superficial observer of Bengali manners must know that their
> games and sports are, for the most part, sedentary ... [h]is maxim being
> that "walking is better than running, standing than walking, sitting than
> standing, and lying down best of all," his amusements have to be for the
> most part sedentary.[1]

He then went on to list the sports that the Bengali engaged in. Besides the
usual suspects like *shatranj* (chess), *pasha* (gambling with dice), cards, marble
throwing, and kite flying, some distinctly nonsedentary sports were included
on the list—wrestling, *hadu-gudu* (better known as *kabaddi*, a team pursuit
game), gymnastics, and swimming. While Smith's description of a Bengali
neatly dovetailed with the prevalent British theories of dividing Indians
into nonmartial—of which the Bengali was the prime example—and martial
races, his list of sports would probably have held true for most of India.

Long before the British entered the scene, Indians were involved in sports. It's not entirely by accident that the premier awards for sportspersons in India are named Arjuna awards and those for coaches are named after Dronacharya, both central figures in the great Indian epic the Mahabharata. In a civilization in which epics such as the Mahabharata still have a greater hold on the imagination than cut-and-dried historical narratives, this is perhaps not unnatural. But the nomenclature of the awards is also a clue to the hoary origin of organized sports in India. Difficult as it might be to imagine, there was life before cricket and the various games introduced to the Indian subcontinent by the British. Not all the ancient sports have survived, and some of them are perhaps lost forever. But many sports, such as wrestling, whose origins go back several centuries, still are played. And others, like cricket, which was introduced along with other sports by the British in the long nineteenth century, Indians have made their own.

This book does not pretend to be a comprehensive history of each and every sport ever played in India. That task is best left to an encyclopedia, of which there are some available. Instead, I look broadly at the evolution of sports and play, especially those that enjoy mass popularity in India, and what it says about Indians. The book is idiosyncratic to the extent that some sports are given more attention, by both choice and accident. Lurking in the background are two questions that will occur to any sports lover, or indeed any observer of Indian society. First, how and why has cricket come to dominate the Indian consciousness? Second, why has a nation of a billion-plus people failed so miserably in international sporting competitions such as the Olympics? There are probably some fairly straightforward answers to these questions, but I have chosen to take a long and sometimes tortuous journey to answer these questions. I hope my travel will reveal much more about Indian society than the response by a prominent sports administrator in the 1980s: "Sport is against our Indian ethos, our entire cultural tradition."[2]

In any study of this sort, it's best to sort out some issues of definition right at the beginning. This is not a pedantic exercise, since either an overtly expansive or a restrictive definition runs the risk of losing sight of the larger connections between sports and society. What does one mean by sports? And do we distinguish between sports and play? Or, indeed, between sports and activities that might be more properly classified as leisure or recreation? While the study of sports has never been central to any of the traditional academic disciplines, from very early on, anthropologists showed a keen interest in understanding the role of sports, particularly in traditional societies. One of the earliest such efforts was by Edward Burnett Tylor—sometimes referred to as the father of anthropology—who in an 1879 article, "The History of the Games," looked at the evolution of various games both complex and simple. Tylor's lead was followed by American anthropologists like James Mooney and Stewart Culin, who were particularly interested in Native American games.[3] Others cast their net in more remote corners of the world, the most notable being Raymond Firth's lengthy article on a Polynesian dart match.

However, it is the 1930s' classic, *Homo Ludens (Man the Player)*, by the Dutch historian Johan Huizinga, that is best remembered today. For Huizinga, nearly every human activity had a "play element." Play was "freedom" or a stepping out of ordinary or real life;[4] play also was the creation of order by bringing a "temporary, a limited perfection" into the confusion of life.[5] In the 1960s, the French anthropologist Roger Caillois critiqued Huizinga's work to come up with a more refined definition of play: "In effect, play is essentially a separate occupation, carefully isolated from the rest of life, and generally is engaged in with precise limits of time and space."[6] Caillois introduced different categories of play, including agonistic games that are competitive and based on speed, endurance, strength, memory, skill, and ingenuity.[7] I also should mention anthropologist Clifford Geertz's classic essay, "Deep Play: Notes on a Balinese Cockfight," which peels away the many layers of a seemingly simple event to say profound things about Balinese society.

In the latter half of the twentieth century, sports studies became a legitimate field in its own right, with a proliferation of books and articles on different aspects of sport. I don't want to go into this literature except to flag two influential authors of the genre. The sociologists Norbert Elias and Eric Dunning analyzed the evolution of sport in the context of a gradual "civilizing process" in which it gradually came to "serve as symbolic representations of a non-violent, non-military form of competition."[8] Another important figure is American historian Allen Guttmann, who, in his *From Ritual to Record*, was critical of Huizinga for lumping together all contests and calling them games. Guttmann makes a sharp distinction between modern sports, beginning around the eighteenth century, and its premodern variants, such as the ancient Olympic Games, the Mayan or Aztec ball games, and the jousting tournaments of medieval Europe. Guttmann, using a self-confessedly Weberian framework, lists seven characteristics that make modern sports what they are: secularism, equality of opportunity, specialization of roles, rationalization, bureaucratic organization, quantification, and a quest for records. In language reminiscent of Max Weber in the *Protestant Ethic and the Spirit of Capitalism*, Guttmann summed up the nature of modern sport thus: "Once the gods have vanished from Mount Olympus or from Dante's paradise, we can no longer run to appease them or to save our souls, but we can set a new record. It is a uniquely modern form of immortality."[9] Indeed, Michael Mandelbaum took this argument forward by pointing out that sports has much in common with organized religion, since it provides "a welcome diversion from the routines of daily life; a model of coherence and clarity; and heroic examples to admire and emulate."[10]

While Guttmann is right on many counts on the recent origins of modern sports, my book's approach is more catholic, as I prefer to look at sports over the *longue durée* and attempt to trace connections between the premodern and modern. For my purpose, the definition of sports by the anthropologist duo of Kendall Blanchard and A. T. Cheska, which brings in a sport's different elements—play, leisure, and, yes, work—works better. They define sport as "a physical exertive activity that is aggressively competitive within constraints imposed by definition and rules. A component of culture, it is ritually patterned, gamelike and of varying amounts of play, work and leisure." This means I won't be discussing cerebral games like chess, which is believed to have its origins in the Indian subcontinent; indoor games of chance like card or board games; and outdoor races or fights involving animals, which were very popular during the Mughal period and can still be seen in parts of India. Indoor games like billiards, snooker, and carrom—a game that holds a special place in Indians' hearts—are also outside the purview of this book. But I will unavoidably be discussing notions of the body, health, and recreation in order to get a more complete picture of the place of sports in India.

A few words are also in order on why I would choose to write a book on sports when India faces so many more pressing problems. The most obvious reason is the ubiquity of sports in India, as in most other societies. In perhaps what was the first serious work on sports, Joseph Strutt wrote: "In order to form a just estimate of the character of any particular people it is absolutely necessary to investigate the sports and pastimes most prevalent amongst them."[11] If we were to add up the numbers of hours the average person spends (or wastes, depending on one's perspective) playing, watching, or discussing sports, we would be very surprised. Besides, huge sums of money and sponsorship are riding on sports in India, particularly cricket. But the more compelling reason is that sports are inherently worthy of study for what is reveals about human nature and societies. As Huizinga put it, "All play means something," going on to add, "Play cannot be denied. You can deny, if you like, nearly all abstractions: justice, beauty, truth, goodness, mind, God. You can deny seriousness, but not play." And in the Indian context, as the historian Sarvepalli Gopal pointed out, "Indeed frequently—too often alas—it [cricket] is the brightest spot of the Indian scene. When we despair of our politicians, Sachin Tendulkar keeps up our spirits."[12]

With these preliminary words, we can map out the plan and scope of this book. If, as Sunil Khilnani pointed out, the agencies of modernity—"European colonial expansion, the state, nationalism, democracy, economic development"[13]—have shaped contemporary India, the same is true of sports in India. I thus tell the story of sports in India through their evolution from elite, kingly pastimes and their encounter in successive stages with colonialism, nationalism, the state, and globalization. This book dwells, among other things, on two issues: first, the intensely political nature of sports in both colonial and postcolonial India and, second, the patterns of the patronage, clientage, and institutionalization of sports.

Chapter 1 traces the history of Indian sports from their mythological origins to around the time of the decline of Mughal rule in the early eighteenth century. For the origin and philosophy of sports in India, it's best to turn to mythology rather than documented history. Just as with every other aspect of Indian life, the epics, particularly the Mahabharata, are indispensable to understanding the place of sports in India. This book thus begins with the Mahabharata. The elaborate training regimen of the Pandava and Kaurava princes under the watchful eyes of their mentor Dronacharya is the earliest example of the *guru-shishya* (teacher-pupil) bond intrinsic to the relationship between a coach and trainee. We also find in the Mahabharata many instances of agonistic competitions bounded by rules. Many of these are for prizes far greater than the medals or trophies of our times. They were literally life and death matters. But interestingly because these contests were so important, rules were strategically broken, often with divine sanction.

Coming to history proper, the sport that has the longest documented history in India is wrestling, with references to it going back to at least the thirteenth century. Of course, sports like hunting have survived over centuries and have now become part of modern competitions in the form of shooting and archery. Sports like polo (known as *chaugan* to the Mughals) also go back several centuries. Then a whole range of sports like *kabaddi*—which for some years have been a part of the Asian Games—still hold sway over parts of rural India and have recently been marketed to a larger audience as a television sport. However, wrestling is different in that it not only has survived over time but still is very much part of the Indian landscape as well as international sports.

As with society, politics, the economy—and indeed everything else—the entry of the British first as traders and then as rulers from the mid-eighteenth century onward had a profound impact on India. Chapters 2 and 3 focus on the fascinating story of this impact on sports and ideas of leisure in India and the complex response it evoked. The British brought with them to India their many organized sports, among which were football (or soccer in America), field hockey, tennis, badminton, golf, and, of course, cricket. British soldiers, along with administrators, sailors, and traders, began playing sports in India from as early as 1721, some thirty years before Robert Clive, the future governor of Bengal, won the decisive Battle of Plassey in 1757, which marked the beginning of the British conquest of India. During this early phase, there was little contact between the sporting activities of the colonizers and those of the natives. A crucial element in the diffusion of English games was the clubs, described as "free associations of gentlemen,"[14] the earliest of which—the Calcutta Cricket Club—was formed in 1792, only five years after the Marylebone Cricket Club (MCC) was established in London. Such clubs, which for a long time were the preserve of whites, spawned several clones set up by the Indian elite. If the clubs were the center of sports activity in India, the other locus was the British regiments and cantonments spread across the length and breadth of India. For British soldiers, the best way to keep themselves occupied and healthy in the unfamiliar climes of India was sport. Accordingly, I focus here primarily on cricket, hockey, and football, the three most popular sports in the first half of the twentieth century. I also spend some time on polo, since it was the one sport that the British picked up in India and took back to England. I include as well a chapter devoted to wrestling, partly because of its unbroken existence from pre-British times but also because of its intriguing evolution.

From the late nineteenth century and after the 1857 uprising, there was a conscious effort to get the Indian elites, particularly the royals, to play English games, especially cricket. At the same time, British administrators and missionaries worked hard at cultivating a Victorian games ethic in Indian public school students. Notable among them were men such as Chester Macnaghten, who taught Ranjitsinhji—who was the ruler of Nawanagar as well as a great cricket player—both Victorian virtues and cricket skills; and Cecil Earle Tyndale-Biscoe, a Christian missionary who introduced football and rowing to Kashmir. Interestingly, Baron Pierre de Coubertin, founder of the modern Olympics, was as much influenced by the ancient games in Greece as by Rugby, the English public school, and its headmaster, Thomas Arnold, that was the inspiration for Thomas Hughes's novel *Tom Brown's Schooldays* (1857).

Another important element in the spread and adoption of English sports in India was princely patronage. This is the subject of chapter 4. Just as rulers in ancient and medieval India sponsored tournaments involving men and animals, Indian princes, such as the maharaja of Patiala (a princely state in northern India), became patrons of cricket, football, and other sports. A few of them, most notably Ranjitsinhji and his nephew Duleepsinhji, were excellent cricketers who also played for England, but some, like the maharaja of Vizianagram, were in it for the power and influence that came with sponsoring and managing teams.

The popularity of English sports was by no means confined to the public schools, princely playgrounds, or club greens. Not only did the common man start taking up English games, but the playing field also became the arena for contesting British supremacy. In chapter 5, I look at how sports and Indian nationalism coalesced in strange ways. The cult of body building in late nineteenth-century Bengal that fed into revolutionary terrorism against the colonial rulers and the odd victory over British teams—the win of the Calcutta club Mohun Bagan over a British regiment in the 1911 Shield (the premier football tournament in India at the time) final being a notable example—was often seen as a triumph for the nascent Indian nation. The connection between a healthy body and nation building was made very early on by influential figures like the Hindu reformer Swami Vivekananda.

Beginning in the 1920s, India also started sending a team to the Olympics, making it the first British colony to do so.

If nationalist euphoria was very much in evidence during Mohun Bagan's victory in 1911, politics infiltrated the playing field in a different form, when race, caste, and, most controversially, communal identities clashed on the *maidan* (an open area or space in a city or town). Chapter 6 examines the two most significant examples of this sort of politics. One was the controversy over the Bombay Quadrangular (later the Pentangular), the most popular cricket tournament in preindependent India played by teams representing different communities, and the other was the spectacular rise of the Mohammedan Sporting Club in Calcutta, both occurring during the 1930s when the Indian National Congress and the Muslim League were bitterly opposed to each other.

Besides India's relatively recent success in international cricket, hockey was the only sport in which India was the unquestioned world champion for several decades. Even more remarkably, India fielded a hockey team in the 1928 Olympic Games—nearly two decades before Indian independence—and won the gold medal. The early history of hockey, documented in chapter 7, is replete with remarkable individuals like the country's first real sports star, Dhyan Chand, and India's first hockey captain, Jaipal Singh, a tribal from Jharkhand (in eastern India), who was educated at Oxford and later become a leader of the Jharkhand movement.

Wrestling can claim to have the longest lineage among Indian sports if one goes back to the epics and medieval texts. It is also the only sport besides hockey in which India won an Olympic medal in its early years as an independent nation. There was a definite connection between wrestling and the efforts of physical regeneration in early twentieth-century India. Wrestlers like the legendary Gama enjoyed the patronage of different princes and was regarded as a "world champion" during his playing days. Others like the Bengali wrestler Jatindra Charan (Gobor) Guha self-consciously touted wrestling and physical culture as a means to nation building. Gama and Gobor are the subjects of chapter 8.

Chapters 9 to 12 take up the story of sports in independent India and trace the complex story of how cricket became the dominant sport, despite both the great popularity of football and hockey in the 1950s and 1960s, and the success of sports stars in individual sports like tennis and badminton. The story of cricket's dominance and the place of India as the de facto center of world cricket is tied in many ways to some remarkable successes like India's unexpected winning of the 1983 cricket World Cup and the ways in which television and radio coverage worked to the sport's advantage. It also had something to do with the identification of the Indian elites with cricket. Now cricket has become much more than a sport in India, combining commerce, entertainment, and politics. Indeed, along with Bollywood films, cricket is the only glue that binds the diversity of India. During this period, though, the country lost its dominance in hockey, in which it had won a string of Olympic medals right up until 1980, and did not place in the top one hundred countries in football. In the Olympics, even a single medal is usually cause for great celebration. At the same time, India's traditional sports like wrestling and more elite sports like shooting have been going through a renaissance of sorts.

This section of the book tries to understand the place of sports in contemporary India and India's relative failure as a sports nation, despite its economic success in the past decade. In doing so, I look at several issues: the link between sport and nationalism—what George Orwell once memorably described as "war minus the shooting"—which rears its head particularly in India-Pakistan contests; the economics of sport, in terms of both its revenue generation and its opportunities for sportspersons; the role of the state, which includes public-sector companies and the armed forces as patrons of sports, plus the quality of sports administrators; the decentering of sport, with nonurban centers producing sports stars and champions; the place of women—absent from much of the story—who are doing increasingly well in sports; and the role of spectatorship at a time when most viewers are watching games on television and are not physically present at the field.

As recently as a decade ago, the entry on India in a handbook of sports studies could claim, though not entirely accurately, that the "sociological study of sport in India essentially remains virgin territory."[15] There are several books on the history of cricket in India, one of them going back as far as 1897. The other sports are, however, woefully underrepresented, with some notable exceptions. India's tryst with the Olympic Games, which goes back to 1920, has been documented in a few books. We also have, of course, several autobiographies and biographies of Indian sportspersons, mostly again of cricket players. In recent times, many more books on and by noncricketers have been written. It is true, however, as historian Dipesh Chakrabarty pointed out, "social historians of India have paid more attention to riots than to sports, to street-battles with the police than to rivalries on the soccer field."[16] Even though cricket figures prominently in my book, I've made every effort to look at the other pieces of India's sports puzzle. Luckily, there are several fine books on the history of sports in other countries, particularly England, which are inspirational role models. The triumphs and tragedies of sports heroes as well as sports organizers and enthusiasts, many of them largely forgotten, are documented in the following pages. Some of them merit separate biographies, a challenge that, I hope, will be taken up by others. Admittedly, some games are given short shrift because it is virtually impossible to do justice to each and every sport in a slim volume like this. Fans of golf, horse racing, and table tennis, to name just a few—all of which are played and followed with great interest in India—will no doubt feel neglected.

One word of caution, though. Despite being a keen follower of many sports, I never graduated beyond games in the neighborhood park or inter-house matches at school. But that is not something I'm particularly ashamed of. If it weren't for people like me, where would sports and the sports industry be? The final word should perhaps be left to the Sri Lankan writer of an intriguing novel on cricket: "Sport can unite worlds, tear down walls, and transcend race, the past, and all probability. Unlike life, sport matters."[17]

1

DOWN THE AGES

SPORT IN ANCIENT AND

MEDIEVAL INDIA

IN THE ANCIENT WORLD THERE WAS NOTHING COMPARABLE TO the Olympic Games of Greece. The games first held at Olympia in at least 776 B.C.E., if not earlier, were among at least four such competitions—the others being the Pythian, Isthimian, and Nemean Games—held in ancient Greece. But the games in Olympia were by far the most prestigious as well as the longest running, as they were held without fail every four years for an astonishing 1,200 years. Though there is a tendency to view the ancient Olympics through rose-tinted spectacles, we now know that it was often a bloody and violent business. As a scholar of the ancient Olympics explained, at both the popular and philosophical levels, it was understood that essentially "all games were war games."[1] While modern sports can, in many instances, be traced back to ancient times, the similarities should not be exaggerated. According to Norbert Elias and Eric Dunning, "Throughout antiquity the threshold of sensitivity with regard to the infliction of physical injuries and even to killing in a game-contest and, accordingly, the whole contest ethos, was very different from that represented by the type of contest which we nowadays characterize as 'sport.'"[2] This was true for ancient India as well.

Sports in the Epics

Even though mention of sports or sports competitions is pitifully scarce in standard histories of ancient India, such references, at least in the martial sense, are plentiful in the great Indian epic the Mahabharata. The Mahabharata is a complex and bloody tale of two sets of warring cousins—the five Pandavas and the one hundred Kauravas—containing 100,000 verses, or *shlokas*, spread over eighteen books. It was most likely composed over several hundred years between 400 B.C.E. and 400 C.E. For nearly every aspect of Indian life, we can turn to the Mahabharata, and this holds true for sports as well. Thus the author(s) of the Mahabharata could boast, "Whatever is found here may be found somewhere else, but what is not found here is found nowhere."[3]

The Mahabharata does not, of course, discuss competitive sports as we understand them today, but it does describe training for the martial arts as well as physical contests within a loose framework of rules. In the stratified Indian society, the martial arts were restricted to the Kshatriya, or warrior, caste, second in the pecking order behind the Brahmins and above the Vaishyas (traders), the Sudras (the lowest caste), and the Avarna (Dalit or Scheduled Caste, formerly called "untouchables") who fell outside the pale of the caste system. This scheme is explained in the Mahabharata itself when the Kuru patriarch Bhishma gives a lengthy sermon to the eldest Pandava, Yudhisthira, over books 12 and 13, which is commonly believed to have been added later to the text. Bhishma described the dharma of the four castes thus: "Brahmins should be self-controlled and study the Vedas. Ksatriyas should give gifts, perform sacrifices, protect people and show courage in battle. Vaisyas should tend cattle. Sudras should obey the three higher classes."[4] This division is quite apparent in the Mahabharata, in which only the princes, such as the Pandavas and Kauravas, were given training in various martial arts, though their teachers were Brahmins. The caste boundaries were rigid, and transgressions, particularly by those lower in the caste hierarchy than the Kshatriyas, were not taken lightly, as the Mahabharata chillingly makes clear. The world of sports also was overwhelmingly male. Likewise, in ancient Greece, women weren't allowed to compete in the Olympics either, although there was a festival dedicated to Zeus's consort Hera, in which virgin girls could take part.

Modern India's Arjuna and Dronacharya awards, which came into being in 1961 and 1985, respectively, draw their inspiration from the teacher of the Kuru princes, Dronacharya, and his favorite pupil, the Pandava prince Arjuna. Bhima, another of the Pandavas, is regarded as a patron saint of Indian wrestlers. Dronachaya was appointed the trainer of the young princes by Bhishma, who was on the lookout for "teachers of recognized prowess who knew archery, since no man of little wit, authority, and expertise in weaponry, or of less than divine mettle, could discipline the mighty Kurus."[5] Drona instructed his wards in archery and swordsmanship and also in hand-thrown weapons like clubs, spears, javelins, and lances, as well as in the art of fighting from chariots, elephants, and horses.

Because of Drona's great renown, young men throughout India flocked to train under him. One of them was Ekalavya, a Nisada belonging to a group of people living in the forest (those who are called Adivasis today), whom Drona refused to accept as a student. Undeterred, Ekalavya practiced his skills in the forest in front of his teacher, a clay image of Drona. But Ekalavya was discovered when the Kuru princes observed him one day displaying amazing shooting skills. When they asked his identity, Ekalavya answered that he was the son of the chieftain of the Nisadas and a pupil of Drona. When Arjuna told Drona that another archer was even better than him, Drona himself went to meet Ekalavya and demanded his reward, *guru dakshina*. Drona's fee was Ekalavya's right thumb, which Ekalavya cheerfully sliced off. Arjuna's position thus remained secure. Among other things, the Ekalavya episode is a powerful allegory of the consequences of transgressing the closed boundaries of martial sports and, indeed, caste hierarchies in general.

With Ekalavya out of the way, Arjuna became the undisputed champion of all weapons, while both Duryodhana, the eldest of the Kauravas, and Bhima excelled in combat with clubs. Arjuna's prowess was shown in the famous episode from the Mahabharata in which Drona tested his trainees' skills. All his trainees were asked to take aim at a clay bird perched on a treetop and to report what they saw before letting fly the arrow. Without fail, each prince said that he saw the treetop, the bird, and his cousins. But when Arjuna was asked, he said he saw only the bird. And when he was asked to describe the bird, Arjuna replied, "I see its head, not its body."[6] On hearing this, a pleased Drona commanded Arjuna to release his arrow, which promptly knocked the bird off its perch.

A dramatic illustration of the closed circle of sport occurred during a public exhibition held by the Kuru princes once they had finished their training under Drona. The star of the show was Arjuna:

> Trained to high excellence, the favourite of his guru hit and shot through fragile targets, and tiny ones, and hard ones, with different makes of arrows. While an iron boar was moved about, he loosed into its snout five continuous arrows as though they were one single one. The mighty archer buried twenty-one arrows in a cow's hollow horn that was swaying on a rope. And in this and other fashions he gave an exhibition of his dexterity with the long sword as well as the bow and the club.[7]

When the rapturous crowds were about to leave the arena, Karna, a central character in the Mahabharata, strode in. Born to Kunti, mother of the three elder Pandavas—Yudhisthira, Bhima, and Arjuna—Karna was abandoned as a baby and raised by a charioteer. He threw down a challenge to Arjuna, who dismissed him as an uninvited intruder. Karna replied, "Ksatriyas excel in heroism, and dharma defers to strength; why trade in insults, the consolation of the weak? Talk with your arrows, heir of Bharata, till my arrows carry off your head while your teacher looks on!"[8] As the two warriors squared off, one of the elders clearly spelled out the rules of challenge to Karna, which meant not only belonging to the right caste but also having a royal lineage:

> Here stands the younger son of Kunti, son of Pandu, descendant of Kuru. He will fight you in single combat, sir. Now that you too, strong-armed hero, must announce your mother, father and the royal lineage of which you are the glory. Once this is known to Kunti's son, he will fight you, or he will not.[9]

A crestfallen Karna hung his head in shame. Then the Kaurava prince Duryodhana, avowed rival of the Pandavas, immediately crowned Karna as the king of Anga to enable him to take on Arjuna. At this point, the charioteer who had raised Karna made an appearance and embraced his adopted son, prompting Bhima to taunt Karna by calling him the lowliest of men. While the drama played out, the sun set, drawing the curtain on this particular episode of an unforced entry into a competition meant only for Kshatriyas.

So much for the training of the Kshatriya princes. Essential to sports is the idea of winning, which often comes with a prize, both material and nonmaterial. Johan Huizinga noted that victory could bring with it honor, esteem, and prestige. But usually every game involved stakes that could be a "gold cup or a jewel or a king's daughter or a shilling; the life of the player or the welfare of the whole tribe."[10] This aspect of sports was shown in the *swayamvar* (the practice of choosing a husband from among a list of suitors) held for the hand of Draupadi, the ravishing daughter of King Drupad. The king announced that he would give his daughter's hand to the person who could string a very strong bow and hit a high target through a small opening. The Pandavas, who were on the run to avoid Duryodhana's evil designs, were at the gathering disguised as mendicant Brahmins. When prince after prince failed to string the bow, Arjuna rose to take a try. This caused some consternation among the princes assembled there, who wondered how a "mere Brahmin boy, untrained in weapons and inferior in strength,"[11] could string the bow in a way that so many Kshatriya princes had failed to do. Once again the hierarchies of caste came into play. But unlike Ekalavya or Karna, who were deemed to be lower in the hierarchy, Arjuna was allowed to proceed because "there is no task anywhere in the three worlds that is beyond the power of Brahmins among the three classes of men."[12] The task that had stumped so many princes was done in a trice by Arjuna: "In the time it takes to blink, he strung it; and he took up five arrows and swiftly pierced the target through the opening."[13]

We find a similar episode of a hero showing his strength to win the hand of a princess in the other great Indian epic, the Ramayana. King Janaka had promised his daughter Sita in marriage to whoever could lift a celestial bow in his possession. When Rama and his brother Lakshman, accompanied by the great sage Vishvamitra, wanted to see the bow, Janaka said that he would marry his daughter to Rama if he could string the bow. Rama did so with ease, winning Sita's hand:

Then, as though it was mere play to him, the righteous prince, the delight of the Raghus, strung the bow as thousands watched. The mighty man affixed the bowstring and, fitting an arrow to it, drew it back. But, in so doing, the best of men broke the bow in the middle. There was a tremendous noise loud as a thunderclap, and a mighty trembling shook the earth, as if a mountain had been torn asunder. Of all those men, only the great sage, the king and the two Raghavas remained standing; the rest fell, stunned by the noise.[14]

A greater contribution of the Ramayana to Indian sports is the character of Hanuman—the monkey god known for his immense strength as well as his loyalty to Rama—who is regarded as the patron deity of Indian wrestling and occupies pride of place in most *akharas* in India.

Arjuna won Draupadi's hand, but the matter did not end there. The fact that a Brahmin had bested the cream of the Kshatriyas in a contest of physical skill did not go down well at all. They said to King Drupad, "Here we are assembled and he passes us by as though we were straw! He wants to give Draupadi, finest of women, to a Brahmin."[15] With these words, they readied to attack Drupad. The Pandavas came to his rescue and warded off the Kshatriya princes, led by such great warriors such as Karna and Salya. Soon the Kshatriya princes beat a retreat, wondering whether these Brahmins weren't the Pandavas in disguise. They left muttering, "The arena has become dominated by the brahmins."[16]

The contests in the Mahabharata were by no means restricted to prowess in archery. A central place is occupied by the gambling match—in fact, according to Huizinga, the main action of the Mahabharata hinges on this game of dice—in which Yudhisthira staked and lost everything, including the Pandavas' common wife, Draupadi. But indoor games of chance, fascinating as they are, are not the subject of this book.

Some of the most riveting, as well as the most ethically troubling, physical contests were those involving Bhima, who excelled in wrestling and fighting with a club. One of the first of such contests was between Bhima and the powerful king Jarasandha. The fight, which lasted for fourteen days (just four fewer days than the great battle that is the centerpiece of the Mahabharata), displayed the full range of the wrestler's skills—smashes, armlocks, and neck locks—which would put any of today's World Wrestling Entertainment wrestlers to shame. The climax is described in chilling detail: "Foe-taming Bhima of great might tossed mighty Jarasandha in the air and whirled him around; with his arms he whirled him round a hundred times . . . then dashed him down, breaking his back, and roared as he trampled him."[17]

The crucial contest was fought at the end of the eighteen-day war between the Pandavas and the Kauravas. Once Duryodhana, the eldest of the Kauravas and the chief villain in the Mahabharata, realized that his cause was lost, he used his powers of illusion to hide inside the waters of a lake. When he was eventually discovered, he repeatedly refused appeals by Yudhisthira to leave the lake and fight. At last, though, he offered to fight the Pandavas one by one, but then Yudhisthira made him an even better offer. Duryodhana could choose to fight a Pandava with a weapon of his choice, and if he could slay him, he would win back his kingdom. An offer too good to spurn, Duryodhana opted to fight with a club any Pandava willing take him on. The only Pandava who had the strength to fight Duryodhana with clubs was Bhima.

It is interesting that after a terrible battle in which thousands were slaughtered and entire clans were wiped out, Yudhisthira was willing to stake the outcome of the war on a single bout of armed conflict. Indeed, even Krishna, the Hindu avatar (reincarnation of Lord Vishnu) and also the chief counselor of the Pandavas and an expert wrestler himself, was upset that Yudhisthira was stupid enough to give Duryodhana a chance to win back his kingdom: "This was great foolishness on the part of the lord of *dharma* [Yudhisthira] to gamble the entire outcome of the war on this single victory."[18] It is noteworthy, too, for the way, and not for the first time, that the rules of the game were bent at the instigation of Krishna, who can be seen as a cosmic referee with a distinct bias toward the Pandavas. Even before the fight began, Krishna warned Arjuna that Bhima would never be able to win if he fought according to *dharma* (law or rules); he could triumph only if he resorted to unfairness. On hearing this, Arjuna, in full view of Bhima, struck his own thigh with his hand, an indication that Bhima must literally hit Duryodhana below the belt. Initially both Bhima and Duryodhana fought each other on an even keel, the clash of their clubs producing sparks and the sound of thunder, with both soaked in blood and sweat. At one point, after having struck a terrible blow, Duryodhana leaped up high to deceive Bhima. It was then that Bhima made his fateful move: "He rushed like a lion to the attack, and as Duryodhana feinted and made to leap up once more, Pandu's son swiftly brought down his club on his two thighs."[19] His thighs smashed, Duryodhana crashed to the ground like a mighty tree. Bhima had won the contest, and to rub it in, he trampled on Duryodhana's head.

Bhima's tactics upset even Yudhisthira, but the strongest response came from Krishna's elder brother, Balarama, who was watching the fight. A furious Balarama shouted, "A curse upon you Bhima, a curse upon you for striking a warrior of blameless valour below the navel! ... The learned texts are clear that no blow should be struck below the navel."[20] He even went to strike Bhima but was stopped by Krishna, who explained that the Pandava had vowed to break Duryodhana's thighs in battle and, as a Kshatriya, was bound to carry out his vow. Later, when a crippled Duryodhana accused Krishna of deceit, he simply replied, "You have been slain ... together with your brothers and sons and kinsmen and friends and troops, because you were pursuing a path of wickedness."[21]

This is not the place to go into the place of *dharma* in the Mahabharata, except to reiterate that the notion of competitive sports, even though restricted to martial arts, albeit with flexible rules, came into existence several centuries ago. Of course, one could object that since the Mahabharata is mythical, it does not say anything useful about the reality in ancient India. But that is missing the point. Irrespective of whether the events in Mahabharata have any grain of truth, the fact is that the great epic has a special place in and has greatly influenced Indian culture. Most Indians have some familiarity with the basic plot of the Mahabharata and have sublimated different elements of the epic. Its enduring popularity was on display in the 1980s when a television series based on the epic had the entire nation hooked on Sunday mornings for several months. As the Marathi scholar V. S. Sukthankar, who guided the Bhandarkar Oriental Research Institute's monumental critical edition of the epic in Sanskrit, once noted, "The *Mahabharata* is the content of our collective unconsciousness."[22] That is perhaps why sports excellence in modern India, too, is associated with the heroes of the Mahabharata—Arjuna and Drona—however mythical and distant they might be.

Sports in Ancient India

Moving from myths to history proper, what references to sports do we find? The standard histories of ancient India provide, at best, sketchy references to recreation and sports. Besides hunting and archery—a necessity for many and a pastime for the royals—we find little mention of sports. A historian of physical education, C. W. Hackensmith, finds mention of yoga, polo, wrestling, and various ball games in India over the centuries.[23] Some, like Renou Louis, believed that games were plentiful in ancient India, but in his list, the boundary between physical, competitive sports and pure amusements, like sword swallowing or tightrope walking, is fuzzy, something that is common to many historians of ancient India.[24]

But even though gambling and board games were popular in India, historian A. L. Basham, says in his classic *The Wonder That Was India* that organized outdoor games were not common:

A form of polo, introduced from Central Asia, became popular among warriors in the Middle Ages, though it is little mentioned in literature, and a kind of hockey was also played. But, in general, ancient India did not put such stress on athletics as did the Mediterranean world. Chariot racing is mentioned in the Rig Veda, and bullock racing was popular in the late medieval period. Boxing and wrestling are often referred to, but were not generally the hobbies of respectable young men, but the preserve of low-caste pugilists, who performed for the amusement of an audience. The archery contest, however, was a much-loved amusement of the warrior class, and vivid descriptions of such contests occur in the Epics.[25]

While sports such as archery and those involving horses—chariot racing and polo—were most likely restricted to the warriors and elites, we find people belonging to the lower castes taking to boxing and wrestling in the guise of performers. What is interesting is that the idea of sports as entertainment, primarily for the elites, as opposed to sports as training for war, was gradually appearing. In other a words, a class of professional sportsmen had come into existence who were performing, just as the acrobats were, for the pleasure of the royals and nobles.

Basham's view of the paucity of evidence for sports in ancient India is corroborated to some extent by nationalist Indian authors who have sought to find an illustrious lineage for Indian sports and physical culture. The most notable among these efforts was Dattareya Chintamani Mujumdar's ten-volume *Encyclopedia of Indian Physical Culture*, originally published in Marathi. (In 1950, a single abridged volume of the encyclopedia was published in English.) Mujumdar, a native of Baroda in western India, was a central figure in reconstructing a history of indigenous sport and encouraging a physical culture movement. He was also the founder of *Vyayam*, a Marathi-language periodical launched in 1915 and dedicated to popularizing sport and physical culture.[26] Mujumdar admits that the Rig Veda, the Brahmanas, the Aranyakas, and the Upanishads are silent on physical activities, but he hastens to add that the strength of famous warriors testifies to the fact that they must have taken part in "effective means of physical culture."[27]

The Rig Veda does, however, refer to riding and *mushti-yuddha* (fighting with fists). For instance, it talks about expert exponents in boxing: "With the constant practice of the skills in boxing and by defeating their opponents, these champions won the honour and respect of the people. People used to adore them."[28] And in another place: "Since these fighters were the ideals before them, naturally the people wished for the brave son, with the grace of these fighters, who would be a good boxer having strong arms and bearer of good horses."[29] Some historians believe that there also were sports festivals during Vedic times called *samana*, in which archers competed for prizes and chariot and horse races were held, but the evidence for these is not entirely convincing.[30] For a later period, S. H. Deshpande makes a fivefold division of sports and physical exercises: martial sports, which include wrestling, archery, and polo; *vyama* or heavy exercises; yogic practices; *krida* or recreational sports, which include swimming and ball games; and gymnastics.

What we can say with some certainty is that wrestling, or *mallayuddha*, was a popular sport in ancient India. Mujumdar writes,

> Wrestling seemed to form the prominent exercise in Pauranic age. The people of all castes practiced it. . . . We read of some descriptions of wrestling bouts, arenas and of seating arrangements for spectators in various Puranas. The idea of the present stadium has its origin in these arrangements.[31]

Engravings, some going back as far as the fourth century B.C.E., show figures engaged in wrestling bouts. There is some evidence suggesting that in the period of the dramatist Bhasa (fourth or third century B.C.E.), wrestling bouts were attended by kings; also during the age of the Jatakas, there existed *mandapams*, or sports pavilions, from which spectators watched wrestling contests.[32]

The popularity of wrestling continued unabated over succeeding centuries. One of the earliest available descriptions of wrestling can be found in the *Manasollasa* of King Someshwara of the Chalukya dynasty who reigned from 1124 to 1138 C.E. The *Manasollasa* refers to many other sports too, including archery (*dhanurvidya* or *dhanur vinoda*), duels with weapons (*anka vinoda*), and a game played on horses (*vajivahyali vinoda*).[33] The chapter entitled "Malla-Vinod" describes in some detail the system of wrestling practiced during the period. There were three kinds of wrestlers, graded according to their skills: the best were the Jyeshthika, below them the Antar-jyeshthika, and at bottom the Govala. A wrestler was known as Bhavishnu when he was twenty and was described as Paroodha at thirty, when he was supposed to have reached his peak. The wrestlers were patronized by the king and were fed a special diet of legumes, meat, and sweets made from milk.[34]

The "Malla-Vinod" describes the wrestler's regimen in some detail. Their lives were strictly regulated, and even conversation with women was prohibited. They were required to practice every other day different positions and holds, and they were prescribed different exercises to increase their skill, stamina, and strength. One of these was lifting heavy sacks full of sand (*bharshrama*); another was practicing heavy club swinging (*bahu-pellanaka-shrama*); and yet another was practicing holds and tricks on a pillar (*malla-stambh*). Wrestling tournaments were regularly held and were presided over by the king and attended by many spectators.

The wrestlers used to wear a strap *langot*. After being ordered by the king the pre-settled pairs with great enthusiasm and keen desire to knock down the opponent, would enter the arena beating and sounding their arms and thighs. In the beginning the two wrestlers of each pair would join hands and touch the feet of each other. Each of the wrestlers after having done this would start the bout, trying to measure the strength of his opponent and finding an opportunity to knock down the other. When it was found that the wrestlers were tired, their bodies wet with sweat, eyes practically closed due to fatigue, and bodies covered with mud, the King would order to stop wrestling and when both were found equally exhausted, both were declared winners. He, whose back did not touch the ground, who was completely successful in overpowering his enemy and who could keep up his stamina even after doing all this, was finally declared the victor. Prizes in the form of ornaments, new dresses, horses etc were distributed to victors.[35]

Another important text on wrestling is the *Mallapurana*, a purana (Hindu religious text) of the Jyesthimallas, a caste of professional wrestlers who were originally from Gujarat but migrated to Rajasthan, Maharashtra, and parts of south India. The text was most likely composed between the fifteenth and seventeenth centuries C.E. The Jyesthimallas were a subcaste of the Modha Brahmins belonging to Modhera, a town in north Gujarat. As we saw in the Mahabharata, even though Brahmins were not strictly prohibited from taking up a sport, they rarely did so. According to the *Mallapurana*, the Brahmins were originally engaged in performing sacrifices in a town called Mayuravam Balam. In the Dwapara age, Krishna, who was passing through town with his brother, was so pleased with the Brahmins that he offered to teach them wrestling, *mallavidya*. Although the Brahmins were reluctant to take on another profession, Krishna, as he was wont to do, convinced them by saying that Brahmins had to take up arts like wrestling to protect dharma in Kalyug, or the age of darkness. Krishna thereupon not only taught the Brahmins wrestling but also gave them detailed instructions about the classification of physical exercises and rules for arranging wrestling matches, making the *Mallapurana* the first wrestling handbook in India.

The *Mallapurana*, as it has come down to us, consists of eighteen chapters. Like the *Manasollasa*, it offers detailed descriptions of the different types of wrestlers, their training regimen, diet, wrestling moves, and competitions. Both the *Manasollasa* and the *Mallapurana* regard any wrestling that is not directed at an enemy as entertainment, which had great significance in its development as a sport. According to the *Mallapurana*,

> Wrestling is considered to be joyful, it develops enthusiasm and removes sorrow. Therefore, it is recommended that the king should always witness the wrestling match. He should invite his friends, ministers knowing the arts and clever citizens, the queen and the princesses. He should also invite the *mallas*. The next day in the morning the king should rise early and make the *mallas* also rise. He should order to bring the earth for the arena.[36]

A ragamala painting from Amer, depicting acrobats lifting weights, sliding down a greasy pole, and two wrestlers. Painting, ragamala, acrobats and wrestlers, Desakh Ragini, opaque watercolor on paper, Amer, ca. 1680. © Victoria and Albert Museum, London

The winners were given prizes, and the victorious *malla* were rewarded twice as much as the defeated. In both the daily routine and the tournaments, wrestling was infused with religious rituals and symbolism. Before going to the wrestling pit, the Jyestimallas were expected to pray to the gods, and on competition days, they prayed to Govinda.

Wrestling contests could be very violent. A particular type of wrestling, *asura*, included "injury to ear and nose, falling of teeth, biting, pulling of hair, throwing earth, scratching with nails, catching the neck, breaking of fingers etc."[37] Another violent form of wrestling was *vajramusti*, in which the wrestler's power was enhanced by an instrument held in his fist. These instruments were known as *maustikam*, *mustim*, or *mutthiya* and were small rings with pointed edges. Some of them were even more deadly, with steel nails and blades attached to the rings and could be considered more as instruments of war than of sports. Until recently, *vajramusti* wrestling continued in former princely states such as Mysore, although the contests were stopped as soon as the first blood was drawn.

We also have evidence of the Jyesthimallas, or *jethis*, in later times. Legend has it that the Mughal emperor Akbar arranged a wrestling match between one of his wrestlers and a *malla* called Lakhaji in which the latter emerged victorious. Later, on the emperor's order, Lakhaji uprooted a neem tree, an act that eventually caused his death. A temple to the goddess Limbja in Delmal village commemorates this event. Later the Gaekwad rulers, particularly Sayajirao I, patronized the Jyesthimallas.[38]

The *Mallapurana* is a particularly interesting document because to some extent it transgresses the caste hierarchy. The Brahmins submitted to Krishna's training only when they were convinced that it was a livelihood that would protect their dharma. As the sociologist Veena Das noted, in the *varna* (broadly defined as caste) theory, each *varna* is "ideally" associated with one kind of occupation. So the Brahmins perform sacrifices, the Kshatriyas are warriors, the Vaishyas are engaged in trade, and the Shudras perform menial services. But this hierarchy ignores a whole range of occupations that cannot be neatly slotted in the *varna* system. "By describing wrestling as 'fighting with hands,' the *Malla Purana* implicitly opposes it to 'fighting with weapons,' which is the occupation associated with Kshatriyas."[39]

According to Mujumdar, evidence of the popularity of wrestling can be found in later periods, particularly in the Vijayanagar kingdom in the Deccan. He described the physical regimen of Krishnadeva Raya, one of the dynasty's greatest rulers, who ruled from 1509 to 1529 C.E.:

He [Krishnadeva] had an excellent physique. He used to practise different physical exercises early in the morning. He was an expert rider too.

He had an awe-inspiring figure.... Sesamum oil about a pound and half was his early morning drink. Then applying oil to all parts of the body, he used to take hard exercise in wrestling and heavy club-swinging to such an extent that all the impurities and the waste matter would come out of his body along with the sweat.[40]

The Portuguese travelers Fernao Nuniz and Domingo Paes left brief accounts of wrestling in Vijayanagar. Paes, who was in Vijayanagar during Krishnadeva's reign, wrote about the violence during wrestling contests, in which "there are blows (given), so severe as to break teeth and put out eyes, and disfigure faces, so much so that here and there men are carried off speechless by their friends."[41] If Nuniz, who was in Vijayanagar during the reign of Krishnadeva's half brother and successor Achyuta Deva Raya, is to be believed, the wrestling matches held during festivals were more like gladiatorial contests but with an odd twist: the loser was rewarded.

The King has a thousand wrestlers for these feasts who wrestle before the King, but not in our manner, for they strike and wound each other with two circlets with points [knuckle-dusters] which they carry in their hands to strike with, and the one most wounded goes and takes his rewards in the shape of a silk cloth, such as the King gives to these wrestlers. They have a captain over them, and they do not perform any other service in the kingdom.[42]

Sports Under the Islamic Rulers

With the coming of the Islamic dynasties, we start getting better records of sports and pastimes, at least those of the elites. The first Mughal emperor, Babur, himself left an invaluable account of his life and time in his diary *Baburnama*. Abul Fazl, the indefatigable chronicler of the Mughal emperor Akbar, also provided a vivid account of the nobility's recreational activities (H. Beveridge, who translated Fazl's *Akbar Nama*, did not think too highly of him, however, labeling him a "great flatterer" who "unhesitatingly suppressed or distorted facts").[43] A flatterer Fazl might well have been, but he also meticulously documented the happenings, both mundane and extraordinary, of Akbar's court. In his *Ain-i-Akbari*, Fazl writes of the various sports in the Mughal court, indoor games such as chess, cards, and *chaupar* (a form of *ludo*), outdoor activities such as *chaugan* (polo), *ishqbazi* (pigeon flying), and, of course, hunting.

In England a few decades earlier, just as a young Henry VIII—before he became obese and afflicted by various ailments—was vigorously taking part in archery contests and hunting, Akbar was a great fan of outdoor sports. Polo, which had been popular in Persia for centuries, entered India with the Islamic invaders from Central Asia. Akbar's ancestor Timur spread both Islam and polo throughout his vast empire, which stretched from Russia to the borders of India. The legendary poet Hafiz blessed Timur by hoping that his enemies' heads would become his polo balls, and Timur apparently fulfilled the poet's wish. The *Manasollasa* has a reference—before the Mughals conquered the subcontinent—to a game played between two teams of eight players, each on a horse, that was very much similar to the *chaugan* played by Persians and Central Asians. Each of the two sides of the playground had a goal (*torana*), toward which the riders, using cane sticks, hit a round ball made of wood. When the ball passed through the goalposts, bugles were sounded to celebrate.[44]

The first Muslim sultan in India, Qutubudin Aibak, is believed to have died during a polo game when he was crushed by his horse. But it was during Akbar's time that the game reached its greatest popularity. Abul Fazl described in detail the polo matches, which usually were played by ten players, with many more on the sidelines.

> The game itself is played in two ways. The first way is to get hold of the ball with the crooked end of the *chaugan* stick and to move it slowly from the middle to the hal [the pillars that mark the end of the playground]. The manner is called in Hindi rol. The other way consists in taking deliberate aim, and forcibly hitting the ball with the *chaugan* stick out in the middle; the player then gallops after it, quicker than the others, and throws the ball back.[45]

When the ball was driven to the end of the ground, loud drumbeats announced the event. Not surprisingly, Abul Fazl showered praise on Akbar's polo skills, which were "unrivalled" and which "astonishes all."[46] He also

A Mughal painting of a polo match from the seventeenth century. Painting, Large Clive Album, polo game, opaque watercolor and gold on paper, Mughal, seventeenth century.
© Victoria and Albert Museum, London

gave his own spin on why the emperor was so enamored of the sport: "Superficial observers look upon this game as mere amusement, and consider it mere play; but men of more exalted views see in it a means of learning promptitude and decision. It tests the value of a man, and strengthens the bond of friendship."[47] So obsessed was Akbar with polo that arrangements were made to play the game at night. Centuries before floodlit games became possible, an ingenious method was devised for playing in the dark by setting the polo balls, made from wood of the *palas* tree, on fire.[48]

Wrestling seems to have been a popular form of entertainment as well. Babur wrote about a celebration in 1528 in which wrestlers staged a show sandwiched between camel and elephant fights and acrobats.[49] Akbar seemed to have been fond of wresting too but may have taken it more seriously. Abul Fazl tells a story, very likely apocryphal, in which when Akbar was a small child of two or three, he took on the older and stronger Ibrahim Mirza and bested him:

> He [Akbar] grappled with Ibrahim Mirza according to the canons of the skilful and of the masters of wrestling and putting his hand before his waist so lifted him up and flung him on the ground that a cry burst forth from the assemblage, and that shouts of Bravo arose from far and near.[50]

Later as emperor, Akbar had in his pay many wrestlers and boxers. According to Abul Fazl, fights were organized daily, and the contestants, who were paid regular salaries, also were suitably rewarded after the event. Fazl listed the famous wrestlers of the time, many of whom were from Central Asia. Some of them, like Muhammad Quli, were given colorful titles like Sher Hamlah, "Attacker of Lions." Religion was not an issue, and among the well-known wrestlers were Sri Ram, Kanhya, Ganesh, and Balbhadra.

Like earlier kings of the Indian subcontinent, the Mughals, too, were fond of hunts, or *shikars*, which were organized on an elaborate scale. Before the emperor embarked on a hunting expedition, some fifty thousand beaters would drive the animals into a ring where they would be trapped. These elaborate hunts were known as *qamargah* during Mughal times. Only then would the emperor make his way into the forest, initially accompanied by a few nobles but finally on his own. Even here Abul Fazl has his own spin, pointing out that superficial observers might find hunting senseless, but in reality it was used as a "means of acquisition of knowledge" and an occasion to inquire into the condition of the people without giving prior notice.[51] It is, of course, questionable whether hunting can count as a sport, even though modern archery and shooting evolved from hunting. Hunting is a bloody business, but just as the upper classes enjoyed fox hunting in England, with its "specific code of manners,"[52] for the thrill of the hunt rather than the actual kill, so too the Mughals probably enjoyed the elaborate rituals and buildup of the *shikar*. As Abul Fazl explained, "Short-sighted and shallow observers think that His Majesty [Akbar] has no short object in view but hunting; but the wise and experienced know that he pursues higher aims."[53] Among these were impressing the might of the emperor on his subjects and testing the skills of the court nobles.

A recurrent feature of Abul Fazl's account of sport in the Mughal court is the instrumentality attached to it. M. N. Pearson observed that in Mughal India, the "most striking aspect of recreation was the absence of pure play or fun, especially among the nobility."[54] In contrast, he noted that the commoners, whose sporting activities were rarely deigned important enough to be chronicled, did enjoy their sports and games. He commented, "One does not wish to create myths of the carefree joys of primitive life, yet clearly commoners could at times let themselves go completely, transcend all bounds and norms. This the nobility seldom achieved. Most of the time they were competing, and they were on show."[55]

Not that *shikar* was a sanitized affair. Indeed it could be life threatening, as was dramatically shown in a famous incident in 1611 when Jahangir's son Shah Jahan and a noble Anup Rai saved the emperor from a tiger.[56] But that did not stop the Mughal emperors from hunting. Jahangir even took the ladies of his court with him on hunts:

I had taken with me to this hunt those who were screened by curtains of honour. The hunt was a good one and came off with great éclat, 200 red and white antelopes were killed. On the 25th another hunt took place in the neighbourhood of Rohtas. In this also my sisters and other women were with me and nearly 100 red deer were killed.[57]

Between 1580 and 1616, Jahangir alone killed 17,000 animals, including 86 tigers. The tradition of *shikar* was continued by Indian princes and senior British officials until the mid-twentieth century when laws and social mores gradually put hunting into disrepute. By then, though, there were plenty of other sports to occupy the attention of the colonial officials, the Indian elites as well as the embryonic middle class in India.

2

EMPIRE OF SPORT

THE EARLY BRITISH IMPACT

ON RECREATION

IN 1615, DURING EMPEROR JAHANGIR'S REIGN, THE FIRST British emissary arrived at the Mughal court. Not long afterward, the British began setting up factories and ships belonging to the East India Company, which had begun operations in London only a few years earlier and now started calling regularly on India. In addition, as a British ICS officer, E. A. H. Blunt, wrote, "Wherever an Englishman goes, he takes his games with him."[1] So it isn't surprising that English sports on Indian shores were first seen in a coastal town. One day in 1721 in Cambay, on India's western seaboard, a bunch of British sailors decided to play a game of cricket. According to one of them, "When my boat was lying for a fortnight in one of the channels though all the country round was inhabited by the Cooleys, we everyday diverted ourselves with playing Cricket and to other Exercises which they would come and be spectators of."[2] Little did the British sailors know that their carefree games were to be the very first act of a sports revolution.

Some sixty years later, and just six years after the Marylebone Cricket Club (MCC) was formed at Lord's, the first sports club—a peculiarly British institution—was formed for playing cricket in Calcutta. The city was then in its early years of existence and a long way from becoming the second city of empire. Although most clubs' early records have been lost, the existence of

Members of the Calcutta Cricket Club, the second oldest cricket club in the world, 1859. Reprinted by permission of the Council of the National Army Museum, London

the Calcutta Cricket Club is vouched for by the *Madras Courier*, which on February 23, 1792, reported cricket matches between the Calcutta Cricket Club and teams from Barackpore and Dum Dum, both on the outskirts of Calcutta and home to British regiments. Despite 1792 being regarded as the beginning of organized cricket in India, an entry on December 16, 1780, in Hickey's *Bengal Gazette*, the first English newspaper in India, points to an earlier date. The report says that the gentlemen of the Calcutta Cricket Club were preparing to take the field for an active campaign, going on to add that the club enjoyed the "use of a splendid site as good as can be found anywhere."[3] A decade later, a two-day "Grand Match of Cricket" was held in January 1804 between old Etonians employed by the East India Company and a team representing Calcutta. One of the players was the son of Sir Elijah Impey, the chief justice of Bengal. The Etonians won the match handsomely by 152 runs, with Robert Vansittart scoring a century and taking eight wickets.[4]

Very soon other clubs were formed in Calcutta and elsewhere, almost all of which were organized around sports activities. There was good reason for the British to take up sports and games in a country where the mortality rate for foreigners was extremely high. In his *Notes on an Outfit for India and Hints for the New Arrival*, published in 1903, the anonymous J. E. D. wrote that the British in India who looked the most fit and in the best of spirits were those who took regular exercise on the playfield or during duty.[5] Besides, as another writer advised a year earlier, the English in India would be wise to surround themselves "with English atmosphere, and to defend themselves from the magic of the land by sports, games, clubs."[6]

In the early days, the club was a basic affair serving as a "meeting place, with a few old books and some drinks," only later evolving into places where "people would be busily chatting among themselves, drinks would be flowing freely and you would repeatedly hear the exclamation 'Koi Hai!' which was the call for one of the servants to come and attend."[7] As novelist George Orwell, a bitter critic of colonialism, wrote in *Burmese Days*, in any town in India, the European Club was "the spiritual citadel, the real seat of the British power."[8]

Of course, cricket wasn't the only game played in these clubs. Clubs in the larger stations usually had badminton and squash courts and, often after the 1920s, a swimming pool. Other sports such as rugby, billiards, croquet, golf, and even rowing, which required navigable rivers as in Calcutta and Pune or lakes as in Nainital, Ootacamund, and Srinagar, also were taken up with gusto. The roll call of clubs that followed the pioneering Calcutta Cricket Club is long and distinguished. The Bombay Turf Club (for horse racing) was founded in 1800, the Royal Calcutta Golf Club in 1829 (making it the oldest golf club outside Britain), the Madras Cricket Club in 1846, the Calcutta Rowing Club in 1858, the Bangalore Club in 1868, the Bombay Gymkhana in 1875, and several more in towns and outposts across the length and breadth of India. The Bombay Gymkhana was fairly representative of the process of bringing together all kinds of sports under one roof incorporating the cricket, polo, football, and gun clubs in 1875 and the boat club the next year. Very soon football, hockey, badminton, tennis, racquets, bowling, and golf were introduced. The membership, too, jumped from 150 to more than 600 within a decade.[9]

What was initially common to these clubs was that all of them were strictly for whites. Even the British had a rigid hierarchy, with the Indian Civil Service officers, the so-called heaven-born (the Brahmins) at the top of the heap, with the ordinary soldiers and Eurasians at the bottom. In fact, admission was so inflexible that when members married, it was the practice for them to resign and be reinducted only after their wives were deemed worthy of the club. Clubs also were rigidly segregated according to profession. An army officer, for instance, would not have been eligible for membership in the Bengal Club in Calcutta, which was meant for the boxwallahs, nor would a man in commerce have been eligible for the United Service Club, which was meant only for those in the army. Even Englishmen belonging to the same family were forced to take up membership in different clubs because of their profession.[10]

Several of these clubs had the word "gymkhana" as a suffix, and for an explanation of this word, we can do no better than to turn to *Hobson-Jobson*, a compendium of Anglo-Indian words and phrases collected by Henry Yule and Arthur Burnell. The authors believe that the word was probably derived from *gend-khana* (ball house), and not from the Urdu *jamaat-khana* (a place of assemblage). According to them, it applied to "a place where the needful facilities for athletics and games of sorts are provided, including (when in fashion) a skating rink, a lawn tennis ground, and so forth."[11] Cricket, however, occupied pride of place, as is evident from a report in the *Pioneer Mail* in 1877: "Their proposals are that the Cricket Club should include in their programme the games, & c, proposed by the promoters of a gymkhana Club, so far as not to interfere with cricket, and should join in making a rink and lawn-tennis, and badminton courts, within the cricket-ground enclosure."[12]

Sir Edward Blunt, who served as an Indian Civil Service (ICS) officer in India from 1901 to 1936, writes that in his time, cricket, rugby, football, hockey, lawn tennis, and golf all were played, alongside polo.[13] He paints a vibrant picture of sports in India. There were numerous competitions in cricket, hockey, and football, in which the teams usually played one another on a knockout system in which the winners of each stage play in the next. The All-India Lawn Tennis Association and its provincial branches organized a number of tournaments. Sports leagues were formed in the larger cities, in which the local clubs, the regiments, and the gymkhana, which was usually attached to the European club, took part.[14]

Sports meets were held at certain periods of the year, particularly in hill stations like Simla, the summer capital during the British Raj, and Nainital. The latter was famous for its early autumn "sporting week," during which civilians and ICS officers challenged the "Rest" at cricket, football, hockey, lawn tennis, golf, polo, billiards, and even rowing, for Nainital has a picturesque lake nestled in the mountains. The schedule was a hectic one, since all the games were played one after the other, with the cricket match and the polo tournament lasting three days each. It wasn't unusual for participants to play a hockey or football match immediately after a full day of cricket, which could be especially exhausting in Nainital's high altitude.[15]

Women were part of the events too. Croquet was equally popular among both sexes. At the end of the nineteenth century, Nainital had a separate "sporting week" for women in which teams were formed according to marital status. In 1901, for instance, the unmarried women (unflatteringly called "spins") broke even with their married counterparts at tennis but won all the other events, including the boat race, hockey, and cricket.[16] In addition, women occasionally played polo,[17] and even cricket matches involving women were not so uncommon. For example, in 1886, a team of women took on men in a match in Simla, with the viceroy in the audience. The playing conditions were that the gentlemen should "bat, bowl, field, and throw left and should use broomsticks in place of bats."[18] Not-so-serious events like the Pagal Gymkhana also were part of the sports "weeks." For example, one of its program of events at Mysore began with pigsticking, followed by a treasure hunt, "running the gauntlet," a potato race, and musical chairs.[19] As an observer noted about the scene in Simla: "The gymkhana events in Simla resemble very closely some of the adventures of Don Quixote . . . charging wind mills, sheep, tent pegs, etc., but there are some less dangerous items; to wit, egg and spoon, cricket ball and affinity races."[20]

For the better part of the nineteenth century, with some notable exceptions like the public schools and missionary institutions, the British were not really interested in extending their sports to the Indians. The English clubs represented a "sanctuary of English life in an alien environment," where one European team played against another and then fraternized over dinner and drinks.[21] Not until much later were "mixed" clubs that admitted Indians and British, such as the Calcutta Club (1907) and the Willingdon Club (1918) in Bombay, formed, at the Indians' insistence and also because the white-only

policy was increasingly becoming an embarrassment to the Raj. The Willingdon Club, for instance, was established because a maharaja accompanying
Viceroy Willingdon was refused entry into the Bombay Gymkhana.

The combination of pleasure with play and the racial exclusivity that accompanied it is well captured in an account of the Calcutta Cricket Club
from around the mid-nineteenth century:

> On the cricket arena stand two spacious tents, not, however, like the pal-
> try affairs bearing the name in England but lined with fancy chintz, fur-
> nished with looking glasses, sofas and chairs, and each player's wants are
> supplied by his turbaned attendants whether it be a light for his cigar,
> iced soda-water, or champagne. The natives do not enter at all into the
> spirit of this manly game, neither do the servants of the players, if desired
> to stop a stray ball, think it at all meritorious to risk stinging their fingers
> by stopping it while in motion, they amble by its side until it has ceased
> rolling and then pick it up.[22]

This attitude was the norm in all the clubs formed by the British. Indians
involved in the British sports were usually either "Fecknee wallers," those
who threw the ball at batsmen during practice, or mute spectators, who occasionally caught boundary hits and returned them to the players. At the same
time, many Indians felt a strange attraction to English sports, as marvelously
captured in Rudyard Kipling's "The Story of Muhammad Din," which tells of
a little boy's fascination with a polo ball—"an old one, scarred, chipped and
dinted"—kept on the mantelpiece of the white sahib's bungalow.[23]

Soldiers and Sports

Besides the clubs, the other center of sports activity in India was the British regiments and cantonments. For soldiers away from home and all things
familiar, the best way to keep themselves occupied was sports. As a former
British soldier explained, "We had one great weapon against boredom. The
answer was sport, sport, sport."[24] Sports were also officially encouraged.
In 1863, the Royal Commission on the Sanitary State of the Army in India
linked the "high rate of sickness and mortality" of soldiers to the "weary idle-
ness of their lives" and "want of exercise."[25] In response to the commission's

inquiries, an officer admitted that there were no "exercising grounds" for soldiers.[26] Later in the early 1900s, Lord Horatio H. Kitchener, the commander in chief of the army in India, recommended "all healthy outdoor games and sports" to keep at bay "impurity and disease."[27]

Around the turn of the century, sports contests between regiments were common. In 1908, for example, the officers of the First/King's Royal Rifle Corps (also known as the Greenjackets) challenged their counterparts in the Jubbalpore garrison. The events included cricket, polo, a road race, a walking race, billiards, golf, shooting, racquets, tennis, and tug-of-war and was spread over six weeks. The Greenjacket officers, who numbered only fifteen, triumphed, even though their opponents numbered fifty.[28]

For a glimpse of regimental life in India, the most readable account (and one that also reflects all the prejudices of the time) is Frank Richards's *Old Soldier-Sahib*, reminiscences of his time in northern India as a subaltern in the Second Battalion Royal Welch Fusiliers from 1902 to 1909. According to Richards, British soldiers played all kinds of sports, but boxing and football tournaments were the most popular. Boxing was compulsory in Richards's regiment. On the day of the "physical training parade," the men were divided into sections and given gloves, after which they slugged it out against one another for five minutes or so and then watched the others doing the same.[29] Indeed, one of Britain's most successful heavyweight boxers in the early twentieth century, Bombardier Billy Wells, was posted in Rawalpindi with the Royal Artillery and won the All-India title twice before leaving the army in 1910 and turning professional. But it was football that really caught the imagination of soldiers in India, prompting Major General Harcourt Mortimer Bengough to comment in 1896 that football was "the only game into which the soldier throws himself with any zest."[30] Later Richards wrote, "If we are ever so unfortunate as to lose our Empire it is a safe bet that soccer will continue to be played all over the world ... in eternal memory of the British soldiers who accidentally brought the game along in their kit-bags."[31]

The institution of clubs and the military overlapped, of course, since soldiers were behind the organization of many clubs. This isn't surprising if we consider the numbers: In 1901, half the British population were military men and their dependents: some 61,000 soldiers, 10,000 women and children, and 5,000 officers. This meant that the cantonments in British India had a large physical presence. Another equally important statistic is that the

The football team of the Twentieth Duke of Cambridge's Infantry, 1920. Note that of the eleven players, only two are British. Reprinted by permission of the Council of the National Army Museum, London

65,000 British soldiers commanded 120,000 Indian sepoys, a ratio of one to two, which had been as low as one British soldier to six sepoys before the 1857 uprising. This meant that the British soldiers and the Indian sepoys had to come in contact, living as they were in relatively close proximity. Sports were one of the rare instances in which their lives intersected. An army doctor testified to the Royal Commission on the Sanitary State of the Army in India that some officers wrestled with native soldiers and "sometimes beat their own [Indian] best wrestlers, and they became very popular with them in consequence."[32] Another officer recalled, "In the evening we used to go to along and have a chat with the Gurkha boys. We would invariably find them playing football and they would immediately split up and demand that we should join them."[33] Although physical contact with native soldiers was not encouraged, beginning in the early twentieth century many regiments had mixed football teams comprising both British and Indian soldiers. Surviving photographs show the football team of the Fifty-Second Sikhs (Frontier Force) posing with an interregimental trophy in 1921 and the Twentieth

Duke of Cambridge's Own Infantry during the same period, when at least half the team were Sikh soldiers.[34]

There were interactions on the cricket pitch, too. Although it is commonly believed that the Parsis were the first Indians to take up cricket, according to news reports published in the *Sporting Intelligence Magazine* (brought out by the *Englishman* newspaper between 1833 and 1850), Indian sepoys were playing cricket as early as 1845. A report of a match played between the European officers and the sepoys of the light company against those of the other companies of the Twenty-Eighth Regiment at Sylhet, in present-day Bangladesh, on March 2, 1845, states:

> The most enthusiastic European cricketers could not have played with more energy and cheerfulness than the native sepoys did. I am not a cricketer myself, but invariably attend as a spectator when the natives are playing; the knowledge that the officers, whether playing or not, take an active interest in their performances gratifies the sepoys.[35]

The reporter observed that as fielders, few Europeans could surpass the sepoys. He singled out one Lungum for his batting prowess and forecast that in a season or two, the Indian sepoys would become very able cricket players. Yet another report advocated cricket as essential to bridging "the distance of the Europeans in the intercourse with the native."[36] In fact, it was this distance between the British officers and the Indian sepoys and the concomitant distrust that it bred that was one of the causes of the great uprising of 1857.

The British Take Up Polo

It wasn't, however, all a one-way traffic of English games being introduced to India by the colonizers. The game that was once the favorite of Mughal emperors was enthusiastically adopted by the British, first in Manipur in the northeast and then gradually across India. The British admitted that polo was an "Indian game before it became an English one."[37] The story of how polo reached the small, rain-lashed northeastern kingdom of Manipur bordering Burma is something of a puzzle. Indeed, whether polo traveled from Central Asia to Manipur, where it was known as *sagol kangjei,* or whether the region had its own variant of the game is debatable. In 1835, a report from the eastern frontier of British India said of Manipur: "The national game of Hockey, which is played by every male of the country capable of sitting [on] a horse renders them all expert equestrians."[38] It is quite possible that the word "polo" is derived from the Tibetan word *pulu* for the wooden ball.

Major General James Johnstone, who was appointed as the political agent in Manipur in 1877, left an early account of polo, which was held in "high esteem" in the region. There was a big polo ground next to the British residency, with a grandstand for the local maharaja on one side and opposite it another for the political agent. Games were held every Sunday, and one of the maharaja's sons, Pucca Sena, was a champion polo player. Johnstone was careful not to play the game himself, however, since he did not want to run the risk of being "hustled and jostled" by the locals, fearing that it might undermine his position. Besides, he was well aware of his shortcomings as a polo player and careful not to be humiliated by the Manipuri players.[39] But one of Johnstone's successors, Frank St. Clair Grimwood, had no such qualms and was an enthusiastic polo player before he was killed in a palace revolution.

Another soldier, Lieutenant Colonel Alban Wilson, of the Gurkha Rifles, captured the flavor of the brand of polo played in Manipur when he was in the region in the 1890s. He described it as the "most exciting thing to watch, for there seems to be no rules beyond that the width of the ground at either side is the goal and the ball has to be got there anyhow."[40] Besides the lack of rules, his description of the atmosphere when the game was played also made it apparent that Manipuri polo was different from the version played by the British:

> The game is watched by a crowd of partisans, who keep up a continuous roar of comment, advice, and encouragement, above which is heard the thudding of the ponies' hoofs, with the rattle of the sticks or clicking of the ball, not to mention the continuous drumming of the players' heels on the big leather shields, which is supposed to encourage their own ponies, whilst making those of the opponents shy off.[41]

By the 1860s, polo had become popular with the British. According to the standard version, a British soldier, Lieutenant (later Major General) Joseph Ford Sherer of the Forty-Fourth Regiment of the (Bengal) Native Light In-

fantry, in the 1850s first observed tea plantation workers from Manipur playing polo and took to the game. The first record of a polo club in India, and
indeed the world, is from Cachar in Assam, started by Sherer and Captain
Robert Stewart, superintendent of Cachar, in 1859. It was composed mainly
of planters and Manipuris. Stewart's brother, General G. Stewart, left an account of polo and its spread in the early days. The general visited his brother
in September 1862 and saw the game being played at Cachar. He returned in
October that year with sticks and balls to Barrackpore, near Calcutta, where
he was stationed. Like a true Englishman, he immediately formed a club,
where polo was played assiduously. On seeing them, some residents of Calcutta became excited and formed a club as well. Soon after, the first match
was played between the Barrackpore Club and the Calcutta Club on the Calcutta maidan in early 1863.[42] Stewart, who by then had become a sort of a
missionary for the game, took polo to Peshawar in the northwestern frontier,
where it was called *kangai*. Eventually polo made its way to England, where
in 1871 a polo match was played in Hounslow Heath.

Not surprisingly, it was widely accepted that only after the British adopted
polo did it acquire the status and paraphernalia of a modern sport. As Briga-
dier General Robert Lumsden Ricketts wrote: "It was not until the game was
taken up by Western races and their more systematic minds and mechanical
efficiency that progress in tactical ideas became possible."[43] The most popular tournaments of the time were the Inter-Regimental and the Indian Polo
Association (IPA) championships. By 1898, the *Indian Sportsman* could confi-
dently assert,

> The ever increasing number of polo tournaments held all over the coun-
> try under IPA rules, affords striking proof, if indeed such proof were
> needed, of the hold the game has taken of the affections of Anglo-Indian
> and native sportsmen. It is as much now the national game of India as
> cricket is of England.[44]

One of the reasons for the popularity of polo was the ubiquity of horse
riding in the Raj, for both exercise and getting to remote places. A British
officer even confessed that everybody was expected to play polo and if he
didn't like it, he didn't have much of an option. He even recalled ticking off
an assistant who didn't want to play, by saying, "Well, if you can't play polo

Lieutenant (later Major General) Joseph Sherer, the "father" of polo, with his Manipuri bearers, 1861. Reprinted by permission of the Council of the National Army Museum, London

you're not much use to me. I'll have to find somebody who can."[45] Polo also held immense appeal to spectators. Frank Richards was an avid spectator at the polo ground and felt that "there are more thrills in watching polo than a football or cricket match ever provided." Polo cost a lot of money, however. Good ponies could cost £100 to £200 each, as ponies were changed after each *chukka* (a period of continuous play lasting roughly seven minutes). As the ICS officer Blunt lamented, "Nowadays, polo is no longer within everybody's reach; the size of the pony has been raised, and its price has risen with it. Thirty-five years ago, polo ponies, and indeed ponies of any kind, could be obtained for less than half their present cost."[46]

More than any other sport, polo was very much a part of army life and cantonments, particularly among officers. Sir Robert Baden-Powell, a huge fan of outdoor sports, wrote in his memoir, "Polo is without doubt the finest game that has ever been invented."[47] Britain's future prime minister, Winston Churchill, was an ardent fan of polo as well and a member of the crack Fourth Hussars team in India. Once at a grand dinner to mark the end of the annual interregimental polo tournament, he waxed eloquent on how polo was not only the finest game in the world but also the "most noble and soul-inspiring contest in the whole universe."[48] In fact, Churchill once traveled from England to India in 1899 solely to take part in the Inter-Regimental Tournament.

It was no surprise that cavalry regiments like the Fourth Hussars excelled in polo. But there were notable exceptions, such as the short-lived revolution led by the curiously named Henry de Beauvoir De Lisle. With the support of his commanding officer, De Lisle began a polo club in the Durham Light Infantry Regiment that successfully challenged the hegemony of the cavalry regiments. The Durham team, which under De Lisle's tutelage adopted tactics borrowed from the regiment's football team, won the Inter-Regimental Tournament three times between 1896 and 1898. But when De Lisle left in 1898, the team's prospects took a nosedive.[49]

Polo and the cost of maintaining horses were paradoxically believed to keep young officers out of mischief. One pamphlet noted that regimental polo players had nothing at all to drink at the polo ground and, after the game, went home to recuperate. Many of them cut down on their drinking and smoking so as to allow them to keep an extra pony.[50] Some, of course, resented the idea that regimental polo clubs and horses had to be subsidized by nonplaying officers. An officer mocked his polo-mad compatriots by asking: "Oh! Ye slaves of the goddess of Polo! Why do you enpinnacle yourselves? Why this lofty supercilious attitude towards the rest of the sporting world? ... Let us cease this intolerance, and agree that all sports are good which are health giving and manly."[51] To this, "A Lover of the Game" had a ready reply:

> I know of no pastime (and I play most games) which so completely absorbs all the faculties. Sit in an office eight or nine hours a days, but play six *chuckkers* three times a week, and they suffice to keep one in trim, even if one owns fully matured ponies across the back of which one never throws leg except polo.[52]

Behind this banter lay a serious question about the expenses incurred by officers in playing polo and the fear that only those with sufficient private wealth could join the ranks of commissioned officers in the cavalry. The situation was serious enough for the War Office in London in 1900 to forbid regimental teams to take part in polo tournaments outside their military districts.[53] A year earlier the lieutenant general of Bengal had ordered all station polo clubs to be disbanded. But such directives were honored more in the breach than in the observance and were met with fierce resistance from cavalry officers. Despite the periodic efforts to curb polo and to regulate the expenses of playing the game and maintaining horses, a 1909 report emphasized that young officers be "encouraged to hunt and play polo."[54]

Hunting and the Raj

Some continuities in outdoor sports and recreation can be found from the Mughal period to the British Raj. As it was for the Mughal kings and nobility, hunting was a passion for many British officials. In this they were aided and abetted by the Indian princes who enthusiastically carried on the centuries-old tradition of organized *shikar* (hunting and shooting). The biggest slaughters took place when viceroys, governors, or the British royal family visited the princely states. C. B. Fry, an English cricketer and longtime associate of Ranji, wrote, "In Indian India, *shikar* holds a prominent place when important events bring important visitors, and in quiet times no guest of an Indian prince would be considered even fairly entertained without being taken out to shoot."[55]

On one such occasion, the maharaja of Bikaner in 1906 organized a two-day session for the viceroy, Lord Minto, during which an astonishing 4,919 sand grouse were shot dead.[56] Six years later, the next viceroy, Lord Hardinge, visited Bikaner and later recorded in his diary: "The best morning I ever had was one thousand four hundred grouse to thirty guns, but I have heard that sometimes as many as four thousand have been shot in one morning."[57] Indeed, hunting was de rigueur for the British, both military men and civilians, and was seen as a sign of masculinity. Literally anything that moved, from ducks to black bucks, was fair game for hunters. The biggest prize was a tiger, whose skin occupied pride of place in many *dak* bungalows. Some people would have nothing to do with hunting, and even if they owned a shotgun and a rifle, they never ever fired them.[58] Sir Alfred Lyall, the lieutenant governor of the North-Western Provinces, wrote to his mother that he felt a "queer sympathy for the tiger when alone and with his claws only he defeats men armed with powerful rifles."[59]

Back home, the British had their storied tradition of fox hunting, and in India they substituted the fox hunt with jackals. One of the most committed civilian hunters, Frank Simson, who wrote the *Letters on Sport in Eastern Bengal*, did not have a high opinion of jackal hunting. But in the North-West Frontier, jackal hunting had its constituents, some of them women, and in Lahore and Peshawar, jackal hunts were common. Participants in the hunt felt that the jackals gave as good a run, if not better, than the fox. Some imported foxhounds from England and reported that the hunt was just as good as in England except that instead of hedges they had to jump over irrigation ditches.[60] Some of the oldest and most elaborate hunts were staged in southern India, the earliest being the Madras hunt in 1776 and the one at Ootacamund in 1844.

Much more popular in British India was pigsticking (or hog hunting, as it was known in western India). According to Blunt, pigsticking had been pursued by Europeans from around 1800. While earlier the spear was thrown in a parabola toward the boar, a civilian named Mills apparently introduced the method of overhead spearing. One of the most ardent proponents of pigsticking was Robert Baden-Powell, who wrote to his mother,

You may think it a cruel form of sport as you sit in your armchair at home, but I am perfectly certain that if you were riding with me here and saw one of these shaggy old devils coming at me you would be the first to cry: "Stick him, Robert, stick him!"[61]

Yet another strong supporter of the sport for its ameliorating effect was the ICS officer Philip Woodruff, who felt that "ugly lusts for power and revenge melted away and even the lust for women assumed reasonable proportions after a day in pursuit of a pig."[62] In contrast, women like Isabel Savory found pigsticking "wildly exciting" and was even moved to compose poetry in honour of the sport.

Over the valley, over the level,
Through the thick jungle, ride with the devil
Hark forward! A boar! Away we go!
Sit down and rife straight!—tally ho!
He is a true-bred one—none of your jinking;
Straight across country—no time for thinking.
There is water in front!—There's a boar as well;
Harden your heart; and, ride pell-mell.[63]

Pigsticking was popular across India, especially in the riverbeds or *kadirs* of the United Provinces. The Meerut Club was the most famous of the pigsticking clubs and the site of the annual pigsticking competition, the Kadir Cup, which took place over three days in March and involved up to 150 horses. The tournament was a grand affair with a contemporary observing that "50 elephants crowded with competitors, spectators and a fair sprinkling of ladies"[64] at the competition. The competition was started in 1865 and was won mainly by soldiers (technically it was the horse and not the rider who won), although Blunt proudly mentions that civilians won the cup twice in 1896 and 1919.[65] According to Simson, Calcutta was one of the best places to enjoy hog hunting, especially if one were a member of a tent club, as the hunting clubs were known. The sport cut across classes, as was evident from the passion for pigsticking of the governor of Bombay, Mountstuart Elphinstone. It is said that when pigs were reported to have been seen, he would declare a holiday to go hunting. The sport wasn't without its dangers, though. One enthusiast recalled how a big boar once charged him and inflicted a nasty wound on his leg. But such injuries were usually shrugged off, and the pigsticking went on as usual.[66] Indeed, injuries sustained during pigsticking were a source of pride. Thus, one entry in a tent club journal reads: "Result of meet—Twenty-four boar, two panther, one sahib badly mauled, one coolie ditto, one broken collar-bone, one dislocated shoulder, one back injured and (only) four horses hors de combat."[67]

The Beginnings of Cricket

Even though English sports were a preserve of whites, their games, as well as their obsession with clubs, soon spread to Indians. The first Indians to take to an English sport in large numbers were the Parsis, who not only embraced cricket enthusiastically but were equally passionate chroniclers of the game. One of the reasons why the Parsis, who were originally traders and merchants, became such fans of cricket was their professional proximity to the British. The Parsis themselves were fond of explaining that they were not Indian at all but Persian and that during Alexander the Great's conquest of Persia, many Greeks married Persians, making the Parsis half Greek.[68] By the 1830s, scores of Parsi boys, wearing their dhoti and *dagli*, were playing cricket. Shapoorjee Sorabjee, who could well be called the first historian of cricket in India, wrote in his *Chronicle of Cricket Among Parsees and the Struggle: European Polo Versus Native Cricket* that the games were most often impromptu affairs: "Parsee boys began with a mock and farcical imitation of European soldiers and officers playing at Fort George, Bombay, their chimney-pot hats serving as wickets, and their umbrellas as bats in hitting elliptical balls stuffed with old rags and sewn by veritably unskillful cobblers."[69]

By 1848 the Parsis were organized enough to form their own club, the Oriental Cricket Club, followed by Young Zoroastrian Club in 1850. This led to a veritable explosion, with several more clubs established. The names of these clubs—Jupiter, Juvenile, Spartan, and Mars—betrayed the Parsis' Anglicization. As Sorabjee explained,

It may strike one why the Parsees should have in their first stage of cricketing styled their clubs after the appellations of the Greek gods. The reason was that during those days the history of Greece was generally taught in the schools that had the least pretence to afford high or classical education. The youths naturally were very much led away by the mighty exploits of the Greek gods and their youthful fancy kept those names vividly uppermost in their minds.[70]

By 1888, the Parsi cricketer Mehallasha Edulji Pavri could list as many as twenty-seven Parsi clubs dedicated to playing cricket.[71] In this enterprise of forming clubs, the Parsis, as an anthropologist put it, were the "bridge community between Indian and English cultural tastes."[72] Even at this early stage, there were monetary incentives to playing sport. Prize matches had begun as early as 1868, and Sorabjee reports that adequate prizes were given away in cricket equipment and cash money. The prize in 1869 was Rs 100, which wasn't a trifling sum at the time.

This had a domino effect among other communities, with the Bombay Union Cricket Club and the Hindu Cricket Club being founded by Marathi students of the Elphinstone High School in 1861 and 1877, respectively. Elsewhere, the Aligarh Cricket Club was established at the Mohammedan Anglo-Oriental College by a Brahmin professor in 1879, and the Madras United Cricket Club was founded by the legendary Buchi Babu Naidu in 1891 to challenge the racially exclusive Madras Cricket Club. The proliferation of clubs made a mockery of an Englishman's claim in 1861: "The game is essentially English and though our countrymen carry it abroad wherever they go, it is difficult to inoculate or knock into the foreigner."[73]

The Parsis' passion for the game was not wholeheartedly welcomed by the British, as is illustrated in the bitter struggle in 1868 for space to play in Bombay. The first clash occurred when a cricket ball struck the wife of a European police constable while she was taking a walk around the Oval in Rotten Row opposite the Secretariat buildings. Shortly afterward, the police commissioner decreed that no more cricket would be allowed at the site. But Sir Joseph Arnould, chief justice of the high court of Bombay, who was a regular spectator of the Parsi boys playing cricket, wrote to the *Bombay Gazette*, "We, English, no doubt are reputed to prefer taking our pleasure sadly and exclusively, but it must be very un-English sport of exclusiveness that feels itself annoyed by a few noisy games of cricket played in its neighbourhood by Parsee schoolboys."[74] Arnould's protests came to naught when the commissioner of police, F. S. Souter, wrote back to the *Gazette* explaining that the "best piece of ground for recreation in Bombay" could not be "wholly monopolized by a few cricketers."[75] He then proposed that another piece of ground be allotted to the cricketers and that the ground in Rotten Row be used only until five in the evening.

A few years later, there was another tussle over a piece of the maidan on which British polo players descended and disrupted cricket matches. Again, Sorabjee provided a detailed account of this extraordinary face-off. Twice a week, polo players belonging to the all-white Bombay Gymkhana played on the public portion of the maidan, not only disrupting cricket games, but also damaging the cricket pitch. Under Sorabjee's leadership, the Parsis first protested to the Bombay Gymkhana, to no avail, and then petitioned the Bombay governor, James Ferguson, in 1881. The petition, signed by 440 cricketers, including both Parsis and Hindus, observed that "it was a little unfair that the comforts and conveniences of the half-a-dozen gentlemen, who generally play polo, should be preferred to the necessary healthful recreation of over five hundred native youths."[76] It even demanded a portion of the gymkhana grounds, since it was "too large for their requirements." When this was rebuffed, the cricketers again petitioned the governor, explaining that "hundreds of cricketers are forced to be crowded into a small space with all its disadvantages."[77] This time Sorabjee and his fellow Parsis were successful, and in 1882 under a resolution by the Public Works Department, the polo players were forced to relocate to a spot farther south.

This victory was short-lived, however, and, in Sorabjee's words, "too much for the Bombay Gymkhana to put up with." A year later, the tables were turned when on a counterpetition by the polo secretary of the Bombay Gymkhana, this time to Governor Ferguson's successor, the earlier order was reversed, and the polo players made a comeback, prompting the gymkhana polo secretary to write to the *Times of India* not to "allow the preposterous notion to take root that a few young Parsee cricketers are going to be allowed to oppose the whole European community and jostle the Europeans off the Esplanade, whether at polo or anything else."[78] This was a clear indication that many of the British in Bombay were opposed to Indians taking up English sports.

The Spread of Football

While the Parsis, and a handful of others, were discovering the joys of cricket, across the subcontinent in Calcutta, Indians were getting their first taste of

yet another great English sport: football (to Americans, soccer). The first recorded football match was a thirty-minute affair in 1802 in Bombay when
a Military eleven trounced an Island eleven, 5-0, but it was in Calcutta that
organized football first took root. The British regiments in and around the
city took the lead in organizing the sport, with the first football match taking
place in 1854. A local newspaper, *The Englishman*, reported, "A Calcutta team
of civilians had challenged the Gentlemen of Barrackpore to meet for a trial
of their skill in the manly game of soccer on Saturday, the 13th April 1854, on
the Esplanade Ground, Fort William, Calcutta, at 5.15 P.M." As in Bombay, the
site was the vast stretch of green, the maidan, located in front of Fort William
in Calcutta, originally intended to provide a clear field of fire. Other matches
followed, in 1868 between the Etonians and the Rest, in which Lord Vansittart scored twice for the Etonians, and another in 1870 between the public
schools of Eton, Harrow, and Winchester and a team composed of a certain
Miss Tina's pupils. Soon Calcutta was being described as a place where "an
unlimited supply of first-rate grounds are at the disposal of football."[79]

Surely but steadily, football clubs followed. In 1878, the first football club
in India was formed. It was initially called the Trades Club, but its name was
later changed to the Dalhousie Athletic Club. The Calcutta Football Club
(which was later merged with the Calcutta Cricket Club) was formed earlier
in 1872 but at first was devoted only to rugby football. Other pioneering football clubs of the time were the Howrah United Club, the Calcutta Rangers,
the Naval Volunteers, and the Armenian Club. The Armenians, who, some believe, were the first Europeans to come to Calcutta, were a particularly sports-
minded community and still field a rugby team in competitions. Similarly to
cricket in Bombay, it was only a matter of time before Indians were drawn to
football. Even though the first Indian to take up cricket is not known, there is
a reasonably strong claim to who was the first Indian to kick a football: Nagendra Prasad Sarvadhikari. We have an account of his initiation to the game:

> How the ten-year-old boy came to introduce football amongst Bengalees
> when related will be read like a romance. . . . One day Nagendra Prasad
> was driving with his mother to the Ganges and the carriage [was] ap-
> proaching the road on the north of the Calcutta F.C. Ground the boy no-
> ticed that on the field a number of Europeans were kicking and throwing
> a pretty roundish thing in air and running and tussling to get it again. The

boy was restless and entreating his mother got down there and watched for a few minutes the game that the Europeans were at. Suddenly the big roundish thing came rolling near the boy. Without hesitation he picked it up and felt it and found to his astonishment that such a large thing was not heavy at all. While holding it a European accosted him and laughingly said, "Kick it to me." The boy was delighted and after the Europeans kicked it in. This was the first time that a Bengali and that too a lad of ten kicked a football. The boy was jubilant.[80]

The boy was hooked, and not long after that, Sarvadhikari took the initiative to organize football games. Having collected subscriptions from classmates at the Hare School (one of the oldest schools in Calcutta, named after the Scottish reformer and watchmaker David Hare), he went and bought a football from Manton & Co, a well-known sports goods store in Calcutta. But in a classic example of the unfamiliarity of Indians with English sports, he actually bought a rugby ball! While Sarvadhikari and his friends were engaged in the bizarre act of trying to play football with a rugby ball on the Hare School grounds, they were noticed by G. A. Stack, a professor in the adjacent Presidency College. He offered to train the boys in the rules of the game, along with one of his colleagues, J. H. Gilligand. Thus was born the Boys' Club, the first football club for Indians. At around the same time, the prominent colleges of Calcutta such as Presidency College (where Sarvadhikari was later a student), Calcutta Medical College, Sibpur Engineering College, St. Xavier's College, and Bishop's College began fielding teams. Other clubs followed, with Sarvadhikari involved in organizing several of them, including Presidency, Wellington, and, finally, Sovabazar in 1887. The late 1880s saw several more football clubs—among them National Association, Town Club, Kumartuli, Aryan, and Mohun Bagan, the last being the team that would make history in 1911. Notably, a club for the Muslims, the Jubilee Club, was established in 1887, which went through a few reincarnations to finally emerge as the Mohammedan Sporting Club in 1891.

Football clubs sprang up in small towns around Calcutta. The Town Club was established in Chinsurah, a town on the Hooghly River, as early as 1883, followed by Ripon AC in 1890 and Chinsurah Sporting in 1893. In the industrial town of Howrah, across the Hooghly from Calcutta, the Howrah Sporting Club was established in 1889. Football also flourished in east Bengal, or what is now Bangladesh. The Wari Club was founded in Dacca by a *za-mindar* (landowner), Surendra Nath Roy, in 1898, while its rival, the Victoria Sporting Club, came into existence in 1903 on the initiative of five *zamindari* families.[81] The proliferation of clubs, both British and Indian, meant that tournaments, too, were held. In this, football was one step ahead of cricket.

The oldest football tournament in India was the Durand Cup, established by Sir Mortimer Durand (more famous for the Durand line separating British India from Afghanistan) and held from 1888 in Simla, in which for a long time only British teams were allowed to compete. The first open tournament, in which Indian teams could participate, was the Trades Challenge Cup, presented by the trading community of Calcutta and inaugurated in 1889. In Bombay, the Rovers Club was formed in 1890, followed by the inauguration of the Rovers Cup in 1891. The Indian Football Association was formed in 1892, without any Indian participation. It announced a "knockout tournament", the IFA Shield, which was an open tournament in name only, with Indian teams not obtaining the right to participate until much later. In 1894 the First Division Football League in Calcutta was born and also was all-British until till 1914. The Punjab–Bengal Cup, established in 1905, was restricted to regimental teams. Other tournaments included the Madras Gymkhana Cup, the Bangalore Brewery Cup, and the local gymkhana cup at Secunderabad, but the regimental teams dominated all the tournaments until the 1930s.

Wherever the British regiments went, they took their games with them. Frank Richards, whose regimental team had won a few tournaments open to British troops, recounts that Indians were enthusiastic about football. When his regiment passed through Roorkee on their march from Meerut, the regimental team generally played a game with native students from the college. The students, who played in their bare feet, were quick, but they could not match the physicality of the British soldiers, which invariably made the difference between defeat and victory.[82] What Richards does not mention, however, is that in those days, the Indian students would never have dared to play roughly, out of deference to the white man. In any event, that football had spread widely is evident from Richards's delightful description of a street game in northern India:

> The most amusing soccer match I ever saw was played on a wide open
> rough road at one end of the Regimental Bazaar. The players were two

picked teams of natives from the Bazaar, who played in their bare feet. Their ages ranged from ten to seventy. They had a proper soccer ball, but the goal-posts were represented by large blocks of baked clay. The chief difficulty of the native referee was to judge whether a high ball which had passed over the heads of the goalkeepers was a goal or not a goal. Most of the male population of the Bazaar had turned out to watch the game and as it progressed they became as excited as the crowd at a Cup Final at Wembley. Most of them had wagered a pice or two on the game, and by the row they kicked up anyone would have thought that there were thousands of pounds in the pot. I heard more bad language than what there would have been in a dozen matches between the Royal Welch Fusiliers and the Highland Light Infantry. Young and old cursed one another with impunity and the referee spent a great deal of his time cursing players and spectators who had dared to question his decisions. Just before half-time the first real stoppage in the game occurred, when the referee awarded a goal for a ball that had passed a good fifteen feet above the head of the white-whiskered old goalkeeper. The goalkeeper called him a something-or-other loose-wallah, and the game was held up to allow these two stand with arms folded on their chests at the regulation interval and go back to each other's pedigrees. The duel lasted about ten minutes, and the referee, who had a bit of a reputation for this sort of a thing, which was his chief claim to the position of referee, was declared the winner. Not many players or spectators objected to his decisions afterwards. Half-way through the second half, a large Indian cart drawn by two slow-moving bullocks came along the road and passed over the playing pitch. The driver and his ancestors were cursed to all eternity by the referee, the players and the spectators, for interrupting the game. The driver halted his team in order to reply suitably, which lengthened the interruption considerably. Just before dusk the game ended in a draw of 1–1.[83]

Competing with the British

The formation of Indian clubs meant that sooner or later there would be encounters on the playing field between the "natives" and the British. The first such contest on the cricket pitch was a rather farcical one between an army regiment and the Parsis, described as "Officers with Umbrellas Versus Natives in Bats." Sorabjee reported that five or six matches were probably played between Mars, a Parsi cricket club, and Union C.C., a European or Eurasian club. In 1877, however, the Parsis played a two-day game against the Bombay Gymkhana, in which the Indian team played well, even managing to take a lead in the first innings. The *Times of India* reported: "The Parsee fielding was remarkably good while the return of the ball was quick."[84] The *Bombay Gazette* had a more detailed description of the proceedings:

> In the afternoon the ground bore a significantly lively appearance. Thousands of natives took up a position wherever they could get a glimpse of the players, and whenever a shot or catch was made, they yelled with an enthusiasm that bespoke much for the future of cricket among them in Bombay.[85]

The *Bombay Gazette* was spot on, since the standard of cricket among Indians had improved by leaps and bounds. Between 1879 and 1883, the Parsis and the Bombay Gymkhana did not play each other. In 1886 a team of Parsi cricketers took the bold step of touring England in the summer, but their record was nothing to write home about, as they lost nineteen matches and won only one match against a certain Lord Brassey's team. Eight of the matches were draws. But they did have the chance to play against the English colossus, W. G. Grace, at Lord's. The same year, the Parsis petitioned the governor of Bombay for land to begin their own gymkhana, and in 1887 they were granted a plot a little to the west of the Esplanade, which had been the site of a bitter struggle earlier. The very next year, a team of Parsis again toured England, acquitting themselves much better this time. They won eight matches, and lost eleven. Eleven matches ended as draws The undoubted star was M. E. Pavri, who was also known as the W. G. Grace of the Parsis, not only by virtue of being a doctor by profession but also for his cricketing skills.

The improvement in the Parsis' cricket skills was reflected in 1889 when the Parsi Gymkhana beat the Bombay Gymkhana in what had now become an annual contest, with Pavri doing the star turn. The Parsi Gymkhana's greatest triumph came in 1890 against an English team led by G. F. Vernon, which included the famous cricketer Lord Hawke. The visiting team had already beaten the Bombay Gymkhana handily when they met the Parsis on

January 30, 1890, in what was billed as the "Cricket Championship of India." The match was watched by crowds numbering more than 12,000, and it roused great passions. The Parsi captain J. M. Framji Patel remembered:

> The canvas tents pitched on the western side of the ground were closely packed with the elite of Bombay society, Indian and European. . . . The "man in the street" was out enjoying his holiday, and in tiers of five and six deep the eastern and northern boundaries of the ground were closely packed by impatient sightseers. Some perched themselves (to get a good view of the game) on the trees surrounding the enclosure. In fine, it required the brush of a Rubens to translate such beautiful sights in to colours.[86]

In a game that oscillated wildly, the Parsis successfully chased a target of 79 to win by four wickets, Pavri again being the man of the moment. The reaction by an Englishman spoke of the larger significance of the match:

> Of that vast multitude not a thousand knew the name of the thing they were looking [at], not a hundred had even an elementary knowledge of the game of cricket. But they were dimly conscious that in some particular or another the black man had triumphed over the white man, and they ran hither and thither, gibbering and chattering and muttering vague words of evil omen.[87]

The Indians' response to the victory was a dual one. On the one hand were the Parsi youth, who "felt for a day or two that he was the victor of the victors of the Waterloo." On the other, Dadabhoy Framjee, presiding over a celebration dinner for the cricketers, as reported by the *Times of India*, talked about "the instinctive fondness of the Parsees for the national game of Englishmen as a proof of their aptitude for cultivating the national spirit of Englishmen— i.e. their courage, their manliness, their perseverance, and their coolness under adverse circumstances."[88]

The Parsis' success spurred the Hindus and Muslims to stake their claim to their own gymkhanas. A Muslim cricket club had been in operation from 1883, and in 1890 the patrons of the club petitioned the Bombay governor to allot it land. These efforts bore fruit in 1891 when a plot adjacent to the Parsi

Gymkhana and one of similar size were allotted to the Islam Gymkhana. Predictably, the Hindus also joined the clamor for their own gymkhana and a plot of land. Their wish was granted in 1892 when they were given the same amount of land as the Parsis and Muslims and on the same terms. This was the genesis of the tournament organized along religious and racial lines that dominated Indian cricket until 1946.

It was not only on the cricket pitch that Indians were taking on the British. In Calcutta, the first club to win the right to compete against the British was the Sovabazar Club. Its formation represented a coming together of the landed elite and the emerging middle class, a story that was repeated in Indian sports during the first half of the twentieth century. The club, formed with the efforts of Nagendra Prasad, was born out of a rift in the Wellington Club over the entry of a low-caste football player named Moni Das, the son of a confectioner. It was certainly not the last time that caste would become an issue in Indian sports. The Sovabazar Club was founded on the premises of the Sovabazar Rajbati, which occupies an iconic place in Calcutta's history. Not only was the city's first Durga Puja (an annual festival dedicated to the mother goddess) held here, which continues to this day, but also the Hindu reformer Swami Vivekananda was given a massive reception on the premises of the Sovabazar Rajbati on his return from the Parliament of Religions in Chicago in 1893. It helped that Nagendra Prasad was a son-in-law of the family. He and a member of the Sovabazar family, Kumar Jisnendra Krishna Deb (who had already shown his interest in sports by forming a tennis club), were the honorary secretaries of the club, and the maharaja of Coochbehar, who later played a pioneering role in organizing sports in Bengal, was the president. The Sovabazar team began playing in the Trades Cup in 1889 and, in its first game against the Xaverians—also the first time that an Indian team played a European one—was handily beaten, 0–3. A highlight of the match was the hat trick scored by Norman Pritchard, a Calcutta-born Englishman who went on to win two silver medals in athletics in the Paris Olympics in 1900. But only three years later, Sovabazar had improved enough to defeat the East Surrey Regiment squad 2–1 in the 1892 edition of the Trades Cup, becoming the first Indian club ever to beat a British team. The National Association, however, had the honor of becoming the first Indian team to win the Trades Cup in 1900.

These early victories over the British came at a time when Indian nationalism was in its nascent stage. The Parsis' victory over the visiting English team
took place just five years after the Indian National Congress was established.
Just as they were in the Indian Congress, the Parsis were at the forefront of
cricket. And just as they were in politics, the Indians playing cricket were a
moderate lot. Even though some hotheaded youths might have felt that they
had bested the English in their own game, it was the rhetoric of Dadabhoy
Framjee—who spoke about emulating the spirit of Englishmen—that was the
dominant mood of the day. This changed radically in later encounters with
the British, beginning in the early twentieth century, when the fires of Indian
nationalism had become stronger and the playing field had become an arena
to challenge and subvert the mighty British Empire.

3

WHITE MAN'S BURDEN

TEACHERS, MISSIONARIES,

AND ADMINISTRATORS

INDIVIDUALS, RATHER THAN THE COLONIAL GOVERNMENT, usually patronized and promoted sports in India, as the British had no formal policy on sports in place in the colonies. This was true even for cricket, the game most beloved by the English.[1] But despite the absence of a policy, colonial officials still played a major role in the "transmission of imperial and national ideas."[2] Beginning in the late nineteenth century, many British educators and missionaries decided that sports and the "games ethic" were beneficial to Indians. This impulse was not restricted to India, however, as Charles Tennyson showed in an aptly entitled essay, "They Taught the World to Play," in which he analyzed the role of the alumni of public schools and universities in spreading English games across the British Empire. Perhaps the best-known expression of these sentiments is Henry Newbolt's poem "Vitaï Lampada" (1898), in which the refrain is "Play up! Play up! And play the game!"

A small army of public school headmasters and teachers in Britain linked sport to empire. One of the most vocal of these proponents was Rev. J. C. Welldon, the headmaster of Harrow from 1881 to 1895—the famous public school where India's first prime minister, Jawaharlal Nehru, once studied—who eloquently summed up the centrality of sport and health to the empire:

> Englishmen are not superior to Frenchmen or Germans in brains or industry or the science and apparatus of war; but they are superior in the health and temper which games impart.... I do not think I am wrong in saying that the sport, the pluck, the resolution, and the strength which have within the last few weeks animated the little garrison at Chitral [in the North West Frontier] and the gallant force that has accomplished their deliverance are effectively acquired in the cricket-fields and football fields of the great public schools, and in the games of which they are the habitual scenes. The pluck, the energy, the perseverance, the good temper, the self-control, the discipline, the co-operation, the esprit de corps, which merit success in cricket or football, are the very qualities which win the day in peace or war. The men who possessed these qualities, not sedate and faultless citizens, but men of will, spirit, and chivalry, are the men who conquered at Plassey and Quebec. In the history of the British Empire it is written that England has owed her sovereignty to her sports.[3]

The contribution of the British public schools was not limited to sustaining the empire; they also were a source of inspiration for Pierre de Coubertin, the founder of the modern Olympic Games. De Coubertin had himself written a treatise more than three hundred pages long entitled *Education en Angleterre* (*Education in England*), and he regarded English public schools and Thomas Arnold, the headmaster of Rugby, as a model. In a speech in 1887, a decade before the first modern Olympic Games, de Coubertin stated, "Two things dominate in the English system, two things that are also means of achieving their ends: freedom and sports."[4]

Likewise in India, public schools modeled on the famous English schools played a pivotal role in spreading sports and inculcating a sporting ethic in the empire's subjects. These schools targeted the sons of princely and aristocratic families and were specifically meant to "fit the young Chiefs and Nobles of India physically, morally and intellectually for the responsibilities that lay before them."[5] According to Viceroy Curzon, the public schools' aim was to familiarize the young princes with English customs, literature, science, modes of thought, standards of truth and honor, and, particularly, with "manly English sports and games."[6] This became imperative after the 1857 uprising in which Indian sepoys in the British army, along with disgruntled princely rulers and landowners, rose up against the British, one of the rallying cries being the threat posed to their traditions by the colonizers. This brought home to the British the acute need for creating a class of loyal Indian rulers educated in English ways to act as a bulwark against any future rebellion. The public schools were one way of achieving this aim, or as the British agent of the Bharatpur agency in Rajputana, Colonel F. K. M. Walter, put it, the goal was to establish an "Eton in India" for the native princes. Walter felt that the most pressing need was a college with ample accommodations for a large number of pupils, as well as a few of their retainers, staffed by "thoroughly educated English gentleman, not mere bookworms, but men fond of field sports and out-door exercises."[7] Many of these schools continue to flourish today, their clientele no longer restricted to the princely families but belonging to the Indian elites and the middle class.

Schools for Princes

The first of the princes' colleges was Rajkumar College in Rajkot in western India, which was established in 1870, a decade or so after the uprising. Mayo College in Ajmer, still a prestigious institution; another Rajkumar College in Nowgong; Aitichison in Lahore; and Daly in Indore followed in the next two decades. Besides these five schools were the lesser-known schools in Murshidabad, Lucknow, Raipur, and Hyderabad. Most of these schools had British headmasters, and sports and outdoor activities were an indispensable part of the curriculum.

Someone typical of the English gentleman who combined the virtues of a man of books and a keen sportsman was Chester Macnaghten, the first principal of Rajkumar College. He was also the person who introduced the great Ranjitsinhji to cricket. Macnaghten came from a long line of officials who had served in India. His grandfather was a judge in Calcutta, and after finishing his service in India, his father was elected a director of the East India Company and subsequently became a member of the Secretary of State's Council. Macnaghten read classics at Cambridge University and, after serving as the tutor to the son of the maharaja of Darbhanga, was appointed the

head of Rajkumar College in 1870. The London *Times*'s obituary of Macnaghten summed up his contribution to India:

> As the young chiefs came under his influence, Macnaghten inspired
> them with a pride in the College games and with an ambition to form
> a squadron of mounted volunteers. He thus appealed to the sporting
> and military tastes which are hereditary instincts with the Indian aris-
> tocracy. . . . The College cricket team would hold a respectable place in
> any country. One of its members, Ranjitsinhji, of the princely house of
> Jamnagar, is at this moment one of the finest batsmen in England. The
> chief of Limri, after he left the College and succeeded to his feudatory
> throne, came to Rajkot to play the College with eleven of his clansmen
> trained by himself. Nor was the book work neglected. Almost every one
> of the hundred and seventy young chiefs and nobles who have passed
> under Mr. Macnaghten's care have signalised their accession to power
> by spreading schools, dispensaries, and useful public works throughout
> their states.[8]

In his introduction to the collection of Macnaghten's addresses to his students, Robert Whitelaw refers to Macnaghten's larger aim of inculcating the
love of sport: "No man was ever less capable of the absurdity of mistaking
cricket and riding for virtue: but he loved cricket and riding himself, and
taught his boys to value such manly exercises, not because they were English,
but because they were conducive to manliness."[9]

Macnaghten himself was aware that in India schools were seen primarily
as places for book learning. But in his address to his students in 1887 he reported that "far more attention is given than formerly to open-air sports and
physical sports."[10] He firmly believed that the long-standing feuds among
rival Rajput clans could be resolved on the school's playing fields. A publication marking the school's fortieth anniversary boasted, "The Rajkumar
College, since its foundation, has been closely following the lines of an English public school on the athletic side, to which a great deal of attention is
deservedly attached in England."[11] Besides cricket, tennis, racquets, football,
athletics, and "gymkhana" sports (mainly tent pegging) were actively played
in Rajkumar College. Remarkably, Macnaghten drew a connection between
the ancient Indian epics and sports:

The demi-gods and heroes of the oldest religions are not only types of moral excellence, but also of perfection of athletic development and of beauty of form. Rama is not only the great and the good; he is also the archer whose shafts never miss. The five Pandus [*sic*], though distinguished each by special attributes—Yudhisthira for piety, Arjuna for bravery, Bhima for strength, Sahadeva for astrology, Nakula for mastery in cattle and horse breeding—were all alike famous for feats of prowess and athletic skill.[12]

He went on to laud Indian sports such as polo, which he described "as an excellent sport, demanding in the highest degree the promptitude of a fearless horseman combined with a calm and practised judgment,"[13] besides encouraging wrestling, boxing, and the use of *mugdals* (clubs) in gymnasiums.

At the same time, Macnaghten was convinced that cricket was the "king of all games" for the "moral advantages" it provided, that more than any other game, cricket taught the quality of fairness and the need to keep tempers in check. He illustrated this with an episode from *Tom Brown's Schooldays*—a bible for many schoolteachers across the British Empire—when one of the masters at Rugby, where the story is set, says to Tom: "What a noble game cricket is! The discipline and reliance on one another which it teaches is so valuable, I think; and it ought to be such an unselfish game. It merges the individual in the Eleven; he doesn't play that he may win, but that his side may."[14] This best encapsulated the role of sports in the eyes of Macnaghten and his compatriots in the British public schools. Macnaghten also seemed to possess a keen eye for talent. Before he and Ranji left for England in 1888, he observed in a speech: "A better or manlier boy has never resided within the College. . . . I speak of him because he has taken so marked a lead in the College that he will be especially remembered."[15]

Tyndale-Biscoe and the Missionary Instinct

Besides the chiefs' colleges, there were other schools meant primarily for children who were not sent to British boarding schools and the children of poorer Europeans or from mixed-race marriages. These were usually run by Christian missionaries, many of whom were themselves products of English public schools and actively encouraged sports and games. Among the earliest

Ranjitsinhji, the most famous alumnus of Rajkumar College, playing one of his trademark shots. Courtesy of Rajkumar College, Rajkot

such schools were the Nainital Diocesan School, founded in 1839, which was later renamed the Sherwood School. Shortly thereafter, the Lawrence Asylums, inspired by Sir Henry Lawrence, opened, first in Sanawar and then in Mount Abu, Ootacamund, and Murree (in present-day Pakistan). Although Anglo-Indians could gain admission to these schools, preference was given to children of "pure European parentage." The British also established several other schools in the hill stations of Mussoorie, Simla, and Darjeeling. Some schools, however, were meant primarily for Anglo-Indians and poor Europeans, such as St. Andrew's Colonial Homes (later renamed Dr. Graham's Homes) at Kalimpong and Goethals Memorial School at Kurseong.[16] In addition, schools for girls were established as well, with the Loreto Convents prominent among them. All these schools emphasized sports. Indeed, the Sanawar Lawrence School's school song is suffused with sports images:

Never Give In, Sanawar
Though the wickets swiftly fall.
And the light is bad and our hearts are sad
And it's hard to see the ball.
Never Give In, Sanawar
It's a cricket motto, too.
Somebody's got to "stop the rot"
And why not you.

The "muscular" Christianity propagated in these schools was not, however, the preserve only of British missionaries. St. Joseph's in Darjeeling, run by Belgian Jesuits, or schools like St. Xavier's in Bombay and Calcutta were equally obsessed with sports. This was true, too, of schools like La Martinière, founded in Lucknow and Calcutta, by the French soldier of fortune Claude Martin.

One of the most colorful missionaries of sport was Cecil Earle Tyndale-Biscoe. Unlike Macnaghten, he was more interested in games other than cricket. Tyndale-Biscoe was educated at Bradfield public school and Cambridge, where he won a Blue (award) in rowing. In 1891 he arrived at the Church Missionary School in Srinagar—still considered one of the premier schools in Kashmir—and remained there until his death. During his first few days in Kashmir, he was informed by J. H. Knowles, the missionary in charge of the school in Srinagar, that a Brahmin boy "never runs, boats or plays games for fear of growing muscle and losing caste."[17] It thereupon became Tyndale-Biscoe's mission in life to change the disposition of his Kashmiri students. He did this by both force and not-so-subtle persuasion. One of his most novel methods was making thirteen the cutoff age for learning swimming; those who could not were penalized by an increase in fees every year until they did learn. Over time, swimming across Srinagar's famous Dal and Wular Lakes became an annual event. The emphasis on sports was quite apparent from the number of marks—1,200 out of a grand total of 5,100—set aside for games in every boy's report card in Tyndale-Biscoe's school.

As a rowing Blue, it was natural that Tyndale-Biscoe wanted to introduce the sport to Kashmir. The perfect opportunity arose when during a visit to Srinagar, Viceroy Lansdowne suggested that the water of the Jhelum River could actually rival that of the Thames. This inspired Tyndale-Biscoe to build a boat, and in typical fashion he convinced two young teachers to inspect it, during which the boat was promptly set adrift. As Tyndale-Biscoe recalled, "They bent their material backbones and ... made a beginning in making that low-caste stuff commonly called muscle."[18] In 1909 an interschool regatta was held that predictably was won by the Church Missionary Society School by thirty lengths. Of course, cricket was played, too, but with the boys loath to touch the leather ball with their hands, for fear of being polluted, they would stop or catch it with their long *pherans* (long, loose Kashmiri dress), making it a "well conducted comic opera from start to finish."[19]

Tyndale-Biscoe's greatest achievement was introducing football (soccer) to Kashmir. Though Tyndale-Biscoe was not the first to introduce football to India, there are some parallels to football evangelists such as the physical education teacher Konrad Koch, who introduced football to Germany in 1874 and Scottish schoolteacher Alexander Watson Hutton who popularized football in Argentina in the 1880s.[20] The first encounter of Tyndale-Biscoe's Kashmiri students with football in the autumn of 1891 revealed the alienness of English sports in India:

TB [TYNDALE-BISCOE] What is football?

BOYS What is the use of it?

TB For playing a game.

BOYS Shall we receive any money if we play that game?

TB No!

BOYS Then we shall not play the game.

BOYS What is it made of?

TB Leather.

BOYS Take it away! Take it away!

TB Why should I take it away?

BOYS Because it is *jutha* [spurious or false] we may not touch it, it is leather.

TB I do not wish you to handle it. I want you to kick ... and today you are going to learn how to kick it, boys.

BOYS We will not play that *jutha* game.[21]

Although Tyndale-Biscoe's first attempt to introduce football did not seem promising, he was not easily discouraged, as evident in his account of the first football game that he organized. Tyndale-Biscoe took elaborate pains to ensure that the game would take place, personally herding the boys "like sheep on their way to the butcher's"[22] from the school gate to the playground with a hunting crop in hand, with other teachers picketing the route with sticks in their hands. The boys were completely ill equipped to play a game wearing long *pherons* and carrying a fire pot under their gowns to keep themselves warm. When the boys were asked to kick the football, no one stirred, but Tyndale-Biscoe had lined up the teachers all around the field with sticks to force the students into kicking the ball. His description of the game is hilarious as well as frightening in its clash of worldviews:

> I called out: "10 seconds left, 9, 8, 7, 6, 5, 4, 3, 2, 1. Kick!!!" and down came the teachers shouting and waving their single sticks. Off went the ball and in five seconds all was confusion, for the boys forgot their places in the field, or that they were holy Brahmans, and a rough and tumble began. As they tried to kick the ball, but generally missed it, their clogs flew into the air and their *pugaris* [turbans] were knocked off while their nightgowns flapped in one another's faces; a real grand mix-up of clothes and humanity.[23]

The game came to a halt when the ball hit one player in his face. His friends took the sobbing player to Tyndale-Biscoe, fearing that he had been polluted, only to be told to wash his face in the nearby canal. Over the next few days and months, the students tried various stratagems to avoid playing football, including carrying pins to deflate the ball. This stopped only after they were asked to pay for each deflated football.

Such a clash of cultures on the playing field was not unique to India. In China, for instance, a man's queue—the braid of hair ordered by the imperial court—and his long gown interfered with playing Western sports. An American sociology professor who toured China in 1911 wrote about young men with queues "skipping about the tennis courts, but they wore their hampering gowns and their strokes had the snap of a kitten playing with a ball of yarn."[24] Yet another eyewitness described a game of football during which the braids of the footballers "would open up and whip the opponent's face, to the point that he could only stop and rub his eyes, whereupon the player would quickly take advantage of the moment to dribble the ball forward."[25] Again in the first Chinese National Games held in Nanjing, a high jumper fouled his jump because his queue knocked off the bar even though he had cleared it. Apparently the athlete came back the next day after cutting off his queue and went on to win the high jump competition.[26]

Even though Tyndale-Biscoe got his students to take up English sports, it was a struggle for him to impress on the Kashmiris the idea of fair play and sportsmanship. Accordingly, when cricket matches were played and the missionary school was batting, it was not uncommon for the opposing team to field more than eleven players or to move the boundary flags. Or during a tug-of-war competition, held in the presence of the maharaja of Kashmir, the opposing team tied the rope to an anchor. But Tyndale-Biscoe noted in his memoirs that one year he watched a keenly contested interclass match during which, despite the referee being a student and not a teacher, his decision was not once disputed, nor was there any altercation. Tyndale-Biscoe could now proclaim that his Kashmiri students had well and truly internalized the English sporting spirit.[27]

When Tyndale-Biscoe first came to Kashmir, he did not hide his disdain for his "dirty, smelling, cowardly" students. But by the end of his tenure, he believed he had truly transformed them. His students were active during epidemics clearing garbage and helping douse fires, saving people from drowning, and chopping wood for the poor in winter. For Tyndale-Biscoe, winning prizes in sports was much less important than coming first in the "race of life."[28] As he proudly wrote in his autobiography:

School life in Srinagar is by no means dull, as we look upon this city of 130,000 as our field of sport, attacking social evils, and trying in various ways to play the citizen. Many of the boys, I think I might say most of them, take a delight in lending a hand in any job where they can be of use, as they have tasted the jolly feeling of giving pleasure and help to their neighbours.[29]

Tyndale-Biscoe wasn't the only missionary encouraging sports. Farther west in Bannu in the North-West Frontier Province, Theodore Leighton Pennell was administering medicines, preaching the message of Christ, and teaching football to his students. In his autobiography, he wrote with satisfaction:

The old order changes and gives place to the new. Tent-pegging will always retain its charm, with its brave show and splendid opportunities for the display of manly courage and dexterous horsemanship. . . . But the simpler native games are gradually giving placed to the superior attractions of cricket and football, and the tournaments which of recent years have been organized between the various native regiments and between the different tribes inhabiting each district and between the schools of the provinces are doing much to create a spirit of friendly rivalry, and to develop among these frontier people a fascination for those sports which have done so much to make England what it is.[30]

Pennell even took a football team from the Mission High School in Bannu for a tour of northern India, during which they excelled, hardly losing a game.

We should also mention briefly the introduction and popularity of football in the tiny Portuguese enclave of Goa on India's west coast. James Mill has argued that unlike in most of British India, where missionaries introduced sports to instill the games' ethics, the church in Goa regarded football as a "means of maintaining congregations and of shoring up existing social structures."[31] Football was introduced to Goa in 1883 by a visiting British priest, but it was the local Catholic church that promoted the game. The Rachel Seminary, which was most important training center for local priests, began fielding football teams. This later caused some consternation, with the local bishop banning participation in tournaments, since he "considered the spectacle of cassocked future priests chasing a ball to be one that undermined the dignity of their calling."[32] Nonetheless, the Catholic schools, such as St. Mary's School in Assolna and St. Xavier's High School in Margao, were eager participants in local tournaments.

Sporting Administrators

It was not only headmasters and missionaries who were promoting English sports. A few British officials, too, were using cricket as an "unofficial instrument of state cultural policy."[33] One of the best-documented colonial administrators involved in sports was Lord Harris, governor of Bombay from 1890 to 1895 and subsequently president of the Marylebone Cricket Club (MCC). In fact, his name still graces the premier interschool tournament in Bombay, begun in 1895, in which India's legendary batsman, Sachin Tendulkar, first displayed his greatness. Harris's biggest contribution—albeit some would say disservice—to sports was initiating the annual cricket match between the Bombay Presidency team, composed of Europeans, and the Parsis. He was also instrumental in allotting reclaimed land to the cricket clubs formed by the Parsis, Hindus, and Muslims. These actions were crucial to the development of the Pentangular—involving the British, Parsis, Hindus, Muslims, and the "Rest"—which was the premier cricket tournament in India until the Ranji Trophy was introduced. Harris's other noteworthy contribution was the 1892/1893 tour of India by an English team led by Lord Hawke.

Lord Willingdon, viceroy of India from 1931 to 1936 and, earlier, governor of Bombay and Madras, articulated a commonly held belief when addressing the Cricket Club of India in 1933: "Cricket was first actively started in this country largely through the influence of that fine British cricketer, the late Lord Harris."[34] Indian writers have been equally deferential, with Framji Patel calling Harris a "true friend and patron of Indian cricket" and Wahiuddin Beg elevating him to the status of "father of Indian Cricket."[35] Harris's role has, however, been disputed in recent times by Ramachandra Guha, who believes that his "contributions to the development of Indian cricket have been vastly exaggerated."[36]

According to Guha, Sorabjee's account of the struggles of Parsi cricketers with the European players over the Bombay Esplanade is clear evidence that Harris sided with the polo players and that he was more concerned with cricket in his own estate in Ganeshkhind in Pune. Even Harris's giving land in Bombay to the Hindus and the Muslim Gymkhana, Guha argued, was only because he had no other alternative. Despite Harris's asserting in his autobiography that cricket would "bring the several races together more and more, in a spirit of harmony,"[37] he never broke the rules of racial segregation. A journalist reported that when the Parsis played Lord Hawke's team, the ground was "divided into sections, one for the Europeans and one for the natives, and no native dared to be seen in the European section."[38]

Harris himself took a completely different view of his tenure in India. In his autobiography, *A Few Short Runs*, he wrote that Indian opinion was generally against playing cricket: "It was popular enough amongst the masses, but it needed a lot of coaxing before the classes would admit that there were such moral lessons to be acquired by youth from playing it to justify their giving their patronage."[39] Naturally, he took umbrage at the abuse heaped on him by the native press, which publicized the fact that because he "occasionally" took part in a game of cricket on the private grounds of Government House at Pune, he was "grossly neglecting" his duties. Moreover, even though Harris fondly recalled the Parsis' "staunchness" and support, particularly that of Framji Patel, he wrote in the introduction to Patel's *Stray Thoughts on Indian Cricket*:

> I was never impressed with Parsee batting, the best of them were liable to throw away their wickets by some rash stroke, due I expect to excitability. To wear down good bowling, and patiently wait for many overs for a run here and a run there, is easier for the phlegmatic Anglo-Saxon than for the excitable Asiatic.[40]

But for all his faults, Harris was prescient about the future of cricket in India: "That cricket is going to stay in India there cannot be any shadow of doubt; it has taken hold all over the country, and *chokras* [urchins] can be seen playing in every village with any sort of old bat and ball hat they can lay hands on."[41] His other wish—that cricket would lay the foundations for friendly relations between East and West—proved far more problematic.

Besides Harris, many other British administrators were involved in cricket. One of the best English cricketers to hold an administrative post in India was Sir Stanley Jackson, governor of Bengal, a former England captain, and the president of the MCC under whom Ranji had played on the Cambridge cricket team. Unlike Harris, Jackson had a more inclusive idea of sports and organized cricket teams in Bengal that included all ethnic communities. But this did not prevent him from being the target in 1932 of a daring assassination attempt by a woman graduate at the Calcutta University convocation. Jackson survived and was appointed chairman of England's Test Match selection committee in 1934.

Other administrators, some in the highest echelons of the service and others much less notable, contributed to Indian sports as well. In the former category was Lord Willingdon, who had played for the MCC and Sussex. He was instrumental in establishing the Willingdon Sports Club in Bombay, which was open to Europeans and Indians. He was a patron of the Board of Control for Cricket in India (BCCI) and might even have had his name associated with India's premier cricket tournament, the Ranji Trophy, if some of his ardent backers had had their way. Yet another administrator of similar disposition was Lord Brabourne, governor of Bombay and, later, Calcutta between 1933 and 1939. He facilitated the purchase of land at a throwaway price for the Cricket Club of India, for which he was the chairman of the Bombay Committee. He was a committed fund-raiser for the stadium of the Cricket Club of India, and to this day his name is associated with it. Englishmen outside government also were associated with cricket. R. E. Grant Govan, a businessman in Delhi, was the first president of the BCCI. R. B. Lagden, a Cambridge Blue in cricket and an excellent hockey player who was nicknamed "Rashbehari" after a prominent Indian nationalist, was a businessman in Bengal and president of the Cricket Association of Bengal.

The availability of lucrative assignments in the princely states meant that English coaches, like Frank Tarrant, Bill Hitch, and A. F. (Bert) Wensley as well as Australians such as Clarrie Grimmett, could work in India and thus play a formative role in the development of Indian cricketers. Some of the British in India also represented their provinces or princely states when the Ranji Trophy began. Wensley was captain of the Nawanagar team in the 1930s, and T. C. Longfield and A. L. Hosie played with distinction for Bengal and were known as Tulsi Chand and Amrit Lal, respectively, in the Calcutta maidan.[42] There is an endearing story of a cultural, albeit unequal, encounter between Indian and British teammates. Apparently when Longfield asked a Bengali spinner named Dutt what field he wanted to set for his bowling, the bowler replied, mixing English and Bengali, "Well, two slips, one third man, one gully or *vchatti chatty char dikey chaddiye paduk na*, sahib."[43] What the bowler meant was apart from the four fielding positions mentioned, the captain could scatter the rest anywhere in the field.

During World War II, occasionally an English cricketer sent to India would play for the Ranji Trophy. The most notable by far was the English legend Dennis Compton, who was posted in Mhow, a cantonment town in central India, and recruited by Nayudu to play for Indore during the 1944/1945 season. Compton played in the finals between Indore and Bombay that season, during which a record 2,078 runs were scored between both teams. Compton ended up on the losing side, despite scoring an unbeaten 249 chasing a massive target on 869 runs in the second innings. Later in 1945, in what was his last match in India, Compton played for the East Zone against a visiting Australian Service team at the Eden Gardens.[44]

We also should mention the journalist E. H. D. Sewell, who was one of the best-known cricket correspondents in India, writing for the *Times of India* and other publications, as well as being a cricket player himself of some skill. He is, however, best remembered for his prejudiced reporting on what was the biggest scandal in Indian cricket in the pre–World War II era: the sending back of the cricket star and a future captain of India, Lala Amarnath, for a lack of discipline during India's tour of England in 1936.[45]

Many minor figures in the civil and military administration contributed to Indian sports in unexpected ways. One was Major John Glennie Greig (whose name was corrupted to "Jungly"), who was a prolific batsman scoring 184 runs for the Europeans against the Parsis in 1889 and a double century for Bombay Presidency against the Oxford Authentics in 1902, besides being an accomplished racquets and tennis player. Apparently, Ranji was so impressed with Greig that he wrote a letter of introduction for him to the Hampshire County team, stating, "Greig is a better bat than I am, and is an excellent bowler as well."[46] Perhaps the most unusual cricket enthusiast was a Yorkshire priest named Joe Murphy who came to Vellore (in Tamil Nadu) in the 1930s and stayed on after India became independent. He apparently died fielding at slip in the 1970s. At one time, teams in the North Arcot district competed for the Murphy Memorial Trophy, named after the priest-cricketer.[47]

To Greig, however, goes the credit for "discovering" Palwankar Baloo, one of the finest cricketers in the early phase of the Indian game. In the 1890s, Greig ordered Baloo to bowl to him at the nets in the Pune Club every day, allowing both players to hone their skills.[48] In subsequent years, Greig and Baloo became worthy opponents on the pitch. But Greig was no lover of Indian cricket, as was evident from an incident in the 1916 Quadrangular against the Hindus in which he was judged stumped for a duck (zero) by a Hindu umpire. On his return to the pavilion, he complained about the umpire, and the game was held up for a full fifteen minutes. This created a huge controversy, with different newspapers carrying their own version of events. Whereas the British-owned *Times of India* was critical of the umpire, the *Bombay Chronicle* labeled Greig's protest "unseemly in the extreme."[49] After the match, which the Europeans won handsomely, Greig sent a letter to the Hindu Gymkhana criticizing the umpire. An official of the gymkhana wrote back, saying that Greig's accusations were "entirely opposed to the character of sport and are calculated to create general unpleasantness."[50]

This incident was an example of the wide gap between the British ideal of sportsmanship and the reality in the colonies. The primary divide was race, as vividly expressed in a blockbuster Bollywood film, *Lagaan* (2001), released more than fifty years after the British left India.[51] The film, which anticipates the multicultural Indian nation, shows a motley band of villagers, belonging to different religions and castes and unschooled in cricket, dramatically defeat a team of colonial officials. At the heart of the film is race, which sports in colonial India and officials like Lord Harris tried, not usually with much success, to bridge.

4

PLAYERS AND PATRONS

INDIAN PRINCES AND SPORTS

IF WE LEAVE ASIDE THE PARSI OBSESSION WITH CRICKET, THE Indian royals were the first group of Indians to take up sports in an organized manner. The Indian princes, of course, had a long tradition of martial sports such as hunting and riding. In 1928, the president of the Indian Olympic Committee, Sir Dorabji Tata, lamented to the head of the International Olympic Committee that in India the maharajas "take interest chiefly in shooting, hunting and Polo and little else."[1] But just as many of the maharajas began going to the English-run public schools in the late nineteenth century, they also started taking up English sports.

In the first half of the twentieth century, the princes rivaled the British in their enthusiasm for outdoor games and sports. This was partly because of the education imparted in British public schools, in which sports occupied an important part of the curriculum, and partly because of the leisure at their disposal.[2] This was very much in evidence in the daily regimen for young royals. As a maharawat of Pratapgarh, a small state in Rajputana, recounted,

> There was nothing that wasn't taught us. Our routine started at six o'clock and followed a very strict schedule. We had physical training and

played football, cricket and hockey mainly in the morning. . . . Then in
the evening we had to play games again, including archery and shooting.[3]

The princes' English tutors could be hard taskmasters, as the experience of
the Mayurdhwaj Singhji of Dhrangadhara, another small state in Rajputana,
shows:

> The ground was always full of school-children from the city, with boys
> at nets and practice games. I remember one practice game when I went
> in to bat. There was one young fellow, a Dewan Sahib's fourth son, who
> used to send cannon-balls down the pitch. When they came, I sort of
> stepped back and my English tutor said, "Did I see you step back? Don't
> do it again." But I stepped back again. "Are you a Rajput?" he said to me
> which was quite galling because all the other boys would understand. He
> said, "Don't step back again," and I did. So he took my bat and said, "Stand
> over there," and he started hitting cricket balls at me, saying, "Why are
> you afraid? The ball is not going to hit you that hard."[4]

Girls weren't exempt from the sports activities. Princess Pravinba of Kutch
recalls that she was "taught to ride, swim, shoot and other sports," along with
her studies.[5] In his "Notes on the Education and Upbringing of the Ruler,"
the maharaja of Scindia advised in 1925, "Children of both sexes should be
taken out shooting once a week without fail and when they have advanced in
years they should, as a rule, be made to spend not less than a couple of weeks
annually on tiger-shooting."[6] This was very much the sort of environment in
which Gayatri Devi, who originally belonged to the Cooch Behar royal family of north Bengal and later married the maharaja of Jaipur, grew up. Over
a period of thirty-seven years, her grandfather shot 365 tigers, 311 leopards,
207 rhinos, 438 buffaloes, 318 antelopes, 259 sambars, 133 bears, and 43 bi-
son.[7] Gayatri Devi herself went on her first shoot at the age of five and shot
a panther when she was twelve.[8]

In the princely states, *shikar* (hunting) was a wildly popular pastime. As
we saw earlier, the maharaja of Bikaner was famous for organizing sand-
grouse shoots in Gajner, where in one morning sometimes as many as four
thousand birds would be shot. Bharatpur occupied a similar position for duck

shoots, and Gwalior, Jaipur, and Alwar were famous for their tiger hunts. As during the Mughal times, the hunts for tigers and panthers, especially in the bigger princely states, were elaborate affairs. Besides the officers in charge of *shikar* information, others took care of the beats and transport. These also were occasions for high British officials, including the viceroy and governors-general, to mingle with the princes. *Shikars* had a dual purpose, enabling princes to exhibit their wealth and their managerial abilities while at the same time to gain the ear of high British officials.[9]

Public School Training

The regimen followed by many princes in their palaces was institutionalized in schools like Mayo College, where sports and recreation took up more than three hours of the working day. The boys were expected to take part in all kinds of activities, including athletics, polo, hockey, football, tennis, racquets, and squash. A history of Mayo College noted,

> From its earliest days the Mayo College developed a taste for sports and games. Outdoor activities soon became popular and the covered play-shed gradually ceased to be required. The report of 1876 stated that attendance at the playground at first enforced had become practically voluntary, that the riding class was attended with pleasure, and that cricket, rounders and football were played with a zest not far short of that shown in an English school.[10]

Mayo's headmaster, Herbert Sherring, also listed two "Indian" games played by the boys, *ghorli attar* and *khoa dhari*, both of which he dismissed as not requiring "great skill, though it causes at times great excitement."[11]

A visitor to Mayo at the beginning of the twentieth century reported that the school had "three cricket and football elevens, each with a capital ground."[12] But it was cricket that was the most popular sport, forming "half the existence of the Mayo school boy" and played even on Sundays.[13] This, of course, had much to do with the active encouragement from the English teachers. Sherring waxed eloquent on the game's many virtues, both physical and mental:

Cricket is an education in itself. It develops every muscle in the body. To the mind it teaches fortitude under defeat, and modesty at the time of victory; for any sudden turn of fortune may even at the last moment change defeat to victory or victory to defeat. It discourages selfishness, and teaches the player the necessity of playing for his side and not for himself.[14]

Polo was another popular sport in the boarding schools. As we saw in the last chapter, the principal of Rajkumar College, Chester Macnaghten, was a great fan of polo for the manly virtues it promoted. In Mayo, though, polo was played by only a few because of the high expense and the absence of a polo ground on the school premises. Sherring writes:

The Rajput, especially the Jodhpur Rathore, is an expert and bold horseman, and if properly mounted can hold his own with any man in India. Many of the young chiefs of the colleges are born riders, full of dash, and with their feather weights and keen eyes need only good mounts and plenty of practice to make them equals of Englishman in this most popular of Indian games.[15]

The school regularly organized sports competitions, and teams in Rajkumar competed for prizes, such as the Football Challenge Cup donated by Khan Saheb Fatehdinkhanji. Rajkumar College often played cricket matches with local or visiting teams. The first match that Mayo played was against the government college, Ajmer, which ended in a tie. From 1887 onward, Mayo played regular matches with the local Ajmer gymkhana, which sometimes had to borrow a few Mayo students to field eleven. The enthusiasm of the Mayo team was evident in 1889 when Mayo was invited by the political agent of Jhalawar to play a match. The school team traveled 120 miles by train to Neemuch, then took a bullock cart and *palki* (sedan chair) for 40 miles, and finally a carriage for another 40 miles.[16] Mayo and Rajkumar also played a series of matches. But because of the distance between the two schools, in 1906 the annual tournament with Rajkumar was replaced by an annual contest with Aitchison College, Lahore, and occasional contests with the Imperial Cadet College, Dehradun, and Daly College, Indore. In 1898

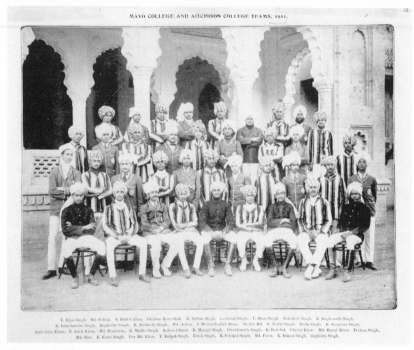

The Mayo College and Aitchison College teams, 1911. The two schools played an annual tournament from 1906 onward. Courtesy of Mayo College, Ajmer

Mayo College first won the cricket shield in the Rajputana Schools Tournament and then went on the repeat the performance every year between 1903 and 1913, except once when it withdrew from the tournament. Starting in 1930, an annual tournament was started with Daly College, made up of five events: cricket, hockey, athletic sports, tennis, and squash.[17]

The Popularity of Polo

It was polo—a game that had had a long history in India but was rediscovered by the British in Manipur and then spread across the subcontinent like wildfire—that first caught the princes' fancy, and it is an association that continues to this day. One of the main reasons was polo's long tradition in India and the preference of many princes for "pastimes which were dangerous, chivalric and equestrian."[18] A sport like polo, confined to the colonial elite, also was a good way for Indian princes to gain access to a charmed circle. Because polo was played on horseback, it had a natural affinity for the princes' traditional leisure activities of pigsticking and hunting. And unlike cricket, which was already attracting players from all classes, polo was confined to the highest reaches of Indian society. This made it popular with the princes, allowing them to mix and curry favor with senior British officials.[19]

All the major princely states—Hyderabad, Gwalior, Mysore, Kashmir (all of which were twenty-one-gun-salute states)—were patrons of polo, but Jodhpur (nineteen-gun salute) and its three-time regent (and later maharaja of Idar), Sir Pratap Singh, occupied a special place in the history of the game. Regarded as the "founder of modern polo in western India," he is credited with designing the Jodhpur breeches that became the approved attire for polo the world over.[20] Sir Pratap was a colorful figure, a die-hard loyalist of the British Empire who enjoyed a special relationship with Queen Victoria, whom he first met in 1887, the year of the queen's golden jubilee. Henry Newbolt even composed a poem entitled "A Ballad of Sir Pertab Singh," describing an idealized Indian prince, and a cartoon in *Punch* magazine once portrayed Sir Pratap with polo mallets crowning his head.[21] According to his biographer, "Sir Pratap's fame as a sportsman will live as long as Polo is played or pigs are hunted and panthers are shot in India. At both games he was in a class by himself, he regarded them as the Rajputs' School for War."[22]

For the high standard of polo in Jodhpur, two persons were responsible: Sir Pratap and Captain Stuart Beatson, who had come to Jodhpur in 1890 to organize two cavalry regiments of the Imperial Service Troops. They were united by a passion for horses and by 1893 had formed a crack polo team made up of Sir Pratap, Beatson, Hari Singh (Hurjee), and Dhokal Singh, which won the Indian Polo Championship (the Indian Polo Association [IPA] was formed in 1892) at Pune, defeating several British regimental teams. Four years later, the Jodhpur team went to England and challenged the English teams on their home turf at Hurlingham. But in subsequent years the Jodhpur team declined, as is evident from the accounts of Amar Singh, a member of the Jodhpur Army Team and a protégé of Sir Pratap. In 1899, the Jodhpur team lost twice to the Alwar team in different tournaments, first at Mhow and then at Nasirabad. But the team eventually won the Delhi Durbar Cup in 1911.

Other states in Rajputana also were known for their good polo players. Even one of the smaller states, Kishengarh, for some time had one of India's best polo teams, and later, Jaipur's polo team prospered. It is said that Dhokal

Singh of Jodhpur taught the young maharaja of Jaipur, Man Singh II, to play polo. The Jaipur quartet, which comprised the maharaja; Hanut Singh and his brother Abhey Singh, who originally was from Jodhpur but married into the Jaipur royal family; and Prithi Singh, won the IPA championship every year from 1933 to 1939. In 1933 the Jaipur team also went to England and won all the tournaments it played in. Such was the adulation for Man Singh that his third wife Gayatri Devi recalled, "Whenever he drove to a match, the police had to clear a path through the crowds, and when the Jaipur team won, his fans poured onto the polo-grounds in thousands to touch his feet in homage."[23] Many years later, an accident on a polo field in England claimed Man Singh's life.

The other great player and patron of polo, and indeed all kinds of sports, was Rajinder Singh, the maharaja of Patiala, a medium-sized state in Punjab. Rajinder's first love was polo and horses, and during his playing time, a Patiala quartet, in which he himself played, was the champion polo team in India. The star player of the team was Heera Singh, who was considered to be "head and shoulders above all other players at that time."[24] In the 1890s the Patiala team won the Punjab Polo Cup four times and the Beresford Cup, played in Simla, three times, and in horse racing, Patiala's horses won two Viceroy's Cups and four Civil Service Cups. Yet another star of the Patiala polo team was Chanda Singh, who was invited to play in Europe. He played for the French Comte Jean de Madre's team, the Tigers, in 1909 and was invited to play for the Spanish king's team in the Spanish Polo Championship, in which he helped the king's team win. Later he played for England in a match against the Americans, which the English won.

Rajinder's sporting interests were not confined to polo. He regularly played tennis and cricket, and every year he organized a "Patiala week" during which horse racing, pigsticking, polo, roller skating, and other activities took place. Not until 1895, just three years before his untimely death, did Rajinder begin playing cricket seriously. According to the *Indian Sportsman*, a contemporary newspaper, the reason for the shift was, ironically, success in polo. It implied that after the Patiala team beat the ace team from Jodhpur in in the 1895 Punjab Polo Cup, Rajinder's ambition was sated and that "from that time polo in Patiala took a back seat to cricket."[25] (It was another matter that more than two decades later in 1922, Jodhpur took revenge by narrowly defeating Patiala, which had Chanda Singh, now a general, playing at the age of fifty-eight, in the finals of the Prince of Wales Tournament with the Prince of Wales himself and Sir Pratap in the audience.)[26] When Rajinder died at the age of twenty-eight, the *New York Times* of November 11, 1900, wrote: "He became the best polo player in India, was a fearless rider, a deadly shot, was second only to Ranjitsinhji at cricket, and was one of the finest amateur billiard players of the day."

Ranji and the Importance of Cricket

The association of the maharajas with cricket ranged from the absurd to the deadly serious. In the first category was the maharaja of Kashmir, who made a mockery of the rules of the game. H. T. Wickham, a member of the Indian Police Service, described a cricket match involving the maharaja:

> At three o'clock in the afternoon that Maharajah himself would come down to the ground, the band would play the Kashmir anthem, salaams were made and he then went off to a special tent where he sat for a time, smoking his long water pipe. At four thirty or thereabouts he decided he would bat. It didn't matter which side was batting, his own team or ours. He was padded by two attendants and gloved by two more, somebody carried his bat and he walked to the wicket looking very dignified, very small and with an enormous turban on his head. In one of the matches I happened to be bowling and my first ball hit his stumps, but the wicket-keeper, quick as lightning, shouted "No Ball" and the match went on. The only way the Maharajah could get out was lbw ["leg before wicket," which is one of the ways a batsman can get out]. And after fifteen or twenty minutes batting he was duly given out lbw.[27]

At the opposite end from the maharajah of Kashmir was a prince who was regarded as one of the finest cricketers of his time. Indeed, Kumar Shri Ranjitsinhji, the Maharaja Jam Saheb of Nawanagar, might not have inherited the throne if it hadn't been for his cricketing genius and destiny. Despite all his impressive-sounding titles, Ranji, as he was better known, was in reality a grandson of a cousin of Jam Vibhaji III, the ruler of Nawanagar in Kathiawar in the present-day western Indian state of Gujarat. Ranji had been adopted by Nawanagar's ruler after he disinherited his only son in 1877. But the birth of another son to one of Vibhaji's Muslim wives in 1882 put Ranji's future claims to the throne in serious doubt, and it was only the sudden death of Jaswantsinhji (also known as Jassaji), Vibhaji's son, in 1906 that put Ranji back into the picture. Exploiting his fame as a cricketer and securing the support of the Rajput states, Ranji maneuvered his way to the Jamnagar throne, cutting out Vibhaji's disinherited son, Kaluba, who technically had a stronger claim. As Richard Cashman points out, "Cricket was one of the languages of the Raj and those who could master its subtle inflections and rhythms could expect to exert a greater influence on colonial policy-makers."[28]

The affection and awe with which the English treated Ranji are quite apparent from the reaction by Charles Kincaid, the judicial officer at Jamnagar, during Ranji's visit to Kathiawar:

> All the agency officials were anxious to meet the famous cricketer; but the situation was rather delicate. The King Emperor's representative at Rajkot was pledged to the support of the young Jam Jaswantsinhji. Fortunately as a Judicial Officer I was not so bound. . . . I took him as a guest to the officers' mess at Rajkot, and everyone was delighted with him.[29]

On the British accepting Ranji's claim to the throne, his biographer Simon Wilde wrote, "Ranji was significantly assisted in his claim by his immense popularity as a cricketer and also by his friendship with the British, perhaps particularly his personal acquaintance with Lord Lamington, the Governor of Bombay."[30]

The reason for this brief description of Ranji's ascendance to the throne is to emphasize that he might not have become the ruler of Jamnagar without his extraordinary cricketing skills. And what is significant too, as we noted earlier, is that Ranji was introduced to cricket by Chester Macnaghten, the principal of Rajkumar College. But we also should not forget Cowasjee Desai, the cricket coach of Rajkumar, a Parsi whose name rarely figures in later accounts of Ranji's career.[31] While in Rajkumar College, Ranji was the captain of the school team from 1884 to 1887, and in his last match for the school, he scored 81 not out in the first innings and took a total of ten wickets.[32] It was Macnaghten who was instrumental in Ranji's going to Cambridge University in 1888. There, although Ranji got his "Blue" in cricket, he did not really shine. It was only when he began playing for Sussex that his talent became evident. In his first season in county cricket in 1895, he piled up 1,775 runs at an average 49.3, second only to the two greats, W. G. Grace and Archie Maclaren. The next year he played for England against Australia and smashed an unbeaten 154 in the second innings. In that series, though, he was left out of the squad in the first Test at Lord's (the host association in those days selected the team) by Lord Harris, who had by then returned from Bombay to become the president of the Marylebone Cricket Club (MCC), on the grounds that "birds of passage" did not qualify to play for England. In 1897 Ranji was part of the England team that toured Australia and finished with an average of 50.77 in the five Test matches. We could go on and on about Ranji's glorious career, but the English response to Ranji was best described by the inimitable Neville Cardus: "No one like him is likely to be born again. It is not in nature that there should be another Ranji. He was the midsummer night's dream of cricket."

There is no dearth of writings on Ranji's cricketing exploits—even in the age of Indian cricket greats like Sunil Gavaskar and Sachin Tendulkar, Ranji probably has more serious biographies to his name—but his contribution to Indian sports has always been a matter of some controversy. Indeed, it is ironic that the premier domestic cricket tournament, the Ranji Trophy, instituted in 1936, is named after a person who wasn't particularly interested in advancing the game in India. This was first explicitly noted by the founder-secretary of the Board of Control for Cricket in India (BCCI), Anthony De Mello, in his history of Indian sports: "Ranjitsinhji was never at any stage prepared to combine his roles of sportsman and Indian Prince. . . . To all our requests for aid, encouragement and advice, Ranji gave but one answer: 'Duleep [Ranji's nephew who, like his uncle, had played for England] and I are English cricketers.'" De Mello added that Ranji "did absolutely nothing for Indian sport and sportsman."[33] While this might be a severe view, it is true that Ranji's contribution to Indian cricket was, at best, limited. His importance was his showing that Indians could excel in the quintessential English sport. As a report in the *Times* pointed out: "The service which Prince Ranjitsinhji has performed for India is not that he has proved one of his race to be capable of the highest achievement in our national sport, but that he has made the fact known to the whole British people."[34]

Back in India from his legendary exploits in England and Australia in 1898, Ranji stayed as a guest of Buchi Babu Naidu, the "father" of Madras cricket, where he was apparently embarrassed in the nets by a local bowler who bowled him a few times.[35] It was as a member of the maharaja of Patiala's team—Ranji had been appointed a colonel in the maharaja's bodyguard—that Ranji played most of his serious cricket in India that season. He scored a century against the Simla Volunteers and a double hundred against a military team in Ambala.[36] He found time to play for the Kathiawar Cricket Club Gymkhana in his home state and also gave coaching tips to boys at his alma mater, Rajkumar College. On a tour of western India, Ranji spectacularly failed against the Poona Gymkhana, being bowled out by a certain Lieutenant Lionel Maury Ross Deas for a duck in each innings. He made up for it, however, in the match against the Bombay Gymkhana, in which he scored 78 runs and took 11 wickets.[37] He played cricket in Calcutta, too, where 10,000 people turned up to see him bat, followed by a grand reception at the town hall. He returned to the city in 1905, playing this time for I. Zingari, the traveling cricket road show, scoring a brilliant century against the Calcutta Cricket Club.[38] He continued playing in Jamnagar even after he ascended the throne in 1907, where he had a cricket ground built, but his appearances outside the state became increasingly rare.[39] In 1910 he took the Nawanagar team on a tour of western India and, four years later, played against the Bombay Gymkhana.[40] Even after Ranji's death, cricket continued to flourish in Nawanagar until at least India's independence. Its patrons were Ranji's two nephews, Digvijaysinhji and Duleep, the latter who, like his uncle, had played for England. The Nawanagar team, led by a Sussex player, A.F. Wensley, even won the Ranji Trophy in 1936, with star turns by the legendary Indian cricketer Vinoo Mankad, then a teenager, and Amar Singh, the fast bowler who played for India.

Ranji last played in England in 1920 at the age of forty-eight, after having lost an eye in a shooting accident. But he steadfastly refused any role in Indian cricket, turning down an offer in 1911 to lead an "all-India" team to England. And when asked to write something for the souvenir program for India's first official overseas tour to England in 1932, he tellingly wrote: "I have not had the pleasure of seeing anything of Indian cricket. It will therefore be a mere presumption on my part to offer any opinion about their cricket."[41] This was not strictly true, though, since he occasionally showed up for matches in the princely states and the chiefs' colleges. During one such match between Mayo College and the Kashmir XI, Ranji had a priceless conversation, even if its veracity is doubtful, with the maharaja (who, as we saw earlier, was never given out when batting) after he returned to the pavilion:

MAHARAJA OF KASHMIR (in Hindi): *"Apne kabhi anda banaya?"* (Have you ever scored a duck?)
RANJI: *"Bahut dafa"* (Many times).
MAHARAJA: *"Maine to kabhi nahi banaya"* (I have never scored one).[42]

The story ends happily, with the maharaja ordering the school principal to give the boys in school an extra day's holiday.

But for all this, cricket was really a minor footnote in Ranji's Indian career. Much has been written about him as the ruler of Jamnagar—in contrast to his early biographers, Mario Rodrigues in particular, offers a revisionist account of Ranji as an autocrat and a poor administrator. Suffice it to say his career as Jam Saheb and later as the chancellor of the Chamber of Princes (a body that was instituted by the British in 1921) was complex. During his coronation ceremony in 1907, Ranji remarked, "I hope to abide loyally by the traditions of this State, in its unswerving loyalty to the British throne"[43] and then used a cricketing analogy in England in 1930 to proclaim fealty to the empire: "You can rely on us in the future, as you have relied upon us in the past, to play the game, and to give every support in our power to the harmony and success of the Imperial team."[44] But he could also rub the British the wrong way, more often than not for selfish reasons. A year before he died, Ranji stated in a contentious speech at the Chamber of Princes: "We, the States, have suffered from the application to ourselves of policies designed primarily in the interests of British India, and we have suffered economically and politically."[45]

If Ranji's reputation as a cricketer far outstripped his contribution to the game in India, the same was not true for the other princes who dabbled in cricket. In the Kathiawar region, home to as many as 282 princely states, many of them only a few acres of land, the princes of Wadhwan, Limbdi, and Porbandar actively promoted cricket; in western India the raja of Jath, a state covering 10,000 square miles, imported the Australian Test player, Clarrie Grimmett, to coach himself; in central India were the maharajas of Gwalior and Dhar and the nawab of Bhopal, along with his more famous son-in-law, the nawab of Pataudi; and in Rajputana were teams from

Jaipur, Bharatpur, Alwar, and Jhalawar. Many of the bigger princely states like Baroda and the Holkars of Indore did not begin patronizing cricket until the 1940s.[46] Baroda had a fine cricket team, with several members of the ruling family excelling, and won the Ranji Trophy three times in the 1940s (and was the runner-up twice). Holkar, whose ruler, Yeshwant Rao Holkar, was a cricket fanatic, won the trophy once (and was the runner-up twice) in the same period.

The House of Patiala

It would not be an exaggeration to say that Patiala was, and still is to some extent, the first family of Indian sports. Beginning with Rajinder Singh, his son Bhupinder, grandsons Yadavendra and Bhalendra, and now Bhalendra's son Randhir, the Patiala royal family has been involved with sport for well over one hundred years. Whatever the reason for Rajinder's shift in allegiance to cricket, within three years Patiala had recruited a wonderful team. The Patiala eleven that played the Calcutta Rangers in 1898 during a tour of Bengal is an excellent example of how the princes assembled a team without any consideration to race, religion, or creed. Besides Ranji and Rajinder himself, the team had three Englishmen, two of them professionals and one amateur, three Parsis—one of them being H. Mistry, the leading Indian all-rounder of the time—a Hindu, a Muslim, and another player who was either European or Anglo-Indian. Coaches were imported, too, with two Englishmen, W. Brockwell and J. T. Hearne. Rajinder himself was a decent bat and, like many of the princes who followed him, preferred to score only in boundaries. To host the matches, Rajinder built the Baradari Palace ground in Patiala, which not only had "no rival in India" but also was thought to match Lord's in its facilities.[47]

Bhupinder Singh carried on from his father. He was a larger-than-life figure, imposing in size with a beard and huge turban, and a compulsive womanizer.[48] He employed several great players, including Nazir and Wazir Ali, Lall Singh, Mohammed Nissar, and Lala Amarnath. Ranji, who had been Rajinder's aide-de-camp, had played for the Patiala team in 1898/1899. Mistry continued in Patiala's service as a coach and the maharaja's personal secretary. Other coaches who served at Patiala read almost like a who's who of world cricket: Wilfred Rhodes, George Hirst, Maurice Leyland, and Harold

Larwood.[49] In addition, Bhupinder maintained a cricket ground in the hill station of Chail in Himachal Pradesh after he was banished from Simla by the viceroy for sexual offenses.

Bhupinder, a product of Aitchison College, was himself a hard-hitting bat. The great English cricketer C. B. Fry believed that during a tour of England in 1911 by an Indian team led by Bhupinder, he hit a six at Lord's that was one of the longest that Fry had ever seen.[50] But Bhupinder was better known for his idiosyncrasies. When he played for the MCC in 1926/1927 against an all-India XI, there was a long break in the match because his one-thousand-pound pearl earring went missing while he was batting. The batsman at the other end, Maurice Tate, a well-known English player, combed the pitch for the missing earring before it was found stuck in the maharaja's hairnet.[51] This was the same player who in an earlier match had refused to appeal when the maharaja, who was this time playing against the MCC, was caught in the slips off Tate's bowling. When asked later why he didn't appeal, Tate replied: "Don't be a fool, we will be staying at this chap's palace later on. I don't want to be poisoned."[52]

That the relationship of the Patiala maharaja with cricket was a peculiar combination of genuine interest and a casual disregard for rules is apparent from another match during the MCC's 1932/1933 tour of India. The MCC team, led by Douglas Jardine, captain of England during the infamous Body-line series in Australia, played a four-day match in Patiala, in which the maharaja's son, Yuvraj Yadavendra, was playing. Edward Docker reported,

> On one day, for instance, play ended at lunch-time, so that the players could get away to the Simla Hills for shooting. On another, after a banquet lasting till three or four in the morning, the Englishman were roused at seven o'clock for a deer hunt, followed by cricket. Again there was an unusual umpiring incident. Bakewell seems to have the caught the Yuvraj [Yadavendra] fairly and squarely at short-leg but indicated to the umpire he hadn't, and the umpire changed his decision. Next ball Mitchell dropped him in the slips.[53]

Not surprisingly, the Patiala XI took the first innings lead.

Bhupinder's interest in sport was a stepping-stone for greater things. As chancellor of the Chamber of Princes nine times between 1927 and 1937, he

Maharaja Bhupinder Singh of Patiala, a patron
of sport known for his flamboyance, playing
an uncharacteristic defensive cricketing shot.
Reprinted by permission of the Mary Evans
Picture Library, London

was more active off the field than on it. During the 1911 tour by an all-India
team to England, in the match against the MCC at Lord's on the last day, the
maharaja was called for a meeting with the secretary of state. He returned to
the ground and was able to bat only because the tea break had been extended.
He even inserted a full-page advertisement for the Patiala state in the London
Times in 1937, which concluded a eulogy to the ruling family by saying that

Patiala "under the benevolent administration of the present Maharaja, will loom large in the politics of India."[54] Bhupinder also was a key player in the BCCI, which came into existence in 1928, as a vice-patron, besides being a huge contributor of funds to the Cricket Club of India, which was founded in 1933 in Bombay. In 1935/1936 he sponsored an Australian eleven, led by J. S. Ryder, to tour India.

Bhupinder's interests were not restricted to cricket. He became the president of the Indian Olympic Association in 1928, after other candidates such as the maharaja of Kapurthala and the maharaja of Burdwan dropped out. He was also a patron of wrestling and helped organize the "world championship" bout in 1928 between the great Indian wrestler, Gama, and the Polish champion Stanislaus Zbyszko, about which we'll have more to say in a later chapter. Indeed, Gama was patronized in succession by several princely courts, beginning with Datiya, Rewa, Orcha, and finally Patiala.

The Bengal Maharajas

The princely patronage of sports wasn't restricted to northern and western India. Bengal had two enthusiastic patrons of cricket. The maharaja of Cooch Behar, Nripendra Krishna, and Jagadindranarayan Ray, the ruler of Natore, now in Bangladesh, tried their best to outdo each other in putting together a quality cricket team. Nripendra Krishna had set up his own cricket ground in Woodlands in Calcutta and maintained three cricket teams. (He was a patron of other sports as well, including football and wrestling.) As cricket coaches he hired two Sussex professionals besides Frank Tarrant, the Australia-born Middlesex all-rounder, who served Patiala after World War I and coached the Indian team that toured England in 1932. The Cooch Behar team competed on an equal footing with the best teams in India, including one led by Ranji and the various Governor's XIs from all over India.[55] Around the same time, Jagadindranarayan bought forty-five acres of land near Old Ballygunge in south Calcutta, spending the huge sum of Rs 100,000 to establish his own cricket ground.[56] Unlike the maharaja of Cooch Behar, Jagadindranarayan was an ardent nationalist and in favor of promoting local talent. He also recruited several Indian stars from elsewhere, including the great Baloo Palwankar as well his two brothers, Vithal and Ganpat, and H. L. Semper. But shortly after the death of the maharaja of Cooch Behar in 1914, Jagadindrana-rayan abruptly gave up cricket, giving credence to the theory that rivalry with his fellow prince was one of his prime motivations for patronizing sports.

Bengal had yet another famous princely patron of sports, the raja of San-tosh, Sir Manmatha Nath Roy Chowdhury, but his interest was primarily in football. The raja became president of the Indian Football Association in 1931 (and a year later he also became head of the Bengal Gymkhana), but he had to fight a running battle with another parallel organization, the All-India Football Association, to decide which body was the legitimate apex organiza-tion of Indian football. Eventually a compromise was reached, with the for-mation of the All-India Football Federation in 1937, the same year the maha-raja died. Santosh was an advocate, too, of a permanent stadium in Calcutta, arguing that sport would "receive a serious check if we fail to provide at the psychological moment a central home for sports." But his dream of a stadium that could accommodate "no less than 60,000 people" wasn't fulfilled in his lifetime.[57]

The Peculiar Case of Vizzy

It might be appropriate to end this chapter with the maharajkumar of Vizia-nagram, or Vizzy as he came to be known, who was associated with cricket as a player, patron, administrator, and finally radio commentator. The title itself, maharajkumar, as Mihir Bose explained, was odd, since it denoted not a ma-haraja but the son of a prince.[58] In reality, Vizzy lost out to his nephew in the race to become the maharaja of Vizianagram, a tiny princely state in Andhra Pradesh. He then set himself up in Benares in Uttar Pradesh on land owned by the Vizianagram royal family. From 1926 onward, he had his own team and private cricket ground in Benares, which the journalist E. H. D. Sewell described in 1934 as "well nigh perfect."[59]

Although Vizzy had played cricket when he was at Mayo College, he was far better at off-field politics and organization. In 1929, the Vizianagram XI—composed of players of the caliber of C. K. Nayudu, the greatest Indian crick-eter of his era; D. B. Deodhar; and Vithal Palwankar—first played in the Roshanara Tournament. Though a favorite to win the trophy, Vizzy's team was unexpectedly beaten. In 1930/1931, he bounced back by organizing a tour of India and Ceylon, where he somehow managed to get the legendary opening pair of English cricket—Jack Hobbs and Herbert Sutcliffe—to join his team. When I visited the MCC Museum at Lord's in 2011, one of the more interesting exhibits was a bat presented by Hobbs to Vizzy, on which was inscribed in Hobbs's handwriting: "I used this bat in my last 'Test' match versus Australia at the Oval, August 1930, also while scoring my first century in India at Benaras, November, 1930." It is rumored that Vizzy even tried to get Don Bradman to play for his team but in the end came away with some cricket tips from the legend. Besides the English openers, Nayudu, his brother C. S. Nayudu, Deodhar, Dilawar Hussain, and other Indian stars, were part of Vizzy's team. In 1934, the team had the West Indian star Learie Constantine in its ranks.

Vizzy's ambitions were much bigger than merely sponsoring his own team. In 1932 he crossed swords with the maharaja of Patiala, already an established patron of sport and a much wealthier prince, by donating Rs 50,000 to cover the costs of India's first official tour to England in 1932. The *Times of India* speculated that on the strength of his donation, Vizzy was likely to lead the Indian team.[60] But Patiala outmaneuvered him by sponsoring the month-long trials for the team selection in January 1932. When the team was announced, Patiala was the captain and Vizzy given the strange position of deputy vice-captain. A shaken Vizzy then pulled out of the tour, prompting the maharaja of Patiala to announce that he was unable to take on the captaincy. Yet another prince, the maharaja of Porbandar—a small princely state in western India where Mahatma Gandhi was born—was appointed captain, with K. S. Ghanyashamsinhji of Limbdi as his deputy. Porbandar, who averaged less than one run in the first four matches of the tour, stepped down from the captaincy, leaving Nayudu to lead the team in the first Test match at Lord's. But the team, depleted by injuries and factional rivalry, lost the Test, even though it performed well in patches.

Vizzy bounced back when India next toured England in 1936. He ingratiated himself with Lord Willingdon by donating a pavilion named after the viceroy in the Ferozeshah Kotla Stadium in Delhi.[61] He even tried unsuccessfully in 1934 to have the trophy for the national championship named after Willingdon and not Ranji, as Patiala had proposed.[62] In between, during the MCC's tour of India in 1933, led by Douglas Jardine, Vizzy's team won the sole victory against the visitors. Jardine even praised Vizzy's captaincy on the occasion. Initially, the nawab of Pataudi, who had already played for England

and cracked a century on his debut in the Bodyline series, was appointed captain but stepped aside because of poor health. Vizzy filled the vacancy and was voted captain by the Indian cricket board. The tour, however, was an unmitigated disaster, with India losing two out of three Tests and losing nine out of the seventeen county games. Vizzy averaged 16.21 runs for the tour and was a poor captain. He cut a sorry figure in the field: "a plumpish, rather hunched figure, perpetually standing in the slips and peering through spectacles at a game he did not seem to understand."[63]

The tour is remembered less for the cricket than for the sensational sending back of India's star batsman and future captain, Lala Amarnath. The incident got plenty of play in the newspapers of the time. Amarnath and Vizzy had been at loggerheads right from the beginning of the tour, and things boiled over during a match against the Minor Counties in which Amarnath was sent in to bat at number seven minutes before the end of day's play. When Amarnath returned to the dressing room, he made his displeasure known vocally. One thing led to another, and the next day Vizzy, in consultation with the English manager, Major Britton Jones, decided to send Amarnath back home.[64] A member of the Indian team, Mushtaq Ali, wrote that this was the "most sensational happening in the history of cricket tours."[65] Later a committee—the first and definitely not the last time that cricket would trouble the government—headed by the chief justice of the Bombay high court, John Beaumont, inquired into the events of the 1936 tour. Even though Beaumont did not find anything wrong with sending back Amarnath, he did say that there was "a strong feeling among most members of the team that he [Vizzy] was not successful as a playing captain."[66] Vizzy remained on the cricket scene, becoming the president of the BCCI in 1954 before losing out in the power struggles on the Indian cricket board. But he continued in the 1950s to give running commentary for cricket matches on All-India Radio. As on the cricket field, his skills left much to be desired, and it was a common joke that Vizzy was extremely successful in hunting because he would play his commentary in the jungle and put the animals to sleep.[67] He is, however, still remembered by a trophy for interuniversity cricket named after him.

Two things are worth noting in the involvement of princes in sports. First, even though many Indian princes schooled in the chiefs' colleges were competent sportsmen, their role as patrons usually made a far greater contribution to sports. And even though their efforts were often aimed at personal aggrandizement and competing with rival princes and occasionally even the British, they nonetheless helped develop and democratize sports in India. Second, it was the smaller princely states that patronized English sports, particularly cricket, with great enthusiasm. Despite the 560-odd princely states in British India, there were huge disparities in size and income among them, as well as in their place in the colonial hierarchy, which was marked by the number of gun salutes. Some of the biggest states, like Hyderabad, covered more than 82,000 square miles, had an annual revenue in excess of Rs 80 million and was accorded a twenty-one-gun (the highest) salute. At the other end of the scale were the nonsalute states covering less than ten square miles and with an annual revenue of less than Rs 10,000. One of the main incentives for the smaller states to take up cricket was greater access to the colonial administrators, which otherwise might have been very difficult, given their size and strength. Besides, fielding a cricket team was much less expensive than maintaining a stable of high-quality horses for polo.

Vizzy was a classic example of a minor royal who used sports to make his name and climb up the social hierarchy. It was only as a patron of cricket that he was able to take on much bigger princes like Patiala, as well as gain the ear of the highest colonial officials. Many other princes used sports to good effect, but none used it as spectacularly as Vizzy did, even surviving the departure of the British in 1947. Who would remember Santosh today if it were not for the national football trophy named after him? Even a medium-sized state like Patiala would probably have been remembered for royal excess if it had not been for its long and varied association with sports. Much rarer, of course, were princes like Ranji, who really were gifted sportsmen. But as Ranji's career showed, without cricket he would have stood little chance of inheriting the Nawanagar throne. As for other princes like the nawab of Pataudi, only their extraordinary talent in sports ensured that their names would figure in the national consciousness.

5

THE EMPIRE
STRIKES BACK

THE 1911 IFA SHIELD AND
FOOTBALL IN CALCUTTA

JUST A FEW YARDS DOWN THE ROAD FROM THE ICONIC EDEN Gardens Stadium in Calcutta and not too far from the free-flowing Ganga is the Mohun Bagan football ground. Step inside the gates and into the members' area opposite the stadium and you are greeted by a large poster with a grainy picture of footballers posing with a trophy. It's the eleven that created history in 1911 by becoming the first Indian team to win the IFA Shield—the blue-ribbon event of the time—by defeating a British regimental team. That momentous event of 1911, ironically the same year the capital of British India was moved out to Delhi, capped nearly four decades of efforts at physical regeneration by Bengalis to shake off the "effeminate" tag bestowed by the British. This was contrasted with the "manly" Englishman as well as the so-called martial races such as the Punjabis, Marathas, and Pathans. The classification was backed up by pseudoscientific studies by colonial officials like Herbert Risley, who believed that Bengalis could be "recognized at a glance" and that climate and diet contributed in great measure to the Bengalis' poor physical condition.[1]

We began this book with an unflattering description of a Bengali by an English journalist. Such views were hardly uncommon among British officials, including such famous figures like Thomas Babington Macaulay, who, among other things, shaped the education policy in India. Among the many disparaging things Macaulay had to say about Bengalis (and indeed Indians in general), the one that stood out was "The physical organization of the Bengalis is feeble even to effeminacy.... His pursuits are sedentary, his limbs delicate, his movements languid."[2] Even more priceless was a British journalist's characterization of a Bengali's physique. According to G. W. Steevens,

> By his legs you shall know a Bengali.... The Bengali's leg is either skin and bones ... or else it is very fat or globular, also turning at the knees, with round thighs like a woman's. The Bengali's leg is the leg of a slave.[3]

These barbs were aimed particularly at the Bengali *babu*, whose rise as a class was predicated on the political economy of colonialism but who over time organized themselves to agitate against colonial rule. The relationship between the British and the Bengalis was a curious one: the Bengalis were, by virtue of being the first group in India to have sustained contact with the colonial rulers, the most "British" of the Indian subjects. Indeed, it was their similarity to the Bengalis—in some senses their mirror image—that may have made the British so wary of them.

Bengalis quickly took to heart these criticisms about physical inadequacy and started believing them. Thus the novelist Bankim Chandra Chattopadhyay could say, without any doubt, that Bengalis always lacked "physical valour," even though he had no tangible evidence of that.[4] In the late nineteenth century, however, the Bengalis began to react to the constant denigration with a concerted effort to raise their self-esteem in both mind and body. Chattopadhyay himself wrote novels like *Ananda Math*, which introduced the patriotic slogan "Vande Mataram," asserting the need for militant resistance against foreign rule. Along with these efforts, a physical culture movement took shape in the 1860s.

In 1866, another Bengali intellectual, Rajnarayan Basu, called for the revival of "national gymnastic exercises,"[5] and a year later the Hindu Mela, which had its patrons the Tagore family, was launched. Particularly active in the Hindu Mela was Rabindranath Tagore's niece Sarala Debi. The festival had on its program wrestling, gymnastics, and other traditional sports, like stick fighting. It also aimed at breaking colonial stereotypes by pitting Bengalis against the so-called martial races. In 1878 the *Sambad Prabhakar* reported on a wrestling contest between a Bengali and a Punjabi in the Hindu Mela: "Even though the Bengali tried very hard to win, he finally failed, but this is not a matter of shame. Last year, the Bengali had defeated the Punjabi, this year he lost ... that the Bengali has succeeded in wrestling with a Punjabi—this in itself is worthy of praise."[6] One of the forces behind the Hindu Mela, Nabagopal Mitra, established an *akhara,* or gymnasium, in Calcutta[7] and was active in recruiting physical education teachers to train the youth. The *National Paper,* the organ of the Hindu Mela instituted by the Tagores in 1865, talked of the need for Bengalis to train as soldiers in order to measure up to the Rajputs, Sikhs, and Marathas. As historian Sumit Sarkar pointed out, it was "natural for young Bengalis to seek psychological compensation in a cult of physical strength and a somewhat exaggerated faith in the efficacy of purely military methods."[8]

Some members of the colonial administration were keen, too, that the Bengalis improve their physical health. Sir George Campbell, lieutenant governor of Bengal in the 1870s, felt that that Bengalis were capable of great things if they set aside their "intellectual vanity"[9] and their love for "literature, law and politics."[10] He introduced physical fitness norms—walking and riding at a prescribed pace—for applicants to the Native Civil Service, emphasized sports in the educational institutions' curricula, and even handed out medals at a Calcutta *akhara.*[11] At a slightly later phase, the YMCA, too, was active in this field. J. Henry Gray, who had been appointed in 1908 as the physical director of the YMCA in Calcutta, wrote that "a large number of the many varieties of physical education that are found in the world are bidding for a place of recognition or a place of prominence here."[12]

Presidency College, the oldest college in Calcutta, was a good example of the interest in physical culture sweeping Bengal. In 1879, the college started offering gymnastics classes. Nagendra Prasad Sarvadhikari, an undergraduate student at the college, along with a British professor, organized the Presidency College Corps to train students in shooting. An athletic, cricket, and football club followed, and shortly afterward, the college was granted a coveted plot of land in the Calcutta maidan. From 1897 onward, it became mandatory for first-year students to attend gymnastic classes.[13] In fact, the college's football team won the Elliot Shield, the premier intercollegiate football tournament, five times between 1904 and 1908. Jitendrananth (Kanu) Roy, who represented Presidency, went on to play for Mohun Bagan.

Both the intellectual strand represented by Bankim Chandra and Sarala Debi and the actual physical culture movement were critical to the growth of the anticolonial revolutionary organizations in Bengal in the early twentieth century. One of the more famous such societies was the Anusilan Samity founded by Satischandra Basu in 1902 in Calcutta. An important part of the *anusilan samities'* anti-British activities was physical culture and the practice of traditional sports. Yet another gymnasium was founded around the same time in Calcutta by a remarkable woman, Sarala Ghoshal, which provided training in sword and *lathi* (stick) play.[14]

Such organizations flourished in the wake of the Swadeshi movement (1905–1911) and were directed against the partition of Bengal. Inspired by publications such as *Bande Mataram, Yugantar,* and *Sandhya,* scores of young Bengalis joined secret groups with the express intention of assassinating British officials and instigating armed insurrection against the colonial rulers. The *anusilan* movement soon spread beyond Calcutta to smaller towns. In 1906, Pulin Behari Das, an expert in *lathi* play, founded the formidable Dacca Anusilan Samity in East Bengal. Nirad Chaudhuri described a "physical-culture" club in his native East Bengal:

> The greatest emphasis was placed on fencing with singlesticks.... In this case the partners stood facing each other from the opposite ends of the lawn, their *dhotis* tucked high, the stick in their right hand, and the cane buckler in the left. They glared at each other and gave the traditional war cry of the Bengal dacoit and fighter—"hare re re re re-e-e-e-e-e-e-e!"[15]

During a later period, another prominent revolutionary formed the Simla Bayam Samity (Simla Physical Culture Club), home to several famous wrestlers, which continues to exist in north Calcutta. Swami Vivekananda, the great Hindu reformist leader, hailed from the Simla area and was said to have been tutored by Khetubabu, one of Calcutta's famous wrestlers. Vivekananda, who was an inspiration for the militant wing of Bengal's nationalist movement, was proficient in several sports: *lathi* play, fencing, boxing, gymnastics, swimming, and horse riding. He also once won the first prize in gymnastics in the Hindu Mela.[16] But Vivekananda is perhaps best remembered for announcing: "You will be nearer to Heaven through football than through the study of the Gita," adding that one "will understand the Gita better with your biceps, your muscles, a little stronger."[17] Oddly, we have no record of Vivekananda playing football, but he was an avid cricketer, apparently even playing one match for the Town Club.[18] Unlike wrestling or bodybuilding, English team games like football and cricket provided Indians the rare opportunity to compete on a relatively level playing field and even beat the British.

The Rise of Mohun Bagan

In this milieu the Mohun Bagan Sporting Club, as it was initially known, was formed and rapidly shot to prominence. Founded in 1889 (just three years after the legendary Arsenal Football Club in England) in the north Calcutta home of Bhupendranath Basu, who later became the president of the Indian National Congress, the club was, right from the beginning, involved in both playing sports and building character. Among the founding members were several of the leading lights of Calcutta society, including the maharaja of Cooch Behar. The club's first playing field was inside a marble palace known as Mohun Bagan Villa, in north Calcutta and owned by the aristocratic Mitra family, from which the club got its name. Later the club relocated to a field in Shyampukur donated by a grandee, Durga Charan Law, and subsequently to yet another field, which it shared with the Aryan and Baghbazar Clubs. Initially the club accepted only students and there was a probationary period of six months. One of the club officials, Jatindranath Basu, often lined up the younger members and quizzed them on their studies. One of them was even expelled for smoking cigarettes.[19]

Interestingly, for Mohun Bagan's first anniversary, a professor of English from Presidency College, F. J. Rhow, was invited to the club and, on discovering that rifle shooting or angling was not part of its activities, suggested that the "Sporting" be replaced by "Athletic" in the club's name. The members agreed, and to this day the club is known as the Mohun Bagan Athletic Club. The composition of the club's founders and of the players was markedly different from that of other clubs, like Vasco da Gama, which was founded around the same time by immigrants and vendors in Brazil, as well as clubs like Arsenal founded by factory workers.[20]

In the early 1890s, Mohun Bagan began playing friendly matches with numerous other Indian clubs in Calcutta like Sovabazar and National Association, as well as educational institutions like Calcutta Medical College and Bengal Engineering College. It also started taking part in the Cooch Behar Cup, a tournament for Indian teams begun by the maharaja of Cooch Behar in 1893, which had as its prize a beautiful silver trophy, to protest the whites-only policy of the major tournaments, but without much success. This began to change in 1900 when the strict disciplinarian Subedar Major Sailendra Nath (Sailen) Bose became the club's honorary secretary. That year the club got its own field in the Calcutta maidan, which it shared with Presidency College for the next fifteen years and also started gathering a mass following. The maidan was a vast expanse of green (which is still in existence), a quarter mile to a mile wide in the early twentieth century,[21] in the center of the city facing Fort William, the seat of the British army in Calcutta. Again, the original intention of creating the maidan was to provide an uninterrupted line of fire from Fort William, but in 1848 it began to be developed for recreational activities, although it remains to this day under the army's control. Despite the maidan's size, there was intense competition among the sports clubs for space, which proved to be a headache for the police authorities, whose job it was to "allot accommodation."[22]

In the first decade of the twentieth century, Mohun Bagan established itself as the best Indian team, winning the Cooch Behar Cup back to back in 1904/1905 and achieving a rare hat trick in the Trades Cup by winning that tournament in 1906, 1907, and 1908. It again won the Cooch Behar Cup in 1907/1908. During this time, Mohun Bagan defeated British teams, too. In 1905, Mohun Bagan won the Gladstone Cup by trouncing the Dalhousie Club (earlier known as the Trades Club), the winner of that year's IFA Shield, 6-1. The next year it beat the Calcutta Football Club 1-0 at the Minto Fete Tournament.[23] These victories over British teams often ended in violence. In the preliminary rounds of the 1907 Trades Cup, when a British team, Dalhousie "B," was losing 2-3 to Mohun Bagan, its players began playing very rough and even used "fists and kicks,"[24] leading the spectators to invade the pitch, resulting in the game's being stopped.

Mohun Bagan's record in the IFA Shield, however, was far from impressive. Even though the IFA Shield had begun later than the Trades Cup, it was quickly established as the blue-ribbon event of Calcutta, indeed Indian, football. The impressive trophy presented to the winning team had been ordered from Messrs Elkington and Company of London and was financed by the maharajas of Patiala and Cooch Behar and two English gentlemen. The IFA Shield was not a happy hunting ground for Indian teams. Sovabazar, which held the honor of defeating a European team for the first time in 1892, was knocked out in the first round of the inaugural IFA Shield in 1893 by the Fifth Royal Artillery team. Mohun Bagan participated for the first time in the Shield in 1909, only to be drubbed 0–3 by the Gordon Highlanders, a British regimental team.[25] This prompted Bagan's rival clubs to circulate pamphlets ridiculing it for "aiming too high." In 1911, Mohun Bagan was thought to have little chance of winning.

The 1911 IFA Shield

Under the stewardship of Sailen Bose and the captain, Shibdas Bhaduri, a remarkable student of the game, Mohun Bagan formed a team that could challenge the best of the British teams in India.[26] Curiously, the team played precisely eleven players in the IFA Shield; that is, it had no bench strength in case of injuries. This was a real gamble, since ten players of the Mohun Bagan XI played barefoot, with, oddly enough, the only non-Hindu in the team, left back Rev. Sudhir Chatterjee, wearing boots. It is tempting to link Chatterjee's religion and his boots, but it was more likely that he picked up the habit when studying abroad. Besides, if popular accounts are to be believed, every effort was made to deter the Bagan players, working in British-run organizations, from training for their team.[27]

The conventional reason given for the Bagan players playing barefoot is that boots cramped their style of play, but it could also have been the expense of buying them. Sutor & Co, for instance, advertised hand-sewn football boots in 1903 for Rs 7 and 4 *annas*, a small fortune at the time.[28] Other companies, such as the Kanpur-based Wense Tannery, sold boots at outlets in Calcutta, Bombay, Kanpur, and Nainital, with "special terms for clubs and regimental teams."[29] Boots were not entirely new to Indian players. The National Association, a south Calcutta team formed by schoolteacher Manmatha Ganguly, played wearing boots and even won the Trades Cup. Dookhiram Majumdar, the founder of the Aryan Football Club, was also a die-hard advocate of boots but was not very successful in making others see his point of view.[30] Whatever the reason for the aversion to boots, Indian teams like Mohun Bagan were at a decided disadvantage on grounds made slushy by the Calcutta monsoon.

Although football is nowadays considered a plebeian sport in India and the rest of the world, the composition of the Mohun Bagan team was a good indicator of how enthusiastically upper-caste Bengalis had taken up sports. The team consisted of ten Bengalis, six of them Brahmins, and one player, Chatterjee, a Christian. The rest were upper-caste Hindus. Only one player, Bhuti Sukul, most likely came from outside Bengal, his surname a corruption of the north Indian "Shukla." Despite belonging to the upper castes, the players were far from well off. Three of the team members were employed in government: Shibdas Bhaduri was a veterinary inspector; Manmohan Mukherjee worked in the Public Works Department; and Habul Sarkar was a clerk in the Calcutta Corporation. In addition to being a footballer, Sarkar played cricket for the City Athletic Club and also was an accomplished hockey player.[31] Three of them were students: Rajen Sengupta and Abhilash Ghosh studied at Scottish Church, and Kanu Roy was at Presidency. Nilmadhab Bhattacharjee was with the Bengal National Bank, and the goalkeeper, Hiralal Mukherjee, once had a menial job at the Martin Brick Company. Bijoydas (Shibdas's brother) and Bhuti Sukul were partners in a small business, which, among other things, traded in opium. Chatterjee, who had a degree in education from England, taught at the LMS College in Calcutta.[32] Not all the players were from Calcutta. Manmohan Mukherjee was from Uttarpara, and Nilmadhab Bhattacharya, from Srirampur. Kanu Roy belonged to a wealthy *zamindari* family from Mymensingh in East Bengal. Much was made of the divide between Mohun Bagan and its latter-day rival, East Bengal, whose support base came from the Ghotis, the original inhabitants of West Bengal, and the Bangals, from East Bengal, or what is now Bangladesh. Eight players of the 1911 Bagan team, including the Bhaduris, were originally from East Bengal. The mixed composition of the team even came in for veiled criticism from *The Englishman* newspaper, which pointed out that Mohun Bagan was a "picked team, several of them being men from up country and from the sister province of East Bengal."[33]

This motley bunch began their IFA campaign by defeating St Xavier's College 3–0, despite playing with ten men (Chatterjee was refused leave by his college to play). Notwithstanding the convincing win, *The Englishman* predicted the next day that "great as the rejoicing was in the Indian camp after last evening's victory, the lamentations on Friday (the day of the second round match) may be much greater."[34] The newspaper's predictions were wrong. Bagan's next opponent, the Rangers Club of Calcutta, was a tougher proposition. But on a slushy ground, which made playing with bare feet extremely tricky, Mohun Bagan edged the British team 2-1, the win riding on two goals by Shibdas. By now, Mohun Bagan's supporters had begun to believe that they had a real chance of winning the Shield.

In the quarterfinal, Mohun Bagan had to face the Rifle Brigade, its first military opponent and the team that had knocked it out in the second round of the previous year's tournament. The regimental teams were traditionally the best football teams in India, with a military team having won the IFA Shield ten times since its inception in 1893. A crowd of about 40,000 had assembled for the "revenge" match, which was held at the Customs ground. The crowds were not surprising considering that Calcutta and its suburbs, according to the 1911 census, had a population of 1,043,307. *The Statesman* reported that a "vast sea of eager, excited faces thronged the galleries" well before the game began at 5.30 P.M.[35] The game was a hard-fought affair, with Bagan winning 1-0, the only goal being scored by Bijoydas in the second half.

In the semifinal, Mohun Bagan was up against yet another military team, the Middlesex Regiment. *The Englishman* reported that "Bengali Calcutta had gone football mad" and that attendance in offices in the city on match day was thinner than usual.[36] The game ended in a tense 1-1 tie, with the English team scoring a disputed goal (many believed that the referee was biased) in the first half. With no system of tiebreakers in those days, the game was replayed the next day, and Mohun Bagan convincingly triumphed 3-0, scoring all three goals in the last ten minutes of the game. The replacement of the referee by H. G. Puller, who was regarded as fairer, and an injury to the Middlesex goalkeeper, who had received a cut in his eye and was playing with his eye bandaged, helped Bagan's cause. A *Times of India* reporter wrote that the only subject of conversation wherever Bengali *babus* congregated was the "rout of the King's soldiers in boots and shoes by barefooted Bengali lads."[37]

The Famous Victory

The stage was now set for the biggest game yet in Indian football: Mohun Bagan versus the East Yorkshire Regiment of Faizabad in the IFA Shield final on July 29, 1911. In the lead-up to the final, emotions had reached fever pitch in Calcutta and its surrounding areas. Tickets for the match, originally priced at Rs 1 and 2, were selling for as much as Rs 15, a small fortune in those days.[38] Such was the enthusiasm that people came from outlying Bengal districts, as well as from neighboring Bihar and Assam. On the day of the match, the transport system was completely choked with spectators trying to get to the Calcutta Football Club field in the maidan. The East Indian Railway ran a special train, and additional steamer services were introduced to ferry spectators to Calcutta from the rural areas.[39]

At the field itself, an estimated 80,000 to 100,000 people gathered.[40] Because most of them could not enter the field, they were kept informed about the proceeding by an ingenious method. As the Reuters correspondent reported, volunteers kept the crowd informed of the progress of the match by flying a kite with the club colors when one of the teams scored a goal.[41] *The Empire*, a local paper, had also installed a temporary telephone connection to the field to relay instantly the game's progress.[42] The weather gods were kind to Mohun Bagan—even though the monsoon had arrived, there was no rain on the day of the final, ensuring that the football pitch was dry and more suitable to playing barefoot.

The fifty-minute match, with a five-minute break at halftime, was thrilling. Both teams were scoreless at halftime. Then, with fifteen minutes left, the East Yorkshire captain, Sergeant Jackson, put his team ahead, but within minutes, Bagan's captain, Shibdas, scored as well, triggering an explosion of maroon and green—Mohun Bagan's colors—kites in the sky. With less than ten minutes before the final whistle, both teams pressed hard for the winning goal. It was center forward Abhilash Ghosh who caught an immaculate pass from Shibdas to put his team ahead 2–1, the final score. History had been made. Mohun Bagan had become the first Indian team to win the coveted IFA Shield. The football correspondent of the *Amrita Bazar Patrika*, the largest circulating English daily in Calcutta, reported: "The scene that followed was beyond description. Hats, handkerchiefs, umbrellas and sticks were waved and the tremendous cheering shook heaven and earth. It was as if the whole population had gone mad and to compare it with anything would be to minimise the effect."[43]

The reverberations from Mohun Bagan's victory were felt way beyond the maidan. The IFA Shield final naturally was widely covered in the local press but also was cited in the international press. Reuters, the *Times, Daily Mail*, and *Manchester Guardian* all sent reports to London. Newspapers from outside Bengal, like the *Times of India* (Bombay) and the *Pioneer* (Allahabad) reported extensively on the victory. But it wasn't just Mohun Bagan's performance on the field that excited people. The local media, primarily the English and Bengali newspapers, read two things into the historic triumph: first, clear evidence that Bengalis did not lack physical prowess and, second, the nationalistic implications of the victory.

In an article entitled "The Immortal Eleven," the *Amrita Bazar Patrika* wrote that Bengalis had proved themselves in the sphere of physical culture, in which they were "so long held to be lamentably deficient."[44] We should point out that a report by the intelligence department in 1911 alleged that the *Patrika*'s policy was "systematic opposition to all measures of Government" and that it had "first started the doctrine of retaliation, advising the children of the soil in dealing with Europeans to return frown for frown and blow for blow."[45] Another newspaper, *The Bengalee*, was more explicit, proclaiming that the Bengali is "no longer the timid and weak-kneed representative of the race whom Macaulay so foully libelled."[46] The Bengali newspapers were even more excited about the humbling of the British by a Bengali team. *The Basumati* wrote that Mohun Bagan had "infused a new life into the lifeless and cheerless Bengali,"[47] while *The Nayak* gushed that the match filled "every Indian with joy and pride to know that rice-eating, malaria-ridden, barefooted Bengalis have got the better of beef-eating, Herculean, booted John Bull in the peculiarly English sport."[48] Other newspapers played up the nationalistic element of the victory. *The Englishman* commented that Mohun Bagan had "succeeded in what the Congress and the Swadeshiwallas have failed to so far to explode the myth that the Britishers are unbeatable in any sphere of life,"[49] and *The Basumati* noted that Bagan had been able to "knit together" people in a way the political parties had not been able to do.[50]

There was some truth in this in the reactions by the Calcutta Muslims to the 1911 victory. When the victory procession after the final was making its way to north Calcutta, several Muslims, accompanied by a band, joined the festivities. *The Mussalman*, a Muslim weekly, wrote that Mohun Bagan had "demonstrated that Indians are second to none in all manly games." But significantly, it added that although the Bagan team was composed of Hindus, the jubilation over the Shield victory was not confined to any particular religion. As proof, it pointed out: "The members of the Muslim Sporting Club were almost mad and rolling on the ground with joyous excitement on the victory of their Hindu brethren."[51]

A poster on the Mohun Bagan Club premises in Kolkata of the team that won the IFA Shield in 1911. Photograph by Pratip Acharya. Printed by permission of Pratip Acharya

Some exploited the victory commercially. The Standard Cycle Company distributed halftone photographs of the Mohun Bagan team along with the July 31 edition of the *Amrita Bazar Patrika*.[52] Even though the victorious team was feted on several occasions, the grand reception in Calcutta's Town Hall proposed by prominent citizens of the city, never took place, and the players did not earn much money from their victory. A proposal by *The Bengalee* newspaper to raise money for Mohun Bagan was voted down by the club authorities.[53] The offers of jobs and money for the players, including employment in Martin Burn Company for all the players, were mostly forgotten after the first flush of victory. Sailendra Nath Bose wrote in *The Statesman* that it was not desirable to "make a fuss" over the Shield victory,[54] and most of the players continued in their earlier jobs. Given the nationalist connotations of Mohun Bagan's victory, perhaps the most unusual career trajectory was that of Kanu Roy. He joined the police after leaving college, retiring as a deputy inspector general of police and, along the way, becoming notorious "for torturing men and women arrested for nationalist activity."[55]

The Aftermath

Mohun Bagan found it difficult to replicate its IFA Shield success, even though it did consistently well in the premier tournaments. Part of the reason was that it became the target of European community, even though *The Statesman* in 1911 suggested that "one great lesson that the English devotion to sports teaches is that defeat should be accepted with good grace."[56] In the 1912 IFA Shield, it was commonly believed, at least by Indians, that the European referee disallowed two legitimate goals by Mohun Bagan against the Calcutta Football Club in the first round. This match was a landmark for an entirely different reason, as perhaps for the first time a sports event was captured on film in India by J. F. Madan and Company, the pioneers of motion picture in India (according to one version, the 1911 final also was filmed), which apparently served only to highlight the referee's bias.[57] Instances of biased refereeing were not unusual. A contemporary commentator wrote that when there was no way "to undermine Mohun Bagan, like a bolt from the blue, without a warning, came a penalty charge."[58]

In 1920, Mohun Bagan reached the semifinals of the IFA Shield only to be thwarted by a lesser-known Indian team, Kumartuli, named after a Calcutta locale famed for its clay artisans. The next year the match between Mohun Bagan and Calcutta Football Club had to be abandoned because of disruptions by the crowd. In 1923, Mohun Bagan reached the final of the Shield for the second time, but this time it was convincingly trounced, 3–0, by Calcutta Football Club. In 1940 Mohun Bagan once again reached the IFA Shield after a gap of several years, but this time it was pitted against another Indian club, Aryan. Before a crowd of at least 80,000, Aryan shocked Mohun Bagan and its thousands of fans by winning 4–1.[59]

Mohun Bagan's performance brought invitations from the big tournaments outside Bengal. In 1923, it was invited to play in the Rovers Cup in Bombay, at which it was the runner-up, losing to Durham's Light Infantry 1–3. According to journalist J. C. Maitra, Mohun Bagan "took Bombay literally by storm."[60] Mohun Bagan came back to Bombay to play a couple of charity matches, raising an impressive Rs 10,000 for the Gujarat Flood Relief Fund.[61] In 1925, it became the first Indian team to compete in the Durand Cup, defeating three British regimental teams en route to the semifinal, in which it lost to Sherwood Forest. In 1914, Mohun Bagan also gained entry into the second division of the Calcutta League, along with Aryan, which until then had been open only to white teams. The next year Mohun Bagan was promoted to the first division, in which it was runner-up in 1916. It went on to win the league much later in 1939. This period was dominated by one of the stars of Calcutta football, Gostho Pal, who earned the nickname "Chinese Wall" for his stout defending. Pal began playing for Mohun Bagan in 1913 when he was only sixteen and still is the only footballer to be honored with a statue on the Calcutta maidan.

There is, of course, the question of how good Mohun Bagan, or its rival Indian teams, was by international standards. Tony Mason noted that the "three bandsman and eight privates who made up the East Yorks side" were, by no stretch of imagination, on a par with the top English clubs of the day.[62] This was perhaps shown by the visiting amateur English football side, the Islington Corinthians, who played a series of matches from Peshawar to Dhaka in the winter of 1937.[63] The Corinthians played four games in Calcutta, winning three, including one against Mohun Bagan by a solitary goal,[64] and tying one against Mohammedan Sporting,[65] possibly the best Indian team of the time. The Corinthians acknowledged that Mohun Bagan had been their "stiffest opposition," even though the visitors lost one game against the Dhaka Sporting Association.[66] But trying to place Mohun Bagan's 1911 victory and subsequent success in the international context is missing the point. Irrespective of the footballing standard, the 1911 triumph should be seen as a great nationalist moment.

Football games, even those involving Mohun Bagan, were not insulated from nationalist protests. On May 24, 1930, during the height of the Civil Disobedience Movement against the British Raj, all matches scheduled for that day, including the one between Mohun Bagan and the Calcutta Football Club—the most popular fixture of the season—had to be abandoned after female members of the Indian National Congress besieged the Mohun Bagan and other club tents. Other matches had to be abandoned because the crowd invaded the field. A week later, at a special meeting of the Calcutta Football League Committee, the Indian clubs decided to withdraw from the league for the rest of the season, making the British wonder why the protesters was putting a stop to "healthy recreation."

It wasn't uncommon for off-field tensions—between the ruler and the ruled, between white and brown—to affect the football pitch. In 1923, Mohun Bagan was forced to play on a field that was partly under water because of heavy rain. Many years later, the historian and communist stalwart Hiren

Mukherjee wrote that the decision was based on the report by the referee R. R. Clayton, who was "enormously competent but unabashedly partisan."[67] This same referee was slapped on the field by a Bengali footballer "out of sheer disgust."[68] Again in 1929, a match between Mohun Bagan and a European club, Dalhousie Club, was marred by violence. The initial provocation was a disputed goal against Bagan awarded by the referee. A little later, the Bagan goalkeeper, Santosh Dutt, collided with Dalhousie's Williams, with Williams having to be carried off with a fractured jawbone. When the referee was seen having a word with Dutt, the crowd invaded the pitch. Only an intervention by some soldiers in the stands saved the referee and the linesman.

At a meeting of the IFA council the next day, the association's president, Thomas Lamb, complained that the "Indian section of the spectators are still lacking in true sporting spirit." He warned that a "racial riot" might have taken place if the Europeans had chosen to retaliate and that the Calcutta Football Club, the top European team, would stop playing Indian teams if such incidents continued. Subsequently, Bagan's goalkeeper, Dutt, was suspended for two years on the evidence of the linesman, Maclaren, who himself was a member of Dalhousie.[69] At a meeting of seventy-one Indian football clubs, it was decided that the Indians would "disassociate from the IFA" and form a separate association.[70] The skewed representation of Indians in the IFA is illustrated by the fact that the fourteen European clubs had eight representatives on the IFA, whereas the 140 Indian clubs had only four. Eventually Lamb was forced to apologize for his remarks; the Indian clubs were given two additional seats; and Dutt's suspension was lifted. Later, parity was achieved in the IFA, with the fourteen members being evenly split between Europeans and Indians.

The acrimony over refereeing continued. Gostho Pal was involved in an incident in the twilight of his playing career that revealed the ill will that the British referees had generated. In 1935 in a league match against the Calcutta Football Club, Pal and his teammates, in a unique form of protest, decided to stay on the field but not to play seriously in the last ten minutes of the match in order to protest the biased refereeing. The Mohun Bagan team "strolled about the field or rested on the ground" and even deliberately handled the ball in penalty area, accepting the penalties. The end result was 6-0 in favor of the Calcutta Football Club. According to the Calcutta historian R. P. Gupta, another time that Pal found a unique method of protesting against racist attitudes was by going to bat wearing a dhoti and shirt in a cricket match between Mohun Bagan and the all-white Calcutta Cricket Club. The Calcutta Cricket Club refused to play unless Pal changed into the traditional whites. When Pal refused, the game was called off.[71] There is a reference to this controversy, although Pal's name is not given, under the heading "Dhoti War" in contemporary newspapers. R. B. Lagden, the president and captain of the Calcutta Cricket Club, wrote to *The Statesman* clarifying that the match at the Eden Gardens was called off on cricketing grounds. He insisted that it was "imperative to play cricket as it should be played in the kit which is recognized throughout the world as being suitable."[72] Mohun Bagan's honorary secretary promptly shot off a reply saying that over the last ten years it wasn't unusual for some members of Indian clubs, including Mohun Bagan, to turn up for cricket matches in dhotis and that there was no intention of insulting their opponents.[73] The *Times of India* even weighed in, with an editorial saying that the "dhoti war" was "most unfortunate and unnecessary from every point of view."[74]

Other parts of India were not immune to such acrimonious incidents on the field, either. In the 1940 Rovers Cup, for instance, a match had to be abandoned because the crowd invaded the pitch after a British team, the Welch Regiment, tied the Young Goans Sports Club. The Western Indian Football Association concluded that the Young Goans refused to play after the regimental team scored a goal and that some of their players egged on the spectators to invade the field. The Young Goans were subsequently handed a three-year suspension.[75] But considering that India's nationalist movement had begun gathering momentum in the 1920s, the number of confrontations between Indian players and fans and the British was surprisingly few. In fact, sometimes British and Indian players played alongside each other on teams representing the Indian Football Association (IFA). For example, when the IFA XI played the Corinthians in Calcutta in 1937, it had two British players, both from the Calcutta Football Club, playing with the best Indian players chosen from the Calcutta clubs.[76] Earlier, when a combined civil and military team played the visiting Chinese football team in 1936, several British soldiers played alongside players from the various Calcutta clubs.[77] The Chinese won that game by 2–0. The Chinese played another match against an eleven selected from the best European and Indian footballers in Bombay, which ended in a thrilling 3–3 tie.[78]

Partha Chatterjee has pointed out that "perhaps rather serendipitously, a competitive domain was created where European and Indian teams met as rivals. This opened up a sphere of public life in the colonial city that was mixed yet deeply racialized."[79] Just as racial animosities sometimes spilled over onto the field, the spectators too would vent their pent-up feelings against their colonial rulers. These sentiments were best expressed by sports journalist Rakhal Bhattacharya:

When someone from my own kin [*jat-bhai*] makes your life hell on the football field, then whether you are an armed soldier or the big boss in my office, you must be inferior to me, or at least in no way superior....When I am sitting in the galleries, there is no rein on my voice and tongue. The torrent of abuse will scare away the ghosts of your forefathers.[80]

The spectators for Mohun Bagan's matches were drawn from all sections of society. Achintya Kumar Sengupta, a member of the judicial service and a writer of some repute, writes in his autobiography about the crowd in the 1920s and 1930s: "Mohun Bagan's match proved to be a great leveller for Bengalis: young and old, father and son-in-law. . . . An enthusiastic pat on a man's back in the gallery, the gentleman turning back proved to be a re-spectable professor. . . . All sailed in the same boat, equal partners in joy and sorrow."[81] Sengupta also pointed out that famous novelists like Shibram Chakraborty were often seen in the crowd.[82]

Mohun Bagan's achievements and the history of football in the Calcutta maidan after 1911 are inextricably tied to its rivalry with East Bengal, whose intensity is comparable to the great football rivalries elsewhere, such as the Celtic Football Club versus the Rangers in Glasgow or Manchester United against Manchester City, which go back over a century. The impetus for forming East Bengal came out of an incident in 1919 when a player from Dacca, Sailesh Basu, felt that he has been unfairly dropped by the Jorabagan Club for a crucial match because of his East Bengali origins. His protests, however, fell on deaf ears. Then he, along with a senior Jorabagan official, Suresh Chaudhuri, who was originally a *zamindar* in Mymensingh District in East Bengal, founded the East Bengal Club in 1920. They were supported by several influential Calcuttans, including Saradaranjan Roy, the cricketer-principal of Metropolitan College, and Pankaj Gupta, who became one of

India's best-known sports administrators. Interestingly, the number of East Bengali players in the East Bengal Club never exceeded that of Mohun Bagan or the other major Calcutta clubs.

Within five years, the club was promoted to the first division of the Calcutta League, a move that was vigorously opposed by Mohun Bagan and Aryan, both of whom were members of the league committee. *The Statesman* surmised that the opposition was due to East Bengal's strength and popularity.[83] The Mohun Bagan and Aryan representatives, however, argued that the promotion of East Bengal was a "petty concession" to Indian teams and did not constitute the removal of the "color bar" for which Indian clubs had been arguing.[84]

The rivalry between Mohun Began and East Bengal on the football pitch began in the 1925 Calcutta League on a dramatic note when East Bengal beat Mohun Bagan 1–0, with Mohun Bagan emerging victorious in the return leg. Interestingly, like Mohammedan Sporting, East Bengal was not averse to recruiting players from outside Bengal. A newspaper reported in 1936 that Bangalore had become the "recruiting ground" for Bengal's football clubs.[85] East Bengal even had in its ranks a player from Burma, Fred Pugsley, who had apparently fled his country during World War II and traveled by foot to India.[86] Pugsley was a mainstay of East Bengal's forward line from 1944 and was the Calcutta League's highest goal scorer in 1945. An indication of the bitter rivalry between Mohun Bengal and East Bengal after 1947 surfaced in 1946 during a league match between the two teams. After the end of the match, the supporters of the two teams hurled bricks, stones, and soda bottles at each other, with both players and spectators suffering injuries.[87] Thus the famous writer Hemendrakumar Ray lamented that in the years following Mohun Bagan's 1911 win, he stopped going to watch football matches because of the unseemly behavior of the crowds.[88]

Much of the history of pre-1947 football in Calcutta has been swept aside by the aftermath of the 1911 victory and the nationalist glow surrounding it. Accordingly, Achintya Kumar Sengupta pointed out that Mohun Bagan was not merely a football club but the "victory symbol of a defeated, downtrodden nation."[89] The 1911 win occurred the same year that Calcutta suffered the signal blow of losing its status as the second city of the British Empire and the capital of British India. If that was a coincidence—or perhaps a conspiracy to defuse the radical, "bomb-wielding" wing of the nationalist movement that had gained momentum in Bengal[90]—another remarkable coincidence is associated with Mohun Bagan. An often-repeated story in Bengal is that just after the 1911 final was over, a person came up to Mohun Bagan's captain, Shibdas Bhaduri, and asked him, "Now that the British have been beaten on the football field, when will the Union Jack flying over Fort William be taken down?" Shibdas apparently replied, "When Mohun Bagan next wins the Shield."[91] His prediction came true. Mohun Bagan regained the trophy again in 1947, the year of India's independence. Little wonder then that Mohun Bagan has forever been identified with Bengali sports pride and Indian nationalism.

6

POLITICS ON
THE MAIDAN

SPORT, COMMUNALISM,

AND NATIONALISM

WHEN INDIAN TEAMS FIRST BEGAN COMPETING AND OCCASIONALLY defeating British teams, they were regarded as exceptional moments. Not only did these events signal that the British were fallible, but they also were celebrated as milestones in the Indian nationalist movement. Traces of the former can be found when the Parsis beat Vernon's team in 1890 and then Lord Hawke's team in 1892. But the nationalist euphoria was much more evident during Mohun Bagan's victory in the 1911 IFA Shield, at a time when India's freedom struggle was first gathering steam and drawing in people from all classes, in contrast to the relatively small elite in the late nineteenth century. If politics infiltrated the playing field on such occasions, it was much more apparent, albeit in a different form, when race, caste, and, most controversially, communal identities clashed on the maidan. The two most significant examples of this sort of politics were the controversy over the Bombay Quadrangular (later the Pentangular) and the spectacular rise of the Mohammedan Sporting Club in Calcutta, both occurring during the 1930s and 1940s when the Indian National Congress and the Muslim League were bitterly opposed to each other.

The Bombay Quadrangular

The Bombay Quadrangular, that peculiar and phenomenally popular cricket tournament organized along religious and racial lines, originated with matches between the Europeans and the Parsis beginning in the 1890s. Later, the Hindus (in 1907) and the Muslims (in 1912) joined to make it a four-way contest. Much later, in 1937, another team, the "Others," composed of Christians and Anglo-Indians, was included, making the tournament a pentangular. The composition of the tournament bore some similarity to the structure of cricket in Trinidad in the early twentieth century, so eloquently described by C. L. R. James. Unlike the religious and racial organization of teams in Bombay, however, the clubs in Trinidad were organized not just along race but also "social strata."[1] What is less known is that tournaments similar to the Bombay Quadrangular that were based on religion and race were also held in Karachi, Lahore, and Delhi. But the Bombay Quadrangular was by far the most popular cricket tournament in preindependence India, at which the best cricketers in India displayed their skills. Because of the way that cricket in India had evolved around gymkhanas begun by different communities, the Quadrangular had its own quirks, one being the question of caste. Among the finest cricketers on the Hindu team in the Bombay Quadrangular in the first quarter of the twentieth century were the remarkable Palwankar brothers, who belonged to a Dalit (untouchable) caste, the Chamars, and whose story has been chronicled by Ramachandra Guha. The eldest of the Palwankars, Baloo, was also one of the most talented cricketers of his time. (We encountered him briefly in an earlier chapter bowling at the nets to the star European cricketer, "Jungly" Grieg, in Pune.) From those humble beginnings, Baloo went on to become the mainstay of the Bombay Hindu Gymkhana. The first time that the Hindus played against the Europeans, in 1906, Baloo established his credentials by taking three wickets in the first innings and five in the second, but did not take Grieg's wicket.[2] Baloo's brother Shivram also played for the Hindus that year. The *Indian Social Reformer* wrote that that the admission of the "chamar brothers" into the Hindu Gymkhana was a "landmark in the nation's emancipation from the old disuniting and denationalising customs."[3] The next year Baloo once again excelled against the Europeans, taking thirteen wickets.

In 1911 both Baloo and Shivram, who was a last-minute replacement for an injured player, toured England with the all-India team under the maharaja of Patiala. Baloo took an astounding 114 wickets on the tour, but despite his phenomenal cricket skills, the question of caste constantly came up. In Pune, Baloo was forced to drink his tea from a clay cup outside the pavilion while his teammates drank from porcelain cups inside. In Bombay, even though Baloo was allowed to have his meals with his teammates, the captaincy of the Hindus eluded him. This controversy came to a head during the 1920 Quadrangular when Baloo's brother Vithal was passed over for the captaincy when the Hindu captain, M. D. Pai, fell ill. The decision was protested by the three Palwankar brothers, who refused to play, asserting that "such matters as caste should be [a] determining factor in Cricket is more than we can quietly bow down to."[4] Before the match against the strong Parsis, the Palwankar brothers relented, and Baloo was appointed vice-captain. Then when the Parsis were batting in the second innings, Pai left the field, perhaps intentionally, to allow Baloo to lead the team.

Ramachandra Guha compared Baloo's breaking the caste barrier with the more famous instances of black sportsmen like Frank Worrell or Jackie Robinson shattering the color bar. In what was the first instance of a sports star cashing on his fame to contest elections, Baloo twice ran in a municipal election in Bombay, but on both occasions he lost, the first time to Homi Pavri, a Parsi doctor, and the second to the great Dalit leader B .R. Ambedkar.

What Baloo couldn't achieve on the playing field his brother Vithal did. In 1923, for the first time a Dalit, Vithal, was appointed captain of the Hindus. Guha's explanation is that the decision could well have been dictated by pragmatism, since the Hindus had lost in the previous two tournaments held in Pune. Now that the tournament was back again in Bombay, where the Banias were more dominant than the Brahmins, the appointment of Vithal as captain was much easier. In his first season as captain, Vithal led the Hindus to victory over the Europeans, scoring a century in the first innings. Under Vithal, the Hindus won two more victories in three years. In 1929, when Vithal was dropped at age of forty, it ended a "thirty years' unbroken connection of the Baloo brothers with Hindu cricket."[5]

Until the 1930s, questions about the tournament's communal organization were rarely raised. A contemporary remarked that from "the one-pie beggar, to the big-bellied Shethia [rich trader] or the *topied* bureaucrat," everybody followed the tournament enthusiastically. He added that "although the tournament is run on communal lines, in cricket there is little or nothing of the communal spirit, and you see a Muslim applauding the hefty hit of Nayudu with the same enthusiasm as any Hindu."[6] The on-field controversies that did occur revolved around racial tensions, as when Grieg disputed the decision of an Indian umpire in 1916. Again in 1929, the European captain A. L. Hosie created a scene when an appeal for a wicket was turned down. The match was stalled for a period and the controversy commented on by the two rival newspapers, the *Times of India* and the *Bombay Chronicle*.[7]

Starting in the 1930s, the communal organization of the Quadrangular began to stir controversy. This was also the time when the Muslim League and the Congress had become bitter opponents. From 1930 to 1933, which coincided with momentous events in India's freedom struggle, including the Congress-led civil disobedience movement, the tournament was not held. In 1934, its resumption coincided with the inauguration of the national cricket tournament, the Ranji Trophy. Even though enthusiasm was sky-high for the Quadrangular, which had been sorely missed by cricket fans, there was some opposition too. One of the principal critics was the Bengali sports editor of the *Bombay Chronicle*, J. C. Maitra, whose avowed goal was the eradication of the "distinctions between caste, creed and colour from the field of sport." But he admitted in 1934 that "if the sale of tickets at the various Gymkhanas is any indication of its popularity among the votaries of the game, communalism has won with all ten wickets in hand."[8] This was also the year that All-India Radio first began live commentary of the matches. The Parsi journalist, A. F. S. "Bobby" Talyarkhan, was appointed to give the running commentary, and the radio broadcasts widened the Quadrangular's popularity even further. Maitra's was thus a lonely voice of dissent who believed that the communal tournament had "outlived its period of usefulness from cricket and national points of view."[9] He even suggested the next year that the Bombay tournament be replaced by a zonal quadrangular, in which teams from different parts of India participated.[10]

Despite Maitra's suggestion, in 1937 the Quadrangular was expanded to include a team of "Others." But the tournament, which was to be played in the brand-new Brabourne Stadium in Bombay, took a hit when the Hindu Gymkhana pulled out, ostensibly on the grounds that it hadn't been allotted enough seats, two thousand for each of the clubs. The Hindus demanded that their share be increased because of their greater numbers, a demand described by the *Bombay Chronicle* as animated by communalism.[11] The Muslims won that year's tournament, which was a lackluster affair with far smaller crowds than usual. The Hindus returned in 1938 and, under Nayudu, won the first real Pentangular by beating the Muslims in front of crowds of more than 20,000. By now, the rivalry between the Hindus or Parsis against the Europeans had been surpassed by that between the Hindus and the Islam Gymkhana.

With the beginning of World War II in 1939, the Pentangular faced its biggest threat. When Britain declared war on Germany, it also included India in the war effort, though without consulting any Indian leaders. The Congress responded by resigning en masse from the provincial governments. The next year, the Muslim League announced its support for a separate homeland for Muslims, and Congress leaders began courting arrest. In this highly charged situation, the holding of the Pentangular was, unsurprisingly, thrown into doubt. Most of those opposed to the tournament were from the Congress, and as Guha pointed out, it was the Hindu Gymkhana that felt the real pressure to withdraw.[12] In these difficult circumstances, the Hindu Gymkhana sought the opinion of the one man whose opinion carried the most weight: Mahatma Gandhi. His answer to the three representatives of the Hindu Gymkhana who met him at his ashram in Wardha in early December was unambiguous. After professing his ignorance of cricket, Gandhi added that his "sympathies are wholly with those who would like to see these matches stopped." He gave as his first reason the incongruity of such "amusements" as cricket matches at a time when war clouds were gathering over Europe and Asia. But what strengthened the hands of the anti-Pentangular lobby was Gandhi's ruling against the tournament's communal organization:

> Incidentally, I would like the public of Bombay to revise their sporting code and erase from it communal matches. I can understand matches between Colleges and Institutions, but I have never understood the reason for having Hindu, Parsi, Muslim and other Communal Elevens. I should have thought that such unsportsmanlike divisions would be considered taboos in sporting language and sporting manners. Can we not have some field of life which would be untouched by communal spirit?[13]

Gandhi's statement sparked a war of words in the columns of the pro-British *Times of India* and the nationalist *Bombay Chronicle*. Gandhi's message naturally went down well with Maitra and like-minded people. But the *Times of India* commented that it could see no "connection between satyagraha and cricket."[14] The thousands of cricket lovers in Bombay were in full agreement with the *Times* on this matter. Letters poured in, decrying the efforts to halt the tournament. One letter writer asked why the Hindu Gymkhana should listen to a man "who had never played cricket."[15] For its part, the *Chronicle* refused to print any letters against Gandhi. The Mahatma's statement was a timely boost, too, for the Indian cricket board, which had recently created the Ranji Trophy and had little sympathy for the Pentangular. As the board president explained, more for instrumental than ideological reasons, the "authorities will be doing the right thing if they abandon communal cricket."[16]

On December 13, 1940, the Hindu Gymkhana held an extraordinary general-body meeting to decide its course of action. After a tumultuous meeting lasting three and half hours, the club decided in favor of a boycott, by a slim margin of 280 to 243 votes. The club's decision was denounced by many, including congressmen like K. F. Nariman, who remarked acerbically on the decision to consult Gandhi: "It passes one's comprehension as to why old and experienced cricketers should make a pilgrimage to the most unsporting spot on earth to consult the least sportive Saint."[17] Without the participation of the Hindus, the 1940 tournament was a sad affair. The radio commentary broadcast was canceled, and not many people turned up for the matches.

After the Muslims won the 1940 tournament, the *Bombay Chronicle* published an editorial headlined "Bury the Pentangular." All opposition to the Pentangular was not as principled. The Indian princes were opposed to the tournament now that they had their own teams playing in the Ranji Trophy; besides, they probably did not want to rub Gandhi and the Congress the wrong way, with Indian independence a distinct possibility. Within days of Gandhi's statement, Vizzy, who was himself associated with the cricket board, proclaimed that it was high time that the Pentangular was given "the burial it always deserved."[18] The next year Ranji prohibited players on his staff from playing in the Pentangular.

But the Pentangular was still some way from being dead and buried. The next year a Maharashtra Cricket Association official again sought Gandhi's opinion. This time, though, the Mahatma was very terse, saying only that his opinion remained the same, adding that he had no time for such things.[19] But even without Gandhi's support, the anti-Pentangular voices kept up their campaign, even forming a body called the Citizens' Anti-Pentangular Committee. Bobby Talyarkhan, who had made his name by broadcasting live commentary of the Pentangular, said in a public meeting in 1941 that the tournament was responsible for propagating communal identities in the city.[20]

The Pentangular was held in 1941 with the Hindus not only taking part but winning it by defeating the Muslims in the semifinal, despite students picketing the grounds. Maitra had no option but to lament that the tournament's supporters "want the edict of Mahatma Gandhi to be thrown overboard and thereby make him the laughing-stock of the sporting world."[21] In 1942, while World War II was raging, the Pentangular was not held. But it returned in 1943, with the highlight being the performance of Vijay Hazare for the "Rest," scoring a 248 in the semifinal against the Muslims and, in a lost cause, a magnificent 309 in the final against the Hindus. In 1944, the Muslims defeated the Hindus in a tense final, winning by one wicket. Some 200,000 people attended the final over four days in Brabourne Stadium, thereby showing that the Pentangular was still extremely popular.[22] In sharp contrast, the attendance for the Ranji Trophy matches was poor, with the tournament final drawing a mere 1,000 people in 1935, the number increasing to 4,000 in 1944. Accordingly, the president of the Cricket Club of India, Homi Modi, pointed out that the "sporting public of Bombay has given a most convincing and resounding answer to the charge that the Pentangular breeds communalism and ill-feeling" and pleaded for a stop to the vendetta against the tournament.[23]

Despite the tremendous response from the crowd, the end was not far. In 1946 with the independence of India and Pakistan just a matter of time and with the shadow of the Calcutta riots looming large, the Indian cricket board finally decided to do away with the Pentangular and replace it with a zonal quadrangular. Unfortunately, the attendance for the tournament, in which many of the stars of the time like Lala Amarnath, K. C. Ibrahim, and Vijay Hazare were playing, was minuscule compared with that of the Pentangular that it replaced.

This incredible popularity of the Pentangular raises the question of whether the love of cricket or communal one-upmanship was at the heart of the tournament. It was probably a bit of both. The players who took part in the tournament, whether Hindu, Muslim, or Parsi, thought highly of the tournament not only for the quality of cricket but also for the camaraderie. The greatest of them all, C. K. Nayudu, categorically insisted in 1941 that the tournament had "brought communities together and not divided them."[24] Yet another great, Mushtaq Ali, said of the Pentangular: "Ripples and roars of genuine applause, from all the stands around, have greeted good performances without distinction, whether it was for Nayudu's sixes, Nissar's ball-taking fizzers or Bhaya's smart pieces of fielding."[25] On the nail-biting encounter between the Hindus and Muslims in 1944, the journalist Vasant Raiji thus could report that "everyone, including the Hindus, cheered the Muslim team at the end of the match."[26]

Such accounts were offset by others that spoke of animosity off the field. Talyarkhan reported that if he criticized the Muslim wicketkeeper, he would get irate telegrams from his Muslim radio listeners about why the Hindu wicketkeeper was being spared.[27] Again in 1941, Vizzy commented that chants of "Down with the Mussalmans" or "Down with the Hindus" were common in the stands.[28] But considering the vitiated atmosphere in which these games were played in the 1930s and 1940s, it seems that such incidents rarely got out of hand or affected the game. In fact, the criticism of the tournament by Congress-minded people like Maitra or Talyarkhan was primarily that it militated against inclusive Indian nationalism. Accordingly, at a meeting organized by the Citizens' Anti-Pentangular Committee in 1941, Syed Abdullah Brelvi, editor of the *Bombay Chronicle*, asked how the supporters of the Pentangular could justify opposing "separate electorates, or even Pakistan."[29] Similarly, the jurist Sir Chimanlal Setalvad wrote in 1941 that the Pentangular encouraged the young to think of themselves in terms of their religion, in which they should be "led to think and act always as Indians first and everything afterwards."[30] Besides the nationalist critique, there were others, like the Indian cricket board, who jumped on the bandwagon, given their vested interest in trying to promote the fledgling Ranji Trophy. As Boria Majumdar noted, "Empty stands at the Ranji Trophy matches, contrasting starkly with attendances at the Pentangular, made the Board, patrons of the former, envious of communal Gymkhanas."[31] Even though the Pentangular rarely saw communal instincts invade the field, this wasn't the case with the football matches involving Mohammedan Sporting Club in Calcutta, and it is

to the fascinating story of Mohammedan Sporting, a club run by and for the
Muslims, to which I now turn.

Mohammedan Sporting

The team that completed the troika in the Calcutta maidan in the 1930s,
along with Mohun Bagan and East Bengal, was Mohammedan Sporting
Club. Even though the 1911 Shield victory is still remembered and memorialized, another remarkable achievement—Mohammedan Sporting's winning
the Calcutta League five times between 1934 and 1938—has largely been forgotten. The story of Mohammedan Sporting cannot be separated from the
extreme passions it generated off the football pitch. Its rise and success was
played out in the Muslim identity and communal politics in Bengal in the
1930s and 1940s.

Mohammedan Sporting came into existence in 1891, more than a decade before the Muslim League was founded, but it had had three earlier
reincarnations in the Jubilee, Crescent, and Hamidia Clubs. In 1891, Mohammedan Sporting had as its patrons many of the prominent Muslims
of Bengal, including the former ruling family of Murshidabad and several
civil servants. It was no accident that Bengal was the site for the club, since
by the turn of the century, the province had not only the largest concentration of Muslims in India but one that was "among the first to be organized
politically to voice their rights as Muslims."[32] The club's first annual meeting in 1894 was presided over by Justice Syed Amir Ali. He was a member
of the Muslim elite, also known as the Ashrafs, who had been trained in law
in England, and he had an English wife. Amir Ali was appointed a judge
in 1890, and with Nawab Abdul Latif, he founded in 1877 the Central National Muhammedan Association, which was restricted to upper-class Muslims. In that sense, his association with football, which was much more a
subaltern sport in India than cricket was, was somewhat out of character.
One of the aims behind the club's founding was to impress on Muslims
the need to take up "manly" Western sports. At the first annual meeting,
Abdus Salam, a member of the Bengal Provincial Service, stated, "We de-
spise, more or less, the indigenous physical exercises of the East, such as
wrestling . . . at the same time we have failed to take, like other elastic and

less conservative races in India, to the manly Western games, such as tennis, foot-ball, cricket etc."[33]

In its first years, Mohammedan Sporting did not have its own field, so it used for practice every other day the field of the Calcutta Boys' School, a well-known private school. Later, when the school found another playground, the club was allowed use of the field full time. One of its early successes was winning the Cooch Behar Trophy in 1909, and in 1927, it created waves by being promoted to the second division of the Calcutta Football League. Beginning in the 1930s the Mohammedan Sporting team was one to reckon with. By 1933 the team was good enough to win promotion to the first division, with eight consecutive wins in the final stretch. Amazingly, in its first appearance in the League in 1934, Mohammedan Sporting became the first Indian team to win the League. The pro-Muslim League newspaper, *Star of India*, gushed that the "Babes" of the first division achieved the impossible by winning the League in their very first year.[34] *The Statesman*, a newspaper with a high British readership, reported that Mohammedan Sporting's victory in the last league match over the unfavored Kalighat was greeted with "unprecedented scenes of enthusiasm."[35] In 1936 the club achieved the rare double of winning both the League and the IFA Shield, becoming only the second Indian team after Mohun Bagan to win the Shield. Only three teams—Royal Irish Rifles, the Gordon Highlanders, and the Calcutta Football Club—had achieved this distinction. Twenty-five years after Mohun Bagan had won the Shield, Mohammedan Sporting repeated the feat by beating the Calcutta Football Club, but only after tying in the first two encounters (There were no tiebreakers in those days). Mohammedan's achievement was reported as far away as Australia, where the *Sydney Morning Herald* carried a news item headlined: "Honour for Islam."[36]

The euphoria over Mohammedan Sporting's victory spread like wildfire. Every match played by the club drew a huge crowd. The nationalist English daily, *Amrita Bazar Patrika*, reported that the "popularity of the team increased with every match" and that the gates would have to be closed long before the match began.[37] One stand in the field was reserved for club members, and two stands were open to the public, who were charged eight *annas* for the enclosure with chairs and four *annas* for the wooden seats. The crowds that thronged to see Mohammedan Sporting were made up of young men as well as older *maulvis* and *maulanas*. One Jan Muhammad would occasionally yell,

"Allah-u-Akbar," thereby galvanizing Mohammedan's supporters.[38] In 1935, for instance, some 60,000 people turned up to watch Mohammedan Sporting defeat Mohun Bagan at the Calcutta Football Club field. After the victory, "fireworks were lit, balloons sent up, pigeons released and the Mohammedans of Calcutta made merry till late in the night."[39]

A souvenir program published by the club in 1935 wrote of the thousands in the outlying areas who "followed each game with the greatest interest, so much so that many used to walk miles to the railway station to meet incoming trains with Calcutta newspapers in order to get the results as soon as possible."[40] There were reports of crowds gathering in towns across Bengal around wireless loudspeakers that broadcast reports of the club matches. Several Muslim sports clubs sprang up in the district and subdivisional headquarters in the wake of Mohammedan Sporting's success. Inspired by the success of Calcutta Mohammedan Sporting, Muslims in Dacca formed their own Dacca Mohammedan Sporting in 1936. Muslims took up sports partly spurred by the proliferation of physical culture association among Hindus in both urban and rural Bengal. At the time, the Muslims of Bengal were hardly a monolithic group, divided as they were by class and location. But the success of Mohammedan Sporting was part of the gradual process of bridging the "factionalism, intrigue and conflicting interests of various Muslim groups"[41] and contributing to the Muslims' communal unity.

The club's astounding success was built on several factors. First, by the 1930s the club had achieved some degree of financial solvency. In 1924 the club's balance sheet was still heavily in the red. It had merely Rs 9 in assets but Rs 3,600 in debts. Very few of the club's 208 members actually paid their membership fees, which amounted to only Rs 25 to 30 per month.[42] This turned around when S. A. Rashid, along with I. G. H. Arif, took charge of the club and began appealing to Muslims to donate generously to the club. The club's turnaround also coincided with the formation in 1932 of a group called the New Muslim Majlis, which included members such as Khwaja Nooruddin and M. A. H. Ispahani and whose aim was to secure India's freedom as well as "capture and re-organise the Muslim sporting club as the premier soccer team of India." Nooruddin (1900–1968) was an alderman in the Calcutta Municipal Corporation and later was elected to the Bengal Legislative Assembly. Besides, he was the secretary of Mohammedan Sporting during the crucial years between 1936 and 1945.

Second, the rise of Mohammedan Sporting Club coincided with the ascendancy of the Muslim League in Bengal and political mobilization around the Muslim identity. Several prominent Muslim League leaders, such as Khwaja Nazimuddin, who later became the second governor-general of Pakistan and subsequently prime minister, became life members. The governor of Bengal, John Anderson, became a patron of the club. In addition, the city's Muslim merchants pitched in to build a fence around the club pavilion.

It wasn't just financial stability and a growing support base that fueled the club's success; there were other, footballing, reasons. Mohammedan Sporting broke with the practice of its main Calcutta rivals, Mohun Bagan and East Bengal, by recruiting players from outside Bengal. In this, it had a significant advantage over its city rivals in that it could recruit Muslim players from all over the subcontinent, recruiting players from as far afield as Quetta and Peshawar in present-day Pakistan. In 1936, for example, the Mohammedan Sporting line-up that took on East Bengal for a charity game had as many as nine players from outside Bengal: Jumma Khan (Quetta); Rashid (Peshawar); Osman and Aquil (Delhi); Serajuddin, Saboo, Masoom, and Rahim (Bangalore); and Noor Mohamed (Fyzabad).[43]

In a significant breakthrough, the club decided to play football wearing boots when the ground was wet. This was enormously important to Mohammedan Sporting's football success, since the major Calcutta clubs usually played barefoot. In fact, the Indian football team played barefoot in international tournaments as late as 1952. But in 1933, for the first time, six Mohammedan players put on boots on a wet day and thrashed the Nebubagan team by an incredible 16–0 margin. The man in charge of the team, S. A. Aziz, even designed a lightweight boot, which was then constructed by local cobblers, that was suited to the conditions in the Calcutta maidan. Even veterans like Samad, who had been playing on the Calcutta maidan for nearly two decades, adjusted remarkably well to boots, running with the "easy grace of a stag," showing "admirable precision in his shots," and proving to be "quite a wonder-man in his new equipage."[44] The club did not, however, give up the advantage of playing barefoot on dry ground.

Mohammedan Sporting must also get credit for producing the first international football player from India, the club's star forward, Mohammed Salim. Born in the predominantly Muslim area of Metiabruz in Calcutta, Salim began his playing career with small club called Chittaranjan before moving to the bigger Bowbazar Club. He had a brief stint with Mohammedan Sporting before being recruited by the Sporting Union Club. Within a couple of years he moved yet again to the Aryan Club, which was being coached by the legendary footballer Choney Majumdar. He then returned to Mohammedan Sporting in 1934 to help it to win its first League title. With his immaculate ball control and passing skills, Salim was the spearhead of the Mohammedan attack.

After Mohammedan won the 1936 League title, Salim was chosen for the All-India XI to play the Chinese Olympic team in Calcutta, which was playing exhibition matches in India. The official in charge of the Chinese team, Ji Zhaoyong, was very impressed by the forward line of the Indian team, which, besides Salim, could boast of players like Rahim, Bhattacharjee, and Abbas. But when it was time for the second match against the Chinese team, Salim had disappeared. The story is that Salim and a friend had embarked on a trip to Europe. He eventually surfaced in Glasgow, though why he chose Scotland as his eventual destination is a mystery. Salim's companion, Hasheem, convinced the manager of the famous Celtic football club to try using Salim. The trial took some time to organize, however, since the local football federation was nonplussed by a barefoot football player. Eventually when the trial took place, Salim so dazzled the club officials that they chose him to play in Celtic's next match. He played two games in which Celtic beat Hamilton and Galston, 5-1 and 7-1, respectively. After the second game, the *Scottish Daily Express* ran a story on August 29, 1936, headlined: "Indian Juggler—New Style." The reporter was mesmerized by Salim's skills:

> Ten twinkling toes of Salim, Celtic FC's player from India hypnotised the crowd at Parkhead last night in an alliance game with Galston. He balances the ball on his big toe, lets it run down the scale to his little toe, twirls it, hops on one foot around the defender, then flicks the ball to the center who has only to send it into the goal. Three of Celtic's seven goals last night came from his moves. Was asked to take a penalty, he refused. Said he was shy. Salim does not speak English, his brother translates for him. Brother Hashim thinks Salim is wonderful—so did the crowd last night.[45]

Even though Salim had offers to stay on in Europe, he decided to return to Calcutta to help Mohammedan Sporting Club win the Calcutta League title for the fourth time in 1937. Salim's story could easily be dismissed as fiction if it weren't for the faded *Scottish Daily Express* news report carefully preserved by his son.[46] The story was picked up much later by the *Junior Statesman*, a Calcutta newspaper, and the *Khelar Ashar*, a Bengali sports magazine. But the remarkable, almost unreal, story of Salim is little remembered today.

It wasn't just Salim who was winning recognition. In a first for Indian footballers, two Mohammedan Sporting players featured in advertisements for the Indian Tea Market Expansion Board. One was Noor Mohamed, the club's "sturdy centre half back," and other, Jumma Khan, was described as "one of India's best full backs." The ads were quite remarkable, considering that no Indian sportsperson, not even a cricketer, had been featured in an ad until then. In fact, C. K. Nayudu, one of the superstars of Indian cricket and captain of the first official Indian team that toured England in 1932, was featured in an ad for the first time for Bathgate's Liver Tonic only in 1941.

The impact of Mohammedan Sporting's astounding success, like Mohun Bagan's 1911 victory, was hardly limited to football. At one level the 1934 League victory was greeted as a landmark event. The popular song— "Mohammedan Sporting *tumko lakhon lakhon salam / ham ab deshka badshah bane, aur sab hai ghulam*" (Mohammedan Sporting, a million salutes to you / We have now become kings of the country, all the rest are slaves)—captured perfectly what the victory meant to Muslims. The successful run by Mohammedan Sporting even inspired Muslim poets like the great Kazi Nazrul Islam to compose poetry in honor of the team:

These feet that have so incredibly woven wonders with the football—
May the power of all of India rise from those very feet,
May those feet break our chains. And our fear, and our dread—
May those feet kick them away! Allah-u-Akbar![47]

In addition, the popular singer Abbasuddin recorded the compositions by the poet Golam Mostafa composed on the occasion of Mohammedan Sporting's winning the Calcutta League five times, which were released by the Gramophone Record Company.[48] The mayor of Calcutta, Nalini Ranjan Sarkar, hailed the win as a "great unifier" and a matter of "pleasure and gratifi-

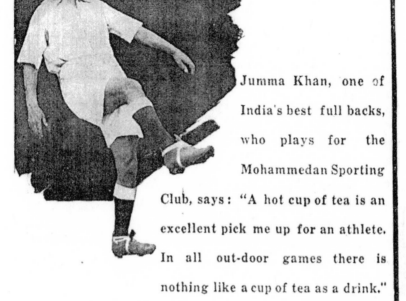

Jumma Khan, one of India's best full backs, who plays for the Mohammedan Sporting Club, says: "A hot cup of tea is an excellent pick me up for an athlete. In all out-door games there is nothing like a cup of tea as a drink."

TEA *for Endurance*

Read our Sports Brochure entitled, "Now for a Cup of Tea" and see why the world's most renowned sportsmen recommend tea as the best refresher and safest stimulant. Please cut out this coupon and send it, together with your name, address and occupation to the Commissioner for India, Indian Tea Market Expansion Board, P. O. Box No. 2172, Calcutta, who will send you free of charge a copy of the Brochure.

INSERTED BY THE INDIAN TEA MARKET EXPANSION BOARD   IK 135

An advertisement by the Tea Market Expansion Board featuring a Mohammedan Sporting player. Calcutta Football Official Program, 1938

cation of all citizens."[49] The president of the Indian Football Association (IFA), the maharaja of Santosh, said the win had "enhanced the reputation of Indian footballers."[50] Similarly, a message from Aligarh University named Mohammedan Sporting's success a "glory to Indian football."[51] There is little doubt that these all contributed to Mohammedan Sporting's expanding footprint.

At the same time, Muslim leaders were claiming the victory as a signal event for the community. The Krishak Praja Party leader and future premier of Bengal, Fazlul Huq, noted that Mohammedan Sporting had "earned a name for Muslims in the sporting world, of which the community may justly be proud."[52] Syed Abdul Hafiz, another prominent politician, wrote in a congratulatory message claiming that the "club came into existence to fulfil a long felt want of the sporting spirit of the community."[53] There also was some reason to believe that the Krishak Praja Party–Muslim League coalition government bent the rules in allotting a plot in the maidan solely to Mohammedan Sporting, when all the major clubs had to share their field with another club. Huq, who had played for Mohammedan Sporting in its early days, and Khwaja Nazimuddin, were present at the field's opening. But the allotment of the new field created such bad blood that a match between the club and a team from the rest of the Calcutta teams, staged to celebrate the occasion, was boycotted by members of Mohun Bagan and East Bengal and the Hindu public in general.[54]

The Communal Rift

Mohammedan Sporting's remarkable run happened at a time when Indian politics was polarized between the Indian National Congress and the Muslim League, and communal tensions were rife in Bengal. The Muslim League had been a marginal presence in Bengal until 1933 when it was revived in the wake of Hindu opposition to the Communal Award. Bengal also had one of the worst records of Hindu–Muslim conflict. Between 1905 and 1947, Bengal was the site of several riots, with Calcutta being one of the province's most violence-prone areas. The situation was such that events like playing music in front of a mosque or a vehicle's running over a child, certain kinds of plays, and, often, a Mohammedan Sporting defeat would lead to violence.[55] The growing tensions between Hindus and Muslims, especially in urban centers like Calcutta, may have influenced the chain of events that split the football world in Calcutta.

Trouble began on June 11, 1937. During a League match between Mohammedan Sporting and East Bengal, an East Bengal official was hit by a Mohammedan Sporting player. The incident was followed by violence outside the ground, which included the stabbing of a thirteen-year-old boy. A day later, the *Amrita Bazar Patrika* reported that communalism had invaded the Calcutta maidan. The situation worsened when the IFA suspended Habib, one of Mohammedan Sporting's best players, instead of Sattar, who had supposedly hit the East Bengal official. The IFA president, the maharaja of Santosh, suggested that the club take steps to rein in its supporters. On its part, Mohammedan Sporting found the IFA's suggestions unacceptable and said it would not play any more League matches until the resolution was rescinded. The club conducted its own inquiry, which found Sattar, and not Habib, guilty and immediately suspended him. When the club secretary, K. Nooruddin, protested the IFA decisions, he was banned from attending the governing-body meetings for the next three years, prompting Mohammedan Sporting to withdraw from the Calcutta League.

A temporary truce was reached after a meeting between Santosh and Nooruddin and after Mohammedan Sporting was given more time to lodge an appeal. During this time, Mohammedan Sporting won the League for the fourth time on July 2, 1937. Four days later, however, the IFA decided that Mohammedan Sporting would not be given any more time and rejected the club's appeal. The controversy dragged for another year, with Mohammedan Sporting meanwhile winning its fifth League title in 1938. Even though Mohammedan Sporting played that year's IFA Shield under protest, it was fed up with what it felt was "repeated bad refereeing, arbitrary decisions with regard to venue of matches and generally the tyranny of the majority of the council of the IFA."[56]

The next year, before a second-leg match against Mohun Bagan in the Calcutta League, Mohammedan Sporting pulled out of the tournament. A few days later, three other teams—East Bengal, Kalighat, and Aryan—pulled out as well, although Aryan did an about-face soon after and rejoined the League. The bridging of the communal divide on this occasion is interesting, although the reason for the other Calcutta clubs' pulling out seems to have been a result of antipathy toward Mohun Bagan's dominance and its policy of opposition to importing players from outside Bengal.[57] The "rebel" clubs, which played exhibition matches against one another for the rest of the season in front of large crowds, even formed the rival Bengal Football Association and instituted the Brabourne Cup that year. In 1940, however, the three clubs returned to the IFA's fold. The off-field controversies did not seem to have affected Mohammedan Sporting's form, since it became the first Indian team to win the prestigious Durand Trophy, held in Delhi, beating the Royal Warwickshire Regiment 2-1, as well as winning the Rovers Cup, western India's premier tournament, in 1940 by defeating another Indian team, the Bangalore Muslims. Interestingly, the only Indian team to have won the Rovers Cup was the Bangalore Muslims—despite its name, the club contained footballers from other communities—who defeated Mohammedan Sporting 1-0 in the 1937 final. It followed this by winning the trophy the next year by beating the Argyll and Sutherland Highlanders.

Contemporary accounts of the events of 1937 through 1939 reveal the deep divisions on the maidan that mirrored the bitter communal politics of the time. The *Amrita Bazar Patrika* laid the blame on the original incident of 1937 on the "disgraceful conduct of some of the Muslims" and commented that "communal partisanship often finds very disgraceful expression in language whenever a Muslim player comes to the grief at the hands of his Hindu opponents."[58] *The Statesman* argued for a ban on intercommunity games, saying that "Calcutta football seems to be not a pale, but a highly coloured reflection of Bengal politics."[59] J. C. Maitra of the *Bombay Chronicle* blamed the situation mostly on Mohammedan Sporting supporters, who celebrated "their successes with fury" and in defeat did not spare players or referees.[60] He added, "The plain fact remains that the sporting life of Bengal, particularly in the domain of football, became so vitiated that any contest was impossible under normal conditions."[61]

The pro-Muslim *Star of India*, which was the mouthpiece of the Majlis, had a completely different take on events. Its editorial on June 20, 1937, indicated how communal thinking had infiltrated the playing field. It spoke about how the "all-conquering Mohammedans" had taken the "glory out of Hindu football." It concluded by noting that the "very idea of so much glory to the Mohammedans seemed to have destroyed appetites and stolen sleep of the thousands of the only loving children of Mother India."[62] Communal events outside the playing field continued to cast their shadow on Calcutta football in the 1940s. Because of the Great Calcutta Killings of 1946, the IFA Shield was not held that year, and the League was canceled the next year.

Communal Versus Secular

Notwithstanding the parallels among the different religious communities fielding teams in the Pentangular and the story of Mohammedan Sporting in Calcutta, the real difference was that Mohammedan Sporting was playing in tournaments that were not organized on communal lines. But as in the Pentangular, the club was playing and winning tournaments at a time when politics was deeply fractured along religious lines. This often influenced spectators, much more so on the Calcutta maidan than in Bombay, and at the same time figured in the prevailing political debates. Mohammedan Sporting had an all-India following, as was evident from a record attendance—described as the "biggest crowd which has ever paid for admission to the Cooperage"[63]—showing up to watch the Calcutta club take on the All-Blues Club in the 1936 Rovers Cup quarterfinal. The same year when Mohammedan Sporting played an exhibition match at Patna against the Duke of Cornwall's Light Infantry team, "several thousand witnessed the match," and the East Indian Railway ran special locals to transport the spectators.[64]

The next year Mohammedan Sporting reached the final of the Rovers Cup, in which it played the Bangalore Muslims before a "crowd bordering on the 10000 mark" at the Cooperage, the venue for the tournament.[65] The *Bombay Chronicle*'s correspondent estimated an even bigger crowd and reported that the Bangalore Muslims "treated 20,000 spectators with their brilliant display of first class football and many a time held their audience spellbound."[66] Despite its name, the Bangalore Muslims, unlike Mohammedan Sporting, was a mixed team with at least four non-Muslims—Kadavelu, Linganna, Laxmi Narayan, and Murgesh—on the team. Ironically it was a Hindu player, Laxmi Narayan, who scored the winning goal for the Bangalore Muslims.

The mixed composition of the Bangalore Muslims team made them poster boys for secular and nationalist organizations. Before the finals, the team was entertained by the King's Circle Sports Club at a dinner party presided over by its president, S. Narayana Iyer. After their victory, the Bangalore Muslims team was feted at a reception held by local Congress Party members. The *Bombay Chronicle* reported that its editor, Syed Abdullah Brelvi, told the meeting: "The most pleasing feature of their victory was that it was achieved by a team which consisted of Hindus and Muslims."[67] When his turn came to speak, the Bangalore Muslim's secretary, Esmail, asserted that there was "no distinction between Hindu and Muslims in Bangalore" and that the Bangalore Muslims "had proved that just as through Hindu–Muslim cooperation they wanted to secure their country's freedom, so, through similar cooperation, they could vindicate their country's name in sports." The Bangalore Muslims proved that their victory was no fluke by winning the Rovers Cup again in 1938 by defeating the Argyll and Sutherland Highlanders.

Three years later, however, Mohammedan Sporting took revenge by defeating the Bangalore Muslims to win the Rovers Cup in 1940, which was also the tournament's fiftieth anniversary. In contrast to the Bangalore Muslims' 1937 victory, soon after Mohammedan Sporting's triumph, Muhammad Jinnah in 1941 told the Muslim students at the Cooperage that the "discipline which sports teach must be harnessed for the benefit of the Muslim community as a whole."[68] For Jinnah and other Muslim League leaders, Mohammedan Sporting's prowess was an important unifying force and a source of pride for the Muslim community at a time when the demand for Pakistan was being forcefully articulated.

Yet another football team that had a majority of Muslims playing for it was the Hyderabad City Police team, based in the southern Indian city of Hyderabad, the seat of the Nizams, who ruled over one of India's largest princely states. The team, also called the City Afghans, the name by which the city's police was known, won the Ashe Gold Cup in 1943 by defeating the Royal Air Force team, which included the English cricket star and footballer Denis Compton. The star of the game was Norbert Andrew Fruvall, the captain of the team as well as its coach. He recruited players like Noor Mohammed and G. Y. S. Laiq, who served the Hyderabad Police team with distinction over the years and also played for India following independence.[69]

Despite the nationalist opposition to the cricket Pentangular in 1940, the Western India Football Association announced a similar tournament in football. The tournament, which was played at the Cooperage, consisted of five teams: the Hindus, Muslims, Europeans, Goans, and the Rest. Naturally the *Bombay Chronicle* was strongly critical of the idea, saying that it was "most unfortunate that while serious efforts are being made everywhere to abolish sporting competitions on communal basis, a new one should have been added to the list."[70] The football Pentangular did not last more than a year, but the Mohammedan Sporting club outlasted Indian independence and continues to exist today. Indian independence and partition saw many patrons of Mohammedan Sporting migrate to East and West Pakistan, dealing a blow to the club from which it never really recovered. It never regained its past glory, though it did have sporadic success and won tournaments until the 1980s. After 1947, however, its relationship with its supporters gradually changed, as did the character of the team, with more and more non-Muslims being recruited by the club. For instance, the team that won the Calcutta League in 1981, after a gap of nearly fifteen years, had as many as eight upper-caste Brahmins turning out for Mohammedan Sporting.

Gandhi and Sports

Throughout the 1930s and 1940s, Indian nationalism was offered as a counterpoint to communal expressions on the playing fields such as those of the Pentangular and the Mohammedan Sporting Club. This brings up the question of whether Gandhi, who in this period was giving new form and direction to the nationalist movement, had any connection to sports. We do know from his autobiography that at a very young age, he was fascinated by both the physical strength of India's British rulers and the eating of meat, which was forbidden in his strictly Vaishnava family. The connection between the two was neatly encapsulated in a doggerel that was popular during Gandhi's childhood: "Behold the mighty Englishman / He rules the Indian small / Because being a meat-eater / He is five cubits tall."[71] Encouraged by a friend, Gandhi even took to secretly eating meat for a year so that he could be "strong and daring"[72] and defeat the English, until he realized the error of his ways. Gandhi's obsession with his body, health, and diet is, of course, well known. Indeed, Joseph Alter has argued that public health was integral to Gandhi's *ahimsa*.[73] Gandhi even went to the extent of saying that it is "impossible for an unhealthy people to win *swaraj* [self-rule]."[74]

This did not, however, mean that Gandhi had much interest in sports. As we saw, he was reluctantly dragged into the controversy over the Pentangular. When he was a schoolboy, Gandhi writes in his autobiography, he "never took part in any exercise, cricket or football, before they were made compulsory."[75]

When Gandhi first went to London to study law, he apparently carried a letter of introduction from the great cricketer Ranji, who arrived to study in England the same year that Gandhi did.[76] This wasn't surprising, given that both were from Kathiawar and had studied in Rajkot, though in different schools.[77] A classmate from his schooldays once spoke of Gandhi as a "dashing cricketer" who was "good at both batting and bowling,"[78] and his only surviving sister told an interviewer that as a young boy, the Mahatma had a "great interest" in "tennis, cricket and such other games," so much so that he would not "remember his meals."[79] But Gandhi himself in 1931 clearly stated his disinterest in cricket: "I have never attended cricket matches and only once took a bat and a cricket ball in my hands and that was under compulsion from the head master of the High School where I was studying, and this was over 45 years ago."[80]

Gandhi's indifference to cricket contrasts with Nehru's great interest in it. Although Nehru wasn't asked to intervene in the Pentangular, as Gandhi was, he was fond of cricket from his boyhood. While at Harrow, Nehru bought a cricket bat and wrote to his father that he was making "slow but steady improvement" and went on to score an unbeaten forty runs in a match. Nehru also sent to his father a detailed description of an Eton–Harrow match,[81] and before his entrance examination for Trinity College, Cambridge, Nehru confessed that it was hard for him to drag himself "from a good cricket match to work."[82]

Gandhi, at least in his South Africa years (1893–1915), had an interest in football. At the beginning of the twentieth century, he founded three football clubs, all of them named the Passive Resisters Soccer Club, in Durban, Johannesburg, and Pretoria. Football was popular among the less well-off Indians in South Africa who played in local leagues such as the Transvaal Indian Football Association and the Klip River District Administration. In 1903, the South African Association of Hindu Football was formed with Gandhi's blessings. Gandhi often showed up at football games and talked to the players during halftime about nonviolent resistance, distributed pamphlets on resisting racial segregation, and even delivered speeches to the crowd. The Passive Resisters did not play in any of the established leagues but engaged in friendlies at the Phoenix settlement or at Tolstoy farm. Gandhi kept up his links with football in South Africa after his return to India. In 1921/1922, the

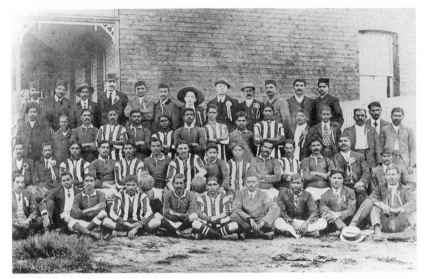

Mohandas (Mahatma) Gandhi (back row, sixth from left), with a football team of passive resisters in South Africa, 1913. Reprinted by permission of Dinodia Photo

tour of a team called Christopher's Contingent, sponsored by a former collaborator of Gandhi, Albert Christopher, was organized by Gandhi's friend and follower Charles Freer Andrews. The team played fourteen matches in India and spent time with Gandhi in Ahmedabad.[83] Ironically, in 1934 there was strong opposition to the proposed tour of the Indian football team to South Africa because of the color bar and discriminatory policies.[84] But the tour, the first foreign trip by an Indian football team, eventually did take place that year, and the Indians won fifteen of the sixteen matches played and lost one.[85]

Even though we have no further evidence of Gandhi's interest in football, he seems to have appreciated the sporting spirit of the British and their ability to accept defeat with equanimity. When World War II was raging, he wrote in the *Harijan*:

Failures do not dismay or demoralize them [the British]. Wars are for them a national game like football. The defeated team heartily congratulates the successful one almost as if it were a joint victory, and then drowns the sorrow of defeat in an exchange of glasses of whisky. If we have learnt nothing worthwhile from the contact with the British, let us at least [emulate] their calmness in the face of misfortunes.[86]

Gandhi's conception of sport, however marginal to his politics, was indeed far removed from the animosities engendered by the popularity of the Pentangular or the victories of Mohammedan Sporting.

7

THE EARLY OLYMPICS

INDIA'S HOCKEY TRIUMPHS

THE TATA GROUP IS ONE OF THE BEST-KNOWN BUSINESS HOUSES in India. The company founded by Jamestji Tata in 1868 as a trading house soon diversified into various sectors such as textiles, steel, electricity generation, and hotels. In recent times, the Tatas have become a global name by acquiring a string of companies outside India. But what is not as well known is that a scion of the Tata family—Sir Dorabji Tata, eldest son of Jamestji Tata and founder of the iconic Tata Iron and Steel Company—was primarily responsible for India's entrance into the Olympic Games. Although the Indian Olympic Association was formally founded in 1927, Indian athletes started going to the Olympics from as early as the 1920 Antwerp Olympic Games.

Many people believe, though, that India's rendezvous with the Olympics began much earlier in the 1900 Paris Games. This is because of one remarkable individual—Norman Gilbert Pritchard, who was born to English parents in Calcutta in 1875 and won two silver medals in the 200 meters and the 200-meter hurdles in the Paris Games. Pritchard was known in Bengal as a champion athlete besides representing the Xaverians' football team with distinction. Between 1894 and 1900 Pritchard won the 100 yards seven times in a row in Bengal. He also won the 440-yard and 120-meter hurdles during this period. In 1900 Pritchard visited London, but he probably did not know about the Olympic Games, which were still in their infancy. During his stay, Pritchard was elected as a member of the London Athletic Club, and within two weeks he had won the club trophies for the 440-yard and 120-yard hurdles and the 100 yards. Subsequently, he competed in the British AAA championship, which served as the trial for the British Olympic team, representing both the London Club and the Bengal Presidency Athletic Club. He placed second in the 120-yard hurdles and did very well in the 100 yards to secure a place on the British team. In the Olympic Games, Pritchard took part in five events, and his affiliation was listed as "British India" in one of them—the 100-meter hurdles.[1] This and his connection with Calcutta have led many Indians to regard Pritchard as one of their own and the country's first Olympic medal winner. Of course, India's singular lack of success, except for (field) hockey, in the early Olympics was also a reason to appropriate Pritchard. Until 1996, in his authoritative *The Complete Book of the Olympics*, David Wallechinsky credited Pritchard's medals to India. But following research by a British historian, in the 2000 edition the medals were awarded to Great Britain. In the next edition, however, Pritchard's medals were jointly credited to both India and Great Britain, which is probably the way it should be.[2]

As for British India's first proper foray into the Olympics, the credit must go to Dorabji Tata. In 1929 in a letter to the president of the International Olympic Committee, Count Bailet Latour, Dorabji recounted his experience of getting Indians interested in athletics. Dorabji, educated in England and a Cambridge Blue in cricket, had been exposed to every kind of English sport. On returning to India, he took an active part in forming associations in schools and colleges to hold athletic meets. Among the institutions with which he was associated was the Deccan Gymkhana in Pune, of which he was the president. Athletic meets were held there, and on one such occasion Dorabji happened to see boys of the "peasant class" taking part in sprints and long-distance races on a rough patch of green that was the gymkhana grounds.[3] This was just before the 1920 games were to be held at Antwerp, and he offered to send three of the best athletes. His proposal was enthusiastically received and "fired the ambition of the nationalist element"[4] in the city. Even though Dorabji was not so eager, members of the Deccan Gymkhana started trying to raise money, but without much success. Eventually, thanks to Dorabji, six athletes were sent to Antwerp, accompanied by India's tennis champion, A. H. Fyzee. The expedition cost Rs 35,000, most of which Sir Dorabji paid himself. Little is known about who represented India, beyond one-line newspaper dispatches reporting that Shimpe of British India had been beaten in nineteen seconds by Bernard of Britain in a featherweight wrestling bout.[5] Because of poor health, Dorabji himself was able to pay only a brief visit to Antwerp and therefore missed out on the sports events.

A bigger contingent of nine athletes was sent to the 1924 Olympics, but this time the trials were a more elaborate affair held at the Roshanara grounds in Delhi. India participated in tennis in the games, with Mohammad Sleem playing well but losing to the eventual gold medalist, V. Richards of the United States, in five sets. This time, funds were available for the Indian contingent, especially from the YMCA. A. G. Noehren of the YMCA, who was also the secretary of the All-India Olympic Committee, the predecessor to the Indian Olympic Association (IOA), wrote to Dorabji (who was the president) before the Paris Games, explaining that people from different parts of the country, including school students from Punjab, had contributed money.[6] Noehren also was hopeful that the government and the military would contribute to the cause of sports in India. The role of the YMCA in furthering sports in Asian countries wasn't unusual, as it had been instrumental in introducing Western sports to China as well as organizing the first two National Athletic Meets in China. China's first contact with the Olympic Games was through the YMCA too, when the organization's Paul Sung represented China at the International Olympic Committee meeting in Amsterdam in 1928.[7] The YMCA also played a critical role in organizing the Far Eastern Championship Games, which were held ten times from 1913 to 1934.[8]

Eight athletes were chosen to represent India: three from Madras, two from Bengal, and one each from Uttar Pradesh, Bombay, and Patiala. H. C. Buck of the YMCA College of Physical Education escorted the athletes. T. K. Pitt from Bengal in the 400 meters and Dalip Singh from Patiala in the long jump performed reasonably well, though India did not win any medals. Dorabji, however, believed that the "leisured class" in India was considerably smaller than that of Europe and that because the majority of people in India were poor, they had little time to devote to sports[9]—a very contemporary conclusion.

In 1927 Dorabji was appointed president of the IOA and Noehren became the secretary. This was not without some controversy, as Dorabji revealed that the India Office wanted Ranji to have the post. But Ranji, according to Dorabji, was not sure about the "amateur" status of the team that was sent to the 1920 games, and in any case "he did not want to have anything to do with it."[10] However, Dorabji's and Noehren's tenures were short-lived—Dorabji because of poor health and Noehren because he was leaving India for good. Although the IOC was loath to let Dorabji go, they reluctantly agreed and asked him to nominate a successor. The only ones in the running were the Indian princes who, as we have seen, had become interested in sports. Dorabji did not believe that any of them had any knowledge of track and field, but he backed the maharaja of Kapurthala, primarily because he went to Europe frequently. In the same breath, he added that the maharaja "takes no interest in this type of sport." The maharaja of Burdwan had also declined the post.[11] According to Dorabji, India was not yet ready for the Olympic Games because field sports were not popular at all; besides, he despaired that "a country with so many religions, so many languages and dialects, so many customs and ideals"[12] would find it impossible to field a national team—an all-too-familiar lament about India's vastness and diversity.

Eventually Bhupinder Singh, the maharaja of Patiala, took charge of the IOA, beginning his family's long association with the Olympics. Guru Dutt Sondhi, Patiala's trusted lieutenant, was appointed secretary and Moinul Haque, assistant secretary. Sondhi, who himself had played hockey at Cambridge and was a university-level runner in Punjab, was an interesting figure who had very early on seen the rewards of being associated with Indian sports. The choice of Bhupinder, however, did not go down well with everybody, particularly the YMCA, which had played a crucial role in sending the Indian team to the 1924 games. Henry Gray, then the YMCA's national physical director for India, Burma, and Ceylon (present-day Sri Lanka), shot off a letter to Latour in 1928 saying that control of the Olympic movement in India had passed to a "semi-interested small group of people" who did not represent the country's interests.[13] But Patiala was too big a fish to be ignored. Moreover, without his financial clout, as well as donations from other princes, the Indian contingent, consisting of the hockey team and seven athletes, would not have been able to go to the 1928 Olympics.[14] Anthony de Mello, who was the brains behind the first Asian Games, noted that Bhupinder Singh was instrumental in sending teams to the 1930 Far Eastern Games in Tokyo (which until then had been restricted to China, Japan, and the Philippines), the 1934 Western Asiatic Games in Delhi, and the 1936 Empire Games (the predecessor to the Commonwealth Games). When Bhupinder Singh died in 1938 at the age of forty-six, the London *Times* paid tribute by writing, "It was in no small measure due to his influence and his purse that India advanced in international rank in cricket, hockey, tennis, and athletics generally."[15]

The Hockey Saga

Amid the several statues of Gandhi, Nehru, and Netaji that dot the Indian countryside, there are precious few of Indian sports heroes. Hockey wizard Dhyan Chand (his last name is Singh in his regimental records, and how it was changed to Chand is not known) is possibly the only one honored with two of them—one in the dusty town of Jhansi, better known for a queen who spiritedly fought the British during the 1857 uprising but also where Chand spent much of his life, and another in Delhi in front of a stadium named after him. (Oddly enough, there is a statue of him in Vienna, where he is shown with four hands and four sticks to illustrate his unreal skills.) Chand was India's first real sports superstar. In many ways, his life mirrors the story of the origin and the rise of Indian field hockey, the only sport in which India had international success and Olympic glory before its independence.

We're lucky that unlike most early Indian sports heroes, Chand left us his memoir, which helps us piece together the early history of hockey and also his exceptional career.[16] Like football, hockey was introduced to India by the British regiments. Indeed, Chand first played hockey seriously only after joining the First Brahmin Regiment (later renamed the Fourth/First Punjab Regiment) as a seventeen-year-old sepoy in 1922 and was encouraged to take up the game by a superior, Subedar-Major Bale (or Bhole) Tiwari. As Chand wrote in his autobiography,

> My regiment was well-known in hockey circles, and hockey was the only outdoor game to which the regiment devoted most of its sporting atten-tion. Bale Tiwari initiated me into this game and gave me my first les-sons. He was my guru. We had no fixed times at the Cantonment to play hockey. We indulged in it at all hours of the day.[17]

India's, and perhaps the world's, greatest hockey player, Dhyan Chand (sitting in first row left), with the hockey team of the Fourth Batallion, First Punjab Regiment, ca. 1923. Chand joined the regiment, earlier known as the First Brahmin Regiment, in 1922, as a seventeen-year-old sepoy. Reprinted by permission of the Council of the National Army Museum, London

He represented his regimental team in the army hockey tournament for several years. Hockey was already being played in different parts of India, and by the first decade of the twentieth century, there were an astounding two thousand clubs playing hockey in India, including an interregimental hockey competition and a native army tournament.[18]

The world's first hockey club, the Blackheath Club, was formed around 1840 in England. A little more than five decades later in 1895 the first hockey tournament in India, the Beighton Cup (strangely named after the legal remembrancer of the Bengal government, T. D. Beighton), was held in Calcutta, followed the next year by the Aga Khan Tournament in Bombay. The Beighton Cup continues to be held to this day, making it the longest-running hockey tournament in the world. In fact, the tournament was such an important fixture that Chand admitted that his "life's ambition" was to win the cup for his home team, the Jhansi Heroes. In his autobiography he even revealed that the best match in his life was not an Olympic game but the 1933 final match in the Beighton Cup against Calcutta Customs, which the Jhansi team won by a solitary goal scored by Chand himself. Chand had less to say about the Aga Khan Tournament, since the Jhansi Heroes made it to the tournament only once, in 1939, and were eliminated in the second round by another fine north Indian team, the Bhopal Wanderers.[19] In 1901, the Madras Hockey Tournament, which was the forerunner of the MCC Hockey Tournament, was inaugurated. In the first match, the Madras United Club XI, composed of Indian players, took on the British Twenty-Fifth Battery, Royal Field Artillery only to be thrashed by fifteen goals.[20]

As in football, Bengal was the center of organized hockey in India. The Bengal Hockey Association was formed in 1908, well before other sports like cricket or football were organized at the provincial level. But unlike in football, the British regimental teams had only limited success in hockey, with the Royal Irish Rifles winning the Beighton Cup twice in 1901 and 1902.[21] Instead, the civilian outfits like the Rangers Club had more success in hockey. In fact, the Rangers team (initially known as the Calcutta Naval Volunteers Club) won the Beighton Cup in its inaugural year and several times afterward. A distinct class element can be detected here, with the British elites in Calcutta and members of the top clubs like Calcutta Cricket Club more interested in sports like cricket and tennis. Those in the lower rungs of the colonial hierarchy like police sergeants and the Eurasians or Anglo-Indians, who usually belonged to the Rangers Club and Dalhousie Club, were greater fans of hockey. Likewise, the employees—again, many of whom were Anglo-Indians, of the various colonial service departments like the Calcutta Customs, the Calcutta Port Commissioners, and the Bengal Nagpur Railways—all had excellent hockey teams. The sports-loving Armenians fielded a hockey team too.

Among the more famous outstation teams in the Beighton Cup were the Jhansi Heroes and the wonderfully named Lusitanians (composed mostly of Goans) from Bombay, which won the Aga Khan Tournament on several occasions, beginning in 1913. Colleges and schools, especially those run by Christian missionaries, were nurseries of hockey all over India. St. James' School, which still is one of the better schools in Calcutta, won the Beighton Cup in 1900. The St. Xavier's College hockey team in Bombay had several fine players, including the Indian Olympian Leo Pinto, and it was the runner-up in the Aga Khan Tournament in 1906. The Xaverian Club of Calcutta won the Beighton Cup twice in the 1920s. The Cathedral School Old Boys won the Aga Khan in 1901 and 1905, while Christ Church School's Old Boys of Jabalpur won it in 1927. Members of the Indian Olympic hockey teams, especially the Anglo-Indians, often learned their hockey in schools like St. George's College and Oak Grove, both in Mussoorie, and Goethals Memorial School in Kurseong.[22] Indeed, the 1928 Indian Olympic hockey team had as many five players from St. George's and Oak Grove.[23] The latter was a school started in 1888 by the East India Railway Company, which oversaw as many as 266 schools, of which 101 were meant for Europeans and Anglo-Indians.[24] The numbers were heavily skewed in favor of non-Indians, though, with more and better-funded schools available to a small group of European and Anglo-Indian employees than to the much larger Indian workforce. But it wasn't just Anglo-Indians or Christian players who benefited from these schools and colleges, some of which had a mixed student body. For example, a Muslim member of the first Indian Olympic hockey team, Feroze Khan (who emigrated to Pakistan after partition), began playing hockey at Lahore's Forman Christian College.[25]

The growth of hockey in India was fundamentally different from that of cricket, which began with communities like the Parsis first taking up the game, or football, which had a substantial middle-class presence, as illustrated by the first overseas tour by an Indian hockey team. Unlike the Parsis, who first sent cricket teams to England or the all-India team led by Patiala in 1911, the first overseas hockey tour by an Indian team was in 1926 when an army team traveled to New Zealand. This wasn't surprising, given the central role of the armed forces in promoting hockey in India, and the tour was the brainchild of Field Marshal William Birdwood, the commander in chief of the British troops in India.

The excitement of this tour is well captured by Chand, who could hardly believe that he had been chosen to represent an Indian team. Pleased he well might have been, since the competition for spots in the team was fierce. The team was selected from 130 regiments and 1,400 players. The touring Indian team, led by a Scotsman, Captain D. T. Cowan, had seventeen members, which included four British and one Indian officer besides twelve non-commissioned soldiers, among whom Chand was one.[26] The exoticness of the Indian team was captured in reports by local papers, which described them on arrival as a "dozen swarthy men, all but three of them turbaned."[27] Even though the team itself had players from all over India, the distinctions between officers and enlisted men were maintained, with the officers being housed in private homes while the rest stayed in the barracks.[28]

Chand described the momentous nature of the tour, noting that this was the "first time an Indian hockey team, more or less representing the country, had travelled abroad."[29] It was a long tour, lasting more than two months, excluding the sea voyage. The Indian team crisscrossed New Zealand, playing various teams and losing only once, aptly enough in the city of Waterloo. The first intimations of the Indian hockey team's future greatness and Chand's genius were very much in evidence on that tour. As the *Auckland Star* reported:

> A revelation in the finer points of the game. Inspired with every tradition of the game, the Indians, forwards and backs, juggled the ball about to the utter astonishment of the Aucklanders. . . . Attacks originated from every direction and any position, being masterly in conception and brilliantly carried out . . . it was impossible to anticipate what the slim son of India would do next with the ball.[30]

Chand was described as "wielding the stick like a magic wand in elusive and uncanny movements."[31] A remarkable aspect of the tour was the sizable crowds that turned up to watch the Indian hockey team play, even though hockey was nowhere near New Zealand's top sport. In fact, in numbers of participants, it was the country's ninth most popular sport. The three "test" matches between the Indian and the New Zealand national teams drew crowds of more than 10,000 people, with the third match pulling in an audience that was definitely more than 18,000, a number that probably has not been matched since for a hockey game in New Zealand.[32]

The 1926 hockey tour was in many ways the precursor to India's fielding a team at the Olympics; the Indian Hockey Federation had been formed a year earlier.[33] The popularity of hockey had much to do with the Indian hockey team's phenomenal success at the Olympic Games. It is remarkable that India was able to field a national hockey team and send it to the Olympics—the first Asian colony of the British Empire to do so—nearly two decades before India became independent. Significantly, a hockey team represented India four years before the country played its first official cricket test match against England in 1932.

The 1928 Amsterdam Games

Hockey had made a comeback in the Amsterdam Olympic Games after being dropped from the program in the 1920 and 1924 games, and the International Olympic Committee agreed to India's request to field a team. Unlike the cricket teams that had toured abroad in 1911 and earlier—organized by the Parsis or captained by a maharaja—a proper trial was held in Calcutta to select a team that would represent India rather than a community or a motley group led and financed by a royal. The trials were held in Calcutta, where the Beighton Cup always drew big crowds. Dhyan Chand attested to the sports-crazy people of Calcutta when he pointed out that the crowds there were always bigger than those at hockey tournaments played elsewhere. The 1928 trials—in which five provinces participated—were no different. Dhyan Chand played for Uttar Pradesh. Although Bengal had a very strong team, it lost in the semifinal to Rajputana. Uttar Pradesh predictably entered the final and beat Rajputana handsomely. A thirteen-member Olympic squad was announced that included Chand, who was now a lance naik (equivalent to a lance corporal) in the army.[34] Three more players, based in England, joined the team later. The team that won the first of India's many gold medals in hockey contained a majority of Anglo-Indians and a sprinkling of players from other communities. Indeed, the team was a good example of the formative role played by Anglo-Indians in the growth of hockey in India. The lineup was Richard Allen, Michael Rocque, Leslie Hammond, Rex Norris, Eric Penniger (vice-captain), Maurice Gately, George Martins, Frederic Seaman, Ernest Cullen, Dhyan Chand, Feroze Khan, Shaukat Ali, and Kher Singh. The three players who joined in England were Jaipal Singh, who was appointed captain, S. M. Yusuf, and the nawab of Pataudi, the star cricketer who represented England in the infamous Bodyline series and later led the Indian cricket team in 1946. Pataudi played for the Indian team in a few of the practice matches in England, but he did not go to Amsterdam.

Trials for the other sports were held in different parts of the country before the all-India trials in early February 1928. In the trials held in Punjab, for instance, Gurbachan Singh and Abdul Hamid were the star performers, both of whom were selected to represent India.[35] The Olympic contingent that was chosen had a nice geographical spread and a mix of diversity. Three athletes were from Bengal (J. Hall, R. Burns, and D. D. Moolji), three from Punjab (Abdul Hamid, Gurbachan Singh, and Dalip Singh), one from Bombay (Dr. B. Chavan), and one from Madras (J. Murphy). G. D. Sondhi was in charge of the seven-man contingent.

There was little expectation, or perhaps even knowledge, of the Indian hockey team, as was evident from only three people seeing off the Indian team on March 10, 1928, when it set sail on the appropriately named *Kaiser-i-Hind*. The Indians players in England, including Jaipal, then a student at Oxford University, joined the team in London. Chand was the star of the team, but Jaipal remains one of India's more enigmatic sports personalities. His appointment as captain proved to be quite controversial. Brought to England by an English missionary from the interior of what is now the state of Jharkhand in eastern India, Jaipal entered St. John's College, where he excelled in hockey and won a university Blue in the sport. The Oxford University student magazine, *Isis*, wrote in 1923 of Jaipal that he was "the greatest find the Varsity has ever had ... there are few more polished and cleverer backs playing in England today."[36] During his Oxford days, Jaipal also was active in organizing sporting activities for South Asians. In 1925, Jaipal got together a hockey team, called Jaipal Singh's XI, made up of Indian students from Oxford, Cambridge, London, Edinburgh, and Manchester, which even took a European tour during the Christmas vacation in 1925. Chand commented that Jaipal's "intimate knowledge of English players and ground conditions" were of great help in preparations.[37] So it was no accident that Jaipal was thought to be the best man to lead the Indian hockey team in Europe. The misgivings about the choice of Jaipal were revealed many years later in 2004 in an interview given by another member of the team, Feroze Khan, on his one-hundredth birthday. Feroze Khan believed that Jaipal was not any better than the left fullbacks who had participated in the Olympic trials in Calcutta and that the British management believed that "an Oxford-educated hockey captain would be better than anyone in India." He also said that Jaipal "mostly kept himself aloof from the players" and joined them only during meals.[38] The differences between the Oxford-educated Jaipal and Chand, a subaltern, were obvious. Jaipal wrote in his autobiography that Chand had only one pair of trousers, and so he took Chand shopping. "I took him to

Austin Reed on Regent Street. . . . Trousers galore were shown. 'Can I take them upstairs and see them in the sun?' That finished me. I told Shaukat the story. 'What else do you expect of a Lance Naik?' he laughed."[39]

The Indian team played eleven matches in England, losing the opener but winning nine of the remaining games and tying one. Chand observed that the country where hockey originated did not much have a following for it, despite the existence of several clubs in the country, with only a "sprinkling" of people showing up for the matches. It was during the England tour that turbans, which for several years were a standard feature of Indian contingents during the Olympic ceremonies, were presented to the Indian hockey team. After their last match in England, at a reception hosted by the National Indian Association, Sir Selwyn Fremantle, a retired Indian Civil Service (ICS) officer, mentioned that each nation was required to wear distinctive dress at the Olympic Games parade and suggested that the Indians wear turbans. The Indian community in London had already raised a subscription to fulfill the need, and each member of the team was given a light blue turban.[40]

The hockey team had reached the Olympics, but the Indian Hockey Federation was in a financially precarious situation. In a letter to the editor in the *Times of India*, Ian Burn Burdock, president of the newly formed Indian Hockey Federation, appealed to the public to make up for the shortfall in funds needed for the team to go to the Olympics. He concluded his letter by saying, "India has every prospect of distinguishing herself at what has now been accepted as her national game Hockey . . . an exceptional effort must be made to give her an opportunity of gaining the highest laurels namely victory in the Olympic Games."[41] He wrote again two months later that despite donations from 128 army units, the federation was still short by Rs 19,714.[42] After the Olympic Games were over, Burdock had to issue yet another appeal saying that Rs 19,000 were still needed to meet the expenses. He pointedly referred to the generosity of the British living in India and asked Indians to follow their lead:

> The Europeans in India have subscribed generously and the Indian Army particularly, has come to our assistance nobly. This appeal is to our Indian friends whose national game is hockey and if only they will come forward and subscribe their mites, however small they may be, there should be no difficulty in raising the balance.[43]

From England the team then traveled to continental Europe, where it played a series of matches in Holland, Germany, and Belgium, easily winning all the games before playing its opening game at the Olympics on May 17, 1928. India beat Austria in the first game by six goals, Chand scoring four of them. It was a similar story in the next few games, with India thrashing Belgium 9–0, Denmark 5–0, and, in the semifinal, beating Switzerland 6–0. Jaipal never played in the final two games, and it still is a mystery why he, who was then a probationer for the ICS and even defied the India Office for refusing to give him leave to play at the Olympics, did not play in the final two matches. Chand provided some hints that communal and racial issues were involved. It also had something to do with the uneasy relationship between the manager, A. B. Rosser, and two ex-soldiers who were accompanying the team. Feroze Khan spoke about Jaipal's strained relations with Rosser as well as his "habit of going back to England in between matches."[44] In an interview several years later, another team member, George Martins, emphatically stated that he regarded Eric Penniger from Punjab as the captain, since he had been "nominated" as captain in India only to be replaced by Jaipal in England.[45] A later historian of Indian hockey blamed the British administrators as well as the Anglo-Indian players for Jaipal's exit. According to him, Jaipal's "staunch nationalistic views" rubbed hockey's "burra sahibs" the wrong way.[46]

In the 1928 games, there were some parallels to the internal politics that divided the Indian cricket teams that toured England in 1932 and 1936 (when Lala Amarnath was sent home). The hockey team, however, proved to be much more resilient and focused. Jaipal said nothing about this in his autobiography. Hockey was only a small part of his story; he rose to become a leader of the Adivasis, a member of the Indian Constituent Assembly, and a three-time member of the Parliament.[47]

Eric Penniger led the Indian hockey team in the finals against the host, the Netherlands, and won, 3–0. The lineup again was Allen, Rocque, Hammond, Norris, Penniger, Yusuf, Gately, Martins, Seaman, Cullen, and Chand. Feroze Khan, Shaukat Ali, and Kher Singh, all of whom were injured, were on the bench. Except for the mysterious incident surrounding Jaipal, it seems from Chand's account that the team's spirit and morale were high. Indeed, Jaipal's absence in the final was not even noted by many. After the Indian victory, the viceroy, oblivious to Jaipal's absence, sent a congratulatory message to "Jaipal Singh and all members of his team."[48] When the winning team returned to India, the reception was very different from when they had left: a huge crowd, including the mayor of the city, awaited them at Ballard Pier in Bombay.[49] Hockey and Dhyan Chand had firmly established themselves in Indians' hearts and minds.

The 1932 Los Angeles Games

A tournament was held in 1932 again in Calcutta to choose the team for the Los Angeles Games, although Chand was exempt, much to his chagrin, from participating. Punjab won the interprovincial tournament, beating Bengal, after which two trial matches were held to select the team. Surprisingly, Jaipal Singh was not even chosen to play for the Bengal team, despite then being posted in Calcutta and captaining the Mohun Bagan hockey squad, and despite Chand's belief that Jaipal was "much better" than the player who was chosen to play for Bengal in the position that Jaipal usually played.[50] Besides Chand, only three players from the 1928 team—Allen, Penniger, and Hammond—were retained. The new faces were Arthur Hind, Carlyle Tapsell, S. Aslam, F. Brewin, Lal Shah Bokhari (captain), Masud Minhas, R. J. Carr, Gurmeet Singh, Roop Singh (Chand's brother), Syed Mohammad Jaffar, and W. P. Sullivan. Bokhari's being appointed captain caused some disappointment, since Penniger, who had been captain in the 1928 finals, felt he was the natural choice. Although he caused a "sensation" by "threatening to pull out,"[51] he was apparently convinced not to by journalist Charles Newham (one of the three who had seen off the hockey team in 1928), who was also one of the founding members of the Punjab Hockey Association. Jaipal was left out, even though a newspaper reported that he was willing to go to Los Angeles "on his own expense," as the hockey federation was short of money to pay for the passage of three players.[52] Five years later in an article, Jaipal had this to say about the selection process and its politics:

> In 1932 when I learnt I had been chosen for the Los Angeles trials I signified in the form each of the candidates had to fill that I would again be willing to pay my own expenses. A prominent member of the I.H.F. had the audacity to tell me I was trying to buy a place in the team. Why did the I.H.F. let me meet my own expenses in 1928?[53]

Despite India's winning an Olympic gold medal in Amsterdam, its participation in the 1932 Los Angeles Olympics was uncertain due to a lack of funds. According to Dhyan Chand, a futile attempt was made to involve Mahatma Gandhi in the efforts to send the hockey team to Los Angeles. Newham wrote to the Mahatma to subscribe to the Olympic Hockey Fund. But just as Gandhi evinced little interest in the cricket Pentangular some years later, hockey was the least of his concerns in 1932, a year after his famous Dandi march, which shook the British. Gandhi wrote back to Newham, "You will be surprised to know that I do not know what really the game of hockey is. I did not know the masses were interested in it. I have never, to my recollection, watched any game either in England, South Africa or in India."[54] He ended the letter by expressing his inability to help the Indian hockey team. However, because of the efforts of the president of the Indian Hockey Federation (IHF), M. Hayman, who was also a member of the Railway Board, and its honorary secretary, Pankaj Gupta, enough money was raised from the Punjab National Bank to at least transport the team. The players also agreed to forgo their £2 allowance after the games as well as to play matches in Europe on the way back to raise money.[55]

The journey of the Indian team to America was as arduous as it was colorful. Assembling in Bhopal on May 14, 1932, the team made its way through India playing games in different venues, leaving Indian shores on a small steamer bound for Colombo. Sondhi was the manager and Pankaj Gupta was his assistant. Both Sondhi and Gupta subsequently had long careers as sports administrators. After playing two games in Ceylon, which the Indians won handily, the team traveled eastward via Singapore, Hong Kong, China, and Japan. In Singapore, they had an unusual request to consider including Sadhu Singh, a Malayan-born Sikh, on the Indian Olympic team. (There was a precedent, since Lall Singh, an Indian born in Malaya, had been selected to play for India in its first official Test match in 1932 against England. However, unlike Sadhu Singh, Lall Singh had been sponsored by a Kuala Lumpur businessman to participate in the trials held in Calcutta to select the team.) Although this wasn't possible, in a token gesture Sadhu Singh played as the right halfback for the Indians when they played the All-Malaya team. Hong Kong was too wet for playing any matches, and no games were scheduled in China. In Japan, the Indian team was given a scare by Waseda University, which lost by a narrow margin of 3–5, the closest result of the tour by far.

India's first port of call in the United States was Honolulu, where they enjoyed the hospitality of the famous Indian merchant Gobindram Jethanand Watamull before disembarking in California, forty-two days after they left India. There the hockey team met up with the four other Indian participants in the Olympics, a swimmer and three athletes.[56]

When the Indian hockey team arrived in Los Angeles, a newspaper reported: "Hockey Kings arrive today. They will be accompanied by their many wives. There are two lions in the team."[57] In reality, the only woman in the Indian contingent was Sondhi's wife, and the two lions were the two Singhs on the team: Rup and Gurmeet. At the opening ceremony of the Olympic Games on July 30, the Indian hockey captain, Bokhari, led the Indian contingent, all of whom were wearing turbans. The tournament itself was an anticlimax, with India needing to play only two games to win the gold. The Europeans had stayed away, apparently because of the economic depression. India beat Japan 11-1 in the opening encounter and then the United States by an incredible 24-1 margin. A story circulated that $1,000 had been bet that Chand would not score more than three goals, and the Americans assigned three players to prevent him from scoring. In any case, he ended up scoring thirteen goals.[58] Not surprisingly, an American newspaper reported that the Indian team was a "typhoon out of the east."[59] The final was played before a crowd of 5,000, among which was the large Indian community in California, which even contributed $200 to the fund for the Indian Olympic contingent.

The coverage of India's Olympic win was a clue to the head start that cricket had, even in those days, compared with other sports. While the *Times of India* barely mentioned the title win—carrying it as prominently as the report on the Harwood League in Bombay—India's win over a county team during the 1932 tour of England found pride of place on the sports page. The headline for that report screamed, "India Wins Match Against Somerset," and went on to describe a great innings played by the Indian cricketer C. K. Nayudu.[60]

The Indian team played a couple of more games in the United States before leaving for Europe, where it played nine matches in four countries, though no games were scheduled in England. The German hockey association offered to pay the expenses of the Indian team while in Europe. Chand's star status was apparent when in Prague a Czech woman insisted on kissing him after the match. Chand got out of the predicament by protesting that he

The 1932 Olympic gold-medal winning Indian hockey team playing a friendly match. The player in the picture attempting to score a goal is none other than Dhyan Chand. Reprinted by permission of the Hindu Archives

was a married man. The Indians played more matches in Ceylon and India to raise money but still ended up with a deficit of Rs 3,000, which Hayman paid. Later, Chand even got an offer from him to join the railways, but he was assured by the army of an officer's commission and so stayed on.[61]

The 1936 Berlin Olympics

In 1935, before the 1936 Olympic Games, the Indian team went on a tour of New Zealand and Australia. The nawab of Manavadar (a small princely state in Kathiawad in western India), a keen hockey enthusiast, was supposed to lead the team but when he declined, Chand was appointed captain. The Indians played forty-eight matches in New Zealand, Australia, and Ceylon without losing a single game, despite the bad ground conditions and weather. The tour by Indians, already two-time Olympic champions, generated considerable curiosity in the Australian media, and their arrival in Australia even made it to the front page of a Perth newspaper.[62] Not surprisingly, the Australians were most impressed by Chand, whom they hailed as "the greatest exponent of hockey of all times."[63] The *Canberra Times* reported, "Dhyan Chand and Rup Singh are brothers and are a remarkable combination. It has been said that the ball seems almost to glue itself to their sticks, and their goal-getting record bears out such a contention."[64] The two other players to attract attention were M. J. Gopalan, who had played one Test for the Indian team against the Douglas Jardine–led England cricket team in the 1933/1934 series (he had also had the honor of bowling the first delivery in the Ranji Trophy in 1934, playing for Madras), and Harbail Singh, the "only man in the side with long hair, beard and turban."[65]

Such was Chand's popularity that a few years later, the Perth Sports Depot even advertised the sale of "Dhyan Chand" hockey sticks.[66] One of the highlights of the tour was a meeting between the world's greatest cricketer, Don Bradman, and the Indian team at Adelaide. Bradman posed with the Indian team for a photograph, one that Chand wrote that he would "cherish" all his life."[67] At a reception for the hockey team, Bradman announced, "I am particularly glad to welcome the Indian players, as they are better exponents of the game of hockey than we are. We will have the opportunity of learning something from them." He hoped that this would be a forerunner to a visit by an Indian cricket team.[68] Then that same evening, he went to watch the Indians play a South Australian XI at the Adelaide Oval. The Indians crushed the opposition, 10–1, and according to Chand, this was the first hockey match that Bradman had ever seen.

Five players from the tour Down Under, including Chand, were selected for the Olympic Games. Gopalan would have made the team but opted instead to tour England with the Indian cricket team. Gopalan was one of many Indian sportspersons, including the great Nayudu, who were proficient in more than one game and thus had to choose between the two. In this case, Gopalan missed an Olympic gold medal only to warm the bench on India's tour of England, and by a cruel stroke of fate, he returned from England on the same ship as the victorious Olympic hockey team. Even though Chand was an obvious selection, he wasn't sure of the captaincy because of his "minor rank" in the army and his social position.[69] As in the 1932 trials, Chand did not take part in the interprovincial tournament in 1936, which was finally won by Bengal, one of the strongest hockey teams in India at the time.

Among the players chosen, Dickie Carr could not make it to Berlin because he wasn't granted leave by his employers, the Bengal Nagpur Railway; the Olympics had yet to make a significant impact in India. The replacement for Carr, Ali Iqtidar Shah Dara, also wasn't given leave by the army. Eventually an eighteen-member squad was announced, and in his third Olympics, Chand's dream of becoming captain was fulfilled, with a majority of the state hockey associations in India backing him. Besides Chand, there were two other candidates for captaincy—Syed Jaffar from Punjab, who withdrew his name, and Mirza Nasiruddin Masood, a former captain of the hockey team of Delhi's elite St. Stephen's College and private secretary to the nawab of Manavadar. Masood, who later held several important government positions, including independent India's ambassador to Saudi Arabia, also left us an account of the Berlin Games.[70] Not surprisingly, Masood's and Chand's accounts differ not only on certain events but also in outlook: Chand, despite being the world's greatest hockey player, was not even an officer in the Indian army, whereas Masood, by no means a vital part of the Indian team, as later events would show, moved around in elite circles. The rest of the team contained the usual high number of Anglo-Indians—Allen, Tapsell, Joseph Philip, Joseph Galibardy, Lionel Emmett, and Cyril Michie—besides Mohammed Hussain, Gurcharan Singh, Babu Nimal, Ahmed Sher Khan, Shabban Shahabuddin, Ahsan Mohammed Khan, Peter Fernandes, and Roop Singh.

The Indian team began its journey in Delhi on the wrong foot by losing 1–4 to the Delhi Hockey XI. This served as a wake-up call for the team, which won the rest of its games in India. The team's final destination before departing was Bombay, where a lunch was organized on June 25, with the guest of honor being the great Parsi cricketer, Dr. M. E. Pavri, who led the Parsis against Lord Hawke's team in 1892/1893. Masood writes that Chand was asked to make a speech but refused, showing that the off-field duties of a captain sat somewhat uneasily on him.[71] The same evening, a dance was organized at the Taj Mahal Hotel where well-wishers and fans turned up in large numbers. The German consul was present and gave a speech on the occasion. On June 27, 1936, the Indian team set sail for Europe on a P&O liner, the *Ranpura*. Just before the ship set sail, the manager, Swami Jagannath, Chand, and the assistant manager, Pankaj Gupta, all delivered farewell messages on the radio. Interestingly, Gupta mentioned that an incident such as the sending back of Lala Amarnath from England, which happened the same year, would never occur with the hockey team, revealing how deep an impression the Amarnath episode had made in India. Besides those traveling to England to take the Indian Civil Service examinations, the hockey team had among their companions on their long sea voyage the maharaja of Mysore, one of India's richest princes in India, who became one of the players' favorites. An unexpected benefit for the team was the Indian vegetarian dishes that were whipped up by the maharaja's large retinue of servants, which he shared with the players. Chand's regiment, the 4/14 Punjab, was posted at Aden, and when the ship stopped there, the Indian team not only was entertained but also got a chance to practice on the regimental field.[72]

The ship's journey ended at Marseilles, in France, where the Indian contingent, which, besides the hockey players and officials, contained six other athletes, made quite an impression. In Masood's words:

> We presented a great variety of ages, colours and appearances. We had amongst us ages ranging from twenty to forty, skins in all shades of white and brown, heights varying from 5 feet to 6 feet, beardless and bearded, from no moustaches to moustaches of every description, from leanness carried to extremities to muscles bulging out of blazers, Aryan, Dravidian and Mongolian features, bare-headed, hats and turbans. What a variety in appearance! And still greater by far in thoughts, habits, temperament and general outlook on life.[73]

The Indian team traveled by train from Marseilles to Paris. The staid Chand merely mentioned that the team took in the famous sights of Paris. The worldlier Masood described in some detail how the Indian team explored the nightlife of Paris. They visited two night clubs and in the second, the Coliseum, some of the players enjoyed dancing with the club girls, paying two francs each for a dance. The show at the Folies Bergère was an equally "fascinating" experience, where the dancers, wearing almost no clothes, made quite an impression on the Indian team.[74] From Paris the Indian team went to Berlin by train in a third-class compartment—a stark contrast to today's athletes. But the reception in Berlin more than made up for the discomfort the team suffered on the train ride.

A large crowd greeted the Indian team, with Dr. Diem, chairman of the Olympic organizing committee, on hand to welcome the team. The British national anthem (the Indian contingent's flag then was a Union Jack but with the Star of India insignia) was played and cries of "Heil Hitler" echoed afterward.[75] All this was reported in a rather prosaic fashion by both Chand and Masood. They weren't, of course, then aware of the significance of the games as a propaganda coup for Adolf Hitler and the Third Reich.[76] Masood published his memoir in 1937, but Chand published his after World War II and still said nothing about the German politics of 1936. Indeed, he recounted how the Indian team excitedly sought autographs from Hermann Göring—Hitler's chief propagandist and one of the key architects of the games—when he was in the athletes' dining hall.[77] Moreover, Masood was very impressed by the German youths whom, he believed, were "growing up in the spirit of self-sacrifice, mutual cooperation and comradeship."

Unlike Chand, who merely stated that the Olympic Village—where the athletes were housed—was much more elaborate than the one in Los Angeles, Masood offered a more detailed description. The village, which covered 1,440 acres, had several cottages with beds, showers, telephones, and refrigerators. The Indians had two stewards looking after them besides an entire contingent of Nazi youths catering to the athletes' needs. The centerpiece of the village, according to Masood, was the dining hall, where every effort was made to cater to the tastes of the athletes from the fifty-three competing countries.[78] The German organizers had made special arrangements for the Indian contingent. They had their own kitchen, and the "chief provisions expert" of the Olympic village had even prepared a "type-written page of instructions on the preparation of curry."[79] But as is still the case, the Indian palate was most difficult to satisfy, with the Indian manager being forced to cook curry on several occasions. Even though this wasn't great food, the Indians usually wolfed it down.

Chand was much more concerned—and this says a lot about his outlook—with India's preparations for the Olympic matches. India was shocked in its very first practice match by German team, losing 1-4. This was such a rare occurrence for the Indian team that Chand said it robbed him of his night's sleep. In fact, Masood was identified as the weak link and a substitute was sought. A cable was sent to Kunwar Jagdish Prasad, president of the IHF, to rush over Dara and, if he were not available, Frank Wells or Eric Henderson. In addition, the services of Penniger, who led the Indians in the 1928 Olympic finals, were sought. It also was decided that Cullen would replace Masood as center half. Eventually, Masood played only one game in the Olympics, the semifinal against France. Despite its constrained circumstances, the IHF sent Dara by air from Karachi, but he reached Berlin in time only for the semifinal.[80] Dara, who played the final two games, later emigrated to Pakistan after Partition and was instrumental in building up the Pakistan hockey team. Not surprisingly, Masood did not have anything positive to say about the "premature decision" to send for reinforcements. In his opinion, India's defeat in the first practice game was due to the team's lack of physical fitness because of the long sea voyage, as well as its poor coordination on the field. He questioned the decision to spend Rs 3,000 to bring a player from India when the IHF was in dire financial straits. He also had something to say about the team's discipline. Although it was mandated that everybody retire to bed by 10 P.M., some members of the contingent, including Jagannath, Gupta, and Chand, went to see a certain Menaka dancing, returning late at night. Eventually a notice was put up, laying out a strict schedule for the team, with the day beginning at 6.30 A.M. and lights out at 10 P.M.[81]

After the shocking defeat in their first game in Germany, the Indians played four matches against local Berlin teams, one against Afghanistan and two against the United States, all of which they won rather easily. The opening ceremony of the Berlin Games was held on August 1. It was a meticulously orchestrated display of the might of the Third Reich, and the Indians were swept away by the spectacle. Unlike Chand, who devoted no space to the opening ceremony, Masood gave a blow-by-blow account of the event. When he heard the 100,000 Germans assembled in the stadium sing the German national hymns in Hitler's presence, Masood had tears in his eyes and felt an upsurge of "national feelings." The American contingent, which had reluctantly come to Berlin primarily because of the efforts of the future International Olympic Committee (IOC) president, Avery Brundage, created some controversy by refusing to dip the American flag to Hitler. The *Times of India* reported of the Indian contingent: "They marched with a dipped flag and eyes right and did not give the raised arm salute."[82] Although this has been interpreted by a recent history of the Olympics as a "grand gesture of defiance,"[83] there is no evidence, in either the newspapers at the time or the players' memoirs, that this was in any way a planned move. This was also the first time that a live radio commentary of the Olympics was available in India. The electronics company, Philips, regularly inserted quarter-ads in the sports pages of the *Times of India* during the Olympics asking readers to tune in to their Philips radio set. An item in the newspaper observed, "Following these programmes will be nearly as good as having a ringside seat at the Great Stadium and you will be receiving the news flashed direct from the arena."[84]

After the inaugural festivities, the games began in earnest. Unlike in Los Angeles, eleven hockey teams were playing. India was scheduled to play Hungary, Japan, and the United States in group I. In its first game on August 5, against Hungary, India won, 4–0, before a sparse crowd. The next match was against the United States, at which India did not come anywhere near the score of the 1932 games but still won easily, 7–0. The final group match was against Japan, and an ever improving Indian team trounced their opponents, 9–0. After each match the Indians were invited for evening engagements, from the visiting maharaja of Baroda to the British ambassador. India played in the semifinal against France, which it defeated, 10–0. Dara was fielded for the first time and netted two goals.

When the day of the finals—August 14, 1936—dawned, India's opponent was Germany, which had given India such a scare in their first practice game. Since it had rained heavily, the field was flooded. The Indians therefore requested that the game be postponed to the next day, which was also the closing day of the games. The organizers decided to hold the match on the morning of August 15—ironically the day on which India became independent eleven years later. A huge crowd of 20,000 turned up for the match, with many turned away because of a shortage of seats. Among the spectators were several Indians, including the maharaja of Baroda and the princess of Bhopal. The first half was closely contested, with Roop Singh scoring the solitary goal from a Jaffar pass. Because the ground was damp, in the second half Dhyan Chand "discarded his studded shoes and stockings and played with bare legs and in rubber-soled shoes." The speed of the Indians picked up appreciably, and the team scored seven more goals, with Germany scoring one, the only one that India allowed in the entire tournament. The August 17 edition of the *Times of India* carried a single-column report on India's triumph, but as in earlier Olympics, it was dwarfed by the double column on England's fine showing against India in the ongoing Test series between the two countries.[85] The

historic nature of India's win over the Germany, given the intensely ideological agenda of the Berlin Games and its emphasis on Aryan superiority, was
overlooked at the time.

India won the gold medal in hockey, but the rest of the athletes—who
had no recourse to modern training methods—were, not surprisingly, a
disappointment. Whiteside and Bhalla finished last in their sprint heats;
Ronak Singh could not finish the six-mile race; and the three wrestlers,
Akram Rasool, Anwar, and Thorat, crashed out in the first round. Only Swami
creditably finished the marathon, though he was sixth from the bottom. An
English newspaper had the following report on Ronak Singh, which summed
up the plight of the Indian athletes:

> In one race, we saw a strange bearded Indian runner, who wears a little
> knot of blue ribbon tied on the top of his head, and is content to trot
> along philosophically far behind the field. He did this in the 10,000 me-
> ters race, a queer character indeed, tall, thin, melancholy and completely
> detached.[86]

Ironically, Menaka, whose dancing proved to be such an attraction to India's
hockey stars, excelled in the "dance section" of the Olympiad (possibly a non-
competitive sideshow of the Olympics), in which fifteen countries competed,
with her troupe winning three out of the ten "first class honours prizes."[87]

Indian Gymnastics Display

The story of the 1936 games wouldn't be complete without mention of the
now-forgotten display by the Hanuman Vyayam Prasarak Mandal in Berlin.
Just as in Bengal, there was a physical culture movement in western India,
particularly in Maharashtra, which fed off the nationalist movement. One of
the more successful and long-standing institutions that propagated the cult
of the body was the Hanuman Club, formed in 1913/1914, which in 1922
came to be known as the Hanuman Vyayam Prasarak Mandal. The organization was founded by Ambadasapant Vaidya, a Brahmin from Amaravati.[88]
Others who were involved in promoting physical education, including yoga,
were Professor Rajratan Manikrao, who established a number of gymnasiums in Baroda. His disciple, Swami Kuvalyananda, founded a research center

for the study of yoga in Lonavla near Pune.[89] Professor Ramamurti Naidu, whom we will encounter again in the next chapter, was a proponent of mass drill exercises.[90] Around this time too, D. C. Mujumdar published his *Encyclopedia of Indian Physical Culture* in Marathi.

In addition was the phenomenon of the export of the so-called Indian clubs (*jori/mugdal*) to England and the United States in the nineteenth century and their movement back to India in ways similar to what happened with polo. Unlike polo, however, the *jori* and *mugdal* were part of the physical education movement in India, which had distinctly anticolonial overtones. Joseph Alter has mapped the fascinating journey of the "Indian clubs," which were picked up by the British army, modified by the Germans and Swedish, popularized by the "muscular Christians,"[91] and then made their way back to India to be "incorporated into an expressly anti-colonial project."[92] Interestingly, institutions such as the Hanuman Mandal, which promoted Indian exercises, did so by fitting them into a Western mold, in particular the one popularized by the YMCA.[93]

At first, the Mandal attracted local students to perform drills and exercises, but later it began organizing summer classes attended by students from all over the country, who were awarded certificates on their completion. Soon the Mandal started performing elsewhere, beginning in Pune in 1928. The same year it gave a demonstration at the annual session of the Indian National Congress in Calcutta on the invitation of the nationalist leader Subhas Chandra Bose.[94] The high point of the Mandal's history was the invitation to take part in the somewhat curiously named World Sports Pedagogic Congress to "exhibit Indian games and exercises."[95] The event was held in Berlin during the Olympic Games. Twenty-four athletes were chosen, and they, along with the Mandal's president, Dr. K. S. Kane, were given a send-off at a function on July 9, 1936, organized by the provincial congress committee. A newspaper report noted the composition of the team, in which the "Harijan and Brahmin rub shoulders together." The report emphasized the nationalist aspirations of the trip, saying that "the team would also have the opportunity of proving to an arrogant people that Indians were physically equal to the West."[96]

On July 25 and 29, 1936, the Mandal gave two informal demonstrations in Berlin, which were "witnessed by thousands of athletes of various nations and appreciated by all."[97] The members of the Berlin Olympic Committee, too, were very impressed. The Mandal team gave wrestling demonstrations and a display of *malkhamb* (pole wrestling). The final demonstration was scheduled for August 11, four days before the Olympics' closing ceremony. At the International Sports Students Congress, which was held in Berlin during the Olympics, the Mandal gave physical demonstrations, and it also sang Bengali poet Rabindranath Tagore's famous song, "Ekla Cholo Re," which was a great favorite of Gandhi's.[98] The team placed second for its physical display and ironically won the Hitler Medal for the "best performance."[99] The Mandal continues to exist today. Alter has interestingly drawn a comparison, and outlined the differences, with the Mandal's "mass drill yoga" in Berlin and the Hindu right-wing organization Rashtriya Swayamsevak Sangh's "mass shakha [unit] drill" in Pune or Nagpur.[100]

Return of the Victors

Even after the Olympics were over, the Indian hockey team was much in demand. After the games, the Indian team played a series of matches in Germany before returning to Berlin to play a game against a city team in the same stadium where it had been crowned the Olympic champions. This time, however, a fatigued Indian team was held to a 3–3 draw before a packed stadium. The team then played one game in the Netherlands before spending a week in England, where it finally got some time off and enough Indian food. Sir Firoze Khan Noon, the Indian high commissioner in London, arranged a reception for the Indian team, at which, among others, the nawab of Pataudi was a guest, as was, oddly enough, Douglas Jardine, with whom the nawab had had serious differences during the infamous Bodyline tour. On the way back to Marseilles where they were to board their ship, the Indian played two more matches in Switzerland. The team journeyed back on the liner *Strathmore*, along with several celebrities: the maharaja of Mysore once again, the nawab of Pataudi, Vizzy, and the British governors of Bombay and Madras.

It is ironic that Vizzy, who had led the Indian cricket team in the disastrous tour of England in 1936, was on the same ship as the hockey team. Even the down-to-earth Chand couldn't help taking pride in the hockey team's achievements: "I felt I was certainly above the ordinary when I posed for a picture with Vizzy on the sun deck. Temporarily I felt I was a couple of inches above the earth with my chest bulging out."[101] Unlike the Indian cricket teams, which were usually led by princes and had a whiff of intrigue surrounding them, the Indian hockey team always seemed more egalitarian and cohesive. This, of course, had something to do with the growth of hockey, which was spurred by the army regiments and Anglo-Indian players. The nawabs and maharajas, with a few exceptions like the nawab of Pataudi, rarely played hockey or football seriously, except perhaps in their days in public schools. Someone like Dhyan Chand, despite his phenomenal skills, would never have been considered a fit candidate to lead India in cricket. In hockey, however, not only did he do so, he also brought back the Olympic gold. This observation was captured by Masood, who did not seem to get along very well with the team management but concluded his book on the Berlin Games by saying, "We had our differences and we had our quarrels, but never once did they come in the way of our duty to the team and the country."[102] Although only two people greeted the victorious Indian team at the Bombay pier, the city mayor organized a grand reception the next day that was attended by a large crowd. On the menu that day was "Dhyan Chand soup," attesting to the popularity of hockey in India and its homegrown legend.

Anglo-Indians and the Character of Hockey

Chand may still be remembered and memorialized for his magical skills, but the role of the Anglo-Indians on the pre-1947 Indian hockey teams has been largely forgotten. According to Frank Anthony, a notable Anglo-Indian, in those days the community "could have produced at least 6 equally good teams." Ten members of the 1928 Olympic hockey team were Anglo-Indians; in 1932, the number was seven; and in 1936, six.[103] Judging by the team's composition, the sport in colonial India was taken up most enthusiastically by minorities—Anglo-Indians, Muslims, and Sikhs. In many ways, however, it was the dominance of the Anglo-Indians in the sport's early years that symbolized the place of hockey in colonial India. The Anglo-Indians occupied a peculiar place in colonial India, as they were given special privileges in securing jobs for being "almost-British" but at the same time were regarded as "not-quite-British" in the social hierarchy, owing to their Asian ancestry.[104] A cultural studies scholar has offered an interesting argument as to why there were so many Anglo-Indians playing hockey:

In a period when all sports—from bodybuilding to cricket—were intensely political, it [hockey] existed in the negative, so to speak, as a mere game. Indeed, the fact that it was so enthusiastically embraced by the Anglo-Indian community, may suggest that its politics, if any, was of a loyalist stripe.[105]

This is plausible considering the role of the army, the colonial service organizations like customs and the railways, and the missionary schools as patrons of hockey.

It's possibly because of the ambiguous place of Anglo-Indians in colonial India that the memory of Anglo-Indian hockey players has largely faded in independent India. One rare instance of recollection was the organization of the Richard Carr (a member of the 1932 Olympics team) Interschool Hockey Tournament by his alma mater, Oak Grove, in 2011 on the anniversary of his one-hundredth birthday. But when Joe Galibardy of the 1936 Olympic team (he missed the trials of the 1948 games because his wife was about to deliver their seventh child), rated by Chand as one of the best ever halfbacks in India, died at the age of ninety-six in London the same year—making him the oldest Indian Olympian at the time—no one in India took any notice. Like many Anglo-Indians, he had left India soon after independence, possibly uncomfortable with the idea of an India no longer under British rule. Indeed by 1947, there already were five Anglo-Indian players in the Western Australia hockey league.[106] It was left to Ashok Mitra, a former communist finance minister of West Bengal and polymath, to mourn the loss in his column in a popular Calcutta daily: "Did Joe Galibardy—or for that matter, Charlie Tapsell [a member of the 1932 and 1936 Olympic teams] deserve a biography? Who knows? Or is it a case of who cares?"[107]

8

LORDS OF THE RING

TALES OF WRESTLERS AND BOXERS

TUCKED AWAY IN A TEXAS LIBRARY IS A RARE PHOTOGRAPH TAKEN in 1928. It shows an Asian man wearing a gown and turban, with a formidable moustache, shaking hands with a white man of similar height and build, and wearing what looks like tights and a jersey, with another formally dressed white man standing in the middle. The men in the picture are Gama Baksh and Stanislaus Zbyszko,[1] a Polish wrestler, with the referee in the middle, before their bout in Patiala in what was billed as the world wrestling championship. Gama, an illiterate Muslim, remains one of the more fascinating characters in Indian sport, a near-mythical figure who bore on his broad shoulders the aspirations of a nation in the making, just as the Indian hockey and cricket teams and Mohun Bagan did. Unlike the exponents of English games, however, Gama was the successor in a centuries-old tradition, albeit one that was also being molded by the marriage of nationalism and physical culture, which I briefly mentioned in an earlier chapter.

Gama's early life and career were a throwback to an earlier time. From medieval times, wrestlers, or *pehalwans,* many of them peasants and from the lower castes, who showed talent were patronized by princes. It wasn't that the upper castes were not into wrestling—the *jyesthimallas* were an example of upper-caste wrestlers, and we have examples of rulers like Krishnadeva

Raya taking up wrestling. Akbar the Great's stable of wrestlers in the sixteenth century was wonderfully eclectic, with both Hindus and Muslims drawn from a wide geographical area being employed in his court. Akbar himself was a fine wrestler. According to Joseph Alter—who has done seminal work on Indian wrestling (or *kushti*) and plumbed the voluminous writings in Hindi on wrestling—beginning in the late Mughal period, most of the well-known champions who caught the eyes of Indian princes were Muslims. One such wrestler was Saddik, who was patronized by Maharaja Sher Singh of Amritsar and was said—we have to take some of the accounts with more than a pinch of salt—to have been eight feet tall, consume fifty-five pounds of ghee (clarified butter) every day, and hang upside down from a gate for three hours every day.[2] Indeed, the descriptions of the diet and the physical regimen of famous Indian wrestlers often beggar description and are a staple of the accounts of their lives. These, along with the stress on celibacy, were held up as examples of their extreme devotion to their discipline. Besides the ruler of Amritsar, several other princes in north India—Baroda, Darbhanga, Datiya, and Indore, to name just a few—were enthusiastic patrons of wrestling. As Alter points out, it was because wrestlers stood for the "ideological principles of a disciplined way of life—physical strength, moral virtue, honesty, respect, duty, and integrity—that they served so well as political emblems."[3]

The Great Gama

Alter constructed Gama's life through the numerous biographies written in Hindi, some of which were surely embellished by his biographers. Gama was probably born in 1878 (according to some accounts, his real name was Gulam Mohammed) into a family of wrestlers. His father, Aziz Baksh, was a famous wrestler in the court of Raja Bhavani Singh of Datiya in modern Madhya Pradesh. After his father died, when Gama was only six years old, he was put under the care of his maternal grandfather Nun Pahalwan, also a wrestler. When his grandfather died soon after, Gama's uncle, Ida Pahalwan (yet another wrestler) took him under his wing and began training him in the intricacies of wrestling. Gama showed his first signs of greatness when as a ten-year-old he sought permission to compete in an exercise competition held by the ruler of Jodhpur in 1888, to which he was taken by another wrestler-uncle, Buta Pahalwan. Gama was given permission to take part only because he was the son of the great Aziz Baksh. The centerpiece of the competition was finding out which wrestler could do the most *bethaks* (knee bends). More than four hundred wrestlers began the contest, but after several hours, only fifteen remained in the fray, one of them being Gama. He was declared the winner because of his young age.[4] By the age of fifteen, Gama already had acquired a huge reputation, and if his biographers are to be believed, his daily routine included three thousand *bethaks* and a one-mile run with a 120-pound stone ring around his neck and a daily diet of five gallons of milk, less than a quarter gallon of ghee, just under one and a half pounds of butter, and almost nine pounds of fruit.[5] Gargantuan amounts of food consumed and an incredible physical regimen were common features in the biographies of Indian wrestlers.

The exaggeration in this construction of life histories was recognized by Gobor Guha, the middle-class Bengali wrestler, who told a story to a disciple about the trip in 1899 made by Indian wrestlers to Europe in the company of Motilal Nehru, Jawaharlal Nehru's father. On the long ship journey, some European travelers expressed a desire to see the Indian wrestlers exercise. The Indian wrestlers protested that the ship would overturn if they exercised. After Nehru convinced them that this wouldn't happen, the wrestlers reluctantly agreed. But as soon they began their exercises, the ship listed, and the wrestlers promptly stopped.[6]

In 1904 Gama showed his skills in a tournament organized by the maharaja of Rewa and moved to the Rewa court. Two years later, he won a tournament organized by the maharaja of Orcha, after which he moved yet again, this time to the court of Orcha. In 1907 at a tournament in Datiya, Gama met his match in Rahim Sultaniwalla, when both of them wrestled for twenty minutes with no clear winner. They wrestled two more times over the next two years, each time the contest ending in a stalemate.[7]

In 1910 the world began hearing about Gama when he was chosen, along with three other wrestlers—Imam Bux, Ahmed Bux, and Gamu—to compete in a world wrestling tournament being organized by the John Bull Society in London. The *Health and Strength* magazine reported the "Invasion of the Indian Wrestlers" in its May 14 issue.[8] In a sign of the times, the sponsor of the trip wasn't a maharaja but a Bengali millionaire, Sharat Kumar Mishra, who saw the venture as a perfect opportunity for Indians to demonstrate their athletic prowess.[9] Gama and his compatriots weren't the first wrestlers to tour Europe. A few years earlier, in 1899, a famous Indian wrestler, Ghulam, and his brother Kalloo had accompanied a delegation to Paris at the time of the Great Exposition headed by Motilal Nehru.[10] There Ghulam defeated Kader Ali, a Turkish wrestler.[11] The details of Nehru's trip are not known, but Indira Gandhi, his granddaughter and the Indian prime minister, referred to it in her speech after receiving the "Olympic Gold Order" in 1983, noting that her grandfather "did a great deal to promote wrestling and even took Indian wrestlers to various cities in Europe."[12] There is another contemporary account by a French writer of Ghulam's domination of the fight with the Turkish wrestler.[13] It wasn't just Europe where Indian wrestlers, or at least Indians with wrestling skills, were going. An Australian newspaper carried the following fascinating news item in 1899:

> What is New South Wales coming to, at least the male population of that colony? There were some sports held up country, one of the items in the programme being a wrestling match and, sad to say, this was won by a Hindoo hawker. . . . New South Wales is now dishonored, disgraced, disgusted, and, distinguished, for one of her "brawny" sons was defeated by a Hindoo hawker! Let us pray.[14]

Gama was apparently not allowed to compete in the London tournament because at five foot eight and 196 pounds, he didn't qualify as a heavyweight.[15] The *Sporting Life* even carried an article entitled "Gama's Hopeless Quest [to find a genuine opponent]."[16] His resourceful manager then arranged to have Gama challenge anyone willing to fight him at a local theater, the Alhambra, with £5 for anyone who could throw him down in less than five minutes. According to Gama's biographers—and again, we mustn't discount some exaggeration—he beat three wrestlers on the first day and ten English wrestlers, as well as thirty Japanese wrestlers, on the second day.[17] But what the London *Times* confirms is that Gama defeated the American champion, Dr. B. F. Roller, on August 8, 2010. The *Health and Strength* reported that the Alhambra was "packed to the point of suffocation" and the "air was electric with excitement."[18] While the *Times* reporter admitted that little was known about Gama except that he had earned the title "Lion of Punjab," Gama was considerably smaller than Roller, who at 224 pounds towered over his opponent. But when the bout began, it was apparent that the "Oriental was not only the swifter but also the stronger man." Within a minute, Gama had thrown Roller off the mat and, in a little over five minutes, not only had defeated his American opponent but also had broken two of his ribs. So impressed was the *Times* reporter that he predicted that Gama would not have any difficulty in defeating Zbyszko, whom he was to fight in September.[19] A short piece in the *New York Times* also took note of the event, describing the match as "$1,000 a side" at a London music hall and reporting that Gama, the "champion of India," had won easily.[20] Before Gama took on Zbyszko, however, his brother Imam Bux fought a bout with a leading professional, John Lemm, at the Alhambra, defeating him in a little over four minutes. The *Health and Strength* reported that the match was "one mighty thrill from start to finish."[21]

In early September, Gama met Zbyszko, who weighed more than forty-two pounds more than the Indian, at Shepherd's Bush stadium in London before a crowd of 12,000 people in what was described as the "catch-as-catch-can championship of the world." But the *Times* correspondent added that this billing could not be technically justified so long as the American, Frank Gotch, who had beaten Zbyszko earlier, and the Russian wrestler George Hackenschmidt were still around.[22] The two men battled for an astonishing two hours and thirty-four minutes, something that would be unheard of in today's make-believe world of professional wrestling, but Zbyszko's defensive tactics ensured that there was no clear winner when the light started fading. As the *Times* reported:

Zbysco, though in perfect condition, and a model of Herculean strength, pursued a policy of passive resistance from first to last. Adhaesit pavimento[23] for nearly three hours: he spread himself face down on the mat, evading his busy antagonist's efforts to fix a half-nelson and breaking other holds by sheer strength, and, when in danger of being pulled over and pinned out, crawling laboriously to the edge of the mat. Thrice he got up and made a futile attack—when the Indian's vast superiority in open play was at once apparent—and he was only too glad to resume his prone position. All this may have been magnificent, but it was not wrestling;

and the spectators were not slow to express their disgust in humorous terms while Gama rode gaily on his back and slapped him contemptuously or dismounted and walked round him.[24]

Even though the crowd was mercilessly critical of Zbyszko, the correspondent pointed out that the Polish wrestler, albeit unsportsmanlike, had not broken the rules, which, he felt, were in dire need of change. Some reports were critical of Gama, too, with the *Sporting Life* saying that Gama "evinced a woeful ignorance of the technicalities of ground wrestling."[25]

It was agreed that the match would be continued the next week, but Zbyszko failed to show up, so Gama was declared the winner and awarded the 100-guinea "John Bull" belt and the £250 stake. The *Times* correspondent once again advocated changes in the rules to penalize defensive wrestlers like Zbyszko if the "Gama v. Zbysco fiasco" was not to be witnessed again.[26] Interestingly, the next year when Gotch fought and beat Hackenschmidt in Chicago on September 4 for what was billed as the "world's Championship," the *Times* wrote before the fight that the winner would "certainly be overthrown without much difficulty when he takes the mat with Gama or Ahmed Bux or any of the heavy-weight wrestlers who cultivate the traditional art in Northern India."[27] This was as clear an affirmation as one could get of the prowess of Gama and his fellow wrestlers in India.

The media coverage of Gama's victories had no explicitly racist or nationalist overtones. The editor of *Health and Strength*, however, wrote, "I actually received letters from readers in India pointing out that if they [the Indian wrestlers] kept on winning, their victories would give a dangerous fillip to the seditions amongst our dusky subjects that menace the integrity of out Indian Empire."[28] Gama's feats were widely reported in India, and he returned a hero. Not surprisingly, the maharaja of Patiala, Bhupinder Singh—who seemed to have his finger in every sports pie—lured Gama to his court at a stipend of Rs 250 per month. Interestingly, even though Gama had conquered the world in London, he still was not the Indian wrestling champion. In 1912, he met his old foe, Rahim Sultaniwalla, in Allahabad, but this time too the contestants were evenly matched. Eventually, Rahim, who was older than Gama, was so exhausted that he left the wrestling pit rather than be pinned down.[29] When the Prince of Wales visited Lahore in 1922, among the entertainment provided was a wrestling bout involving Gama. The *Times's* report did not mention it, but according to Gama's biographers, the prince awarded Gama a thirty-pound silver mace.

The Patiala Bout

Nearly two decades after the original bout between Gama and Zbyszko in London, a rematch between the two was arranged on January 28, 1928, by the maharaja of Patiala as part of an industrial and agricultural exhibition at Patiala. A special stadium was constructed to accommodate the spectators. Ranji, who arrived by a special train, opened the exhibition. A day before the Gama– Zbyszko bout, another Patiala wrestler and Gama's brother, Imam Bux, fought Goonga. In the audience, which was estimated at 10,000, were several Indian princes, including Ranji, the nawab of Bhopal, and senior British officials like Harcourt Butler and Leslie Scott.[30] But it was the Gama–Zbyszko fight that "thousands of visitors from all parts of the country" had flocked to watch.[31] Obviously, wrestling bouts were a spectacle that was eagerly devoured by urban and rural spectators.

The bout itself was an anticlimax, with Gama throwing Zbyszko flat on the ground in under a minute. The *Hindustan Times* had banner headlines on the front page of its edition of January 31, 1928, announcing the victory. Detailed reports inside stated that "over a hundred thousand visitors" witnessed the bout. "Gama jumped like a lion and in only 30 seconds threw Zybysko to the ground amid loud and continuous cheers. Gama sat over Zybysko for half a minute and the referee declared Gama victorious and winner of the World Championship."[32] The maharaja of Patiala rewarded Gama with a mace of gold and silver. According to another newspaper, Zbyszko was "deeply dejected" after the humiliating loss and declared that Gama was a "tiger and sportsman."[33] The quick end to the bout caught everyone by surprise, including the organizers, who had installed electric lamps and a searchlight in case the bout lasted for two hours, in a repeat of the 1910 bout between the two wrestlers in London. To make up for the thoroughly one-sided contest, Gama and Imam Bux gave a display of "wrestling feats" for the assembled dignitaries and the large crowd.[34]

According to one observer, nationalist feelings ran high—remember that this was 1928 and Gandhi already had organized his successful Non-Cooperation Movement against the British—and the crowd shouted, "India

Gama and Zbyszko before their bout in Patiala, 1928. The bout ended in Gama's victory in less than a minute. Courtesy of H. J. Lutcher Stark Center for Physical Culture and Sports, University of Texas at Austin

has won!"[35] Since Zbyszko was not British, explicit nationalist sentiments did not find expression in the contemporary news reports of the time. But such was Gama's fame at the time that there is a story that Mahatma Gandhi, in jest, challenged him to a bout. Gama replied with a ready wit that one wouldn't associate with an illiterate wrestler: "How could I possibly hope to win against you who have flipped an empire on its back?"[36]

Gama's renown also periodically attracted wrestlers to India who were willing to travel a long way to challenge him in the wrestling ring. The same year as the Patiala bout, Jess Peterson, who claimed to be the champion of all the champions of the world of wrestling, challenged Gama through a letter to the editor in the *Times of India*. The Paris-based Peterson claimed to have defeated Zbyszko three times and appealed to the maharaja of Patiala to arrange a bout. He concluded his letter by requesting the maharaja "to be so kind as to interest himself in this meeting," since it was sure to be "great sporting attraction."[37] When the fight did take place in early 1929 in Patiala before a crowd of 10,000, which included royalty from Patiala, Kashmir, and Jind, Gama won easily. After the victory, the crowd chanted not only "Victory to Gama" but also "Victory to India" and "Victory to the East." Peterson, despite losing, went home richer by £1,500.[38]

Such challenges continued to come Gama's way. In 1936, when India won its third hockey gold in Berlin, a Romanian wrestler, George Lonesco, was camping in Lahore giving demonstrations of feats of strength at the Regal Theatre, in the hope of fighting Gama. Lonesco claimed to have received a letter from Patiala in response to a telegram that the terms for meeting Gama was Rs 100,000 and less for the other wrestlers such as Imam Baksh. A news report said that the six foot-plus Lonesco was an Olympic champion who had beaten thirty-three famous wrestlers from different countries.[39]

That there was money to be made in wrestling is evident from a news item in 1937 reported that no fewer than twenty-five leading wrestlers, the majority of whom were heavyweights, were visiting India, calling it the "biggest invasion of India by European wrestlers."[40] They were to challenge India's best in a series of bouts culminating in an all-India championship in Bombay. The prize money announced was Rs 10,000 and a gold cup for the winner, Rs 5000 for the runner-up, and Rs 2,500 for the third place.

Gama apparently kept wrestling till the early 1940s and, even at the age of fifty, was still doing six thousand knee bends every day.[41] At the age of sixty-five, he was issuing challenges to "all comers" and lamenting the deterioration in the standards of wrestling.[42] Again, we must assume some exaggeration. When in 1939 the famous sports writer A. F. S. "Bobby" Talyarkhan interviewed Gama, the latter insisted he was fifty-three years old and ready to defend his world wrestling title. Talyarkhan, however, felt Gama looked like he was on the wrong side of sixty and more like a "kindly and elderly Muslim gentleman."[43] Later, in a tribute to Gama after he died, Talyarkhan criticized him for not agreeing to fight challengers unless they first defeated his juniors and disciples.[44] In 1947, when the subcontinent was partitioned, Gama and his brother left for Karachi and later settled in Lahore in Pakistan, living in obscurity, only to flicker briefly in the public consciousness at the time of his death at age eighty. The man who had once been the emblem of India's physical prowess died in penury in 1960 and lived in a "tumbledown riverside hut" near Lahore before he was moved to hospital.[45]

Gobor Guha and Middle-Class Wrestlers

While there were others, like Goonga and Imam Bux (Gama's brother), with a background similar to Gama's, who made a name for themselves in the world of wrestling, yet another strand had little to do with the traditional story of peasant boys taking up wrestling and finding a place in a princely court if they were good enough. In the late nineteenth and early twentieth century, wrestling and bodybuilding had become an important part of the nation-building exercise and an answer to the repeated British insult to certain communities in India, particularly the Bengalis, as being physically inadequate. This wasn't peculiar to India. In early nineteenth-century Germany, for example, *Turnen*, or gymnastics, was an important part of nationalism and resistance.[46] In the first half of the twentieth century, Mao Zedong was exhorting the Chinese to improve their physical condition. In an earlier chapter in this book, we discussed the physical regeneration movement in Bengal at the turn of the twentieth century and how wrestling, gymnastics, and bodybuilding was an integral part of it. The popularity of wrestling among the upper classes is evident from the fact that as a child, the great Bengali writer, Rabindranath Tagore, began his day with wrestling. He wrote in his memoirs about his childhood routine:

> What we were taught at home was much more than the school syllabus. I had to rise before sunrise to wear a wrestling costume and wrestle with a professional. Then I put on my body smeared with earth (from the wrestling arena) a dress and took lessons in Physics, Geometry, Arithmetic, History and Geography.[47]

The Tagore family was not unusual in this regard. Indeed, many of the elite families of Calcutta employed *pehelwans* to teach wrestling to youngsters. These families sponsored wrestling matches, too. The *Englishman* newspaper in 1851 carried the following account of a contest between a Muslim and a Hindu wrestler held in Calcutta before a large crowd:

> On Sunday ... a display of wrestling took place at the Seven Tanks, the country-house of Prankissen Mullick and his brothers, being one of a series of similar exhibitions got up by these Baboos, wherein professed wrestlers competed for prizes. The crowd of natives outside the barrier, and on the walls and trees, was tremendous; and there were, perhaps, 500 persons of the better sort within the barriers, including some European gentlemen of the civil, military, mercantile and legal profession.[48]

Among the many wrestlers in Bengal from that era, the name of Jatindracharan (or "Gobor," as he was better known, which in Bengali literally means cow dung) Guha stands out. That Bengalis weren't expected to excel in physical activities is well illustrated by the comment, perhaps apocryphal, made by Indians in San Francisco after Gobor won a famous bout: "You are a Bengali? Never!"[49]

Unlike Gama, Gobor was born into a wealthy family in Dorjipara in north Calcutta. But like Gama, Gobor's family was full of wrestlers, the most notable being Ambikacharan Guha (Ambubabu) and Kheshtracharan Guha (Khetubabu), who had several famous disciples, including Swami Vivekananda. Gobor's father, Ram Charan Guha, was Khetubabu's brother, and it was Khetubabu who introduced Gobor to wrestling at the age of thirteen. Among the training staff for Gobor were wrestlers from outside Bengal, such as Rahman and Gurta Singh.[50] But the young Gobor wasn't being trained only in wrestling; at the same time, he also was being introduced to Hindustani classical music under the tutelage of the maestro Kukubh Khan.[51] While this combination might seem somewhat odd, in reality there is a remarkable similarity between the practice of wrestling and Indian classical music, in which skills are handed down from a guru to a disciple. Much later, the writer Hemendrakumar Ray recalled spending hours in Gobor's living room listening to some of the finest Hindustani classical musical artists, like Ustad Zamiruddin Khan and Ustad Karamatullah Khan.[52]

We don't know how good a musician Gobor was, but even as a teenager, he had developed into an exceptional wrestler. He fought his first professional bout in 1910, when he was only eighteen, against Nowrang Singh, a Punjabi wrestler patronized by the maharaja of Tripura.[53] Gobor made his first trip to Europe that year, the same year that Gama was wrestling his way to glory in London. According to one account, written by a contemporary of Gobor, he was part of Gama's team.[54] He returned to Europe in 1913 and, by his own account, fought and defeated several of the leading lights of European wrestling, such as Jimmy Campbell and Jimmy Essen. Several stories are told about Gobor. One is that he met the first black heavyweight boxing champion, Jack Johnson, in Paris during his trip to Europe. Johnson apparently asked Gobor to hit him on his neck, which Gobor proceeded to do so several times in the middle of the ring. But Johnson withstood all the blows directed him at him.[55] Such mixed fights were not unusual at the time. A news item in the *New York Times* from 1913 reports that Johnson had vowed to wrestle "any man in the world."[56] Gobor went back to Europe in 1920, along with a disciple, Banamali Ghosh, and fought several bouts there.

The next year he went to the United States for bouts in both the big cities and the smaller ones in middle America. Gobor's entry into America was not easy, however. A New York newspaper, the *Evening World*, carried a small news item entitled: "Hindoo Wrestler Grapples [with] Immigration Authorities." It said that "Gobar Goho," who claimed to be "champion wrestler of the British Empire," and his trainer "Banoman Ghosh," had arrived at Ellis Island aboard the *Adriatic* with only $5 between them.[57] They were trying their best to convince the immigration authorities to exempt them from the laws excluding Asians on the grounds that they were entertainers. This was a time when wrestling was going through a renaissance in the United States. Another New York newspaper reported that professional wrestling, "which suffered a knockout blow because of the sins of unscrupulous promoters and performers many years ago, appears to have come back almost to its pristine glory of popularity."[58]

Gobor eventually made it past immigration and fought his first bout against Tommy Draak in Brooklyn on January 31, 1921.[59] The *New York Tribune* reported that the "gold eating prince" (a reference to Gobor's professed habit of eating gold leaf) lost his first match on American soil to Draak at Prospect Hall in Brooklyn in eighteen minutes.[60] Another newspaper confirmed that Draak defeated the "Indian prince from Calcutta" in eighteen minutes and fifteen seconds.[61] But Bengali chroniclers noted that later that year, Gobor avenged his defeat to Draak, though there is no mention of this revenge bout in the American newspapers.

Gobor Guha's fame in India rests on his victory over Ad Santel, who was described by American newspapers of the time as the light heavyweight champion of the world and who had made a name for himself by defeating several champion *judokas*, or practitioners of judo, in the San Francisco Coliseum on August 30, 1921. The *San Francisco Chronicle* described Gobor as a "Hindu giant" with a "speaking acquaintance with English, the American habit of chewing gum, that he's picked up in the States, and plenty of tonnage." The newspaper's correspondent wrote that little was known about Gobor's skills, and he put his money on Santel.[62] But the reporter was in for a shock as Gobor, "chewing gum and all," proved too big and strong for Santel and won the bout in one hour and three minutes with a crotch hold.[63] This fight has become part of folklore, and seventy-five years later the government of India released a stamp to commemorate the platinum jubilee of the "world wrestling championship" between Gobor and Santel. What is no longer remembered is the rematch two weeks later in San Francisco, at which Santel took his revenge by defeating Gobor in an action-packed fight in seventeen minutes, and the *Chronicle* declared that it was now "fifty-fifty" as far as Santel and the "Hindu" were concerned.[64]

After his San Francisco bouts, Gobor traveled across the United States. An account of his fights in the United States, published in the periodical *Servant of India*[65] and in which Gobor wins a majority of his bouts, is, however, at odds with reports from American newspapers. The *Morning Tulsa Daily World* reported that Gobor has been picked to fight the world heavyweight champion Ed "Strangler" Lewis on April 6, 1922, at the local convention hall.[66] Tickets to the bout were priced between $2 and $3, and an ad in the newspaper called him "Jatrinda Goho-Gobar," described as a "giant Hindoo" who "claims to be the heavyweight champion of his native land."[67] The newspaper wrote that he was six feet two inches tall, weighed 240 pounds, and became a sensation when he "threw more than two hundred men in a tournament in his native city." This was not the first time that Gobor had met Lewis in the ring. The newspaper reported that on October 8, 1921, Lewis had won in a questionable manner against Gobor in Kansas City. It quoted a Wichita paper asserting that "Lewis fouled the Indian." Apparently, Lewis caught Gobor unaware with a flying headlock when the latter was about to register a protest with the referee.[68] Later that year, Gobor suffered another defeat to Joe Stecher, a former heavyweight champion, in Kansas City.[69] Lewis also continued to get the better of Gobar. In early 1922, the *New York Times* carried a report, datelined Fort Wayne (Indiana), that Lewis defeated "Jatindra Gobar, of India, in straight falls ... winning the first in twenty three minutes and the second in one minute."[70]

The Tulsa fight received a lot of publicity, not least because of the rarity of an Indian, let alone a wrestler, in Oklahoma. Three days earlier, the local newspaper carried a report on Gobor, saying that his massive girth had made quite an impression on locals. Gobor, wearing a "picturesque Hindu headdress," was taken around the city and introduced to baseball fans before a game. But what was played up were his exotic habit of "eating gold" and his hands, which were small compared with his huge frame. Gobor was quoted as saying, "Gold gives you stamina. I eat six or seven leaves every day and on the day of the match I eat fifteen or twenty." The newspaper was also impressed by Gobor's personality, calling him a "well educated young fellow of pleasing personality." It also found him "highly intelligent" and able to carry on a conversation on any subject. One of the newspaper reports gushed that Gobor "seems to have the temperament of a bushy Newfoundland pup, the strength of an unusually mild mannered elephant, the manners of an Oriental nabob and the general line of intellect of George Bernard Shaw."[71]

That Gobor also had a sense of humor is apparent from his response to a question about whether his small hands were a handicap. "Well, I seem to have got along very well. You see I've never had any different—so I can't know how it would be. Of course I'd like to have big hands like Stecher—or Lewis." The bout itself was a bit of an anticlimax. Before a big crowd, Lewis used his "wicked headlock" to good effect, felling Gobor in twenty-nine minutes in the first round and less than seven minutes in the second.[72] Gobor's fortunes did not improve thereafter, losing to Alan Eustice, the heavyweight champion of Kansas, in Topeka the next week[73] and yet again to Lewis in May that year.[74]

Outside the ring, Gobor had firm political opinions. At a lecture in London in 1926 on India given by Charles Sissons of the University of London,

Gobor, who was in the audience, disagreed with the speaker's arguments. He later wrote a letter to the *Standard Examiner*:

England had never kept her promise in India, since the proclamation of the late Queen Victoria, right after what is known as the Sepoy Mutiny of 1857.... India gave many men and vast sums of money ... and what did she get? As soon as peace was declared, came the Rowlatt Act, and later, a massacre of innocent men, women and children by General Dyer in Jallianwalla Bagh in Punjab.... One question I asked the learned doctor was: "How much money was drained from India since the British advent." He said he did not know.[75]

Guha's Last Bout

Back from his American adventure, Gobor squared off against Chota (junior) Gama, who is described as the son of Kaloo Pehelwan and a disciple of the original Gama (elsewhere Kaloo Pehelwan himself is described as Chota Gama),[76] in a famous bout on January 20, 1929, organized as part of the Calcutta Congress Exhibition. The month-long event included all sorts of physical displays, like *lathi* and sword play, besides ticketed events such as boxing bouts and freak shows that included a three-year-old "Boy Hercules" lifting heavy weights with his teeth and a sixteen-year-old girl with two heads. Professor Ramamurti Naidu, a man of astonishing strength who ran a circus, was also present displaying his "wonderful physical feats along with European, Chinese, Japanese and Indian performers."[77] But the star attraction undoubtedly was the bout between Gobor and Gama, which was billed as a "gigantic demonstration of physical strength" and a "colossal sporting event of the day unheard and unseen in India."[78] The tickets were priced between Rs 1 and Rs 25, no mean sum of money in those days.

The ticket prices did not prevent a huge crowd from turning up at the Park Circus Maidan well before the wrestling bouts began at 2 P.M. After the bouts between other wrestlers were over, the big fight between Gobor and Gama was announced, little after 4 P.M. The two wrestlers presented a striking contrast, with Gama looking "splendidly knitted all over with big strong muscles," while Gobor was "somewhat flabby and had not much to show by way of bulging muscles."[79] In the first minute, Gama pushed Gobor against the ropes and sent him crashing to the ground. The judges separated the two and asked them to move to the center of the ring. But once again Gama pushed Gobor to the ropes and held him in a tight embrace. One of the judges walked into the ring and declared the tactics unacceptable, but in the meantime Gama had Gobor on his back. Immediately Gama leaped into the air and declared victory in "an ecstasy of delight" while Gobor walked out of the ring with "an ill-concealed look of disgust." One of the judges, the nawab of Murshidabad, asked the two wrestlers to enter the ring once again, but Gobor refused to do so. Not surprisingly, a popular Bengali daily, the *Ananda Bazar Patrika*, declared that Gama had won unfairly.[80]

In a statement to the press, the two judges, the nawab of Murshidabad and Surya Kanta Banerjee, explained what had happened. They said that despite having told Gama that he had not won the bout, he began shouting that he was the winner. This was the judges' version of the event:

> The gong which is usually rung was not gone and we two had a consultation and held that it was not a win for Gama. Both of us requested Gobor Babu to come back to the ring and start wrestling again. But he refused to continue the wrestling: we decided thereupon according to the rules of wrestling to declare Gama the winner.[81]

The controversy did not end there. Gobor decided to quit wrestling that day, but the feeling of being cheated never left him or his followers. In a slim booklet to mark the 111th anniversary of the great wrestler's birthday, a disciple wrote that Gobor used to claim that he was never defeated in wrestling except by unfair means. In the same essay, the writer noted that Gobor's defeat by Gama rankled him for several years after the bout. In the 1950s when the Congress Party invited Gobor to a function to honor eminent sportspersons, he refused to attend, saying that he had been treated like a "villain" in 1929.[82] When Gobor formally retired in 1944, he had built up a following, according to one estimate, of more than five thousand disciples. The *akhara* that he had established continues to exist in a narrow lane in north Calcutta. When I visited it a few times in 2012, the mud pit in the *akhara* had a forlorn look, and more activity could be found in a gymnasium on the premises. Gobor's followers have, however, preserved his bed, exercise equipment, and newspaper reports of his fights in a small room meant to be a memorial to the great wrestler.

Other wrestlers from Calcutta built up a formidable reputation around the same time that Gobor was traveling around the world. Bhabani Charan Saha, or Bhim Bhabani, was not only a contemporary of Gobor, having been born two years earlier, in 1890, but he was also trained in the *akhara* of Khetubabu from Gobor's family. But like many strongmen of the time, he was lured away. At the age of nineteen, he secretly left home and joined Ramamurti Naidu's circus. Naidu himself was one of the most famous strongmen of his time.[83] As part of Naidu's troupe, Bhabani toured Southeast Asia. Legend has it that he could pull three cars, support two elephants on his chest, and even pull vehicles with his teeth. In the wrestling ring, he defeated an American in Shanghai and won a small fortune of $1,000. Later he left Naidu's troupe and joined another famous circus run by Krishnalal Basak of Calcutta. Eventually he formed his own circus troupe, but his career was cut short when he died at the age of thirty-two.[84]

There was an explosion of circuses in Bengal, with Krishnalal Basak's Hippodrome Circus and Priyanath Basu's Great Bengal Circus being two of the more famous ones. They provided an avenue for young men, mostly from a poor background, to display their strength and make a decent living. These circuses not only offered entertainment but also gave vent to nationalist feelings. Basu regularly sang the nationalist hymn, "Vande Mataram," during performances and even composed a nationalist song himself. Similarly, Naidu gave a lecture and demonstration in 1909 in Calcutta supporting the movement to boycott government schools.

An introduction to a manual on wrestling that Gobor Guha wrote in 1934 described wrestling now as having changed from that of the past, when it was seen by educated people as "thuggery" (*goondami*) or a "rampage among buffaloes." Now, he explained, it does not occur to the youth that "if they wrestle in a loincloth they will be mistaken for *durwans* (watchmen)."[85] But despite what Gobor might have felt, there was more than a whiff of disrepute attached to boys belonging to landed families who took up wrestling as a profession instead of merely regarding it as a means of physical improvement. As Rosselli pointed out, "There seems to have been a tension throughout the history of the physical culture movement between the ideal of the gentleman amateur and the temptation of professionalism."[86] Thus, a Bengali strongman, Amarnath Roy, also known as Barsati Babu, did not take up an offer to join the court of the maharaja of Cooch Behar as a wrestler because of family pressure. Instead, he gave up wrestling and became a surveyor for the government, only to die in his mid-thirties.[87]

Boxing in Bengal

I must briefly mention here India's experience with another contact sport, boxing. This sport, as we saw earlier, was very popular in British regiments. The first record of an Indian fighting professionally, however, was when Baboo P. N. Mitter, trained by a British boxer, George Smith, took on a series of British servicemen at John Wilson's Great World Circus in 1888 in Calcutta. The prize for the challengers was the princely sum of Rs 10 if they could give "three clear taps with the gloves on the face in the space of three minutes."[88] Mitter bested his opponents quite easily. As *The Englishman* reported:

> The Bengalee gentleman who appeared was much too good for his opponents, and has a fair idea of the noble art. He is a fine specimen of a man, over six feet in height, and weight, we should say, upwards of fourteen stones [196 pounds], and he certainly would be able to astonish many Europeans with whom he might come in contact.[89]

After this fight, we do not hear of any public fight involving Indians until 1903 when two Indian boxers, M. N. Mitra and L. C. Sanyal, took part in a "native" boxing championship organized in Calcutta by a retired American lightweight champion, Jack McAuliffe, who had set up shop in Calcutta. From 1907 the Minto Fete, which was organized by the British army and attracted boxers from all over India, became an annual fixture. But Indians weren't part of the tournament; other foreign boxers practiced their trade in India. One was Albert Fleming, who established the All-Allies Boxing Tournament in 1919 and, more important, took boxing to some of the prominent Bombay and Calcutta schools. One of the star boxers of the All-Allied tournament was Calcutta's Kid D'Silva. He went to Bombay, the other center for boxing in India, to fight the local star, Milton Kubes. D'Silva lost the bout as well as a rematch in Calcutta. He later went to fight in Australia in the 1930s, where the media christened him the "Hindoo wizard of Sock."[90]

It was a Bengali boxer, Paresh Lal Roy, who could claim to be the father of Indian boxing. Like Gobor, he made a name for himself abroad, but unlike the wrestler, Roy went to England to study. Born into a rich landowning family, Roy was sent by his barrister father to be educated in England. He studied at St. Paul's School and later at Cambridge University. Roy's initial training in boxing was from Jim Driscoll of Cambridge. Roy was a quick learner, and in 1912 he won the featherweight title at the Public School Championship in Aldershot. In Cambridge, Roy won a boxing Blue by representing his university in the bantamweight category against Oxford. His first appearance in a boxing bout at the famous Empire Theatre in Calcutta was a dramatic one, according to Clary Miller, who wrote the first history of boxing in India:

It was at the Empire, that a dapper Bengali was persuaded at the bar to gulp down his scotch and soda and substitute for a boxer who had failed to turn up. Ringsiders watched as dress bow, stiff shirt and dress suit were peeled off, and into the ring stepped a man with black silk socks and patent leather shoes. . . . Mr. Brown displayed a stiff and starchy left—typical of the old English school—a few left jabs, followed by a crisp right, and it was all over. Mr. Brown left the ring as dramatically as he had come.[91]

Two years later, in 1924, Roy fought another famous bout, this time against the flyweight and bantamweight champion of India, Edgar Brighte, an Anglo-Indian from Bombay. Roy was apparently the superior boxer and, in the sixth round, sent Brighte crashing through the ropes. Even *The Englishman* newspaper noted that Roy had "all but defeated Brighte and put him through the ropes, which in itself is an achievement hitherto unaccomplished by the many fighters Brighte has met."[92] But in the final verdict Brighte was declared the winner. This was Roy's final fight, and after retiring he joined the Indian Railways.

The first Inter-Railway Boxing Championship was held at the Grand Opera House in Calcutta in 1928. Besides the railways, the YMCA and the police were doing their bit to encourage the sport. Roy formed the Bengal Amateur Boxing Federation in 1930, and under his tutelage, several Bengalis took up boxing. Among them was Santosh Dey, who, along with Roy, formed the Bengalee Boxing Association in 1941. Dey ran as many as thirty-six training centers in Bengal, and his trainees were good enough to defeat the Royal Air

Force boxers in 1944 and a U.S. Army team the next year. Unlike wrestling, however, princely patronage for boxing was rare. An exception was the backing by the sports-loving maharaja of Cooch Behar of local boxers, including Rabin Bhatta, a qualified medical doctor, who represented India in the 1948 Olympics.[93]

The Place of Wrestling

Even though boxing gained popularity in some urban centers, it was wrestling that occupied a special place in preindependent India. Unlike the various sports introduced to India by the British—and polo, which was adopted by the British and played by the Indian elites—professional wrestling was very much a preserve of rural and often illiterate Indians. Bengal was a notable exception, where the cult of bodybuilding and wrestling coalesced with militant nationalism and attracted several middle-class youths. The more famous wrestlers like Gama or Gobor, who were seen as symbols of Indian masculinity and national pride, were made out to be figures larger than life. Their astonishing physical regimen, their fantastic diet, and their invincibility in the wrestling ring all were part of the construction of supermen. Exaggeration or the "scope of excess,"[94] as Alter puts it, was an essential part of this construction. Indeed, it was perilous for normal men to emulate a wrestler's diet. When posted as a soldier in India between 1842 and 1849, the famous British explorer and polyglot Sir Richard Burton (who also translated the *Kama Sutra*) tried following the diet of an Indian wrestler, with disastrous consequences. Apparently he was "so disturbed by bile as to be quite incapable for a period."[95] At the same time, much more than other sportspersons, wrestlers were positioned outside the matrix of modernity embodying both moral and physical strength.[96] Hence, they were appropriated for the nationalist project but also represented a link to the premodern age.

There was, however, a dichotomy, particularly in the late colonial era, between the perceptions of Indian wrestlers and their admirers and those of the outside world. This had something to do with the changes in global wrestling, in which the unregulated world championships used as yardsticks for excellence were gradually replaced by the Olympic events in freestyle and Greco-Roman wrestling. Alter writes that after the 1940s, these changes turned Gama into a "somewhat ambiguous, anachronistic, colonized person;

a person with great fame, to be sure, but a hero whose ethnicity, along with his class, national and global status, had become increasingly problematic."[97] This was somewhat evident in Talyarkhan's encounter with Gama in 1939, about which he wrote after the wrestler's death in 1960: Gama had "the far-away look in his eyes which told more of a man wrestling with the problems of life than wrestling with his fellow mortals in deadly combat."[98] The class dimension of professional wrestling, which was largely a lower-class sport, was the other source of tension. This was best expressed by Gobor Guha's anguish when he wrote in the 1930s about how wrestlers were once mistaken as thugs (*goondas*). These tensions have persisted in independent India, where wrestling has remained for the most part a lower-class, provincial sport that occasionally attracts the public's attention with success in international competitions.

9

FREEDOM GAMES

THE FIRST TWO DECADES

OF INDEPENDENCE

THE YEAR 1948 WAS A LANDMARK FOR SEVERAL REASONS. NOT only were the Olympic Games being held after a gap of twelve years because of World War II, but also several newly minted nations, including India, Pakistan, and Ceylon (in 1972 it became Sri Lanka), took part in international events for the first time. For India, of course, this was its first Olympic Games as an independent nation, having won its freedom just under a year earlier. When the eighty-strong Indian contingent, including sports officials, dressed in their now-trademark turbans, marched in the opening ceremony, they for the first time were carrying the Indian tricolor.

But undercurrents of tension revealed the prickly relationship between the former colony and its imperial master. Reporting on the inaugural ceremony, a London newspaper wrote that during the march, the Indian flag-bearer did not dip his flag in salute to the king. This was hotly disputed by the Indian manager, G. D. Sondhi, who said that the standard bearer had to be changed at the last minute and was under the belief that "eyes right" was sufficient when marching in front of the king and hence did not lower his flag.[1] An even greater irritant to the Indians was the change in accommodation for the Indian contingent, from the Richmond Park Olympic Village to an empty school in London's northwestern suburbs, where they had only the Burmese for company. But even though the Indians were unhappy, Sondhi stated on his arrival in London that he was pleased that the move was not due to a "colour bar."[2]

Nonetheless, it was apparent that feathers had been ruffled by reports of other countries, as well, expressing their disappointment with the transfer from Richmond Park to the London suburbs. The chief of the Iranian team said that they were disappointed, and the Pakistanis observed somewhat more diplomatically, "We did not like the move but we obey orders."[3] The controversy burst into the open when the manger of the Indian swimming squad complained that his team had been "badly upset" by the cramped accommodations and training difficulties in the new quarters.[4]

The Indian contingent had few expectations, although the hockey team, which had won the Olympic gold three times in a row before World War II, was expected to do so once again. This despite the observation by A. F. S. "Bobby" Talyarkhan, who, after watching the national championship in 1944, commented that "Indian [field] hockey is definitely on the decline."[5] The 1948 team was completely different from the one that had won in Berlin in 1936, with all the greats from the prewar era, including Dhyan Chand, having long retired. The team was led by Kishen Lal, with the brilliant K. D. Singh Babu as vice-captain, and it had as many as eight players from Bombay and five from Bengal. The number of Anglo-Indians had dropped dramatically, with only three members—all from Bengal—from the community in the twenty-man squad. By the 1956 games, Leslie Claudius was the only Anglo-Indian on the team.

As for the earlier Olympics, we are fortunate to have the memoir of a member of the Indian hockey team—Balbir Singh (senior), who made his debut in London and played for India in the next two Olympic Games too.[6] Even though his account of the London Games is, at best, sketchy, his memoirs offer an insight into the significance of an independent India taking part in the Olympics as well as a peek into the intense sports relations between the two newly created nations of India and Pakistan, especially in hockey and cricket. This was particularly evident for someone like Balbir, who used to play for the pre-Partition, undivided Punjab team, on which many of the Pakistani players had played earlier. He was acutely aware of the changed situation:

The Indian and Pakistani teams were billeted at different places. We first met at Wembley Stadium during the ceremonial opening of the games. Niaz Khan, A. I. S. Dara, Shah Rukh, Mehmood and Aziz saw us, but I was surprised to see that our old friends were deliberately keeping a distance from us. The openness of old was gone.[7]

Dara was the captain of the undivided Punjab team that had won the Indian nationals in 1947 and had played for India in the 1936 Olympics as a young man; Shah Rukh, Mehmood, and Aziz all were friends of Balbir from his Lahore days.

India faced the possibility of two encounters—one against Pakistan and the other against Britain—both of which would be a first for the newly independent nation, with plenty of emotional baggage. Pakistan and Great Britain were in a different group, and India was expected to meet one or the other in the final. In the first two games, India won by big margins against Austria and Argentina. The final group game against Spain was tougher, but India still won. There already were predictions of an India–Pakistan final, with a newspaper correspondent writing that the Pakistanis and Indians "were the two outstanding teams in the event not only because of their high-scoring and comfortable victories, but because of their brilliant individual play."[8] But it was not to be. Although India overcame the Netherlands in the semifinal, Great Britain beat Pakistan handily in the other semifinal.

The stage was now set for India to meet its former imperial master. Oddly enough, although Britain had won the hockey titles in 1908 and 1920, it had not entered a team since India started playing in 1928. Some believe that it was fear of losing to India that might have prompted Britain to keep away from Olympic hockey, though we have no evidence of this. So this was the first time that India was to meet Britain on the hockey field. Unlike in earlier Olympics, some had doubts about India's ability to win a fourth successive gold. The Europeans had improved their game, and the Indians weren't accustomed to playing on heavy, wet turf. Against Spain, India "found their stick-work lacked the certainty it had on the dry turf in earlier games."[9] Against the Netherlands, it was felt that "a draw would have been a fairest index to the game."[10] Not surprisingly, before the finals the Indians opted to scrap their practice in order to focus on the "tactics to be used against the heavier British side."[11] The *Times of India*'s Alex Valentine predicted, "The

Indians want hot sunshine for the next two days; the British want rain, or at least no heat."[12]

When the final was held at Wembley Stadium before some 10,000 spectators on August 12—just three days before India's independence day—neither the persistently wet weather nor a ground made muddier by the play-off for third place before the final (which was protested by the Indian officials) could stop the Indian team. As a correspondent reported, despite "the heavy, muddy turf and the light rain," the Indians "outclassed the British team with their superb ball control, accurate passing and intelligent positional play."[13] Balbir, who scored twice in the final, recalled that both Kishan Lal and Babu played barefoot on the slippery surface, with the Indians winning handily, 4-0. In the crowd was the staunch anti-imperialist and close ally of Nehru, V. K. Krishna Menon, independent India's first high commissioner to Britain, to whom the Indian victory must have seemed especially sweet. He was among those who ran onto the field to congratulate the Indian team, and later he hosted an official reception for the team at India House.[14]

Unlike their Olympic victories before 1947, when the Indian team returned home after a brief tour of Europe, they were given a rapturous welcome in Bombay. Later the victorious team played an exhibition match at Delhi's National Stadium before a crowd of 70,000 that included Nehru and India's future president, Rajendra Prasad. After the match, Nehru is said to have remarked that the crowd was so large that he could not see the "match at all." The crowd had its fill of the Olympic heroes, celebrating what was "free India's first major achievement in the world of sports."[15]

This also was the first time that India played football in the Olympics, the first real test for India on the world football stage, despite initial fears that not enough money to send the team would be raised. This wasn't, however, the first time that Indian football players had played outside India. An Indian team had toured South Africa in 1934 to play against teams formed by Indians settled in South Africa. In 1936, an Indian team played the Chinese Olympic team in what was the "first soccer international to be played in India."[16] The match, played before a crowd of 20,000, with another 100,000 spectators outside, ended in a thrilling tie. In 1938, another team selected from the best players in the Bengal clubs, led by Mohun Bagan's Karuna Bhattacharjee and with the irrepressible Pankaj Gupta as manager, toured Australia. The Australian tour was quite a success, and the Indians, particularly those playing

Dhyan Chand (extreme left) with India's first health minister, Rajkumari Amrit Kaur; Governor-General C. Rajagopalachari; India's first defense minister, Baldev Singh; and the 1948 Olympic gold-medal winning hockey captain, Kishen Lal. The occasion was an exhibition match between the Indian Olympic hockey team and a provincial team led by Chand, who by then had retired from international hockey. Reprinted by permission of the Hindu Archives

barefoot, was widely covered by the media. Indeed, the reports had more than a whiff of the Oriental magic associated with Ranji's leg glance or Dhyan Chand's dribbling skills. The headline in a Perth newspaper—"Barefooted Indians Will Show Us Tricky Soccer"—and its report about the Indians' "tremendous speed" and "clever control of the ball" were typical of the coverage.[17] The Indian team played five "Test" matches against Australia and also matches against other state teams. The matches were well attended, with the game in Brisbane, which hosted the second soccer Test, attracting as many as 16,000 spectators and raising £800 as gate money.[18]

In the 1948 London Olympics, the Indian team, the majority of whom still played barefoot, were impressive in the only match they played, at Ilford, some twenty-five miles from London, losing 1–2 to France. The score might have been different if India had not missed two penalties and conceded a goal seconds before the final whistle. The noted sports commentator Berry Sarbadhikari, who was at the match, wrote: "I have never seen before or since the vanquished team given as big a hand as the Indians were that evening at Ilford."[19] Many of the players were from Bengal (both Bengalis and those like

Taj Mohammed, originally from Quetta, and Mahabir Prasad, from Bihar, who played for clubs in Bengal) as well as from Mysore. The imprint of Calcutta football on the team was evident from the fact that the coach for the London Games also was from Bengal—Mohun Bagan's Balaidas Chatterjee. The captain of the 1948 team was Talimeran Ao, a Naga footballer who had played for Mohun Bagan for nearly ten years, beginning in 1943. Ao, who later qualified as a medical doctor from the prestigious R. G. Kar Medical College in Calcutta, proved to be a forerunner, since some of the best footballers in India today hail from northeastern India.[20] Also on the team were the brothers Anil and Sunil Nandy, who belonged to a remarkable football family, all four brothers of which played for India at one time.[21] The budding star of the team was Sailen Manna, who played almost his entire career with Mohun Bagan and went on to captain both India and his club in the 1950s. When he died in 2012 at age eighty-seven, *The Economist* paid a handsome tribute by publishing an obituary, perhaps the only Indian footballer to have had that honor.

Even though Indians had been playing barefoot for decades, this was the first time that the Indian football team played barefoot in an international tournament. For the Indians, playing against booted footballers wasn't unusual; in fact, it contributed to their on-field skills. As a veteran sports commentator pointed out, "There was a certain Indianness about it, which was as unique [as] the rope trick or shall we say Ranji's leg glance."[22] For the rest of the world, it was an unusual sight, as evident in the reaction in London and the several legends that grew up around the Indian team's exploits. At a reception in Buckingham Palace, when Princess Margaret reportedly asked Manna if he weren't afraid to play barefoot, he replied that it was "easier to keep the ball under control."[23] Another story was that King George VI made Manna roll up his trousers to see whether his legs were made of steel.

Obviously, India's barefoot footballers had made quite an impression, despite getting knocked out in the first round. After the Olympics, the Indian team showed its mettle by beating a Wales team and the famous European club, Ajax Amsterdam, 1–0.[24] Not surprisingly, India received an invitation from the international football federation to play in the 1950 football World Cup in Brazil, the first one in twelve years. Despite doubts about whether India's players would lose their amateur status if they played in the World Cup, practice began in Calcutta under the supervision of their foreign coach, Harry Wright. There was even a suggestion, which was accepted by the organizers, that the Indian team be "picked up" from Cairo and not Calcutta, which would result in a saving of Rs 40,000 for the Indian football federation.[25] But eventually it was decided that India wouldn't participate in the tournament. It was widely believed that India pulled out because the players would have had to play in boots, but the official reason cited by the All-India Football Federation was the lack of funds to travel to Brazil. Thus was lost the only opportunity that India has had until now to take part in the football World Cup.

The rest of the Olympic contingent, which included athletes, boxers, wrestlers, weight lifters, cyclists, and swimmers, had a largely forgettable outing. The notable exception was Henry Rebello, a nineteen-year-old Anglo-Indian from Bangalore who was considered one of the favorites to win a medal in the triple jump. Before the Olympics, at an athletic meet held in Motspur Park, Rebello had placed first. Despite easily qualifying for the final of the Olympics, Rebello had to pull out with a torn hamstring, having failed to warm up adequately on a typical drizzly London afternoon.[26] Another strong performance came from wrestler K. D. Jadhav, who finished sixth in the bantamweight category and was destined for glory in the next Olympic Games.

Although India had resumed its pre–World War II hockey supremacy as an independent nation and caught the attention of the world in football in 1948, its cricket team had not done as well. India's first Test series as an independent nation was against Australia in 1947/1948. It was a sign of the times that the captain of the Indian team was none other than the controversial Lala Amarnath, who was completely different, in both background and temperament, from the Indian captain just before independence, the nawab of Pataudi (senior). The Indian team (with Pankaj Gupta making his third trip to Australia as the manager of three different sports teams) was advertised by the Australian press as a beacon of hope for the newly independent and recently partitioned country. One of the newspapers wrote that the Indian cricketers may "well prove the magic elixir to banish national and inter-racial bitterness."[27] Because of Partition, several talented players had emigrated across the border, the impact best illustrated by the great Pakistani bowler Fazal Mahmood. He was part of the Indian squad to Australia, which was chosen in March 1947, and was training in Pune with the other team members at the time of Partition. On his journey back to his home in Lahore, he was accosted by Hindus on the train. It was only because of the quick action by the former India captain C. K. Nayudu, traveling on the same train, who pulled out his bat and warned the attackers, that Mahmood survived to represent Pakistan in its first-ever Test match against India in 1952.[28]

Besides Hindus, the team to Australia consisted of two Muslims, a Christian, a Sikh, and a Parsi. As Lala Amarnath proclaimed, "We come from all over India, and when we play cricket we look on ourselves as playing for all of India."[29] Nonetheless, the Indian cricket team had a disastrous tour, losing all four Test matches to the Australian "invincibles" led by Don Bradman. *Wisden* reported:

> India cannot have happy memories of their tour in Australia during 1947/1948. Of the 14 first-class matches played, only two brought victories compared with seven defeats. In the Test matches they were outclassed: four were lost; in three Australia batted only once; and such was the superiority of the Australians that except in one instance the result looked a foregone conclusion before the end of the first day.[30]

Among the bright spots of the tour was Vijay Hazare, who struck two memorable centuries in the fourth Test at Adelaide and was described by the Australian writer Jack Fingleton as a "batsman of the top world-class."[31] Hazare, along with the captain, Lala Amarnath, were the only two batsmen to score more than one thousand runs in the fourteen first-class matches on the tour. All-arounders Vinoo Mankad and Dattu Phadkar did well, too. In addition, some legends grew around Don Bradman's first contact with the Indians on the cricket pitch. One of the more amusing ones was of wicketkeeper Probir Sen from Bengal, warning Bradman that he was going to stump him off Mankad's bowling, which he then did. There is, however, no record of Bradman's being stumped by Sen in any of the Test matches, except in a first-class match between India and South Australia. Despite such bright spots, concocted or otherwise, of India's sports performance in 1948 in cricket, hockey, and football, cricket was the least inspiring.

The 1951 Asian Games

Beginning in the 1950s, a newly independent India under the stewardship of Jawaharlal Nehru was looking to play a leadership role in Asia, with the first Asian Games held in New Delhi in 1951 as a symbol of India's assertive new role. There were, of course, earlier attempts to bring together Asian nations to compete against one another. The Far Eastern Championship Games (FECG), which took place from 1913 to 1934 and in which the YMCA played a major role, were sometimes described as the "Oriental Olympic Games." Indeed, the International Olympic Committee believed that the Far East and India were "backward areas" with regard to sports and that events like the FECG would help them make progress.[32] The FECG did not, however, by any means include all Asian countries but was confined to Japan, China, and the Philippines, with India taking part only once, in the 1930 games held in Tokyo.[33] The Western Asiatic Games (WAG) was the West Asian counterpart of the FECG, and here India, under the enterprising G. D. Sondhi, took the initiative. In 1934, Sondhi, who had by then become a member of the International Olympic Committee, with the backing of his patron, the maharaja of Patiala, organized the first and only WAG in Delhi. He wrote to Pierre de Coubertin, the father of the modern Olympic Games, explaining that his "great example in founding the world international brotherhood of sport" was being "imitated on a small scale in the East."[34] Besides India, only three countries—Ceylon, Afghanistan, and Palestine—eventually took part in the event. Delhi's Irwin Amphitheater was the site of the hockey matches and athletics, and the swimming and diving events took place in Patiala. India was the winner in all events except the shot put and the relay race, which Ceylon won. The next WAG were supposed to be held in Palestine in 1938 but were canceled because of the uncertain times leading up to World War II.

The idea of the Asian Games came up even before India's independence, during the Asian Relations Conference in New Delhi's Purana Qila (Old Fort) called by Nehru in March 1947. Sondhi proposed the idea of Asian Games to the assembled representatives from twenty-five Asian countries. The next year he went to London to present his case during the Olympic Games, taking advantage of the presence of thirteen Asian countries, including India. The chief managers of the Asian teams were invited to a meeting at which they enthusiastically supported Sondhi's proposal to hold the Asian Games every four years. Then on February 13, 1949, the Asian Games and the Asian Games Federation were formally established at Patiala House in New Delhi, where representatives of nine countries met with the new chair, the maharaja of Patiala, Yadavendra Singh. They decided to hold the Asian Games every four years, in the even years between the Olympics, beginning in 1950. Delhi was selected as the venue for the first games, with the maharaja of Patiala elected as president and Sondhi as honorary secretary and treasurer.

But the games had to be postponed because of the lack of infrastructure and other problems. Sondhi, who was the director of the organizing committee, resigned in 1950, and Anthony de Mello, president of the Board of Control for Cricket (BCCI), stepped in to salvage the situation.[35] The cost of the games, Rs 600,500, was contributed by the Cricket Club of India and the National Sports Club of India.[36] The Indian army lent two buildings next to the National Stadium to house the athletes and officials, and the games eventually began on March 4, 1951.[37]

Although they were a decided improvement over their predecessors such as WAG, the Asian Games were still modest by current standards. Over eight days, around four hundred athletes from eleven countries took part in six disciplines: swimming, water polo, cycling, weightlifting, football, and basketball. Besides India, the other participants were Afghanistan, Burma, Ceylon, Indonesia, Iran, Japan, Malaya, Philippines, Singapore, and Thailand. However, Pakistan, which had taken part in the 1949 meeting in Patiala House, refused to attend the games, setting in motion a process in which the acrimony between the Indian and Pakistani governments regularly spilled over onto the playing field.

Before the games began, Nehru, addressing the Asian Games Federation, stressed the ties that bound those Asian nations recently freed from the colonial yoke and called for their cooperation.[38] Nehru's message for the assembled athletes echoed de Coubertin's ideals of Olympism. "Athletic contests are good for developing friendly rivalry among the youth of our nations," Nehru explained. "Each one must try his best whether winner or loser, must play his part gracefully and must enter into the spirit of the games."[39] This message was adapted to serve as the games' motto: "Play the game in the spirit of the games." The Asian Games were an important milestone for postcolonial Asia, which was picking up the pieces after the ravages of World War II. An Indian newspaper headlined its report on the opening of the games—"Important Landmark in the Reawakening of Asia"—noting that Japan would be making a bid "to regain her forgotten glory in the sports arena."[40]

The Asian Games generated a good deal of enthusiasm in India, with 40,000 people packing the refurbished Irwin Amphitheater, renamed

National Stadium, for the opening ceremony. Like Nehru's message, other aspects of the Asian Games had been borrowed from the Olympics, like the torch relay carried by forty-four runners, with the honor of the final lap inside the stadium going to one of India's oldest Olympians, Dalip Singh, who was greeted by "wild cheering."[41] In the competition, Japan topped the medal tally with twenty-four golds, but India acquitted itself well, winning fifteen gold medals. The star of the games for India was a Goanese Christian, Lavy Pinto, who won both the 100- and the 200-meter races. India also won the football gold under the captaincy of Sailen Manna, beating Iran in the final, the only goal being scored by Sahu Mewalal, a star of the early years of independent India. In the Mr. Asia contest—which was subsequently scrapped from the Asian Games program—Parimal Roy, a Bengali, won the competition for the best physique in Asia.[42] India's performance confirmed that it was a sporting power to reckon with, at least on the Asian stage. Besides, the successful staging of the Asian Games paved the way for India to hold other international competitions, such as the World Table Tennis Championship held in Bombay in 1952.

The Helsinki Games

In the first decade after Indian independence, two more Olympic Games were held, in Helsinki in 1952 and in Melbourne in 1956. In both games, the Indians won the hockey gold, but used different styles. The buildup to the Helsinki Games was marred by the jockeying of rival state associations to include players from their state. The Uttar Pradesh state association wanted O. P. Malhotra on the team, whereas Bengal wanted C. S. Gurung. One of the bargaining chips was that Bengal was willing to pay Gurung's expenses if he were selected. A newspaper described the "attempts to wangle in players" as depressing and noted that in 1948, the selection of players from Bengal had been allowed because their association was willing to bear the expenses. The final team included Gurung but not Malhotra, who was on the team for the Melbourne Games. These incidents were a precursor of the bitter politics that later held hostage hockey and, indeed, all sports in India.

The Indian hockey team, captained once again by K. D. Singh Babu, had to play only three matches en route to the gold. The final against the Netherlands was expected to be close, but the Indians won in what was a "one-sided final" riding on a Balbir Singh hat trick. Pakistan's hopes of an Olympic medal were dashed once again, and the seriousness with which the event was treated was apparent from a resolution passed in Pakistan that termed the loss as a "setback to national aspiration."[43] As in 1948 the Indians were given a rousing reception when they returned home. The players were mobbed by fans, and when four of the Punjab players, including Balbir, were taken around Jullundur City in an open jeep, they were showered with gifts, baskets of fruit, sweets, and garlands of flowers.

For the first time, too, India won a medal in a sport other than hockey. Although the country's initial medal hopes were pinned on long-distance runner Sohan Singh, it was Khashaba Dadasaheb Jadhav who won a bronze in the bantamweight category in wrestling.[44] Astonishingly, this would be India's only individual medal for more than four decades until Leander Paes won a bronze medal in tennis in 1996. Equally surprising is the neglect of Jadhav's memory by sports fans. His remarkable journey to Olympic glory and his subsequent descent into oblivion nicely capture the story of sports in the early years of independent India. Jadhav, the youngest of Dadasaheb Jadhav's five children, living in Goleshwar Village in Karad Taluka in India's western state of Maharashtra, began wrestling in an *akhara* early in life. Besides wrestling, Jadhav actively took part in weight lifting, running, and swimming. His first trip to the Olympics in 1948 was funded by the maharaja of Kolhapur, a small princely state in Maharashtra, but in 1952, no generous patron was available. Remember that the Indian Olympic Association's financial state was precarious, as the Indian government had reduced its grant-in-aid from Rs 100,000 to Rs 70,000, and the various state governments did not give much priority to sports. Requests for funds from the Bombay (the state of Maharashtra had not yet been created) chief minister, Morarji Desai, were refused. Help for Jadhav came from an unexpected quarter. The principal of Rajaram College, where Jadhav had studied, mortgaged his house to raise funds to send him to Helsinki.[45]

Jadhav did not disappoint his former teacher when he created history by winning a medal. But the reporting of the event—a mere single column in the *Times of India*—and his reception back home in India were nothing compared with the rapturous welcome given to the hockey team. It was left to Jadhav's native village to organize a hero's welcome. A victory procession, complete with 150 bullock carts, was organized from Karad Station to a local temple in

Goleshwar. An eyewitness recalled that such was the throng of well-wishers that the fifteen-minute journey took seven hours to complete.[46] Jadhav received no financial rewards, and in 1955 he joined the state police as a subinspector. For the next twenty-two years he held the same rank, despite several requests to the government for promotion. In a cruel twist of fate, Jadhav was promoted to assistant commissioner in 1982 just six months before his retirement. Two years later, he died in an automobile accident. Honors and money had eluded Jadhav in his lifetime; only in 2001 was he awarded the Arjuna Award posthumously for his lifetime achievement.

For the rest of the Indian participants, the Helsinki Games were not memorable, particularly for the football team, which had impressed everybody at the London Games. But in the bitter cold of Helsinki, the barefoot Indian footballers, led by Manna, literally got cold feet. Playing against the eventual runner-up, Yugoslavia, India allowed ten goals and scored only one, a debacle that prompted the All-India Football Federation to make wearing boots compulsory.

Women in Sports

Helsinki was notable for other reasons. For the first time, Indian women—who were largely absent from the history of sports in preindependent India—participated in the Olympics, with athletes Nilima Ghose and Mary D'Souza being part of the Indian contingent. Except for the Olympics, however, women had only occasionally taken part in international sports. Jenny Sandison, an Anglo-Indian from Kharagpur, played at Wimbledon in 1918 but lost in the first round. The honor of being the first Indian woman to win a match at Wimbledon went to Leela Row, another Anglo-Indian, who won in the first round in 1934.[47] In postindependent India, Rita Davar was the runner-up in the junior women's event at Wimbledon in 1952. Indian women did have some success in the Asian Games. In the 1954 Manila Asiad, the Indian women's relay team won the gold medal, and in the next games in Tokyo in 1958 Stephie D'Souza won a silver medal.[48]

Before 1947, hockey and basketball were the two most popular sports among women in India, even though it was mostly Europeans, Anglo-Indians, and Parsis who played them.[49] As Anthony de Mello pointed out, "The most Westernised communities—the Anglo Indians and the Parsis—were the first in which women came to the forefront in sport."[50] The Women's Hockey Association was formed in 1928 by Lady Kathleen Tegart, wife of Charles Tegart, the infamous police commissioner of Calcutta from 1923 to 1931, who was the target of a failed assassination attempt by Indian revolutionaries. A hockey tournament for women had begun in 1947, and an Indian women's hockey team took part for the first time in an international hockey tournament in 1953 in England.

Around the same time there was a remarkable occurrence in the male-dominated world of professional wrestling. In an inversion of Indian mythological tradition, Hamida Banu, a woman wrestler who was also known as the "Amazon from Aligarh" (Banu's hometown in Uttar Pradesh), challenged male wrestlers to decide who her husband would be. On May 2, 1954, the Associated Press reported that in a bout held in Bombay, Banu, who at five foot three weighed a substantial 230 pounds, defeated Baba Pahelwan in less than two minutes, the third time she had felled a suitor since February of that year. The two other unfortunate claimants for Banu's hand were Kadag Singh and a "Hindu from Calcutta."[51] Banu even announced plans to challenge leading wrestlers from Europe, prompting a reporter to quip that her visit might put a strain on the continent's resources, since her "daily diet consisted of 12 pints of milk, six bowls of soup, four large glasses of fruit juice, a chicken, two pounds of mutton, one pound of butter, six eggs, two pounds of almonds, two loaves of bread and two plates of *biriyani* (rice and mutton)."[52] A *Times of India* columnist rhapsodized, "One look at the mighty Amazon from Aligarh is enough to send the shivers down your spine. She is more than a match for any woman, and the lack of rivals must have driven her to the point of challenging members of the opposite sex."[53]

The victories of Banu over male wrestlers and the "mixed" events did not, however, go down well with the patrons of wrestling. A bout between Banu and a male wrestler, Ramchandra Salunke, could not be held in Pune because of the opposition of the Rashtriya Talim Sangh, the city's controlling body for wrestling.[54] Again during a bout in Kolhapur in Maharasthra, Banu was booed and stoned by wrestling fans after she defeated a male opponent, Somasingh Punjabi. The police had to control the crowds, who labeled the bout a "farce."[55] The blurring of sports and entertainment in these events is illustrated by the fact that Banu's bout was to be followed by a bout between two wrestlers, one lame and the other blind. That matchup was eventually abandoned when the blind wrestler complained of a toothache and gave his opponent the victory.

The controversy over Banu even required the intervention of the Bombay's dour chief minister and future prime minister of India, Morarji Desai. Banu had appealed to Desai regarding the "banning" of her wrestling bouts on, according to her, grounds of her gender. Desai reportedly told her that the bouts had been banned not on gender grounds but because of several complaints about the promoters, who were apparently putting up "dummies" to challenge Banu. We might never know the truth of such allegations, but Banu continued to fight and not always against male wrestlers. She defeated Vera Chistilin, advertised as Russia's "female bear," in under a minute in the Vallabhbhai Patel Stadium (the site of many freestyle wrestling events from the 1950s to the 1980s) in Bombay.[56] A month later she was invited to fight Singapore's woman wrestling champion, Raja Laila.[57] Subsequently, however, she disappeared from the pages of the English press, leaving us hanging about her fate in the male-dominated world of wrestling and her marriage plans.

The Melbourne Games

By the time of the 1956 Olympics Games, India was, for the first time, facing a serious challenge in hockey. The Europeans were rapidly improving, as was Pakistan. In the first three matches in Melbourne, the Indians, led by Balbir Singh, beat Afghanistan, the United States, and Singapore—all relatively weak teams—convincingly. In the semifinal, though, India met its first real opposition in the Olympics: West Germany. India scraped through, however, setting up a final against Pakistan, something that had been in the offing since 1948. Even though the Indian and Pakistani national teams had never played each other, the Punjab Police team had toured Pakistan to play its counterpart, the West Punjab Police, in 1955. The two matches played in Lahore and Montgomery generated great enthusiasm. In Lahore, banners were put up welcoming the "friends from neighbouring India," and according to official estimates, some 60,000 Indians were expected to cross the border to attend the matches.[58] These numbers were early clues to the passions that India–Pakistan contests would generate, as well as proof of the two countries' relatively porous borders and flexible visa regime, which, however, ceased to exist after the 1965 India–Pakistan war.

India's and Pakistan's journeys to the final of the Melbourne Games diverged. India had scored thirty-nine goals in four matches, and Pakistan had scored ten goals and conceded three. In the semifinal, Pakistan had edged past Great Britain in a nail-biting game. But the semifinal match against Germany showed that India was no longer the invincible force that it had been in earlier days. It was unable to play with its "usual smooth combination," and the second half was "marred by rough tackling" and exchanges of "heated words."[59]

The mood in the Indian camp before the big day was best described by Balbir Singh: "I could not sleep that night, and after tossing about restlessly for a while, I went out for a stroll. It was quite late in the night when someone called out my name."[60] Also up at that late hour was Ashwini Kumar, who took Balbir back to his room and gave him a pill to soothe his nerves. Only then could Balbir go to sleep. On the morning of the match, the Indian camp was very jittery, as evident in an incident on the team bus. Just as the bus was about to leave for the stadium, an official sneezed, considered a bad omen by some in India. Ashwini Kumar immediately asked Balbir to get off the bus, go back to his room, lie down for five minutes, and then return. The match itself was a close one, with India winning by a solitary goal scored by R. S. Gentle in the second half. Balbir, who already had two gold medals, admitted that the Melbourne victory was special, since it was against Pakistan. His sentiments are unsurprising, considering Balbir was from Punjab, which had borne the brunt of the Partition violence in 1947.

As usual, however, the rest of the Indian contingent was disappointing. After Jadhav's performance in the 1952 Olympics, high hopes were placed on the wrestlers, whose "prospects were rated next best only to the hockey team."[61] The Indian athletes, including the women, were particularly disappointing, with Mary Leela Rao withdrawing from the 100-meter heat after straining her leg muscles. The American track star Jesse Owens, however, believed that Indian athletes had no reason to despair, saying that he had found a "wealth of potentially outstanding athletes" during a visit to India.[62]

Indian Football's "Golden" Era

Besides the hockey triumph—the sixth consecutive time that India had won the Olympic gold medal—the 1956 games represented the best-ever performance by the Indian football team in a global tournament, although the team's performance needs to be put in perspective. Because several countries pulled out, only eleven took part. Consequently, India got a walkover against Hungary, one of the stronger teams, in the first round. In the second round, India decisively beat the host, Australia, the highlight being a hat trick by center forward Neville D'Souza from Bombay. As one journalist described the triumph, the Indian team that "paid its way to Melbourne today got its money's worth."[63]

But the game wasn't without drama. There was an argument before the game about whether the Indian team could play barefoot, and there was some confusion about whether World Cup football rules applied to the Olympic Games. The secretary of England's Football Association, Sir Stanley Rous, asserted that nothing in the rule book said that a player must wear boots. Eventually, India's players agreed to play wearing boots, on the understanding that if any of them suffered from cramps, he could remove them.[64] The Indians won quite easily, never needing to take off their boots. Only the inside right S. Banerjee got cramps in the closing stages and removed his boots, but that did not make any difference, since he had to leave the field shortly afterward. In the semifinal, India played Yugoslavia, which eventually won the silver medal, before a crowd of 25,000 spectators. After a goalless first half, Yugoslavia won convincingly, 4–1. In the play-off for the bronze medal, India was beaten by Bulgaria. So what was India's best football performance on the world stage involved only one victory in three matches played.

One of the real architects of what was arguably India's "golden era" in football was Syed Abdul Rahim, coach of the Hyderabad Police Club and the Indian team in the 1950s and early 1960s. Many believe that it was his innovative tactics, coupled with strict discipline, that were responsible for India's football triumphs. Besides his team's success in the 1951 Asian Games, India won the Asian Quadrangular Tournament (also known as the Colombo Cup)—involving India, Pakistan, Ceylon, and Burma—four times in succession from 1952 to 1955.[65] It was in the inaugural tournament in Colombo that India first met Pakistan on the football field and played to a goalless draw. Both countries had an equal number of points at the end of the tournament and were declared joint winners. But this wasn't without controversy, as India claimed that it was the rightful winner because it had scored more goals. India's appeal was turned down, so the trophy stayed with India for six months and then traveled to Pakistan for the next six.[66] In the 1960 Olympics, even though India was disqualified in the group stage, under Rahim's stewardship, the team played impressively, losing narrowly to European powerhouse Hungary, which had at least three players who went on to play in 1962 World Cup, tying France and losing to Peru.

The pinnacle of Indian football may have been reached at the 1962 Asian Games in Jakarta, where it won its second gold medal, but against a much stronger field than in 1951. To win the gold, the Indian team, led by Chuni Goswami and with stars like P. K. Banerjee and Jarnail Singh, beat Japan and South Korea, both future Asian football powers. The 1962 Asiad was significant not only for India's football success but also for the peculiar circumstances in which it won the gold. Even before the games began, there was controversy over the participation of Israel and Taiwan, both recognized by the International Olympic Committee (IOC) and the Asian Games Federation (AGF) but not by the games' host, Indonesia. The Indonesians did not allow athletes from Israel and Taiwan to participate, prompting G. D. Sondhi, representing India at the Asian Games Federation Congress being held in Jakarta, to lodge a protest. He even went to the extent of proposing to strip the Jakarta Games of its Asian Games status. A compromise was eventually reached, but many Indonesians saw Sondhi's actions as a direct threat to their country and their president, Sukarno. On September 3, 1962, a mob attacked the Indian embassy as well the hotel where Sondhi was staying, although he had already left and was preparing to fly back to India. That same evening Sukarno declared that the actions by the AGF were a breach of the "Bandung spirit"—a reference to the famous 1955 Bandung Conference that was meant to foster closer ties between postcolonial nations and was attended by both Sukarno and Nehru—and that Indonesia would host the Games of the New Emerging Forces (GANEFO) in 1963.[67] It was in this extraordinary situation that India played in the football finals on September 4 and won against South Korea, 2–1 in a stadium packed with hostile spectators.

One of the goal scorers, the turbaned Jarnail Singh, who later was captain of the Asian All-Stars XI in 1966 and 1967, recalled that on the way to the stadium, he sat on the floor of the team bus to avoid the Indian team's being noticed.[68] Chuni Goswami remembered in his autobiography that the words "Indian team" were erased from the bus that ferried the players from the games village to the stadium on the day of the finals.[69] Describing the situation inside the stadium, an Indian official reported: "A very large section of the crowd of a hundred thousand persistently booed the team. Not satisfied it continued to boo when the victory ceremony to present the Gold medals to our team was performed."[70] As coach, Rahim used the adverse circumstances to India's advantage. Before the game, he made the entire team hold hands and sing the national anthem. He then repeated this routine during halftime to pep up the team in the face of the crowd's relentless hostility.[71]

The Rome, Tokyo, and Mexico Games

The 1960 Olympic Games in Rome were a landmark for Indian hockey, but for the wrong reasons. For the first time since India had begun playing Olympic hockey, it failed to win the gold medal. Some had noticed the warning signs in the 1956 games. Sports administrator Pankaj Gupta, writing in 1958 in *Sport and Pastime*, pointed out,

> India maintained her supremacy in world hockey at Melbourne by a short whisker and this, I say, must make us pause. We can no longer take anything for granted. The standard of world hockey has improved and other nations like Holland, England, Germany and Pakistan have caught up with India in technique as well as in standard.[72]

Gupta proved prophetic. In the Rome Games, in which an unprecedented sixteen teams took part, India trounced Denmark's weak team in its opening group match, but in the next match, India had to fight hard against the Netherlands for a win. In the quarterfinal, India beat Australia by a solitary goal in a match in which a tie would have been a "fairer result."[73] The story in the semifinal was similar, with India winning, 1–0, against Britain.

This set up a final once again against Pakistan. Pakistan, too, had won hard-fought victories against Germany and Spain in the quarterfinal and semifinal, respectively. India had already met Pakistan on the cricket field in two Test series, but an Olympic gold added to the tension that always permeated India–Pakistan sports contests. The final was watched by the "biggest crowd ever" for a hockey match, and it was also televised throughout Western Europe.[74] In an evenly fought match, Pakistan scored the only goal early in the first half and hung on to the lead to win its first gold medal and, indeed, its first Olympic medal. Toward the dying minutes of the match, Pakistan apparently resorted to "time-wasting tactics," which was greeted with jeers by Indian supporters. But this was par for the course for what was an eagerly awaited victory for Pakistan. This was apparent from the message wired from the Pakistani chef-de-mission to the then Pakistani president, Field Marshal Ayub Khan, describing the victory in military terms: "On behalf of hockey team I report successful completion of job."[75] For his part, the Indian chef-de-mission, Ashwini Kumar, desperately tried to hide the nation's disappointment by looking ahead: "The reverse should not dampen or demoralise us but we should gird up our loins for the next encounter."[76]

Nineteen sixty was a heartbreak year for the Indian hockey team, but even more grief was in store for the country. For the first time since Rebello had failed in the triple jump in 1948, India had a medal prospect in the track-and-field events. Milkha Singh had represented India in the Melbourne Olympics but had done nothing of note. In the 1958 Asian Games, however, he had won gold medals in both the 200- and 400-meter races; he had also won the 400-meter race in 1958 in the Cardiff Commonwealth Games. In Rome he was strongly favored to win a medal, and in the heats he finished second on every occasion, raising hopes of a medal finish. But in the final, Milkha only narrowly finished fourth, despite breaking the Olympic record for the event. There was another close miss in 1960 when Gurbachan Randhawa placed fifth in the 110-meter hurdles. But it is Milkha, still hailed as the Flying Sikh (a sobriquet bestowed by Pakistan's military ruler, Ayub Khan, when Milkha beat Pakistan's fastest runner, Abdul Khaleq, in an Indo-Pak sports meet in Lahore in 1960),[77] who is symbolic of the many near-misses of Indian sports. Such is the aura about him that in 2013 he was the subject of a biopic entitled *Bhaag Milkha Bhaag*. It also says something about India's lack of success at the international level that a man who missed an Olympic medal, however narrowly, is revered as one of the greatest Indian athletes.

India had to wait four years to renew its rivalry with Pakistan in the next Olympic Games, in Tokyo. In the 1964 games, for the first time, the Indian team did not have a single Anglo-Indian player, as most of them had emigrated to the United Kingdom or Australia. Instead, the team was dominated by players from Punjab, with as many eleven players, including the captain, Charanjit Singh, of the eighteen-member squad having "Singh" as their last name. Indeed, starting in the 1950s, players from Punjab formed the backbone of the Indian team, with a small village called Sansarpur (near Jullundur city) providing a steady stream of hockey Olympians in the 1950s and 1960s. This in many ways confirmed the "minority" character of hockey, which in preindependent India had been dominated by Anglo-Indians and Muslims. Along with the Sikhs, in independent India the two other groups that played hockey in large numbers were the tribals, or Adivasis, and the Coorgis, a distinctive ethnic group from the southern state of Karnataka.

The Rome Games had decisively proved that India was no longer the undisputed champion of hockey when the only talking point was the margin of Indian victory. This was evident right from the first game that India played in Tokyo. The number of teams in the competition was fifteen, just one short of that in Rome, and they were divided into two groups. As in Rome, the Indians struggled in the group matches against the top European teams, barely managing to defeat Belgium and the Netherlands and tying Germany and Spain. Only against the weaker teams like Malaysia, Canada, and Hong Kong did India win overwhelmingly. In the semifinal, India played one of its better games, defeating the strong Australian team. India's opponent in the final was, once again, Pakistan, which had been placed in the other group and had won all its games en route to the final.

The final was tense, even occasionally turning ugly. Both teams were locked goalless for most of the match, with the game briefly stopped after a quarrel between the players from the two sides. It took a penalty stroke for the stalemate to be broken. Mohinder Lal converted the penalty to give India the lead and reclaim the gold medal from Pakistan. *The Statesman*'s S. E. Friskin reported: "On a cold and miserable afternoon, symbolic of the gloom of the past four years, Indian hockey emerged from darkness into light with the triumph today of its Olympic team."[78] The "day's greatest hero" was the goalkeeper Shankar Laxman—the same player targeted for abuse for letting in the sole goal against Pakistan in the 1960 Olympics—who foiled many Pakistani attacks. Except for India's triumph in the largely boycotted Moscow Olympic Games in 1980, this turned out to be the last time that India won a gold medal in the Olympics. The match was followed with feverish interest in India: "Work stopped, shops closed, schools, colleges and offices were half-empty, crowds cloistered round roaring radios and transistors in all parts of Delhi as, at the other end of the world, India came to the hour of decision in the Olympic final."[79] When the team returned to Delhi, they were taken in a procession from Red Fort to the Lady Hardinge ground, with hundreds of people lining the route. The government even released a special newsreel on the hockey final to be shown in movie theaters across the country.[80]

By 1964, sportswriters were already forecasting the end of India's reign as the hockey champion. Rex Bellamy reported in *World Sports*,

> In Tokyo, as in Rome, one goal separated India and Pakistan in the Olympic hockey final.... But that goal and the manner of it was hardly convincing evidence of India's supremacy. All that final proved, if proof were needed, was that India and Pakistan had the world's finest teams, and that there was nothing to choose between them.

He also predicted the dominance of Australia by pointing out that when the "Australians get their teeth into a game ... they tend to make a meal of it, and at the Tokyo Olympics they sank their teeth firmly into world hockey."[81]

These dire predictions finally came true in the 1968 games, at which in Mexico, for the first time, India failed to reach the finals of Olympic hockey. Even though it won a bronze medal, this was treated as a national calamity. A newspaper report captured the mood: "Quietly, almost as if they had done something wrong, the Indian Olympic hockey team, bronze medallist returned to their take-off point.... What a contrast it was to previous occasions."[82] Commenting on the defeat, Prime Minister Indira Gandhi said that it reflected "lack of discipline."[83]

There were several possible reasons for India's decline in hockey. Besides the charge of administrative inefficiency, hinted at by Pankaj Gupta,[84] the Europeans, most notably the Netherlands and West Germany, as well as Australia and Pakistan, had vastly improved since World War II. This was pointed out by a former Olympian, R. S. Bhola: "Let us accept defeat gracefully and with it also the fact that we are no longer overlords.... Other nations like Australia, West Germany, Spain, Japan, Belgium, Kenya, Holland, New Zealand apart from of course Pakistan are now the same standard as us."[85] He demanded that hockey be made compulsory in schools in order to stem the decline. Other hockey greats, such as K. D. Singh Babu and Balbir Singh (senior), voiced similar sentiments, stating that the defeat at the Mexico games was "deserved."[86]

Among the rapidly improving hockey-playing countries, Australia benefited the most from the immigration of Anglo-Indians, particularly in Western Australia where several Anglo-Indians set up base. The Pearce family of Perth was noteworthy, with all five brothers—Cecil, Melville, Eric, Gordon, and Julian—who were born in Jabalpur in central India and went on to represent Australia in hockey between 1950 and 1970. Other Anglo-Indians, such as Kevin Carton, who played for Australia in two Olympic Games, and Fred Browne, who was Australia's first Olympic hockey coach, were crucial figures in the development of hockey in Australia. The Anglo-Indian migration paid dividends for Britain too, with John Conroy playing a pivotal role on the British team of the 1950s. Many of India's Anglo-Indian Olympians also set up base in Australia and Britain. The legendary Eric Penniger, who played in three Olympics, emigrated to Britain; R. J. Carr and Carlyle Tapsell left for Australia.

Early Contests on the Cricket Pitch

The 1950s set a trend for Indian cricket: formidable at home and dismal abroad. After the disastrous Australia tour, India played host to the West Indies in 1948/1949, losing one Test and the series. Even though the cricket was mostly uninspiring, with both teams hampered by a lack of quality bowlers, the popularity of international cricket was evident. As *Wisden* commented: "Enthusiasm for cricket in India proved unbounded and record attendances almost everywhere assured financial success or the tour."[87] It was England that India was most eager to challenge, however. In 1949/1950 the Marylebone Cricket Club (MCC) decided not to send a team to India, with the Indians making do with a tour by a Commonwealth team composed mostly of professional players from the Lancashire League. The reasons for the MCC's avoiding India were made clear in a report submitted to the International Cricket Council (ICC), in which the MCC bluntly stated that it was "bound to give priority of consideration to their older traditional foes i.e., Australia and South Africa."[88]

Not until 1951/1952 did the MCC send a team to India. The English team was admittedly "second string." Besides being hindered by the slow and lifeless pitches as well as the heat and humidity, the lurking threat of the infamous "Delhi belly" was felling players, with the MCC team in later tours bringing canned food with them, much to the dismay of their hosts. India went into the fifth Test match in Madras, which began on the day that King George VI died, 0-1 down. But once India bowled out England cheaply, thanks to a magnificent spell of bowling by Vinoo Mankad, India held the upper hand. On a wearing pitch, England capitulated, with Mankad and Ghulam Ahmed proving to be the principal destroyers. The victory was doubly historic. India not only won its first-ever Test match, but it also was against England. As the *Times of India* reported, "For 20 years they have tried and at their twenty-fifth attempt success has come. And what a triumph it was—by an innings with more than a day to spare."[89] When India toured England later that year against a stronger English side, it lost three of the four Test matches and was saved only by the weather in one. The tone was set in the first Test at Leeds when in the second innings, India lost four wickets without a single run on the board, the worst start ever in a Test match.

Playing Ball with Pakistan

Although the summer of 1952 was a poor one for India, it had the opportunity later that year to play Pakistan for the first time. This marked the beginning of an enduring and often bitter rivalry, not only on the cricket pitch, but also on the hockey field. The Pakistan team was led by Abdul Hafeez Kardar, who had played for the Muslims in the Pentangular and also had represented the Indian team in the 1946 tour of England. An Oxford Blue in cricket, Kardar had a "deep commitment to the idea of Pakistan"[90] and later became a prominent politician. Ramachandra Guha named him "perhaps the greatest cricketer-ideologue born outside the West."[91] On the Pakistani team were cricketers who had played with Indian players before Partition; Amir Elahi and Vijay Hazare were teammates in Baroda, as were Kardar and Lala Amarnath in Lahore.

The first Test match between the two neighbors—which also was Pakistan's first ever—was played in Delhi's Ferozeshah Kotla Stadium. Considering the occasion, India's president, Rajendra Prasad, opened the match. India won decisively, with Vinoo Mankad once again doing the star turn. However, in the next Test match at Lucknow, the home of high Muslim culture and nawabi cuisine, Pakistan leveled the series just as convincingly as India had won the first Test. In the third Test in Bombay, India won easily. Hazare and Mankad, who missed the second Test, were the two main contributors. The fourth Test was rained out, and the final Test in Calcutta was a draw. The series was played in good spirit, despite the Hindu groups' attempts to disrupt the matches. In Nagpur, where Pakistan played a match against Central Zone, the president of the right-wing Hindu Mahasabha, N. B. Khare, announced that his party would stage protests outside the stadium. In a preemptive move, he was arrested, prompting the Pakistani paper *Dawn* to proclaim that the Hindu leader had been "bowled out."[92] In Calcutta, too, Hindu Mahasabha members shouted anti-Pakistan slogans outside the Eden Gardens Stadium, but that did not affect the Test match in any way. The stands were packed every day of the match, and a Mankad double century was a highlight of the drawn game.

Three years later India, led by Mankad, went to Pakistan for a five-Test tour, playing its first match in Dhaka in East Pakistan and then flying west across the subcontinent to continue the tour. Kardar was not only the captain of the Pakistan team but also a selector and a columnist for *Dawn*. A dull draw in the first Test at Dhaka was a sign of the safety-first cricket that was to follow, resulting in all Test matches ending in a draw. It seemed that the fear of "defeat seemed upper most in the minds of the two teams," and *Wisden* described the cricket as "two boxers tentatively sparring for an opening, but being afraid to strike the first blow in case some unexpected counter might be forthcoming."[93] Kardar was even more scathing in his newspaper column: "Mr Toynbee characterizes history as a challenge and response. When the history of the present series is written it will go down as the series without a counter-challenge to the challenge of negative tactics."[94] But the lack of excitement on the field was adequately compensated by the enthusiasm off it. The bitterness of Partition was momentarily forgotten in the festival of cricket. Among the special invitees was Talyarkhan, the star commentator, who was invited by Radio Pakistan for the second Test at Bahawalpur. For the third Test match in Lahore, which was the premier city in undivided Punjab, 10,000 Indians crossed the border at Wagah every day and returned in the evening. *Dawn* called it the "biggest mass migration across the frontier since Partition."[95] The city literally closed down, and "almost the whole of Lahore—minus [those] who were lucky to go to the stadium—listened to the radio from 10 A.M. to 5 P.M. every day."[96]

In the next series between the two neighbors, held in India in 1961/1962, the cricket was as dull as it had been previously, with all five Tests as well the fifteen first-class matches ending in a draw, a dubious record of sorts. The stakes were too high for either of the two teams to risk losing, which was pointed out by *Wisden*: "The chief aim of the contestants appeared to be to uphold national prestige by avoiding defeat rather than to take the risk of trying to enforce a decision. Cricket was a secondary interest."[97] Much of the goodwill of the two earlier series had evaporated. In the first match of the tour at Baroda, an Indian fan shook Pakistani opener Hanif Mohammed's hand and apparently cut his fingers with a sharp object. Despite the Pakistani newspapers calling it a "treacherous handshake," Mohammed was fit to play in the first Test in Bombay. Indian batsman Abbas Ali Baig, a Muslim, received threat letters accusing him of deliberately playing poorly, prompting Talyarkhan to condemn the notion that Pakistan–India contests were between "Hindus and Muslims only."[98] Off the field were ominous rumblings about the Kashmir issue, which eventually led to full-fledged war in 1965 and the breaking of cricket ties between the countries for more than a decade.

Individual Stars

Besides the team sports and Olympic events, a few Indians performed admirably well in other individual sports. Foremost among them was Ramanathan Krishnan, who was not, however, the first Indian tennis player to play on the international stage. Like the team sports, tennis too was brought to India in the nineteenth century by British officials and soldiers. In 1885 the Punjab Lawn Tennis Championship was established organized in Lahore, and in 1887 the Bengal Lawn Tennis Championship began in Calcutta. The first All-India Lawn Tennis Championship was played in Allahabad in 1910. For the first two decades or so, though, hardly any Indians played in the tournaments, which were dominated by the Europeans.

For obvious reasons, Wimbledon, the oldest tennis tournament, which was played in London, was the preferred tournament for Indians. The first Indian played at Wimbledon as far back as 1905 when a walkover by B. K. Nehru gave the victory to his opponent. The first Indian to actually play in Wimbledon was Sardar Nihal Singh in 1908.[99] In 1910 Nihal Singh was joined by two more Indians: the brothers A. Fyzee and A. H. Fyzee. In 1921 S. M. Jacob, an ICS officer, and the India-born Briton L. S. Deane—members of India's first Davis Cup team—even reached the Wimbledon semifinal, which they lost in five sets. That year India reached the Davis Cup semifinal, beating the heavily favored French team on the way, but losing to Japan.[100] In fact, a tennis team was representing India in an international tournament well before its hockey team did in 1928 and its cricket team in 1932. In 1920 the Davis Cup authorities had, oddly enough, decided that India possessed "a constitution and independent national representation," only to reverse their decision in 1923.[101]

Deane's success in Wimbledon continued in 1923 when he reached the semifinal in the men's doubles, teaming up with A. H. Fyzee, as well as in the mixed doubles. In this period, Mohammad Sleem was the top Indian player, having been the first non-European to win the Punjab Championship in 1915. In 1924 he represented India at the Olympics, and in 1928 he won the Wimbledon Plate title, contested by players who had lost in the first and second rounds. Another talented player was Cotah Ramaswami, a Cambridge Blue and the adopted son of Buchi Babu Naidu, who played for India in the 1922 Davis Cup. Sixteen years later Ramaswami represented India in cricket against England at the advanced age of forty-one, becoming the only sportsperson to have played both tennis and cricket for India. But it was Ghaus Mohammed in 1939 who bettered his predecessors by becoming the first Indian to reach the final sixteen in singles in Wimbledon.[102]

The rise of Krishnan, a Tamil Brahmin, was due in large measure to his father. Long before tennis dads became the norm, Krishnan's father, Tenkasi Krishnaiyer Ramanathan, or TKR as he was known, pushed him toward playing tennis. TKR got his first glimpse of tennis in 1930 at the Madras United Club and became besotted by the game. Not having the means to buy expensive tennis equipment, he bought his first racket by selling his wife's jewelry. By 1937 he was the Mysore state champion, and in 1939 he was a finalist in the All-India hard-court tennis championship, at which he lost to Ghaus Mohammed. Krishnan's initial interest clearly lay in team games, but his father pressured him to play tennis. Krishnan's coaching began in a tennis court in Tenkasi, a town in southern Tamil Nadu. He won his first tournament in the same town when he was only twelve, teaming up with his father in doubles. In 1950 the Krishnan family moved to nearby Madras City where the thirteen-year-old Krishnan won the Stanley Cup, a tournament open to college students, organized by the city's elite Loyola College. At the age of sixteen, he was good enough to play for India in the 1953 Davis Cup. The next year Krishnan appeared on the world stage, winning the junior Wimbledon championship and going on to achieve in 1959 the highest ever world ranking, third, by an Indian player. In 1960 and 1961 Krishnan reached the semifinals, but both times the eventual champions, Neale Fraser[103] and Rod Laver,[104] respectively, stood in his way. During this time, other Indians, such as Premjit Lall and Jaidip Mukherjea (both losing finalists in the junior Wimbledon), also did well in Wimbledon but faltered in the final stages. Mukherjea did, however, reach the Wimbledon quarterfinal on four occasions in the 1960s and early 1970s.

Like many future Indian tennis players, Krishnan had the habit of performing well above his potential in the Davis Cup, in which he played until 1975. In the 1959 Davis Cup, Krishnan beat Laver, one of tennis's all-time greats. But when Krishnan played in his last Wimbledon, in 1968, the transition from the amateur to the professional era had just begun, which was just as well, since his easygoing, gentlemanly style might have not been well suited to the rigors of professional tennis.

Indeed like Ranji and Dhyan Chand, Krishnan was known in tennis circles for his Indian, or Asian, style of play, which eschewed power for grace. The noted actor Peter Ustinov once wrote of Krishnan: "Tennis does take on national characteristics so very easily. Krishnan, for instance, is capable of beating anyone with his soft, accurate shots, psyching opponents with a game that is obviously related to the Indian character."[105] The image of Krishnan as a "touch artist" lingered well after his retirement. Krishnan himself, however, believed this was a misrepresentation. Speaking to me at the tennis academy in Chennai run by him and his son Ramesh, he explained, "All good players have power, accuracy and control."[106] Ranji and Chand might have well said the same thing if they were alive today.

Krishnan wasn't the only Indian successful in an individual sport. In badminton—a game whose modern form originated in the British cantonment of Pune in the mid-nineteenth century and enjoys remarkable popularity in India despite a shortage of indoor courts—the now-forgotten Prakash Nath reached the final of the All-England Badminton Championship (the most prestigious international badminton tournament) in 1947. He lost to Denmark's Conny Jepsen in straight sets but began a career with the tournament that produced two Indian champions in subsequent years. Nandu Natekar from Maharashtra—which was really the seat of badminton in India—was another prominent player in the 1950s. In 1956 he won the Selangor International tournament in Malaysia[107] while still a student of Bombay University, and in 1963 he won the singles title at King's Cup tournament in Bangkok. Like Krishnan, however, he was unable to win a major title, his best performance in the All-England Championship being a finish in the quarterfinals.

Partition created an enduring rivalry between India and Pakistan in hockey and cricket, and the only individual sport in a contest (albeit brief) between the two countries was squash. The Western India Championship played at the Cricket Club of India (CCI) was the premier squash tournament of the time. The man who dominated the early years of the tournament, which began in 1943, was Hashim Khan, from Peshawar. His rival was Abdul Bari, a member of the CCI who was said to be a distant relation of Hashim. After Partition, Bari decided to stay on in Bombay, and in 1950 he competed in the British Open, the sport's unofficial world championship. He reached the final, at which he lost to the Egyptian, M. A. Karim, who had already won the tournament twice. In 1951, Hashim won the first of his seven British Open titles, becoming the first of many Khans to dominate the championship. Unfortunately, Bari's rivalry with Hashim was cut short in 1954 when he died in London of a brain hemorrhage at the age of thirty-two.[108] With him died India's hopes on the international squash court.

The Dara Singh Phenomenon

The story of Indian sports in the 1950 and 1960s would not be complete without mentioning a unique "sports" hero, someone who was less a sportsperson in the conventional sense and much more of an entertainer. This was the wrestler Deedar Singh Randhawa, or Dara Singh as he was universally known. Like his predecessors such as Gama, Dara made his name not in the Olympic arena but in the freewheeling and often make-believe world of professional wrestling, a precursor to the World Wrestling Federation (now the World Wrestling Entertainment) fights of more recent times. Little is known about Dara's early life. He was born in 1928 in a village near the holy city of Amritsar in Punjab. When he was barely out of his teens, after having trained in traditional Indian wrestling, he went to the Far East to fight professionally. One of the earliest mentions of him was in 1946 when he lost to Jeff Conda.[109] By the early 1950s, Dara, who was initially known as the "Champion of Malaya,"[110] had returned to India and made a name for himself taking part in freestyle wrestling bouts that pitted him against men with such exotic names as Hulk Hogan, Red Scorpion, Boston Crab, Mad Monk, and Mighty Cheng. Many of Dara's opponents, such as Flash Gordon, Dracula, Black Shadow, and Son of Zoro, wore masks, and considerable interest was drummed up over whether Dara could unmask them and reveal their identity.[111] As early as 1953, Dara was fighting "American freestyle wrestling" bouts at Bombay's Vallabhbhai Patel Stadium before crowds exceeding 15,000,[112] and a newspaper claimed that wrestling was "the craze" in Bombay, overtaking for the moment the city's two other sporting passions: cricket and racing.[113]

In the "morality play"[114] of professional wrestling, Dara, a symbol of Indian masculinity, was the good guy fighting the big, bad brutes from the West and usually ending up winning. Some of the most famous of the five hundred–odd bouts that Dara fought in his lifetime were with King Kong— the professional name of the nearly 441-pound Hungarian wrestler, Emile Czaja (or Tzayea, as the Indian newspapers referred to him), who, despite his fearsome reputation, was described by a women's magazine as a "portly but courtly gentleman."[115] Dara and King Kong had fought each other in Malaya earlier,[116] and one of the first fights between the two wrestlers in India was at Vallabhbhai Stadium in 1953 where the two fought before a crowd of nearly 40,000. Though there were justifiable doubts about the authenticity of these fights—Czaja himself was the promoter of many of the fights between himself and Dara—King Kong won that bout.[117] The return fight between the two attracted an even bigger crowd when 50,000 people turned up at the Vallabhbhai Stadium.[118] Such was the electrifying effect of these fights that the *Times of India*'s correspondent wrote:

> The Englishman seeks his thrill in football arenas and the American gets his excitement from watching baseball stars in action, but when it comes right down to the final analysis they have little on the Indian, who loves nothing better than to see King Kong and Dara Singh come to grips at the Vallabhbhai Stadium.[119]

The same writer pointed out that though some of the fights were clearly "stage-managed," the better man usually won. Tag teams were popular, too, with Dara usually joining his brother Randhawa and occasionally crossing borders by teaming up with the Pakistani wrestler Akram.[120] There were even Dara clones, with a wrestler going by the name of "Killer" Dara Singh who challenged the original Dara and, predictably, lost.[121] The fights were often "freestyle," in the truest sense of the word, with attacks on referees[122] or foul means, bringing a premature end to the bout.[123] Possibly the biggest-ever crowd—numbering around 60,000—assembled to watch Dara wrest the "world title" from the American, Lou Thesz.[124] On the way to the "world championship," Dara had picked up such fancy titles as Rustam-e-Hind.

Dara's fights were widely advertised in newspapers and on billboards. *The Hindu*, for example, in 1960 advertised an "All-India Championship" on Madras's Salt Cotaurs ground, where Dara was challenged by several foreign wrestlers, including Russian Rocket, Blonde Tiger, and, invariably, King Kong.[125] Wrestling bouts involving Dara were held in smaller towns too and sometimes with unanticipated outcomes. In Jabalpore, Madhya Pradesh, the lights went off in the stadium before a Dara fight, provoking the crowd of 20,000 to go on a rampage. The galleries of the stadium were damaged, spectators were injured, women were molested, and even some furniture was stolen.[126] It wasn't unusual for crowds to vent their ire if they felt that the bouts were too obviously stage-managed.[127] Sometimes events turned serious, as in Delhi in 1968 when the police has to use teargas and batons to disperse the fans, who, despite having valid tickets, could not be accommodated inside the stadium.[128] Such incidents had not been uncommon in the past either. Newspapers report an incident in 1933 when a wrestling match in Bombay had to be abandoned when a crowd of 40,000 went on a rampage after Nizam *pehelwan*, a disciple of Gama, was apparently unfairly defeated by his opponent.[129]

Contrary to what some people believe, however, wrestling bouts involving Dara and his colorful competitors, which continued until the late 1970s, didn't attract only the unlettered masses. P. Lal, a professor of English, a writer, a publisher, and something of a legend in Calcutta, wrote the following about freestyle wrestling:

> Cricket is cricket. But to have seen Dara Singh execute an Aeroplane Spin; to savor the cunning intricacies of the Egyptian Deadlock applied by Wadi Ayoub; to clap Goldsky on to the Boston Crab, to receive the full aesthetic impact of Harbans Singh's Flying Dropkick; to enter into the warmth of King Kong's Octopus Embrace—these are nutmegs of delight for which Haroun-al-Raschid would have parted with a small fortune. Bowling googlies are trivial when compared to fifteen-minute nelsons.[130]

Dara and his ilk, of course, had many detractors. One was the evergreen sports writer A. F. S. "Bobby" Talyarkhan, who lamented on the death of King Kong that he and his fellow wrestlers could get "get away with anything under the labels of styles and codes of wrestling unknown to the purist of the great art."[131] On another occasion he wrote that he would "welcome these alleged wrestling displays as part of a Big Top entertainment," but not as part of the "great and traditional" art of amateur wrestling.[132] The paying audience for Dara's fights, however, wasn't too bothered about such niceties. As Roland Barthes pointed out in a short essay, professional wrestling is not a sport but a "spectacle."[133] He went on to explain, "The public couldn't care less that the fight is or isn't fixed, and rightly so; the public confines itself to spectacle's primary virtue, which is to abolish all motives and all consequences: what matters to the public is not what it believes but what it sees."[134]

Dara was also the first sportsperson to bring the sporting and the film industry together (The other sportsperson from this period who did this literally was the cricketer Mansur Ali Khan Pataudi, who married the famous actress Sharmila Tagore in 1969). Dara acted in his first film in 1952 and went on to star in more than 115 films, mostly B-grade and popular among the underclass, the last one being released in 2007. The first film in which he was a hero was *King Kong* (1962), whose success spawned several more action films that showcased Dara's strength: *Iron Man*, *Samson*, and *Rustom-e-Hind*,

A poster of a popular Dara Singh film from the 1960s. Reprinted by permission of Dinodia Photo

to name a few.[135] Later, in the 1980s, he played the Hindu god Hanuman in the phenomenally successful tele-serial *Ramayana*. Dara was fighting—or performing, if you will—at a time when Indian amateur wrestlers were doing reasonably well in the Commonwealth Games and the Asiad. But it was Dara, rather than Olympic medalist Jadhav or his successors, who grabbed the imagination of the masses and outlived the 1950s and 1960s. To borrow from Barthes, Dara's fights, unlike amateur wrestling, could give the public the "great spectacle of Suffering, of Defeat, and of Justice."[136]

When Dara died in 2012, there was an outpouring of tributes on the front pages of newspapers (and television channels), prompting a noted newspaper columnist to write that Dara was the "first Indian superhero."[137] That claim contained some hyperbole, since wrestlers like Gama from an earlier era had fought and won against foreign wrestlers—admittedly with less colorful names than those of Dara's opponents—in front of huge audiences. It is, however, undeniable that few could match Dara's popularity as well as his longevity on the public stage in independent India.

The Nationalization of Kabaddi

If Dara Singh and his promoters turned freestyle wrestling into mass entertainment for the urban population, another indigenous sport with a long lineage, kabaddi, was undergoing a fascinating transformation. Some people suggest that kabaddi goes back to the Vedic age. The *Oxford Companion to Sports and Games* describes it as a "traditional team pursuit game" requiring the players to "hold their breath for a long time."[138] The sport, which was always more popular in rural than in urban India, is played by two teams in an open space, with one player, called the "raider," who must try to tag out members of the opposing team. What makes kabaddi distinctive is that the raider must tag his opponents in one breath while repeating a cant that has to contain the word "kabbadi." Kabaddi is known by various names across India—*hu-tu-tu* in Maharashtra, *chedu-gudu* in Madras and Mysore, *jabarjang* in Punjab, and *hu-du-du* in Bengal. In addition, there are three variants of the sport: *surjivani* (or *sanjivani*), *gamini*, and *amar*. This diversity, as Joseph Alter has argued in an insightful article, began to be tamed in the twentieth century, and kabaddi was turned into a "civilized sport . . . designed by various nationalist groups and state bodies to conform with international standards for rules and regulations."[139]

In modern India, kabaddi was cited first in 1911 when it was one of several sports, including wrestling and other assorted entertainment, held at the Badshahi Mela in Delhi.[140] Then in the 1920s, mainly through the efforts of enthusiasts in western India, kabaddi began to take the form of an organized sport. In 1923 the first all-India kabaddi competition was organized in Baroda by the Hind Vijay Gymkhana.[141] At the same time, different organizations like the Maharasthra Sharirik Shiksha Mandal and the YMCA attempted to standardize the rules. But it took more than a decade before kabaddi could make it to the program of the All-India Olympic Championships (or the Indian Olympic Games), which were later known as the National Games. In 1937 there was a proposal to include kabaddi in the program for the Indian Olympic Games, and it was added to the schedule in 1938.[142] Indeed, Alter found a link between the demonstration of indigenous games by the Hanuman Vyayam Prasarak Mandal in 1936 in Berlin (discussed in an earlier chapter), in which kabaddi was part of the routine, and its formal status as a "sport."

It was in independent India that kabaddi became an organized sport. The All-India Kabaddi Federation was formed in 1950, and a national competition was held every year, in which both state and institutional teams took part. In fact, kabaddi was included as the only demonstration sport in the 1951 Asian Games in Delhi, giving it legitimacy on the international stage.[143] This paved the way for kabaddi to eventually be included in the Asian Games in 1990. The standardization and internationalization of kabaddi have helped what was and still is essentially a rural sport acquire the semiofficial status of a "national" sport. In his entry on kabaddi, John Arlott writes that the sport is not only one of India's "national games" but also "reflects a philosophy of simple living and high thinking."[144] Kabaddi invariably figured in recommendations by government-appointed committees as an example of an indigenous sport that needed to be encouraged. The connection between the philosophy of the sport and strong character was made by many, including Nehru, who, when opening a kabaddi tournament in Bombay, noted that the sport helped build "sturdy men."[145] The makeover of the sport was forcefully articulated by a proponent of the sport:

> Before independence when people were imprisoned by their infatuation for the depravities of Western civilization there were some people who said that kabaddi was a low-class village game. But now that we Indians have cast off the yoke of Westernization and have given birth to a new patriotic spirit this sport is finally receiving the recognition it deserves.[146]

Government Policy in Nehru's India

In the early years of Indian independence, Jawaharlal Nehru's government had plenty to worry about, and sports weren't a top priority. At a time when the Indian economy was inward looking and stagnant, the financial outlay for sports in the First Plan was a paltry Rs 150,000, but this increased substantially by the Third Plan to Rs 110 million. However, as with the 1951 Asian Games, Nehru understood the potential of sports to project India's image and forge international ties. In 1948 a commission to study schools, headed by Tara Chand, made several recommendations regarding physical education. Acting on the recommendations, the Central Advisory Board of Physical Education was established in 1951, followed by the All-India Council of Sports (AICS) in 1954, headed by the retired military chief K. M. Cariappa, to act as a liaison between the government and the various national sports federations. Although there was no sports ministry yet, India's first health minister, Rajkumari Amrit Kaur, herself a tennis player and president of the All-India Tennis Federation in the 1950s, had a keen interest in sports. In 1953 a coaching scheme named after the Rajkumari was initiated, and when Kaur died, in a touching tribute Talyarkhan wrote that "no Indian woman has so interested herself in the country's sport nor known so much about the subject."[147]

In 1958 the Sports and Welfare Department was created under the Ministry of Education. The next year a high-profile, eleven-member committee, appointed by the government, submitted a report to the minister of education suggesting ways to improve standards in sports and games. The committee, which included luminaries like the maharaja of Patiala, Amrit Kaur, Duleepsinhji, Naval Tata, and Jaipal Singh, recommended forming a central training institute for coaches. Among other things, it also stressed the need to encourage sports in rural areas and to provide playgrounds in all schools and colleges. Interestingly, three members, including Kaur and Singh, dissented.[148]

In 1961 the National Institute of Sports (NIS)—which was later renamed the Netaji Subhas National Institute of Sports—was founded in the maharaja of Patiala's sprawling palace and grounds. The next year the Rajkumari coaching scheme was merged with the National Coaching Scheme of NIS. This did not go down well with Kaur, who resigned from the chairmanship of the governing body of the NIS in 1962 primarily on the basis of her disagreement with the policy of a training course for experienced coaches.[149] In 1961 the Arjuna Awards for outstanding Indian sportspersons were instituted, with twenty, including one woman (hockey player Ann Lumsden), receiving the award from India's president, Sarvepalli Radhakrishnan, in 1962.[150] The awards, too, were not without controversy, as the maharaja of Baroda publicly criticized the manner in which the awardees were chosen.[151]

The government's position on sports was articulated by M. C. Chagla, minister of education and a former chief justice of the Bombay High Court, in his inaugural address, delivered at the All-India Congress of Sports in 1962. Unlike in the Soviet Union, which Nehru so admired, or Mao's China, where sport was seen as a natural extension of nationalism, Chagla put a Nehruvian spin on the role of sports: "The best way of achieving national integration is by playing games," he said. "After all, there are no castes, no communities, no religion as far as sports is concerned." He recognized the importance of India's performing well in international meets but said it was more important to have "more and more playgrounds and playing fields."[152]

Two other things came through in Chagla's speech. The first was an emphasis on indigenous games and rural sports, particularly wrestling, with Chagla pointing out that "sports must be taken to the villages in order to make the nation sports-minded and physically fit."[153] Second, he talked about the need for more coordination between the government and the national sports federations and for all sports to "come under one umbrella" so as to ensure that the best sportspersons represented India in international competitions.[154] Both these issues influenced the government's sports policy and also caused some controversy in the coming years.

As we shall see in the next chapter, it was not so much bodies designated for sports, such as the All-India Council of Sports (AICS), but state-run organizations like the railways, armed forces, and police that better served the cause of sports in India. Jaipal Singh, who headed an investigatory committee appointed by the AICS in the 1960s, told a newspaper, "Sports is in a very big mess in India and, surprisingly, it is the bigwigs of sport who are responsible for the current state of affairs."[155] Even at the early stage, General Cariappa, in his capacity as the president of the sports council, sounded a warning about the state alone taking up the burden of promoting sports, advising that "sports should be in the private sector than in the public sector."[156]

Overall Picture

In the first two decades since Indian independence, we find an unusual contradiction. While India remained a power in hockey and was among the top football nations in Asia, cricket, despite India's poor performance, was still phenomenally popular. Even though India was tough to beat at home, in matches away, India lost by wide margins in Australia, England, and the West Indies. It managed its first Test victory abroad against a weak New Zealand team only in 1967.

India's underperformance in cricket in its first years as an independent nation was powerfully expressed in 1959 in an article by Vijay Merchant (an outstanding batsman for India and a *Wisden* cricketer of the year in 1937) in *Wisden* before an Indian tour of England:

> After 27 years in the international sphere we seem to have got nowhere and have only five victories to our credit in Test matches. Of these one was registered against a second-rate England eleven in 1951–52; two against Pakistan on their initial tour of India in 1952 and two against a weak New Zealand team in 1955–56.[157]

He went on to criticize the role of politics in sport, an issue that was increasingly cited as a reason for India's poor performance in sports: "I do not know how much cricket there is in our politics but there is a lot of politics in our cricket."[158] India's record had no impact on the popularity of the game, however. *Wisden* reported that during the 1964 MCC tour of India, in which all five matches were dreary, with draws in every match, the Test grounds, whose capacity was between 30,000 and 50,000, were nonetheless packed.

The philosopher Sarvepalli Radhakrishnan, who was India's second president, commented during a function in 1954 that "like the other symbols of British civilization—the ballot box, the limited liability company and the revised version of the Bible—cricket has come to stay in India."[159] This sentiment was echoed by commentator and sports writer Dicky Rutnagur a few years later:

> Of all the forms of their culture the British brought to India, none thrust its roots as deep as cricket. Though India has dominated international

hockey for almost four decades, cricket is far more a part of the national scene than the only team game at which we have been world champions.[160]

Why did cricket, when India's performance on the international stage was decidedly mediocre during this period, attract such a following? This is the subject of a later chapter.

10

DOMESTIC SPORTS

STATE, CLUB, OFFICE, AND

REGIMENT (1947-1970)

WHEN MOHUN BAGAN PLAYED EAST BENGAL IN THE 1950S AND 1960s, thousands thronged to the stadium. The same was true for the premier hockey tournaments such as the Beighton Cup and, to a lesser extent, cricket's Ranji Trophy. After the first two decades of independence, team games like football, cricket, and hockey thrived in India. In football and hockey, most of the preindependence tournaments survived and continued to flourish through the 1950 and 1960s. New tournaments and new clubs were established, some of which were located away from the traditional sports centers. In cricket, the Ranji Trophy became the focus of interstate rivalry (the interzonal Duleep Trophy began in 1961), although the demise of the princely states meant that some of the prominent teams from colonial India, such as Nawanagar and Holkar, were replaced by the newly created linguistic units. The end of the princely states also changed the patronage of sports. The princes were gradually replaced by sponsors, from both the public and private sectors. This was more the case in cricket than in football, which already had a club structure, and hockey, which always had had support from public-sector organizations and the armed forces. In Nehru's socialist India, in which the "commanding heights" state had an inordinately large presence, it wasn't surprising that the public-sector organizations were the biggest employers of sportspersons. This resulted in two things. First, unlike other many other parts of the world, Indian sports remained semiprofessionalized, so sportspersons could not depend on sports for their livelihood. Indeed, many of them played for their clubs for free or for a fairly small amount and depended on their regular salary from their employer to make ends meet. Second, for many sportspersons, a career in a company, public or private, became the ultimate goal, sometimes to the detriment of their sports ambitions.

From Princes to Corporates

In preindependence India, many professional sportspersons were employed in the princely states. Whereas wrestling and polo had been favored in an earlier period, by the twentieth century many Indian princes had switched to cricket, and several of India's leading cricketers were in the employ of princes, both minor and major. C. K. Nayudu, who has been described as "the embodiment of the game"[1] in India, was brought to Indore in the 1920s by its ruler, Tukoji Rao III. Nayudu not only was made a captain in the Holkar State Army, but he also led the Holkar cricket team to four Ranji Trophy titles in the 1940s and early 1950s. Nayudu was so revered that the maharaja of Holkar, Yeshwant Rao, a die-hard cricket fan, once said of him: "I may be the ruler of the state, but C. K. is surely the King of Outdoor games."[2] This wasn't surprising, since by the 1930s Nayudu was so popular that "C. K. Naidu" bats were on sale for the considerable sum of Rs 10.[3]

Several of independent India's star cricketers, such as Vinoo Mankad (Nawanagar), Vijay Hazare (Baroda), and Mushtaq Ali (Holkar), were employed by princes. In fact, Hazare, who came from a poor family, first learned cricket in Jath, was then taken on by another small princely state, Dewas Senior, and was finally recruited by Baroda.[4] But once India became an independent republic and the princely states were abolished, most of the princes disbanded their teams, and others were forced to cut back on expenses. Some teams, like Baroda and Holkar, that were funded by princes who had been relatively less affected by the creation of a republican India, continued for a while to exist and prosper. Over time, all the states in the Indian union had their own teams playing in the Ranji Trophy, though exceptions were made for the traditional cricketing centers such as Bombay, Hyderabad, Baroda, and Saurashtra. These coexisted with state teams of Maharashtra, Andhra Pradesh, and Gujarat, where, respectively, these centers were located.

When Baroda won the Ranji Trophy for the fourth time in 1957/1958, five members of the team were the maharaja's employees, with three players, including Hazare, being aides-de-camp to Fatehsinghrao Gaekwad.[5] The former maharaja himself was part of the team as well. Under Nayudu, Holkar continued to play for the Ranji Trophy until 1955 and won the tournament twice in the 1950s. The Holkar team, led by Nayudu, even toured Ceylon in 1948.[6] But these were the exceptions and not the rule. There was little money to be made in India playing cricket then, as perhaps most graphically illustrated by the case of D. D. Hindlekar, who played four Test matches for India but died in 1949 at the age of forty, unable to afford medical treatment. It was only after his death that a cabaret show was organized to raise funds for Hindlekar's wife and seven children.[7]

The majority of cricketers had to seek other patrons, both inside and outside India. In democratic India, even the former royals were recruited by private companies. The most famous cricketer among the former princes, and also India's captain, M. A. K. Pataudi, was briefly employed by JK Chemicals. Two minor royals, Yajurvindra Singh and Hanumant Singh, both of whom played for India, worked for Mahindra and the State Bank of India, respectively.

Even before Indian independence, some sportspersons joined the Lancashire League in England as professionals. Among the first to do so were Amar Singh and Lala Amarnath, before World War II. Then in the 1950s, with the decline of princely patronage, several more headed to Lancashire. The leading player of this group was Vinoo Mankad, who had to seek other sources of employment after the Nawanagar team disbanded in 1947 and played in the Lancashire League for fifteen years. He was one of the highest-paid professionals of the time in the league, earning as much as £1,400 a season. The famous sports commentator and writer, John Arlott, wrote that Mankad "follows in the tradition of the great English professional all-rounders. Like them he is a craftsman who lives his craft so deeply that it becomes almost an art."[8] Several other leading players who played for India, including Hazare, G. S. Ramchand, Polly Umrigar, Dattu Phadkar, Chandu Borde, C. S. Nayudu (C. K.'s brother), Subhas Gupte, and Vijay Manjrekar, followed Mankad's lead and joined the Lancashire League. While he was in India, Mankad lent his exceptional skills to as many as six states, including Bengal, as did his India teammate Vijay Manjrekar, who played in four. Even the great C. K. Nayudu played for four teams, making his last appearance in the Ranji Trophy as the captain of Uttar Pradesh in 1956 at the age of sixty-one.

Mankad's professional status did not, however, go down well with the Indian cricket board. This was evident during the run-up to India's tour of England in 1952 when he, having already signed up for Haslingden in the Lancashire League, was asked to attend the team trials in India. Mankad responded reasonably, saying that he was willing to attend the trials on the condition that his selection was assured. As India's top all-rounder, Mankad was well within his rights to make this demand, as playing for India would deprive him of income. But the Indian selectors decided not to pick Mankad, much to the dismay of the Indian press. In a delicious twist of fate, the Indian team was forced to recall Mankad before the first Test after two members of the team suffered injuries. Although he was not released by his club for the first Test, he returned in the second to slam 72 and 184 runs and claim five wickets in the first innings.

Richard Cashman has made the point that in colonial India, the best cricketers were from two ends of the social spectrum. At one end were players from princely families (Nawab of Pataudi), well-off professional families (C. K. Nayudu), and business families (Vijay Merchant). At the other end were players from low-income backgrounds, such as Amar Singh (whose bowling was famously described by the great English batsman Wally Hammond as coming off the pitch like the "crack of doom") and Lala Amarnath. Few players were from middle-income families. This changed dramatically after 1947, and the change was most apparent in Bombay, which was the Indian cricket's headquarters (the Board of Control for Cricket [BCCI] was based in the city, and Bombay also won the Ranji Trophy fourteen times in a row between 1958 and 1972). Many of the players playing for Bombay and, indeed, India in this period were from middle-class families who had learned and played cricket in the city's two legendary clubs, Dadar Union Sporting Club and Shivaji Park Gymkhana.[9] As a visit to Shivaji Park in the winter of 2013 revealed, the *maidan* is still dotted with pitches where several cricket matches are being played at the same time.

There was, however, a preponderance of upper-caste cricketers in the higher echelons of Indian cricket. The Indian cricket team that won the first

Test series against England in 1971 listed eight Hindus, of whom seven were Brahmins, including the captain, Ajit Wadekar. According to one calculation, since 1970 more than a third of Indian Test players have been Brahmins, even though they account for less than a fifth of India's population.[10] This was perhaps natural, considering that until the 1980s, most Test players were university educated and English speaking, which was still the preserve of the upper castes. We also might note that by this time, being a Brahmin did not necessarily denote wealth and privilege; hence many of the Brahmin cricketers had an urban, middle-class background. Some people even believe that Brahmins took to cricket because of the lack of physicality in the game.[11] In addition, the upper castes tended to be batsmen, which was less physically demanding, and not bowlers, which was usually more arduous.

Certain schools and colleges in Bombay, too, were nurseries for middle-class cricketers. The Parsi-run Bharda New High School produced a long line of cricketers who played for India, beginning with Vijay Merchant. The same was true of King George School, which is now known as Raja Shivaji School. Among the colleges in Bombay, the rivalry between St. Xavier's and Elphinstone and between Siddharth College and Ruia College was legendary.[12] Wadekar considered the matches between Ruia and Siddharth in the 1960s as "trying as any first-class match."[13] The same could be said for the St. Stephen's–Hindu College contest in Delhi. In Hyderabad, Nizam's College produced many star cricketers, from Ghulam Ahmed to M. L. Jaisimha to Abbas Ali Baig, all of whom played for India. Some of the traditional centers, such as Ranji's former school, Rajkumar College, kept producing decent cricketers, with eight princes from the school playing for Saurashtra in the Ranji Trophy.[14] Indeed, Ramachandra Guha believes that an all-time eleven (including players who emigrated to Pakistan after Partition) from Kathiawar, where Jamnagar is located, would be able to challenge the best that the rest of India might have to offer.[15]

According to Cashman, from the 1960s a majority of players on the Indian cricket team were college graduates, in contrast to the "leading hockey and soccer players of the country who were mostly matriculates or non-matriculates."[16] This meant that white-collar jobs were available for cricketers, though not for many of their counterparts in football and hockey. The railways had traditionally been an employer, with the B. B. & C. I. Railway recruiting players in the 1920s. In independent India, the railways continued this policy. India's future captain, Nari Contractor, whose international career was cut short in 1962 by a head injury, joined the Western Railways in 1957 at a salary of roughly Rs 200 per month (at current rates, less than US$4). The railways also took part in the Ranji Trophy, having assembled a strong team in the 1950s, which included an aging Lala Amarnath, who at one time was not only captain of the railways team but also a national selector.

Customs, Bombay Port Trust, and B.E.S.T. were some of the other state-run organizations that employed cricketers. Among the private companies, Burmah-Shell was a prominent employer of cricketers. All these companies took part in India's oldest interoffice tournament, the Times Challenge Shield, founded by the *Times of India* in 1930, which, along with the Kanga League (described as the "most competitive club competition in the world"),[17] were the premier tournaments in Bombay. Before 1947, in all but two years, the state-run companies had won the shield. But after 1947, the private companies began aggressively pursuing cricketers and building formidable teams. The Tata Group was the first to begin corporate sponsorship of sports, founding the Tata Sports Club in 1937. The Tatas' association with sports begun by Sir Dorabji was continued by Naval Tata, who headed the Indian Hockey Federation and was also a member of the International Hockey Federation. The Tatas won the Times Shield for the first time in 1941 and ten more times between 1947 and 1977. This was because of the company's aggressive recruitment policies in the 1950s and 1960s, which attracted several cricketers who had played for India, including Bapu Nadkarni, Naren Tamhane, Farokh Engineer, and Nari Contractor. In fact, in 1959 Contractor had joined the State Bank of India from the railways, at a salary that was double his earlier pay. When he shifted allegiance to the Tatas in 1960, he was receiving more than four times his salary from the railways.[18] The Tatas' rationale was that by building great sports teams and figuring regularly on the newspapers' sports pages, the firm could become a "household word."[19] Other private companies, such as Associated Cement Corporation (ACC), followed suit, building strong teams during that period and tasting success in the Times Shield. Mahindra was another company that actively recruited players, although winning tournaments was apparently of "marginal interest" to the firm.[20] During a later period, teams formed by textile companies, such as Mafatlal and Nirlon, were remarkably successful, not only in the Times Shield, but in tournaments elsewhere in India too.

State-run companies like the State Bank of India (SBI), with literally hundreds of branches across the country, were equally interested in investing in cricket. In the 1960s the SBI got together a formidable team that won the Times Shield four times. The SBI's unique feature was that it recruited players from all over the country and not just Bombay. Such was the success of its recruitment that the 1967 Indian team to England had as many as thirteen SBI employees.[21] Interoffice tournaments were held in other cities as well, with the Sport and Pastime Trophy (named after a weekly magazine of the same name), a limited overs tournament in Madras sponsored by the *Hindu* newspaper, being one of the more prominent ones. Later, after the *Sport and Pastime* weekly magazine closed, it was later renamed the Hindu Trophy. It also wasn't uncommon for office teams to play in regional tournaments like the Buchi Babu tournament in Madras and the Moin-ud-Dowla Gold Cup in Hyderabad.

The States of Football

The tournaments set up before before 1947, such as the IFA Shield, Durand, and Rovers, continued to flourish and draw sizable crowds in independent India. Unlike cricket, whose Ranji Trophy often fought a losing battle with international cricket to draw crowds,[22] domestic football attracted healthy crowds. Newer tournaments like the DCM Trophy, instituted by a textile company, the Delhi Cloth Mills, were established as well. The DCM Trophy, played in Delhi for the first time in 1945, began with only five participants and had one team named Jinnah Sporting and another named Hindu Sporting, which were reminders of the tumultuous politics leading up to Partition. The DCM tournament was also the first one to invite foreign teams in the 1950s, including such Pakistani clubs as the Pakistan Mughals, Young Men, and Zamindara. Pakistani teams playing in India were not uncommon in the 1950s, with the Raiders Football Club of Lahore winning a "sensational" victory over Mohun Bagan in the quarterfinal of the 1952 Rovers Cup[23] around the same time that the Pakistani cricket team was on its first tour of India.

Calcutta and the intense rivalry between Mohun Bagan and East Bengal was the epicenter of Indian football. The "ferocious binary," as one analyst termed it, meant that all other clubs in Calcutta (with the exception of Mohammedan Sporting) played the "purely formal function of providing an opponent for the Big Two."[24] The rivalry between the two clubs received a boost after the huge influx of refugees into Calcutta from East Bengal (or what was then East Pakistan) after Partition who supported the East Bengal club. Mohun Bagan and Mohammedan Sporting were the star teams in pre-1947 India, but East Bengal dominated in the first years after Indian independence. Thanks to a forward line collectively known as the "Pancha [Five] Pandavas" (after the mythical brothers from the Mahabharata)—made up of Appa Rao, P. B. Saleh, P. Venkatesh, K. P. Dhanraj, and Ahmed Khan—all of whom were from south India, East Bengal between 1949 and 1953 won all the major football titles in India: the IFA League and Shield three times, the Durand Cup and the DCM Trophy twice, and the Rovers Cup once.[25]

Massive crowds would turn up to watch the Mohun Bagan–East Bengal matches. A sports commentator noted when the two teams played, Calcutta was split into "two distinct camps," where after the game, "if one half of Calcutta is glad, the other half inevitably becomes sad."[26] The humorous side of this was reported in a newspaper in the 1950s about how Mohun Bagan–East Bengal games had created marital discord in a Bengal village in which the husband was a Mohun Bagan supporter and his wife's loyalty lay with East Bengal. The rivalry was also the subject of a popular Bengali film, *Mohun Baganer Meye (The Daughter of Mohun Bagan)*, in which a diehard Mohun Bagan fan is unwilling to let his son marry an East Bengal fan.[27] But there was a dark side, too, with the fans often resorting to violence. The very first IFA Shield final after independence in October 1947 between Mohun Bagan and East Bengal had to be abandoned because of crowd violence, with the police having to resort to firing to disperse the spectators, injuring eleven people. Part of the problem was due to the large numbers outside the ground who "clamoured for admission" and subsequently "gate-crashed and swamped the galleries."[28] Crowd violence was, of course, a serious problem elsewhere in the world as well. For instance, beginning in the early 1900s, violence was endemic in Celtic-Rangers games in Scotland, with pitched battles between spectators and the police being a common occurrence.[29] It wasn't only Mohun Bagan–East Bengal matches that led to violence. When lesser teams looked as though they might defeat either Mohun Bagan or East Bengal, the crowds often turned violent. In 1949 this happened when the Aryan Club, always an irritant to the Big Two, was leading by a goal against East Bengal at halftime. Unfortunately, the referees often bore the brunt of such violence,

Chuni Goswami, Mohun Bagan star and India captain, during a Calcutta League match against archrival East Bengal, 1963. The packed stands are testimony to the popularity of the rivalry between the two clubs. Photograph by Monojit Chanda. Printed by permission of Monojit Chanda

and in the 1949 incident, the referee was beaten unconscious by spectators.[30] Such incidents occurred so often that in 1951 the chief minister of West Bengal, B. C. Roy, was forced to call a meeting of the football clubs and come up with a plan to stop the violence.[31] Even though the police presence in the ground was increased, it had little effect. Again, therefore, in 1957 Roy suggested that club names like East Bengal or Mohammedan Sporting, which encouraged "localism, provincialism and communalism," should be disallowed, but no avail.[32]

The Calcutta clubs and their enormous fan base were the leading football outfits, but regional football centers flourished as well. In 1948, for instance, Bangalore Muslims won their third Rovers Cup by defeating a Mohun Bagan team that contained as many five Olympic players.[33] Indeed, Mysore (later renamed Karnataka) was a nursery for India football, with as many as six players from the state playing on the 1948 Olympic team. Most of them, however, were recruited by the big Calcutta clubs. For instance, Ahmed Khan, who played for India in the 1948 and 1952 Olympics as well as in the 1951 Asiad, started his playing career in Bangalore, first with the Bangalore Crescent and then the Bangalore Muslims, but was recruited by East Bengal in 1949, where he played for more than a decade.[34] While these teams lost steam in the 1950s, the state-run Indian Telephone Industries team was a regular in national tournaments.

Hyderabad was another prominent football center, and the premier team from the southern city was the state-owned Hyderabad Police, which continued its dominance in the post-1947 period. One of the great games involving the Hyderabad Police was the Durand Trophy in 1950, the first in postindependent India, when it was up against Mohun Bagan. Hyderabad Police was down, 0–2, for most of the game, managing to tie in the dying minutes.[35] In the replay, the Hyderabad Police won a famous 1–0 victory. That year, the Hyderabad Police won thirteen of the fifteen tournaments it participated in, including the Rovers Cup.[36] Over the next five years, Hyderabad Police won the Rovers Cup five times in a row. The team was composed predominantly of Muslims, with the odd Hindu or Christian player turning out for the club. The 1952 Hyderabad Police team for the Rovers had at least one Hindu, Doraiswamy, and a Christian, Patrick, playing.

Football thrived in Goa, too, but a peculiar situation prevailed there, with Portugal loath to let go of its enclave in India, even after the British left in

1947. In fact, the Portuguese government used football to bring Goa closer to Portugal and even established a Goa league, the Conselho de Desportos da India Portuguesa. The first title was won by the Clube Desportivo Chinchinim, with the Clube de Desportos de Vasco da Gama subsequently winning the league three times. Foreign clubs were invited to play in Goa, including the famous Portuguese club Benefica, which visited in 1959. It played a military team and a Goanese team twice, winning all the games. Outside Goa, the sizable Goan population in Bombay organized the Young Goans team, which played in the local tournaments and won the Nadkarni Cup three times in the 1940s.

In 1961, the Salgaocar Sports Club, which was founded by a big mining company, won the last football league in Goa held under Portuguese rule. It also was the first Goan team to play in a major national tournament, the Durand Cup, in 1962. In fact, coming as it did right after Goa was annexed by India, Prime Minister Jawaharlal Nehru made it a point to have himself photographed with the Salgaocar team at his residence.[37] Other mining companies had their own clubs in Goa as well, the most notable being the Dempo Sports Club and the Sesa Goa Sports Club. This trend, of industrial houses setting up football clubs, had earlier begun in Bombay. The Tata Sports Club won the city's Harwood League first in 1945 and several times afterward. Caltex and Mahindra, two other clubs founded by corporate groups, dominated Bombay football in the 1950s. One of Caltex's stars was Neville De Souza, who scored India's only hat trick in Olympic football at the Melbourne Games. De Souza also scored two goals when Caltex won its only Rovers Cup in 1958 by defeating Mohammedan Sporting.[38] Mafatlal, another Bombay club sponsored by a corporate group, was a force to reckon with, not only in Bombay, but also on the national stage, winning the Rovers Cup in 1965 and the DCM Trophy twice in 1966 and 1967. But it was left to the curiously named India Cultural League—a team backed by Bengalis associated with the Bombay film industry such as Ashok Kumar, Sachin Deb Burman, and Manna Dey—to become the first Bombay team to annex the IFA Shield in 1953. The India Cultural League, with the well-known actor Pran Krishan Sikand, or simply Pran as he was better known (who made his name playing a villain in Bollywood films), as the manager, beat Mohun Bagan in the semifinal to set up a final against East Bengal. The final was played three times, resulting in a tie on each occasion. The India Cultural League was, however, declared the winner after East Bengal was penalized for playing with two Pakistani recruits, Masood Fakhri and Niaz Ahmed, who had been suspended by the Pakistan Football Federation.[39]

The southern state of Kerala is another part of India that takes its football very seriously. Kerala also shares with Bengal its taste for fish and communism. The 1948 Indian Olympics team had one member from Travancore, the princely state from which Kerala was created. Subsequently, the state has produced several good football players, but only in the 1970s, when Kerala won the Santosh Trophy for the first time, did the state's club teams, like the Kerala Police, begin to have a national impact.

Strong football clubs emerged in other parts of India. In north India, the Jullundur-based Leaders Club was three times the runner-up in the DCM Trophy between 1966 and 1968 and shocked Mohun Bagan in the 1967 Durand Cup quarterfinal. The biggest star of the Leaders Club, and of north Indian football after Jarnail Singh, was Inder Singh, who played for the Indian team from 1963 to 1975, and in the early 1970s he joined another Punjab outfit sponsored by a textile company, JCT (Phagwara). The Punjab Police team was another worthy team from Punjab, winning the DCM Trophy in 1966.

Alongside the vibrant club scene, the national interstate tournament, the Santosh Trophy, enjoyed its heyday in this period. Not only did big crowds watch the Santosh Trophy matches, but they showcased the best available talent in India. The first Santosh Trophy, which was held in 1941, was predictably won by Bengal. The next time it was held, in 1944, Delhi won the title by shocking Bengal in the final. Bengal was dominant from 1945 onward, winning the title eleven times until 1970, much like Bombay's record in the Ranji Trophy. Bengal not only benefited from its abundant local talent but also could draw on outstation players who represented Bengal by virtue of being registered with the Calcutta clubs. Mysore won the title in 1946 and again in 1952, 1967, and 1968 (the last two times as Karnataka), and the Hyderabad team under coach S. A. Rahim won for two years running in 1956 and 1957 and once again in 1965, by which time it was part of Andhra Pradesh state. The other notable winners were Maharashtra in 1954 and 1963 and the railways three times in the 1960s, when it had on its roster one of India's finest football players, P. K. Banerjee.

Pay in Football

There was not much money to be made as a footballer in the 1950s, though some playing for the bigger Calcutta clubs could get by on their earnings there. One of the biggest stars of the early years of independent India, Sailen Manna, was not paid by his club, Mohun Bagan, which he joined in 1942 and remained for nearly two decades. All that Manna got was his travel expenses, which amounted to Rs 19 (according to one of his biographers, only Rs 13) in his first years.[40] His primary source of income came from a job with the government's Geological Survey of India. This was not unusual. Players from the next generation, like Chuni Goswami, India's captain from 1962 to 1966 and a state-level cricketer to boot, who played his entire career with Mohun Bagan (1955–1968), was not a paid professional. During his playing career, he worked initially for a state-run company, Indian Aluminium, and then from 1961, with State Bank of India where he spent the rest of his career. For lesser-known teams, the rewards were scant. For instance, each player on the Bombay Amateurs team, which lost narrowly to the Hyderabad Police in the 1952 Rovers Cup final, was given Rs 500 and two bush shirts by the Western India Football Association in appreciation of their "splendid achievements."[41]

Of course, some players were paid by the clubs, with East Bengal's "famous five" receiving between Rs 3,000 and Rs 5,000 per season in the 1950s. The Calcutta clubs aggressively recruited players from all over India. For instance, East Bengal officials went to Rajahmundry, in present-day Andhra Pradesh, to recruit Appa Rao, who was then working for the Imperial Tobacco Company. Rao professed his inability to get leave for four months from the company to play during the Calcutta football season. But that wasn't a deterrent for East Bengal, which got one of its influential members to talk to an ITC official to obtain a leave for Rao, who joined the club in 1941.[42] When in Calcutta, the outstation recruits often lived together so they wouldn't be homesick. Anand Bhavan, a hotel in central Calcutta, was a favorite of players from south India.

The Calcutta clubs' talent scouts even looked outside India for players. At the first Asian Quadrangular tournament (which came to be known as the Colombo Cup), held in Colombo, Ceylon, in 1952, the Pakistani forward Masood Fakhri caught the clubs' attention, and the next year, East Bengal recruited him. Fakhri, however, played for only two seasons for East Bengal before moving to Mohammedan Sporting in 1955.[43] In fact, in the 1955 Rovers Cup, Mohammedan Sporting specially arranged for Fakhri to play in only the finals against Mohun Bagan.[44] Another Pakistani, Niaz Ahmed, had played for East Bengal in the 1953 season under controversial circumstances because his transfer documents were not in order. The free movement of Pakistani players to India was a reminder that in the 1950s, ties between the two neighbors still were cordial.

The Santosh Trophy was another recruiting ground for the Calcutta clubs. A member of the 1962 Asian Games squad, I. Arumainayagam, was recruited by Mohun Bagan in 1961 after he had represented Mysore against Bengal in the Santosh Trophy. In this he was following an established tradition of football players from south India who were recruited by Calcutta clubs in the 1930s, initially by Mohammedan Sporting, and, in the 1940s, by East Bengal and Mohun Bagan. Arumainayagam came from a neighborhood in Bangalore called Guntroop (now known as Gautama Puram), from which players, like Olympians A. A. Basheer and K. P. Dhanraj, had already played for Calcutta clubs. Arumainayagam was recruited by Mohun Bagan's captain, Mariappa Kempiah, who himself was from Bangalore.

Arumainayagam began playing for Mohun Bagan for Rs 3,000 a season in the early 1960s, and when he quit the club in 1968, his pay had increased substantially to Rs 20,000. Subsequently he joined the Southern Railways, which afforded him the stability of a regular job as well as the opportunity to play for another ten years.[45] Not only Mohun Bagan or East Bengal were willing to pay big money to lure outstation recruits. Smaller clubs, too, often paid big money to compete with the Big Two. For instance, in the 1950s the Rajasthan Club, bankrolled by the wealthy Marwari community (which originally came from Rajasthan) in Calcutta, won the IFA Shield in 1955. Three years later, the same club persuaded the future star and captain of India, Jarnail Singh, then a schoolboy, from Punjab to play for them.[46] Jarnail, who transferred to Mohun Bagan in 1959 for Rs 6,000, went on to become one of the highest-paid players in Calcutta in the 1960s, receiving as much as Rs 25,000 per season in the 1960s. Pay for professional footballers elsewhere in the world was much higher than in India, but if living standards were taken into account, it did not amount to a great deal. For instance, a top English footballer of the 1960s, Jimmy Greaves (who played for Chelsea,

Tottenham Hotspur, A. C. Milan, and West Ham), was earning £100 per week near the end of his career.[47]

The fierce competition for players between the two big Calcutta teams (and periodically Mohammedan Sporting) usually encouraged plenty of intrigue and hard bargains during the transfer season. Chuni Goswami, for example, in 1955 was offered a Fiat car, worth a princely Rs 14,000 at the time, to move from Mohun Bagan to East Bengal. He refused the offer.[48] Others like Goswami's Mohun Bagan teammate Arumainayagam, who recalls being kept confined to a hotel room during the transfer season and even being escorted to the bathroom. Such drama during the transfer season had a long history. A newspaper report in 1936 spoke of the "intimidation and bribery" during the transfer of players in the Calcutta League:

> Stories are going [sic] the round of the maidan of a first division player who moved from one club to another under the charm and guileful persuasion of a well known cinema "star" after all other methods of persuasion having been tried by the club that wanted him and failed to get him.[49]

Such situations have continued to be a feature of Calcutta football to the present day, sometimes even posing law-and-order problems. The Bengali writer Moti Nandy even wrote a fictional account of the intrigues around club transfer called *Dalbadaler Aage* (*Before Changing Club*).

State Funds for Hockey

Like football, hockey, too, enjoyed considerable popularity in the 1950s and 1960s. The international success of the Indian hockey team translated into big crowds for tournaments like the Beighton (Calcutta), the Aga Khan (Bombay), and the MCC Gold Cup (Madras). Former India players like Leslie Claudius, a four-time Olympian who played for Calcutta Customs, told me a year before he died in 2012 about the huge crowds that thronged the Calcutta maidan to watch the Beighton Trophy matches.[50] Claudius himself was a star on the maidan, as Trevor Vanderputt, the Anglo-Indian captain of the Rangers hockey team who later settled and coached in Australia, recalled: "'Eh ta ["this is" in Bengali] Claudius!' or 'Hail Claudius!' was the awed cry of praise, making him sound like a victorious Roman senator when he pulled off an impossible save."[51] Yet another Olympian, Gurbux Singh, remembered that crowds of more than 25,000 people, many of them outside the stadium watching the game through periscopes, would be present for the premier Beighton Cup matches.[52] Vanderputt said of Calcutta hockey in the 1950s: "Crowds of up to ten thousand were common at a top game. The ladies with their parasols (umbrellas), the men with their Panama hats and 'solar topees' (pith hats) graced the occasion. A band played at half-time and good-natured barracking and much laughter could be heard."[53]

Once it caught the popular imagination, thanks to India's Olympic victories, hockey was patronized by the state-run institutions such as Customs, Port Trust, railways, and the state police departments. Some of the better teams in the Calcutta Maidan were the Calcutta Customs, the Port Commissioners, which won the first Beighton Cup in independent India in 1948, and the Bengal Nagpur Railway (BNR). These institutions were able to attract many Olympians, with Customs in the 1930s and 1940s having in its ranks as many as six national players. Claudius, for instance, was born in the railway junction town of Bilaspur in central India and began his career with the BNR before joining Calcutta Customs in 1949. He served out the rest of his career in Customs, playing for its hockey team until 1965 and subsequently retiring as an assistant collector. Others, such as the two-time Olympian Gurbux Singh (1964 and 1968 games), joined Customs in 1957 as a grade I officer, with a monthly salary of Rs 440, and stayed with the organization for just under a decade. By that time, he had started his own business in motor parts, a rare example of a hockey player going in to business. Pat Jansen, another Olympian, played for the Calcutta Port Commissioners before joining Union Carbide and emigrating to Australia. The railways had on its rolls players of the caliber of India's 1948 captain Kishen Lal. The strength of the Railways team was evident from the fact that it won the national championship twice in the 1950s. Like the armed forces, such was the depth of the Railways' talent that its regional centers fielded separate teams for premier tournaments. In 1955, for instance, two railway teams—North Eastern Railway and Western Railway—made it to the semifinal of the Beighton Cup, with the latter going on to become a cowinner.

In the 1950s, the Calcutta football clubs like East Bengal and Mohun Bagan built strong hockey teams that bested their institutional rivals. In 1957 East

Bengal, with players like Gurbux Singh, won the Beighton Cup by defeating Mohammedan Sporting. This was only the second time that one of the major Calcutta football clubs had won the Beighton, sparking "scenes of jubilation, hitherto unseen in local hockey." East Bengal's supporters "shouted slogans, clapped, pealed bells, blew conch-shells."[54] The very next year East Bengal's archrival, Mohun Bagan, which had players like the Olympian Keshav Dutt (1948 and 1952 games) on its team, won the Beighton Cup, beating the Corps of Engineers, Kirkee.

In Punjab, which was really the nursery of Indian hockey in independent India, Punjab Police was a major employer of hockey players and sportspersons in general. Some of the brightest stars of hockey in independent India worked and played for Punjab Police, including Balbir Singh (senior), a three-time Olympian who played for the Punjab Police for more than two decades between 1941 and 1961; and Udham Singh, a four-time Olympian, who played for the same team for eighteen years, beginning in 1947. The dominance of the Punjab Police was evident from the composition of the Punjab state team in the 1950 national hockey championship, in which fourteen of the sixteen players were policemen. Again, India's team for the 1956 Olympics had five players—Balbir Singh (senior), Udham Singh, Raghubir Lal, Gurdev Singh, and Bakshish Singh—all from the Punjab Police, and another four in the 1952 games.

Bombay was the other great center for hockey, with as many as seven members of India's 1948 Olympic squad from that city. Besides the Tatas' team, some of the pre-1947 teams, such as the Lusitanians, were still in existence, winning the Aga Khan Tournament in 1953 and 1954 and reaching the finals twice in the 1950s. Four players from the Lusitanians were on the Indian team in the 1948 Olympics: Walter D'Souza (who was also a football player on the Young Goans team), goalkeeper Leo Pinto (who cut his teeth playing for the Byculla Rovers at the tender age of thirteen), Maxie Vaz, and Lawrie Fernandes.[55] In the 1950s, Dhyan Chand's home state, Uttar Pradesh (known as the United Provinces in pre-1947 India), also fielded a team known as the UP Selected XI, which jointly won the 1955 Beighton Cup. The star of this team was India's former captain, K. D. Singh Babu, whose artistry, as one newspaper reported, was "so absorbing that he left both the opposition and the spectators spellbound."[56]

Unlike cricket or football, few private companies fielded hockey teams. The Tatas were an exception, with the Tata Sports Club fielding a hockey team that included the Olympians R. S. Gentle and Leo Pinto (who had moved from the Lusitanians). In the late 1940s and 1950s, the Tata Club won the Beighton Cup four times and the Aga Khan Cup three times. The Tata Sports Club also went on a foreign tour to East Africa, with Pinto as player-cum-manager.[57] Hockey received a boost in Calcutta because of the intense rivalry between Mohun Bagan and East Bengal, with both clubs vying to win the Beighton Cup. East Bengal, for example, recruited Gurbux Singh in 1957 and won the Beighton Cup, breaking the institutional teams' stranglehold on the tournament. Singh again helped East Bengal win the Beighton Cup in 1967, after which he joined Mohun Bagan for the rest of his playing career. When he began playing for East Bengal, Gurbux was paid Rs 2,000 for the entire season. A decade later, when he was playing for Mohun Bagan, he was paid Rs 6,000 for the season.[58] Other Calcutta clubs, too, sometimes spent heavily on outstation players in order to keep up with Mohun Bagan and East Bengal. The Bhowanipore club, which was never one of Calcutta's major sports clubs, succeeded in bringing the great K. D. Singh Babu to Calcutta for a couple of seasons, 1953 and 1954, and even winning the Calcutta Hockey League in 1953.[59] Trevor Vanderputt cited the phenomenon of "shamateurs" in Indian hockey, in which the players held low-paying jobs and were given financial "incentives" by the major clubs so that that their amateur status and prospects of playing the Olympics would not be hindered.[60]

The interstate hockey championship also was popular, with Punjab the dominant team in independent India. In 1947 Punjab won the championship, following it by winning the championship three times in a row from 1949 through 1951, once again in 1954, and twice in the 1960s. The Railways were equally dominant in this period, winning the title nine times. The 1952 national championship was a particularly eventful one, with Bengal, led by the Anglo-Indian Olympian Dick Da Luz and a heavy concentration of Anglo-Indian players, snapping Punjab's three-time championship streak. In the championship played in Calcutta, the two teams played out a thrilling 1–1 tie in the final, with the sole Armenian in the Bengal side, Zaven "Bulbul" Carapiat, playing an excellent game. In the replayed final, Bengal won, 2–1, much to the delight of the packed stands.[61]

The Armed Forces

Besides the sports clubs and state-owned companies, we need to say something about the involvement of the armed forces in sports during this period. Like the railways and the State Bank of India, the armed forces were able to attract talent from across India. Unlike the two other state-run organizations, however, the army had a much longer tradition of patronizing sports, besides being able to draw on a pool of personnel who were recruited after rigorous physical tests. The role of the army in the development of sports in British India has been well documented, so much so that Anthony de Mello, in his pioneering book on Indian sports, wrote that the "principal source of sporting inspiration" in modern India was the British army.[62] This was especially true for hockey.

Beginning with Dhyan Chand and his brother Roop Chand, many hockey players in British India were members of the armed forces. After 1947, the army's role in nurturing hockey talent continued to some extent. The village of Sansarpur, near Jalandhar Cantonment, may be the best example of the army's place in hockey's history. The British army introduced hockey to Sansarpur at the turn of the twentieth century, and by the 1990s the village of 3,000 had sent twenty-five hockey players to the Olympics, which is probably a "per capita Olympic record."[63] Not surprisingly, the first hockey Olympian from Sansarpur was an officer, Colonel Gurmit Singh, who played for India in the 1932 Olympics. In independent India, several more Olympians from the village were associated with the army. One was Colonel Balbir Singh Kular, who represented India in the 1968 Olympic Games and also has written about Sansarpur's unique hockey tradition.

The armed forces fielded the Services team in the national hockey championship, which fared very well in the 1950s and 1960s, winning the title five times and becoming the runner-up the same number of times. The strength of the Services team was apparent from the fact that the 1956 Indian Olympic squad had as many as five Services players, including the three-time Olympian goalkeeper Shankar Laxman. That year a Services team also won the Beighton Cup, defeating Mohun Bagan.[64] Besides the combined Services team, regimental teams from different parts of the country participated in the various hockey tournaments. Some of the notable teams were the Sikh

Regimental Centre, Madras Sappers, Corps of Signals, Maratha Light Infantry, and the Indian Air Force, which had several Olympians in their ranks, such as Hari Pal Kaushik, V. J. Peter, Hardyal Singh Garcchey, R. S. Bhola, and Shantalal Jadhav.

In cricket and football, the Services also took part in the Ranji Trophy and the Santosh Trophy probably fielding its best teams in the 1950s and 1960s. The Services cricket team, led by India batsman Hemchandra "Hemu" Adhikari, reached the Ranji finals in 1956 and 1957. The Services football team, led by one of India's finest goalkeepers, Peter Thangaraj,[65] won the Santosh Trophy in 1960 and was the runner-up twice in the 1960s. As in hockey, regimental teams also did well in the premier national tournaments. The standout teams in the 1950 and 1960s were the Madras Regimental Centre and the Dehradun-based Gorkha Brigade. The Madras Regimental Centre, with Thangaraj as the goalkeeper, won the Durand Cup twice in 1955 and 1958. The Gorkha Brigade featured in three Durand finals, each time playing against a military team. In 1958 the Gorkhas lost to the Madras Regimental Centre; in 1966 it beat the Sikh Regimental Centre to win the trophy; and in 1969 it repeated its triumph, beating the paramilitary Border Security Force (BSF). The BSF team also had an enviable record, winning the Durand in 1968 and subsequently four more times in the 1970s.

Besides the three big sports, the armed forces had a stranglehold on athletics and sports generally, from basketball to boxing. Starting in the 1950s, many of the medal winners in the Asian and Commonwealth Games were from the armed forces. Accordingly, in 1962 the Indian Olympic Association's journal stated that "no fewer than nine of the major national championships in various branches of sport are held by the Services teams or individuals."[66] The first Indian wrestler to win a gold medal in the Commonwealth Games (1958), Lila Ram, as well as India's first gold medal winner in boxing in the Asiad (1962), Padam Bahadur Mall, and subsequently two-time Asian Games gold medalist, Hawa Singh, were soldiers. The most famous athlete from the armed forces was Milkha Singh, a lowly *jawan* (junior soldier) who had fled, at great risk, from present-day Pakistan during the 1947 Partition.[67] He was recruited by the army in 1952 and joined the Electrical Mechanical Centre at Secunderabad in south India.[68] It was in the army that Milkha first participated in a trial for a six-mile race, on the promise that those selected for training would be "exempted from fatigue duty" and also be given "an extra

Milkha Singh, in his prime, practicing. Reprinted by permission of the Hindu Archives

glass of milk every day."[69] Milkha made it to his unit team in 1953 and, in the 1955 Services Athletic Meet, placed second to India's national champion in the 400-meter event. From there Milkha never looked back, going on to win, as mentioned in an earlier chapter, in several international events.

Conclusion

There was good reason why state-run organizations and private companies played a big role in Indian sports in the years immediately following independence. None of the major sports, with the partial exception of football, paid enough to sportspersons for a secure livelihood, so most of them had to look for stable jobs that allowed them time for their sports. The state-run organizations like railways, Customs, or the state police departments had a long tradition of employing hockey players, which they continued in independent India. As government-owned organizations, they were helping what was effectively India's "national" game. This was also the time when the Indian state, under Nehru's guidance, played a huge role in nearly all sectors. By having players on their rolls and building up strong teams, the state-run organizations not only advertised themselves as good employers but also burnished their credentials in general. Many of the hockey players who were not college graduates, however, were employed in lowly jobs and were not paid very well. For athletes, who were not playing one of the three big sports, a job in one of the state-run organizations or the armed forces was often the only hope of a stable source of income.

Unlike hockey, cricket and football saw a greater involvement of private companies. Except for the Tatas, who sponsored teams in all three major sports—hockey, football, and cricket—most private firms preferred cricket or football. This was probably because hockey, despite India's international success, had a smaller following compared with that of football or cricket. This was true all over the world, where hockey never really counted as a mass sport even in countries like Australia, the Netherlands, or Germany, which had been successful since the 1960s. The private firms that put money into football and cricket had good reasons for doing so. One was getting mileage for the firm through its sports success. A Tatas' publication in 1972 explained that when its teams did well, the company became well known, something that the management felt no amount of advertising could accomplish. But the firms differed in their approach to those employees who were recruited for their sports prowess. The Tatas preferred to offer employment to young sportspersons and groom them both on the playing field and in the office or factory. The Tatas' mantra was that even after retirement, a sportsperson would be able to have a career and "be an asset rather than a liability."[70]

A similar philosophy was followed by Mahindra, which, like the Tatas, seriously sponsored both cricket and football and competed in open tournaments. Like the Tatas, the company was interested in grooming young talent and was known to turn down established players seeking employment. The Delhi Cloth Mills followed a different strategy by sponsoring a football tournament, which quickly became one of the premier tournaments in India, providing tremendous publicity for the company.

Other companies like ACC and Mafatlal were more interested in quick success and recruited players who had already made a reputation. The outlook of the company's management was, of course, critical to its recruitment policies. For instance, in the late 1960s, the new chairman of SBI, which was so active in recruiting sportspersons, was against the "ad hoc recruitment and employment of players which resulted in too many special privileges for sportsmen."[71] This ended in a change of policy in the 1970s. All things considered, however, Indian companies and government institutions played the role of benefactors and patrons in the absence of a professional sports structure. Such a structure, according to Richard Cashman, compared well with that of other countries. Speaking of cricket, he wrote that the relationship between an Indian patron and a cricketer was "potentially lifelong," whereas an English country contract—at the time the highest-paying proposition in cricket—was limited to a cricketer's playing career.[72] This was true of hockey and football, too, with the difference that unlike cricket players, football and hockey players tended to be less educated and hence more likely to be employed in lower-level and less lucrative jobs. This in turn meant that after their playing days were over, even football players or hockey stars who had once played for India languished in lowly jobs and struggled to make ends meet. A notable example is India's hockey goalkeeper and double Olympic gold medalist, Shankar Laxman, who spent his career with the Maratha Light Infantry. After retiring in 1979, he lived in poverty. When he was diagnosed with gangrene in 2006 and eventually died from it, he did not have enough money for treatment.[73] Similarly, when a football great, Sahu Mewalal, who scored the winning goal for India in the 1951 Asian Games, died in 2008, his children had to struggle to get him treated. Even though Mewalal had been an employee of the railways all his life and a star forward of the Eastern Railways team, his postretirement pension was a pittance.

For every Laxman and Mewalal, there were several hundred unknowns who played for their club and state teams with little to show by way of money for their athletic prowess. Possibly the most remarkable story of a former national-level sportsperson who fell on tough times is that of Paan Singh Tomar, from the hardscrabble district of Morena in Madhya Pradesh. Tomar, who represented India in the 3,000-meter steeplechase in the 1958 Asian Games and whose national record in the event stood for more than a decade, was a *subedar* (equivalent to a petty officer) with the Bengal Engineers at Roorkee. In 1977 he killed three of his cousins over a land dispute.[74] Although the subsequent chain of events is, at best, uncertain, Tomar had been on the run ever since becoming a dreaded name in the bandit-infested Chambal valley of Madhya Pradesh. When he was shot dead, along with gang members, on October 1, 1981, in a police ambush, he had been indicted for fifty crimes, including eleven murders. Tomar's death was not only reported in some detail by the London *Times*,[75] but his life was also the subject of a critically acclaimed biopic in 2012. Albeit an extreme case, Tomar's life is a reminder of the vagaries of being a sportsperson in India.

The uncertainties as well as the joys of being a sportsperson, particularly a football player, were vividly portrayed in the fictional writings of Moti Nandy.[76] That fiction is close to real life is evident from the concluding lines of the autobiography of Surajit Sengupta, a star football player in the 1970s and 1980s. When describing the complex emotions on the day his son was born, Sengupta recalled only one thought: "Whatever he does in life he must never become a footballer."[77]

11

1971 AND AFTER

THE RELIGION CALLED CRICKET

THE YEAR 1971 IS BEST REMEMBERED IN INDIA FOR INDIRA Gandhi's winning a resounding majority in India's first-ever midterm general election and for the war of liberation in Bangladesh. That year, momentous events were taking place on the cricket pitch as well that would change the face of sports in India for good. The sports drama of 1971 had two acts. The first was at the Queen's Park Oval in Port of Spain where India was playing the West Indies in the second match of a five-Test series. India had gone into the series never having won a Test match against the West Indies, despite having played it on twenty-three occasions from 1948 onward. In 1971 the West Indies was going through a rebuilding process, having lost the services of its formidable pace attack of the 1960s. But the team, led by the mighty Gary Sobers, had a strong batting lineup that included Roy Fredericks, Rohan Kanhai, Clive Lloyd, and, of course, Sobers himself. On March 10, 1971, the day the Indian general elections ended, the Indian cricket team was left with the task of chasing a paltry target of 124 runs to win the match. India reached the target comfortably, thanks to a twenty-one-year-old called Sunil Manohar Gavaskar who, incidentally, made his debut in that match. The next three Tests were draws, and India won its first its first overseas series victory against a strong cricketing nation. (The only other series that India had won abroad was against New Zealand, a perennial also-ran in world cricket, in 1967.) Significantly, Gavaskar ended up scoring a mammoth 774 runs in the series, becoming a legend in the Caribbean to the extent that a calypso was composed in his honor.[1]

The second act of 1971 was played out five months later in a setting much more central to the imagination of any Indian: London. When India began its tour of England in July, it had not won a single match of the nineteen Tests it had played on English soil, beginning in 1932. Indeed, in its last two visits, the Indian team had been soundly beaten in all the eight Tests that had been played. Compared with the West Indian team, the English cricket team in 1971 could also lay claim to being the top team in the world. After the first two Tests ended in rain-hit draws, the two teams headed to London's Oval ground for the final Test. The Oval Test, too, seemed destined for a stalemate until on the fourth day of the match, England was bowled out for 101 runs, its lowest-ever score against India, due to a magnificent spell of bowling by Indian spinner Bhagwat Chandrasekhar. The fifth day of the Test marked the beginning of the eleven-day annual Ganesh festival held in honor of the elephant-headed Hindu god of fortune. The significance of this was not lost on Indian supporters, who went to the extent of arranging for an elephant from Chessington Zoo to parade around the outfield.[2] The Indian team managed to hold itself together to chase down 173 runs in the second innings, despite Gavaskar not scoring a run.

Only around 5,000 Indian supporters were at the field to see the historic moment, but they made the most of it. As the London *Times* reported, "The Indian supporters celebrated the winning boundary by Abid Ali by rushing from the terraces as the players made a dash for the pavilion."[3] This is how Gavaskar described the finale in his best-selling *Sunny Days*:

> Abid was swallowed up by the huge crowd of spectators, mostly Indians, who had rushed on to the fled. Farokh, who was at the other end, had no chance of making it to the pavilion. Both players were engulfed by the crowd and they were hoisted on willing shoulders and held high up in the air. Their trousers were stuffed with money and it was good ten minutes before they could go the dressing room where there were equally wild scenes.[4]

The iconic photograph of the joyous scene represented in equal measure the sheer thrill of beating the colonial masters at their own game and the liberation of Indian cricket from decades of mediocrity. The next day's *Times of India* confirmed the significance of the win on its front page: "Indian cricket achieved its ultimate ambition here today—a victory over England in England."[5] An editorial the next day spelled out the ramifications: "Glorious to be living at this hour and to be an Indian! Days, months, years will pass, but our cricket team's magnificent triumph over England in England will remain unforgettable."[6]

The events in faraway London were followed with avid interest in India. All through the final day of the Test, people in Delhi "were seen glued to their radio sets, tight-lipped and fingers crossed, praying for an Indian win." Those without access to a radio "kept in touch with the progress at the Oval, ringing up the news agency and newspaper offices for the latest information." Once the winning run was hit, "crackers burst and cricket fans marched through Bombay's streets in gay abandon."[7] When after a fortnight or so, the Indian team returned to India, their flight was diverted to Delhi so that they could first meet Prime Minister Indira Gandhi. A reception was organized at the Kotla cricket ground, where the team got a standing ovation from a packed stadium. The next day the team landed in Bombay to a rapturous welcome. A newspaper reported:

> The police band struck the tune of "Welcoming the Conquering Heroes" as skipper Ajit Wadekar and his men alighted from the plane and walked to the specially erected rostrum at the airport. More than 10,000 people, including a large number of girls, in their best costume, turned out at the airport hours before the arrival of the team and cheered the heroes as they were led to the rostrum.... From the airport the players were taken in an open motorcade to the City Hall and all along the route, they were showered with petals, garlands and bouquets by millions of people ranging from school children, workers and the common man.[8]

The *Times of India* even launched a fund in appreciation of the victory.

This was obviously was no ordinary victory. While the victorious hockey teams of the past had been feted and had even beaten England in the first

Olympics after Indian independence, that did not compare with the reaction to the 1971 victory at the Oval. This was a transformative moment for Indian cricket. Indeed, Ramachandra Guha has called 1971 "the year that would mark Indian cricket's coming of age."[9] It is no coincidence that 1971 was also the year that Gavaskar—the first real pan-Indian sportstar after Dhyan Chand and one of the finest batsman of his time—burst on to the international scene. A sports writer has written, and many would agree, that Gavaskar's debut divided Indian cricket into two eras: BG (before Gavaskar), a period generally marked by debacles and defeats, and AG (after Gavaskar), when Indian cricket won some famous victories and much greater international respect.[10] Yet another historian described the effect the great batsman had on other sports in a cleverly entitled article, "How Gavaskar Killed Indian Football."[11] The year 1971, then, is a useful starting point to discuss one of the questions posed at the beginning of this book: How did cricket become the dominant sport in India, and why did hockey and football, so popular in the 1950s and 1960s, gradually decline?

Formation of a Cricketing Public

Even though 1971 was a defining year for cricket in that India showed it could compete with the very best, a "national" cricketing public was being constituted well before that. There were several reasons—some due to the way the different sports were organized globally and others because of way they developed in India—why cricket was able to lay claim to being the real "national" sport and to being the first among equals. The first was the nature of world cricket, in which only six nations were members of the small circle of Test-playing nations when India began playing Test matches in 1932. This meant that for the better part of fifty years, from 1932 to 1970, India was able to rub shoulders with the top cricket-playing nations despite having a poor record. In this, cricket was very different from football and hockey, both of which were very popular in India through the 1950s and 1960s. From early on, Indian football was built on city-based clubs, which developed a passionate fan base. In contrast, the Indian national football team had a much lower international profile with only sporadic success, never playing in the World Cup and making its last appearance in the Olympics in 1960. Even in the Asian Games, football's success dried up by the 1960s. As Satadru Sen

The cover of the *Sportsweek* magazine featuring the Indian team on its arrival in India
after its historic win over England in 1971. Front row, from left to right, Bishan Singh Bedi
(wearing turban), Abid Ali, Eknath Solkar, Captain Ajit Wadekar, Sunil Gavaskar (with
trophy), Erapalli Prasanna, D. Govindraj, and K. Jayantilal. Note the price of the magazine,
which at 50 paise is less than one U.S. cent at the current conversion rate. Courtesy of the
personal collection of Clayton Murzello

noted: "Even though India's record in cricket in the period between its international debut and its first victory overseas in New Zealand is not significantly better than its record in football, its presence in world cricket was much greater than what it was on the football field."[12]

Unlike football, a lack of international success wasn't a factor in hockey until the late 1960s, since India was still among the top teams. But here too, we must remember that besides the quadrennial Olympics (the hockey World Cup was started in 1971, by which time Indian hockey had slipped into decline), the Indian team itself was a not a very visible entity. Besides, as I pointed out earlier, hockey's popularity was increasingly confined to small pockets of the country, such as Punjab; what is now the state of Jharkhand; the tribal areas of Orissa; and the district of Coorg in Karnataka. In short, by the 1970s hockey was no longer a mainstream sport. Above all, in most of the countries where the game was played, hockey did not have the kind of following or glamour that either football or cricket did. As one scholar observed, outside India, hockey within a few years of its birth became "a game for middle-class women and a handful of middle-class men," with hardly any mass following.[13] Visits by international hockey teams to India were rare, though occasionally teams from top hockey-playing nations, such as the Netherlands and Germany, played matches in India. Even rarer were international tournaments hosted by India, such as the hockey tournament held in Ahmedabad in 1962 in which nine teams, including those from Germany and the Netherlands, participated.[14] It was only when the Pakistani hockey team toured India, as in the 1977 and the subsequent Test series, was there real enthusiasm among sports fans. Again, unlike football, hockey did not have a comparable club following. National-level tournaments, such as the Beighton Cup, were popular, but institutional teams like the regional units of the Railways or the Punjab Police were never likely to have a committed fan base. Some clubs, like Bombay's Lusitanians, composed mostly of Goan players, and the hockey teams of the Calcutta clubs, such as Mohun Bagan or East Bengal, had a larger following, but they were the exceptions. In the case of the two big Calcutta clubs, the following for hockey games had fallen dramatically since the 1960s.

Radio Republic

The one critical factor in creating a national audience for cricket was the radio. Radio commentary of matches—usually accompanied by the crackle of airwaves and the listener's imagination to conjure up the scene in a distant cricket field—brought about at first an India-wide community of cricket fans huddled around the radio sets and, later, with technological progress, glued to a transistor at home or work or even on the move. In 1933, when Test matches were played in India for the first time, radio commentary was first broadcast, although it was limited to only part of the day's play. In addition, the listening audience was minuscule, since the broadcast was restricted to certain parts of Bombay where the first India–England Test match was held. Besides, there were just under 11,000 licensed radios sets in the city at the time.[15] The very next year, there was radio commentary for the Pentangular by A. F. S. "Bobby" Talyarkhan. It wasn't just cricket, however, that was being broadcast live. In 1934 there was running commentary for a Calcutta football league match between Mohun Bagan and Calcutta Football Club, with the commentators being the star duo of Raichand Boral (a legendary music composer) and Birendra Krishna Bhadra (an equally famous broadcaster, though he was far better known for his rendition of the *Mahishasurmardini* on radio before the annual Durga Puja festival).[16] But the real difference between cricket and other sports became apparent after 1947. In the 1948/1949 India–West Indies series, the state broadcaster, All-India Radio (AIR), organized running commentary in the major cities for all five Test matches. A few other first-class matches were broadcast live as well. Richard Cashman pointed out that these broadcasts dominated AIR's daytime programs that winter and "played a significant role in creating a mass audience for cricket."[17] The number of radio sets being manufactured increased dramatically, too, from only 3,000 in 1947 to 150,000 a decade later.[18]

More important, cricket matches involving India that were played abroad could be followed from India, with the BBC commentary for matches in England having a wide following. As noted earlier, India's victory in England in 1971 was avidly followed on the radio by cricket fans. At the time there were an estimated 15 million radio sets in India, but the number of people of listening to cricket commentary would have been many times more. By one estimate, 80 million people were listening to radio commentary in the mid-1970s.[19] Most accounts by Indians, except for the lucky few who were at the field, of the 1971 victory revolved around the radio. Even those who weren't able to listen to the running commentary had their own radio-related story, listening in the privacy of their home or in crowded public places. Guha has a charming recollection of the 1971 Oval Test when he was at boarding school:

> My cricket-mad House Captain, Vivek Bammi, went as privilege to listen
> to the BBC, disregarding my pleas to let me accompany him. For a while
> I thumbed distractedly through my books till, minutes before we had to
> turn into bed, Bammi rushed into the study to announce: "England 101
> all out, Chandra 6 for 38!"[20]

Not surprisingly, the likes of John Arlott and Brian Johnston and their British accent have instant recall for older Indian cricket fans.

Some in the AIR commentary team acquired reputations almost rivaling those of the players. The greatest commentator was undoubtedly A. F. S. Talyarkhan who, with a scorer by his side, single-handedly broadcast in 1948 the entire proceedings of the second Test against West Indies.[21] But that was also his last stint as a commentator (he made an exception for the 1954/1955 series in Pakistan), since he was unwilling to abide by the AIR's policy of having a three-person commentary team. Talyarkhan is probably the only Indian commentator to have inspired a poem, by the well-known poet Dom Moraes:

> Seen by the sun, you have memories,
> ... Nayudu who covered the sky with sixes
> Merchant snarled cuts way on panther feet,
> Your voice and pen erected them like trees,
> ... From my generation, and for others, thank you.[22]

Other well-known commentators included Dicky Rutnagur, Bijoy Chandra "Berry" Sarbadhikari, Pearson Surita, Devraj Puri, Anant Setalvad, Ananda Rau, and, of course, Vizzy, who was more famous for his gaffes. In the 1960s, in addition to English, cricket commentary in Hindi and few other Indian languages, such as Bengali and Tamil, were introduced, which further widened cricket's reach. The multiplicity of languages also contributed much to the "indigenization"[23] of cricket and the "domestication" of the vocabulary of cricket.[24]

The popularity of the cricket broadcasts can be gauged from the fact that 60 percent of the radios in Bombay during the Test match against the West Indies in December 1978 were tuned in to cricket. Outside Bombay, the figure was 45 percent in urban areas,[25] dwarfing the audience for other radio programs. In the 1950s, radio commentary was provided for club football in Calcutta—with commentators like Ajay Basu becoming legends in their own right—and sometimes for other sports, but its audience was a fraction of the nationwide cricketing public. This was pointed out in 1970 by a magazine: "Why this partiality for Test cricket, the running commentary of which is on the national hook-up, it is difficult to understand. . . . Occasionally the finals of a premier football or tennis or badminton final get time on AIR, but mostly it is not on the national hook-up."[26] The partiality of radio (and later television) to cricket was captured by a letter to the editor in a newspaper in the early 1980s from Punjab (at a time when the state was in the grip of militancy), threatening dire consequences if the India–Pakistan cricket matches were broadcast:

> In case the running commentary will be telecast/broadcast we will blow off the commentator box. . . Hence it is wise for the AIR and Doordarshan [India's state-run broadcaster] officials not to come to the stadium for the sake of their own lives. They should have to think of hockey, football, athletics etc, in which India is lacking (sic) behind due to wrong policies of AIR and Doordarshan.[27]

Radio was critical to the formation of a mass audience for cricket in India in the 1970s, but other media fed into the popularity of cricket as well. As Sujit Mukherjee—who in the 1990s published a charming book on cricket—noted, "If there are nine ways of getting out at cricket, there are at least five media through which one can explain why or recall how it happened—newspaper reports, magazine articles, published books, radio broadcasts, Doordarshan telecasts."[28] I mentioned earlier the partiality of newspapers to cricket in pre-1947 India, and this continued in independent India. (I discuss the role of television later in this chapter.) In the sports magazines and books in the 1970s and even earlier, cricket was by far the most common topic. By the late 1970s, India could "boast of three sport weeklies, mostly sustained by cricket, two cricket quarterlies, one annual, an increasing number of books on the game in English and many Indian languages."[29] Indeed, journals on cricket had a long history in India, going back to the monthly magazine *Indian Cricket*, published by the Cricket Club of India from 1934 to 1940. In the 1940s, the *Hindu* newspaper group began publishing the annual *Indian Cricket* as well as the popular *Sport and Pastime*, which folded in 1968. By the late 1970s, there were three sports magazines in English—*Sportsweek* (begun by the journalist Khalid Ansari),[30] *Sportstar* (published by the *Hindu* and still in existence), and *Sportsworld* (with M.A.K. Pataudi as its first editor[31])—being published. In all these magazines, cricket coverage occupied the lion's share of the pages.[32]

A National Obsession

Although cricket had a reputation for being an elite sport in colonial India, as we saw in an earlier chapter, it also attracted cricket players from lower-class backgrounds. After 1947, however, the middle classes provided the bulk of state-level and national players. At the same time, cricket was avidly followed by both elites and plebeians. The Congress Party's politics was avowedly socialist and autarchic in the first three decades of independent India, but cricket was one imperial import that flourished. The Harrow-educated Jawaharlal Nehru was a regular in the annual cricket match between the two houses of Parliament. An iconic picture shows Nehru in the 1950s, dressed in cricketing whites and with his chin on the handle of his bat, as if for a moment divested of the cares of running the country. Indeed, during his daughter Indira Gandhi's imposition of emergency rule between and 1975 and 1977, a picture of Nehru walking onto the cricket field was reprinted on the cover of a government brochure with the title "The Skipper of Modern India." Even those who publicly condemned cricket often privately followed it. Guha tells a wonderful anecdote about the socialist leader Ram Manohar Lohia, who was no friend of cricket, which he regarded as a colonial sport. But in 1960, when Pakistan was playing a Test series in India, after giving a press conference in which he harangued Nehru, the English language, and cricket, Lohia walked to the nearest *paanwallah* and asked about Pakistani batsman Hanif Mohammed's score.[33]

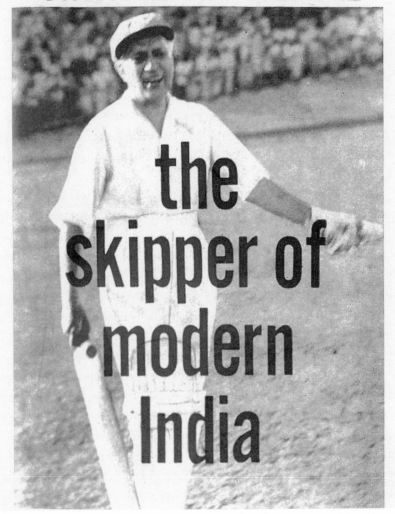

The cover of a government brochure featuring Jawaharlal Nehru, which was published during the emergency imposed by Prime Minister Indira Gandhi. Courtesy of the personal collection of Ramachandra Guha

Unlike football or hockey, there was plenty of glamour associated with cricket, and individual players tended to have a bigger following than football or hockey stars. In colonial India, the glamour was provided by the princes and high British officials. But in independent India, a few of the princes were still playing, most notably the debonair, Oxford-educated

M.A.K. Pataudi, who was appointed India's cricket captain in 1962 as a twenty-one-year-old, the youngest ever in Indian history. When he married film star Sharmila Tagore in 1969, he literally united the two great passions of India, cricket and Bollywood. Despite losing one eye in an accident, Pataudi continued playing cricket at the highest level. Historian Mukal Kesavan wrote: "His pedigree, his poshness, his flair, his epic disregard for his handicap, spoke to the anxieties and aspirations of a young republic, and to its hunger for heroes."[34] A contemporary of Pataudi's, the England cricket captain Mike Brearley, noted that Pataudi was the "first cricketing superstar in India whose appeal involved so heady a mix of brilliance, charm and charisma."[35]

Several Indian cricketers from humbler backgrounds also lent color and glamour to the game in the formative years of independent India. These included Mushtaq Ali, Salim Durrani, and M. L. Jaisimha. Durrani, who was known for hitting sixes on demand, even acted in a film in the early 1970s, becoming the first Indian sportsperson (if we omit Dara Singh) to do so, starring opposite the Bollywood star Parveen Babi. And when he was dropped from a Test match, spectators turned up at the field with signs saying "No Durrani, No Test," something first seen when Mushtaq Ali was dropped in 1946 from the Indian team playing against the Australian Services team.

The obsession with cricket and its impact on national pride were evident during India's disastrous tour of England in 1974. Having raised the bar in 1971, India was decisively beaten in 1974, with the second Test at Lord's marking a new low when India scored its lowest-ever Test total of forty-two runs in the second innings. If the events on the cricket pitch did not go well for India, the events off it underscored the place of cricket among India's elites. The day after the Lord's Test, the Indian team was invited to a reception at the house of the Indian high commissioner, B. K. Nehru (a cousin of Jawaharlal Nehru). When the team showed up late (one of the reasons was that an Indian player had been caught shoplifting at Marks and Spencer's and the team manager was busy trying to hush up the incident; the other was London's evening traffic), the irate high commissioner apparently asked the Indian captain, Ajit Wadekar, to leave—an incident without precedence. The Indian media, however, went hammer and tongs at the Indian team. The *Times of India*'s cricket correspondent wrote about the players that "thanks to the publicity showered on them, they have been inclined to regard themselves as being above the law." A spokesman for the Indian high commission was quoted as saying, "They don't only play bad cricket, they also display bad manners."[36] Even though the matter was eventually sorted out and the Indian team spent some time at the high commissioner's reception, the incident was a reminder of how seriously Indians took wins and defeats on the cricket field. India's star spinner and a man not known to mince his words, Bishan Singh Bedi, summed up the situation in his inimitable way that day on the team bus: "If we had won, and turned up late there would have been no problem. But just because we've lost, we get the stick."[37]

From the 1970s, India's performance on the cricket field was important enough to merit discussion in Parliament, giving cricket the imprimatur of the nation's most important sport. After the disastrous 1974 tour, the issue of the players' behavior came up. Two members of the Lok Sabha (the Lower House) asked what action the government had taken against "certain improper actions on the part of the Indian cricketers" while they were in England. In his written reply, the education minister, Nurul Hasan (at the time, sports were under the education minister's watch), stated that the president of the Board of Control for Cricket in India (BCCI) and the team manager had apologized more than once, prompting the government to close the case.[38]

The same year, there was a controversy over cricket when Bedi was not included on the Indian team to face the West Indies in the first Test of the 1974/1975 series. The ostensible reason was the Indian cricket board's decision to look into Bedi's unauthorized appearance on a television program and his refusal to cooperate with the captain in the 1974 England series. But even before Bedi could be heard by the board's inquiry committee, the selectors were apparently instructed not to choose him for the team. This came up for discussion before Parliament, as did the larger issue of the board's riding roughshod over players and paying them a pittance, despite the sport's incredible popularity. A member of the Rajya Sabha (the Upper House) strongly objected to the attempts being made to "humiliate the world class spin bowler" and demanded his reinstatement on the Indian team. He questioned the BCCI's authority to drop Bedi and asked for a government inquiry headed by a former judge of India's Supreme Court.

He also brought up the question of payments to players. An amount of £17,200 was originally given to the Indian team as foreign exchange, which was subsequently raised to £25,000. The players, however, got only an additional 50 pence in their normal daily allowance of £2 and not for the full duration of the tour.[39] Bedi refused to sign the receipt for payment, and this, it seems, was the real reason for the board's actions.[40] Popular displeasure was expressed in Delhi, Bangalore, and Amritsar, where a cry of "No Bedi, No Test" gathered momentum.[41] Eventually the protests inside Parliament and on the streets resulted in Bedi's coming back on the team in the third Test.

Four years later, Bedi, as India's captain, was once again at the center of a controversy, but this time it was a potent cocktail of cricket and nationalism. The occasion was an India–Pakistan series, the first after seventeen years, during a period in which the two countries had fought two wars. In the final one-dayer at Sahiwal when India was twenty-two runs short of victory with eight wickets in hand, Bedi conceded the match after Pakistani bowlers kept bowling bouncers. The *Times of India*'s K. N. Prabhu reported, "Even had Viswanath stood on Gaekwad's [the two batsmen at the crease] shoulders he would not have got at the ball."[42] The tour, however, continued, with India losing the final Test at Karachi, a match that was telecast live in the major Indian cities. The Indian team returned to find demonstrators at the airport shouting angry slogans, and the team's "miserable" performance was raised in the Lower House, with a demand for an inquiry by a committee into the loss.[43]

Crowds at Cricket Grounds

Despite the game's elitist connotations, cricket was very popular with the masses even when India lost more matches than it won. The frenzy for tickets in every Test match center was a forerunner to the hysteria surrounding cricket in later years. It was routine for stadiums to be filled beyond capacity, and playing on Indian grounds was an intimidating experience for visiting teams. The spectators came from all sections of society, and the crowds thronging cricket stadiums developed a reputation for volatility. In the very first series after 1947, when India against the West Indies, the crowd for the second Test played in Bombay set off firecrackers and blew bugles inside the stadium, behavior that was unheard of on cricket grounds. Both teams complained about the crowd, prompting the president of the Indian cricket board to appeal to the spectators before the fifth Test, which also was in Bombay, to refrain from making "all indecent noises."[44] There were worse incidents in other centers, like Kanpur, an industrial city not far from Delhi, which didn't have much of a cricketing tradition. In the 1964 series against England, the fielders were pelted by missiles, from relatively harmless fruits to more dangerous bricks. Such behavior was roundly condemned by contemporary writers, one of whom chastised the Kanpur crowd, somewhat mildly, as behavior befitting a "fair or Charity Bazaar."[45]

Even worse followed in 1967 in Calcutta, which was known for its discerning but equally explosive crowd, when the West Indies was touring India. On the first day of the Test match, the crowd spilled out into the field.[46] On the second day, which also was New Year's Day, the police beat up some spectators in an attempt to clear the ground. This led to riots in the stadium, with spectators setting fire to the awnings and lighting bonfires inside the ground. The violence spread outside, with a few buses set ablaze. Some 200 people, including 52 policemen, were injured. The game was stopped that day but resumed two days later after both teams were assured of safety. The BCCI even announced a bonus of Rs 100 each for the Indian players as an incentive to play. Violence during football matches was not uncommon, but this was the first time that violence on this scale had occurred during a cricket match. The West Bengal government appointed a commission headed by a judge to investigate it. The commission's report, based on interviews with 74 witnesses and 181 written statements, which was released later that year, squarely blamed the cricket administrators for not ensuring the spectators' basic comforts.[47] The English sportswriter Scyld Berry, who covered an English cricket tour of India in the 1970s, had this to say about the Calcutta crowds: "Riots have undeniably occurred, but they have been sparked by two acts of provocation that have inflamed reasonable people elsewhere: police brutality and the over-selling of tickets."[48] The utter disregard for spectators' comforts, despite the riches that the BCCI have accumulated, continues to this day. The authors of a recent book on cricket asserted, "Going to the stadium to watch an important match is not for the weak. From buying a ticket to surviving the heat, hunger, and bird-brained security arrangements, it is a supreme test of human endurance and courage."[49]

Barely two years later, tragedy struck again at the Eden Gardens when the Australians were touring India in the winter of 1969. Calcutta was then in chaos, with thousands of refugees from East Pakistan having fled to the city. On December 16, 1969, before the start of play of the fourth day of the Test match against Australia, some 25,000 people had queued up for tickets. When the counters opened, there was a mad rush, prompting the police to intervene. The crowd faced off against the police, resulting in six deaths and several injuries. Ironically, the day's play began on time, with more violence inside the stadium. In fact, that tour was a particularly violent one, as the first Test match in Bombay also was marred by crowd disturbances. The violence in Bombay concerned an incident on the field when an Indian player, Srinivas Venkataraghavan, was controversially declared out by the umpire in India's second innings, with India on the verge of losing. The radio commentary, which was relayed to the spectators on their transistors, said the umpire was wrong, provoking a violent reaction inside the stadium. Stands were set on fire and missiles were hurled at the players. The match concluded with thick clouds of smoke billowing in the background. The *Times of India* reported the next day: "It is a novel and sad state of affairs that violence latent in our public life should spring to the surface on our cricket fields." This was a crowd that obviously did not think much of the advice on the official program given to spectators watching a visiting Australian team play a Sind XI in 1935: "Don't query the umpire's decision, he is nearer the wicket than you."[50]

It would be a mistake to think, as many do, that only international cricket drew crowds. While the early rounds of the Ranji Trophy drew only a sparse crowd, in the 1970s it was not uncommon for crowds of up to 30,000 to turn up for the final stages of the Ranji Trophy. As a spectator at the ground, Ramachandra Guha recalled the "thunderous reception" that star batsman, Gundappa Viswanath, got during the historic 1974 Ranji Trophy semifinal when Karnataka defeated Bombay to end the latter's incredible winning streak of fifteen consecutive titles. But Ranji Trophy matches weren't immune to crowd violence either. In 1969, a match between Mysore and Bengal had to be abandoned after the crowd invaded the field, protesting what they believed was a questionable decision against a Mysore batsman.[51] Again in 1977, a match between Bombay and Baroda suffered the same fate when the

Crowd violence at the Eden Gardens on New Year's Day, 1967, during an India–West Indies match. Photograph by Monojit Chanda. Printed by permission of Monojit Chanda

crowd pelted players with stones and dug up the pitch.[52] It wasn't just the Ranji Trophy that drew an enthusiastic response. Other city-based tournaments, such as the Buchi Babu tournament, named after the "father" of Madras cricket, and the Moin-ud-Dowla Gold Cup, begun by Nawab Moin-ud-Dowla of Hyderabad, were very popular during this period. Gavaskar wrote in his memoir that during the 1971 Buchi Babu tournament, in which he was representing Associated Cement, the crowd at the college ground was so large that "he had to be escorted by the police to the wicket."[53] Even today, the tournament occupies an important place on the cricketing calendar, even though the crowds disappeared long ago.[54] In 1980, a cricket writer noted that the Moin-ud-Dowla Cup offered the privilege of "being able to watch, for a week or ten days every year, all the leading Indian players of the time."[55] This, however, changed in the television era when the attendance at domestic matches plummeted. In the 1999/2000 season, for instance, a Ranji Trophy semifinal match between Mumbai and Tamil Nadu drew a daily average of 5,000 spectators, while the early-round matches involving Mumbai were watched by only a few hundred spectators.[56]

Women in Whites

Despite all the hype about men's cricket, the women's game, too, got an encouraging start in the 1970s when a women's national cricket championship was started in 1973.[57] A journalist described the enthusiasm for the championship held in Pune, which, he felt, predicted a healthy future for the women's game.[58] In the international arena, Richard Cashman wrote about the first women's Test series in 1974/1975 against the visiting Australians, attracting up to an average daily crowd of around 5,000 to 10,000.[59] India's first Test match win, against the West Indies in 1976 in Patna, was watched by some 25,000 spectators.[60] Players like Diana Edulji and Shanta Rangaswamy, both captains in the 1970s and 1980s and Arjuna awardees, became household names in their time. Rangaswamy said in an interview that in the 1970s, crowds of 40,000 used to be the "normal attendance" at women's Test matches.[61] But another former Indian player pointed out that many in the largely male audience came for the novelty of watching "girls play in skirts."[62]

The initial expectations were overly optimistic, however, and even in the 1970s, newspapers noted the "microscopic" following for women's cricket. Most women cricketers have complained about the stepmotherly treatment of women's cricket and the lack of funds. In an interview, Edulji recalled that team members were asked to pay Rs 10,000 each to participate in the 1982 women's World Cup in New Zealand.[63] Then in 1997, the women's World Cup was held in India for the second time, but it turned out to be a logistical nightmare, with the BCCI not cooperating with the Women's Cricket Association of India on the matter of venues. Nonetheless, the finals in Eden Gardens between Australia and New Zealand in Calcutta drew a full house of 80,000.[64] By the time the women's cricket World Cup came to India again in 2013, the BCCI had taken over women's cricket. But even that didn't stop the World Cup matches from being moved from Mumbai's (Bombay's) premier Wankhede Stadium to smaller venues because of the Ranji Trophy matches. According to Edulji, the BCCI has done little to fund women's cricket, with the players receiving a paltry Rs 2,500 per domestic match. Another former Indian women's captain, Anjum Chopra (one of the few women in the male-dominated world of cricket commentary and talk shows on television), took a more pragmatic view when she said the situation was a "reflection of reality and of market forces."[65]

The Decline of the Rest

The dominance of cricket in the 1970s was also due to India's lack of success in the other team sports. For Indian football, the 1970 Asian Games bronze medal was the last notable international success. In hockey, India had slipped to third place by the 1968 Olympics and in 1972 could not improve its bronze medal position. This was to be India's last Olympic medal against a full field, without counting the 1980 gold medal in the largely boycotted Moscow Olympics, in which most of the top hockey-playing countries did not participate. India had a fleeting triumph in 1975 when it won its first and only hockey World Cup before a sellout crowd of 50,000 at the Merdeka Stadium in Kuala Lumpur. In Delhi, huge crowds of hockey fans were seen standing outside banks and government offices listening to the radio, and the celebrations following the victory were testimony to the popularity of hockey, especially in north India. The *Hindustan Times* reported: "Delhi fans danced to the rhythm of drums and distributed sweets. In Connaught Circus, a huge clapping and dancing crowd followed two drummers and a group of *bhangra* dancers. A restaurant owner treated his customers for free when the news came out."[66] On the players' return, 10,000 people were at the Palam airport in Delhi, causing a near-stampede. Later, cash awards were announced for the players.

The 1975 victory proved to be a false dawn for Indian hockey, however, as the very next year India had its worst showing ever in the Olympics, finishing seventh in the Montreal Olympics, even though before the games it was regarded as "favourites."[67] The introduction of astro turf grounds was touted as a reason for India's dramatic fall, but *The Statesman*'s sports correspondent, K. N. Mohlajee, reported that it would be "churlish to attribute India's destruction to astro-turf."[68] He squarely blamed the Indian administrators for the debacle in what would become a recurrent complaint about Indian sport: "What a fall. From crowned kings to humble seekers of minor placings. That briefly is the tale of Indian hockey. . . . And the seeds of all these disasters were sown by the bosses who pick and choose the team."[69] There were even reports of a letter signed by all sixteen players of the Olympic team leveling serious allegations against officials.[70] The cartoonist Ranga summed up the cruel irony of the situation when he portrayed a returning Indian hockey player telling a customs officer at the airport: "Nothing to declare, Sir. . . . No Gold, No Silver. . . . Not even Bronze."[71]

India had some international success in individual sports such as badminton and tennis. In 1980, Prakash Padukone won badminton's premier tournament, the All-England. The same year he also won the Danish Open and the Swedish Open but never achieved the same kind of success after that. In tennis, Vijay Amritraj was once spoken of in the same breath as Bjorn Borg and Jimmy Connors, the world's top players in the 1970s and 1980s. But despite reaching the quarterfinals in two Grand Slam events in 1973 and repeating the feat in one Grand Slam tournament in 1974, Amritraj did not fulfill his early promise, instead achieving his highest ranking of 16 in world tennis in 1980. He reached the Wimbledon quarterfinal in 1981 only to lose a five-setter to Connors, despite being two sets ahead.[72] That loss in a way typified Amritraj's career, in which he occasionally came close to beating Borg and Connors but failed to clinch the match. Ramesh Krishnan, seven years younger than Amritraj, has had some success on the international circuit, reaching the quarterfinals of Grand Slam events on three occasions in the 1980s. But at the end of the day, these were niche sports in the Indian context and did not in any way dent the popularity of cricket.

The Television Revolution

When Nehru died in 1964, only fifty-eight television sets were licensed in India. The first television broadcast came in 1959 when AIR beamed programs to twenty-one television sets within a 15.5-mile radius of Delhi.[73] Over the next decade, the number of sets crept up to just over 84,000 sets in 1972, at a time when the Indian population stood at around 550 million, and each television set cost a considerable Rs 2,000. Of these, Delhi and its surrounding areas had about 50,000 licensed TV sets, and the greater Bombay area, another 16,000.[74] Only in 1969 was a sports event broadcast live on television, and not surprisingly, it was a cricket match—the third Test between India and Australia in Delhi. The telecast was restricted to Delhi, and given the limited number of television sets, only a few would have watched the match on TV. It took another three years for the next live telecast, when the Uttar Pradesh government requested AIR—there being no state television broadcasting entity yet—to set up a television transmitter to telecast the fourth Test match of the 1972/1973 series in Kanpur. The broadcast, which was meant to mitigate the rush of seats for the match, was restricted to a radius of five miles around the stadium and watched on around three hundred TV sets provided by a local manufacturer on the instructions of the state government. In the same series, the fifth Test in Bombay also was broadcast live. Groups of spectators watched the live telecast through the glass panes of electronic stores or, in one instance, a college library. For the first time, a television-watching public was created, albeit in a small way, for a live event, and significantly it was for cricket matches. In the 1978/1979 series against Pakistan, the audience was greatly expanded, as the entire Test series was telecast live in the major Indian cities. But even in the early 1970s, a prescient observer predicted that the future will "belong to the transistorized TV as surely as the present belongs to the transistorized radio."[75]

The real impetus for television broadcasts came during the 1982 Asian Games, which were being hosted for the second time in Delhi. In 1976, when a national emergency was still in place, Prime Minister Indira Gandhi had created a separate state entity, Doordarshan, to handle television. It was only during the Asian Games that both "national" programming and color transmission began. In Parliament, the information and broadcasting minister announced that the government, on the recommendation of an expert committee, had decided to introduce color television in a "phased manner."[76] This process was accompanied by India's indigenous satellite program, which saw the launch of the INSAT-1A satellite in 1982 and another one the next year. The government's report on the Asian Games explained the strong link between the games and national pride by announcing that television would "stimulate interest and muster a national will, behind Asiad 82, and make the people realize that as hosts both our national honor and prestige was involved."[77] By this time, the number of television sets in India had also jumped significantly, to 2 million. The color television coverage of the Asian Games, especially the opening ceremony, won "near-unanimous praise" from Indian viewers.[78]

It was a coincidence that just as a national television audience was forming, India had its greatest cricketing triumph since its 1971 victory over England. On June 25, 1983, India caught everybody by surprise by winning the cricket World Cup (which until then was played over one day with sixty overs for each team). The win was completely unexpected, since India had performed abysmally in the two earlier tournaments and was considered a novice in the limited-over version of cricket. The iconic image of India's young captain, Kapil Dev, holding up the cup at Lord's was seen by millions of viewers across the country. The viewership wasn't restricted to households that owned TVs, as those without television sets watched the semifinal and the final—the only two matches shown live—in someone else's house or in common spaces. Guha's recollection of the final is testimony to this fact as well as to the capriciousness of the telecast:

> I myself watched the 1983 World Cup final in a college common room in Calcutta. When India batted first and were all out for 183 few gave us any hope. . . . The great [West Indian batsman] Vivian Richards came in and started ominously well. After his second boundary the television went on the blink. Doordarshan had lost its signal from London.

I, too, was one of the millions of Indians glued to the TV and the unreliable broadcast. The signal did come back shortly after Richards was out, and by then India was on its way to a famous victory.

Despite the fortuitous link between cricket and an ever expanding television audience, it ironically hastened the decline of football and hockey. For football, television coverage of international football opened the eyes of sports fans to the vast difference in standards between Indian football and that of the rest of the world. This was true even in Calcutta, which was India's most football-obsessed city. The first international match to be shown live was the final of the 1978 World Cup, and by the next World Cup in 1982, the entire tournament was shown live. This had the effect of impressing on football fans the "gap between their own local heroes and the great international stars."[79] In the case of hockey, the introduction of television coincided with a particularly heavy defeat and that, too, at the hands of Pakistan in the 1982 Asian Games final. A sports enthusiast, who was then studying at an engineering college in northern India, recalled having watched the game with several of his fellow students on campus on a brand-new color TV set provided by the college:

> When India scored a goal, the cheering was beyond any I have experienced in my life. After all, it was the final, we were watching it in colour, and India had taken a lead against Pakistan—how much better could a

hockey game get? And then, in a disaster of gigantic proportions, Pakistan mauled us 7–1. The silence in the room was deafening.[80]

The Indian goalkeeper, Mir Ranjan Negi, was villified[81] (his reputation was partially redeemed after the success of the Bollywood film *Chak de India*, based on his time as the coach of the Indian women's hockey team), and many Indians switched off from hockey forever. Success in international hockey has dried up since, with India winning an Asiad gold in 1998 but having no success in either the Olympics or the World Cup. Thus an editor of a national daily lamented, "One of the greatest tragedies of our hockey is that its most glorious phase preceded the era of live television in India."[82]

The Business of Cricket

From the 1980s onward, the popularity of cricket reached an all-time high, made possible by, and intrinsically linked to, the phenomenal growth of television during this period. By the mid-1980s, three million sets were being produced in India, and in the early 1990s 34 million Indians owned TV sets. Also during this time, the reach of television increased significantly, with the number of transmitters jumping from 172 in 1985 to 698 in 1995.[83] The BCCI—which had Rs 200,000 in its coffers during the 1983 World Cup[84] and did not even have enough money to reward the members of the Indian team—was quick to spot the immense opportunities presented by the happy convergence of an ever widening television audience and an upswing in the fortunes of Indian cricket. It even dared to bring the World Cup, which had been held in England since its inception in 1974, to the Indian subcontinent. Legend has it that the idea of the World Cup in India originated in a snub by the Marylebone Cricket Club (MCC) of the BCCI president (and Congress politician) N. K. P. Salve, who had asked for extra tickets to the 1983 cup final at Lord's.[85] But it was Jagmohan Dalmiya, a Marwari businessman from Calcutta who had joined the BCCI in 1978, and Inderjit Singh Bindra, a former bureaucrat from Punjab, who were the real brains behind getting the World Cup to the subcontinent. The Indian textile giant Reliance Industries bankrolled the tournament and, in a masterstroke, India's traditional enemy, Pakistan, was brought on board as the cohost. Even though both India and

Pakistan lost in the semifinal, the matches were played to packed stands, and the live telecast of matches did wonders for the popularity of cricket.

The marriage between cricket and television was cemented from the early 1990s when the Indian economy was unshackled from decades of state control. For the first time, private satellite and cable broadcasters were allowed to enter the Indian market, breaking Doordarshan's monopoly over cricket. The BCCI gave the sports production company, TWI, the right to broadcast the 1992/1993 England–India series for $600,000.[86] The broadcast was a marked improvement from Doordarshan's usual unprofessional performance. That same year TWI won the right to telecast live the Hero Cup, organized by the Cricket Association of Bengal to celebrate its diamond jubilee. But Doordarshan and its parent body, the Ministry of Information and Broadcasting, prevented the broadcast of the first few matches, citing the British-era Telegraph Act. Eventually India's Supreme Court had to intervene, convening on a holiday—an unusual occurrence—and overruled the government. The remaining matches were telecast live. Since the court's ruling was limited to the tournament, the very next year the ministry again opposed the BCCI's deal with the cable television station ESPN to telecast the India–West Indies series.

The controversy also brought under a cloud the 1996 World Cup, which was being held on the Indian subcontinent for the second time in a decade, but this time jointly by India, Pakistan, and Sri Lanka. Once again the matter was taken to court, and this time the Supreme Court, in a landmark judgment in 1995, undermined the government's position by ruling that the airwaves could not be a state monopoly, thereby ushering in the cable television revolution.[87] This opened the door to lucrative deals, the likes of which were unheard of in Indian cricket. For the 1996 World Cup, the WorldTel company, through the then unknown Mark Mascarhenas, offered $10 million to the organizing committee for television rights.[88] This was ten times more than the previous World Cup rates. A blitz of corporate tie-ups followed, with an "official sponsor for every conceivable product, including the official World Cup chewing gum."[89]

This kind of marketing for any sport was unheard of in India, and it raked in an estimated $50 million in profits for the World Cup's organizing committee.[90] It must be noted, too, that cricket is perfectly suited to television and its advertisers, "with its many pauses, its spatial concentration of action and its extended format."[91] By this time, the one-day version of cricket had become the most popular format in India, and the crowds for Test cricket, spread over five days, had started thinning. Besides, the percentage of revenue earned from gate money had been steadily falling, making the spectators at the field, who had always gotten a raw deal, virtually redundant in the Indian cricket board's scheme of things.

Not only the cricket board made money. The players, who had gotten a pittance until the 1980s, were now much sought after. In fact, after the 1983 World Cup win, the Indian team had to literally corner the BCCI for a cash reward for their great achievement.[92] Gavaskar, whose career spanned the 1970s and 1980s, was the first cricket player to really benefit, with his earnings shooting up from Rs 2,000 per endorsement in the early 1970s to Rs one million per endorsement in the late 1980s.[93] Yet another cricketing superstar, Kapil Dev, signed a three-year deal in the early 1990s with Pepsi that was worth Rs 1 million per year. The earnings of cricket players who represented India also jumped dramatically, from Rs 1,000 for an entire tour in 1971 to Rs 9,000 per Test in the late 1980s. The real game changer, however, was the deal that Mascarhenas struck in 1996 with India's all-time biggest sports star and one of the finest-ever batsman in the world, Sachin Tendulkar, guaranteeing him $7.5 million over five years.[94] By the time he retired in 2013, his estimated annual earnings stood at $22 million. It is instructive that one of the few names, besides those of his family and coach, whom Tendulkar singled out in his emotional speech during his farewell Test match was Mascarhenas, who died in a car accident in 2002.

By this time, cricket had swamped the other sports in India, and the country was on its way to becoming the de facto headquarters and engine of growth for world cricket. Since then, the amount of money in cricket has risen exponentially, giving the sport a unique status in India and making the BCCI the world's richest and most powerful cricket body. From 1999 to 2003, Doordarshan paid the BCCI $11.5 million per year for cricket broadcasts rights inside India. In 2004 when the TV rights came up for renewal, a private channel, Zee TV, bid $260 million. When Zee was disqualified in 2006, another company, Nimbus Communications, bought the rights for more than double the amount, $612 million.[95] The reason why broadcasters were willing to stake such large amounts of money on Indian cricket was the country's cornering of nearly three-quarters of the global market for cricket. In 2012, the BCCI signed a six-year deal with Star TV for approximately $750 million for broadcast and digital rights to Indian cricket.[96] In addition, the board made another Rs 43.4 million from endorsements, sponsorship, and advertising. By this time, television penetration in India had also increased dramatically, from twenty-six people per TV set in 1992 to ten per set in 2011. The number of television households also tripled in that decade, to nearly 145 million.

The phenomenal rise in the BCCI's revenues meant that administrative positions in cricket now came with incredible clout and hence were very attractive to Indian politicians. Accordingly, in 2010, two-thirds of the state associations were run by politicians, with one of India's most powerful politicians, Sharad Pawar, heading the BCCI from 2005. Pawar was appointed as the president of the International Cricket Council (ICC) in 2010, the second Indian to occupy the chair after Jagmohan Dalmiya in 1997. This merely confirmed the BCCI's position as the body that called the shots in world cricket. According to Gideon Haigh: "As India's proportion of global cricket revenue has grown with each passing year, so have its political ambitions, to the extent that the ICC has begun resembling a subsidiary of the BCCI—exactly the relation, of course, that the ICC once had with the MCC."[97]

The players' salaries also kept pace, with the top-tier (grade A) contracted players with the BCCI receiving an annual fixed income of $186,000 for 2012/2013 and the lowest-tier (grade C) contracted players getting around $46,500. In addition, each player got Rs 700,000 per Test match, Rs 400,000 per one-day international, and Rs 200,000 for a Twenty20 match. This, however, was only small fraction of the top cricket players' earnings, with many of them making much more from endorsements. India's most successful-ever captain, Mahendra Singh Dhoni, who led India to two World Cup triumphs in different formats in 2007 and 2011, was the world's highest-paid cricketer in 2011, making $26.5 million. Sachin Tendulkar was second on the list, with $18.6 million.[98] Not surprisingly, the world's five highest-paid cricketers in 2011 were from India. It's not just cricket players for India who make big money. Those playing domestic tournaments for their state teams also make a substantial amount when compared with that of other Indian athletes. A domestic cricketer can earn between Rs 600,000 and Rs 1.2 million if he plays only the Ranji trophy, and he is most likely to be employed by a state-run or private company. And thanks to the Indian Premier League

(IPL), Indian cricket players are able to make money they wouldn't ever have imagined making, without even playing for the national team.

During this period, too, the heady combination of money and popularity mired cricket in its biggest-ever scandal: match fixing involving several international cricketers. And again not surprisingly, the Indian subcontinent was at the epicenter of the controversy. The scandal, whose lid was blown off in 2000, made a mockery of the term "gentleman's game" to describe cricket. The investigations, which spanned several continents, ended the careers of the Indian captain, Mohammad Azharuddin (ironically elected an MP on a Congress Party ticket in 2009), who was found guilty of match fixing and banned from the game for life, while several other players were given lesser penalties for having links with bookies. That Indian cricket was able to turn the corner was due in no small measure to the next Indian captain, Sourav Ganguly, and his teammates like Tendulkar, Rahul Dravid, V. V. S. Laxman, and Anil Kumble, who not only were some of the best Indian cricketers of all time but, more important, cricketers of integrity.

Beyond the Metros

The potent combination of television and the lure of big money had a salutary effect nonetheless. It has ensured the spread of cricket beyond the metros and traditional centers to small-town India. This was illustrated by the emergence of cricket stars from towns and states that never really had a cricketing tradition, as well as those from poorer backgrounds. Not that there weren't cricket players from lower-class backgrounds earlier. Eknath Solkar, who played for India in the 1970s, was an example of a cricketer who came from a poor family. But he was an exception besides being from Bombay, the great nursery of Indian cricket. The difference in the last decade or so has been the emergence of players from what was considered the hinterland of Indian cricket. Perhaps the best example of such a cricketer was Mahendra Singh Dhoni. He was born and raised in Ranchi in the eastern state of Jharkhand (carved out of the state of Bihar in 2000) where his father was an unskilled worker in the state-run Hindustan Steel Authority. As a schoolboy, Dhoni represented his school, DAV, in the interstate tournament and later was chosen to play for an undivided Bihar. He caught the eyes of the national selectors during a Deodhar Trophy match in 2002/2003, and by 2004 he was playing for India.[99] Since then, the Pathan brothers, sons of a *muezzin* in Baroda; Munaf Patel, son of a cotton farmer in Gujarat; Praveen Kumar, born into a family of *pehelwans*; and several others like them have played for India. Television played a key role in this phenomenon. One of the recent stars of the Indian team, Virender Sehwag, who grew up in Najafgarh on the fringes of Delhi, explained:

> In 1992 I saw Sachin Tendulkar for the first time on TV during the World Cup. I was in Class VII and the exams were on, but I skipped them because the games used to be telecast early in the morning and clashed with the school timings. . . . I just loved the way he batted—that first memory is still fresh.[100]

The rise of the IPL has also meant that cricketers who may never play for India are able to get substantial remuneration, something that was not possible in an earlier era. Of course, this has its downside, too, with some cricket players turning out to be one-tournament wonders who are rarely heard about afterward. The story of Kamran Khan, the son of a woodcutter from Uttar Pradesh, is particularly poignant. Hailed as a tear-away fast bowler when he was picked by one of the IPL teams in 2009, he had been dumped by 2011 and was back in his native village working in the fields.[101]

The rise of Uttar Pradesh (UP) is perhaps emblematic of the decentering of Indian cricket. UP, which never really had a tradition of playing cricket, won the Ranji Trophy for the first time in 2005. Since then, several players from UP, many of them from smaller cities in the state, have been selected for the national team. The first player from Uttar Pradesh ever to play for independent India, Gopal Sharma, who later coached the state team, had this to say about the spread of the game:

> Now, the state team has very few players from the main cities like Lucknow or Kanpur. Among the main reasons for the game becoming popular was the spread of TV and the increase in its glamour quotient. Earlier, they used to listen to the commentary on radio and very few households had TV. But now every house has a TV set, and cricket is obviously a big deal now.[102]

The decentering did not happen outside the metros; it happened inside them, too. For instance, the great Tendulkar did not study in one of the fancy Bombay schools but at Shardashram Vidyamandir, not far from the famous Shivaji Park, whose alumni include more than a hundred Ranji cricketers, some of whom played for India as well.[103] In fact, the record partnership of 664 runs with his schoolmate and later India cricketer, Vinod Kambli, that first brought Tendulkar into the limelight was achieved in 1988 for Shardashram against the elite St. Xavier's School in the Harris Shield. Even today, people point reverentially to the Sassanian Cricket Club ground at Bombay's Azad Maidan where the match was played.[104]

The decentering of cricket and the massive infusion of money into the game have changed the way the sport is played in India. For the better part of its cricketing history, India has been extolled, as well as derided, for its lack of killer instinct and for adhering to norms of a past era's sportsmanship. This spirit was best exemplified by India's great batsman and two-Test captain, Gundappa Viswanath, who in the 1979/1980 Jubilee Test against England recalled English wicketkeeper Bob Taylor after he had been declared out by the umpire. This was a one-of-a-kind act of sportsmanship in the modern era of cricket. Thus Scyld Berry wrote in the 1970s:

> The traditions of sportsmanship which the British had originally brought with them, and which their emulators—the Parsis and princes—had adopted and helped to propagate, were still being upheld. India had preserved this ethos in the same way as it preserves servants, tea strainers or circuses, which are also becoming extinct elsewhere.[105]

This ethos has now become extinct in India, too.

The Indian Premier League

In the late 1970s, the Australian media tycoon Kerry Packer unleashed a cricket revolution with his World Series of Cricket, which rocked the cricket establishment. Nearly three decades later, another revolution was set in motion, but this time by the pillar of the cricket establishment: the BCCI. Depending on which side you're on, April 8, 2008, either revolutionized cricket or completely destroyed it.[106] That day, the first match of the Indian Premier League (IPL)—a tournament involving city-based franchisees playing twenty overs a team—was played on a balmy evening in Bangalore. India had been slow to take to the Twenty20 format, which was first played in England in 2003. It was once again a surprise World Cup win by India—this time in the inaugural Twenty20 World Cup in 2007 in South Africa, in which India was a reluctant participant—that woke up the BCCI to the potential of the shortest format of the game (cricket is unique in having three formats of the game at the international level). As the cricket writer Gideon Haigh put it,

> The final at Wanderers [in South Africa] was comparable in historical significance to the World Cup final twenty-four years earlier. Now the televisions stayed on, and for weeks afterwards. Fifty-over cricket was suddenly passé and twenty-over cricket hot to the point of radioactivity, as India embraced the game of which it was now the unlikely world champion.[107]

If Jagmohan Dalmiya monetized cricket in the 1980s and 1990s, it was another Marwari businessman, Lalit Modi, who was responsible for realizing the potential of Twenty20 cricket. Modi, whose family owned a business empire, had dabbled in cable television in the 1990s. His meteoric rise (and equally rapid fall) was caused by the IPL. His real connection to cricket began when he became president of the Rajasthan cricket board as well as vice president of the BCCI in 2005. Inspired by the franchise-based sports model in America, where Modi was once a student, he floated the idea as early as 1995 of an international cricket league based in Indian cities. At first, Modi's proposal found no takers, but once an Indian business group, Essel, challenged BCCI's monopoly by unveiling its own Twenty20 league—the Indian Cricket League (ironically the same name that Modi had once proposed) without the BCCI's permission—the Indian cricket board sat up and took notice. This, coupled with India's win in the inaugural Twenty20 World Cup, completed changed the BCCI's outlook. Under Modi as commissioner (the designation also was borrowed from the United States), the IPL proved to be a spectacular success in its first year. Its first auction to pick the franchisees and their owners raised $723.5 million, and television rights were sold to Sony for more than $1 billion. As one writer put it, "Modi wasn't the first person to monetize cricket; he was, however, the first to reckon its worth in billions of dollars rather than mere millions."[108] Besides mega industrialists like the Reliance Group's Mukesh Ambani, who bought the Mumbai franchise, Bollywood's biggest star, Shah Rukh Khan, and other film stars bought stakes in the franchisees. This brought about a marriage between two of India's biggest passions: Bollywood and cricket.

At the player auction held later, the major Indian players raked in millions, with Dhoni coming out on tops with an astronomical $1.5 million bid from the Chennai franchise. But there were several surprises, too, with obscure Indian players being sold for huge sums (even as established international stars like Australian captain Ricky Ponting were acquired for very low sums), completely inverting the incentive structure of Indian and, indeed, international cricket. Traditionally, Indian cricketers had to shine in junior tournaments and the Ranji Trophy before they could think of representing India and making money and achieving fame. Now they could become famous and wealthy merely by putting on an IPL jersey. The international impact of the IPL was revealed in a players' survey in Australia, which found that nearly half the cricketers, who had signed a central contract with Cricket Australia and the six state associations, were willing to give up international cricket for the IPL.[109] Club versus country, a feature of most international team sports, had suddenly become a reality for the first time in cricket.

The IPL made several innovations that shook the staid world of cricket. Besides the high-profile auctions, the IPL offered cheerleaders, music at the grounds, and for a while a mandatory postmatch party for players, which lasted until the wee hours of the morning and created plenty of controversy. This naturally brought scathing criticism from many who saw the IPL corrupting the game. But whatever the purists thought, there was little doubt that IPL was a big hit with cricket fans. By 2010, just two years after the IPL was started, a consultancy firm pegged its value at $4.13 billion.[110] The TV ratings for the first three IPLs were impressive, elbowing out prime-time serials in the race for eyeballs. The tournament's high rating was helped by the high number of women tuning in to the games. Even though both the IPL's television ratings and its advertising rates have been falling since 2011,[111] it still remains a popular product. By this time, Modi, too, had lost elections to the Rajasthan cricket board, and he was suspended by the BCCI as the commissioner of IPL on the day of the 2010 IPL final, after having been accused of corruption and bypassing due processes. Just few days earlier, a controversy over the bidding and ownership of a new IPL franchise based in Kochi (in the southern state of Kerala) had claimed the scalp of the Congress minister and cricket buff Shashi Tharoor. Here Modi was the chief protagonist as well, publicly declaring himself against the consortium, backed by Tharoor, which eventually won the bid for the Kochi franchise. The controversy snowballed to the extent that the principal opposition party described the IPL as the "biggest ever" scam in the country, once again showcasing the links between cricket and politics in India.[112] The Kochi franchise was dissolved in 2011. The financial health of the franchisees was a concern too, and according to one estimate, by 2011 all the teams had lost a combined $25 billion in value since 2008. The IPL's unsavory reputation was confirmed in 2013 when it was found to be part of a betting scandal, involving players and owners.

The IPL is part cricket, part commerce, and part *tamasha*, which sports writer Mihir Bose describes as a "rich Indian word which means fun, excitement and glamour all rolled into one."[113] Describing the first two iterations of the IPL under Modi, the authors of the first in-depth study of the organization concluded: "IPL was not about cricket at all. It was definitely about commercial interests—of the players, of the franchise owners and the BCCI."[114] Commercialization, of course, is not a bad thing, as some Indian commentators like to believe. Indeed, as one writer put, it, "Cricket and commercial interests have always gone hand in hand."[115] But what has irked many about the IPL and its administrator, the BCCI, is making cricket beholden to commerce, to the detriment of the game. Guha described the IPL as "representative of the worst sides of Indian capitalism and society."[116] Having watched a few IPL games in the stadium, I found that the cricket was often a sideshow for the spectators, who were more interested in the music being belted between every delivery by the DJs on the ground, in the cheerleaders in hot pants, and, if you were lucky enough to be in a VIP box, in the free food and alcohol. Indeed, the IPL can be seen as a metaphor for the increasingly affluent and growing Indian middle class, which thrives on spectacle and excess.

More Than Just a Game

"Cricket is an Indian game accidentally discovered by the English."[117] So wrote Ashis Nandy in the memorable opening line to his book on cricket.

One of the reasons that he offered to back up his statement is civilizational, as he believes that the nature of the game is particularly suited to the Indian temperament: "The duration of a test match, lasting up to thirty three hours and even then often ending in a draw, would tax the patience of most people except the Gita-devouring ahistorical Indians, who continue to try and see it as pleasurable and as an epitome of desireless, *karmic* life."[118] Ramachandra Guha, who usually is critical of Nandy's understanding of cricket,[119] seems to agree with him on this score. "Indians have more time; Indians like doing things together; Hindus don't really mind a 'draw'; Hindus are culturally syncretic and choose to absorb foreign imports rather than reject them: those are the lines on which we might begin to explain the extraordinary Indian love for cricket."[120]

We may not agree with Nandy's civilizational argument, but the success of the IPL and its links with Bollywood is a validation of another strand of Nandy's argument—cricket as a spectacle and a "consumable commodity"—to explain the sport's phenomenal popularity in India. He argues that in the "Indian popular culture of entertainment, cricket-as-spectacle is closer to film-as-spectacle than to cricket-as-sport."[121] Similarly, Mihir Bose draws a parallel between cricket and *tamasha*, in which Bollywood film stars, politicians, and, of course, cricketers are part of the cast.[122]

This is particularly true of the IPL, whose games are compressed into an evening's worth of entertainment and attract spectators who wouldn't want to watch a five-day Test match. What Nandy wrote about the longer version of cricket is equally, if not more, applicable, to the IPL:

> Cricket in India is most popular exactly in those sectors which cannot distinguish a silly mid-off from a long-off and a third man from a china-man [terms that denote fielding positions and a particular type of bowling delivery]. The modal viewer sees cricket as a relatively simple affair in which the vocabulary of the game is exhausted by less than twenty words: boundary, century, victory, defeat.[123]

He also noted a quasi-religious element in watching cricket in India. In an earlier era when India's cricket grounds did not have forbidding fences around them, it was common for spectators to put garlands (one Babu Tangewale possibly held the record for garlanding) on the cricket players—as they would Hindu deities—when they reached a milestone such as scoring a century; and radio commentary was akin to a religious chant so that even spectators at the ground felt it necessary to carry a radio with them. Televisions lent another dimension to the links between cricket, on the one hand, and film and religion, on the other: "For a country whose cinema stars are its major celebrities, television lends cinematic authority to the sports spectacle. In a civilization where seeing (*darsan*) is the sacred instrument of communion television has intensified the star status of the great Indian cricket players."[124] That is perhaps why posters proclaiming "Sachin is God," a reference to Sachin Tendulkar's iconic status in India, are so common on Indian fields.

Besides cricket's easy identification with traditional forms of entertainment and worship, it also arouses in spectators what Arjun Appadurai calls the "erotics of nationhood."[125] Hence, defeating England in 1971 in what was the quintessential English sport and also on English soil was what brought such intense celebrations in India. But as the power of England has shrunk and memories of colonial rule have faded, nationalist emotions have usually been reserved for Pakistan, with whom India has fought three full-fledged wars and one serious border skirmish. Since the 1980s, though, it has mostly been on the cricket field where India and Pakistan have fought their battles. As Appadurai pointed out,

> Cricket matches between India and Pakistan are thinly-disguised national wars. Cricket is not so much a release valve for popular hostility between the two populations as it is a complex arena for re-enacting the curious mixture of animosity and fraternity that characterises the relations between these two previously united nation states.[126]

The importance attached to India–Pakistan matches is reflected on the long list of Indian cricket captains who lost their jobs for leading teams that lost, or even had a draw in, a Test series against Pakistan.[127] Accordingly, a sports writer noted: "In both countries a special stigma is attached to failure against the sub-continental rival, while success is doubly rewarded. In the eyes of the more ardent cricket nationalists, the inescapable vagaries of luck and form are always suspect. On either side of the border, there's a tendency to respond to defeat with allegations of betrayal."[128]

Cricket has often been a casualty of strained relations between the two countries, with long gaps between tours. Between 1962 and 1978, a period punctuated by two wars, there were no cricket matches between India and Pakistan. For most of the 1980s and 1990s, which saw unprecedented communal violence and riots in India, the little cricketing contact between the two countries took place on neutral venues, with a large expatriate South Asian population, such as Sharjah in the United Arab Emirates and as far away as Toronto. Cricketing ties were resumed in 1997, but the Kargil conflict in 1999 nipped in the bud further sports contact for five years. At the same time, cricket has been used to improve relations between the two countries, despite the best efforts of Hindu right-wing groups to disrupt visits by the Pakistani team. Threats by the Shiv Sena, the radical Hindu party from Maharashtra, ensured that Pakistan did not participate in the Hero Cup in 1993, not long after a disputed mosque in Uttar Pradesh, the Babri Masjid, was destroyed by Hindu nationalists. In 1998/1999, months before the Kargil conflict, when the Pakistani team visited India for the first time in twelve years, the Sena dug up the pitch in the Ferozeshah Kotla ground in Delhi, site of the first Test match of the series. Even though the Sena leader Bal Thackeray described the act as "true patriotism," it did not have any impact whatsoever on the series, with the first Test moved to Chennai and the second played in the hastily restored Kotla ground (where for only the second time in the history of Test cricket, a bowler—Indian spinner Anil Kumble—took all ten wickets in an innings). Unlike the Sena and its supporters, Indian cricket fans were very happy to watch Pakistan play. In the Chennai Test match, 50,000 people turned up every day to watch the game. Pakistan won that match, and the captain, Wasim Akram, led his team on a victory lap to a standing ovation from the Chennai crowd. It was a scene that would have left the Sena and its supporters deeply puzzled.

The ups and downs of the India–Pakistan contests were amply reflected in the one-off Test (as part of the Asian Test Championship) that was held in Calcutta in February 1999 during the same tour. Around 100,000 spectators attended each of the first four days of the match. On the fourth day, however, after the controversial dismissal of Tendulkar, angry spectators stopped play for more than an hour. I was part of the seething crowd at Eden Gardens that day, and it seemed to me that it was a combination of the dislike of certain Pakistani players combined with the perceived injustice done to Tendulkar that brought emotions to the boil. Play resumed, but on the fifth and final day of the match, when India was on the verge of losing, the 65,000 people who had turned up at the stadium that day turned violent. Not for the first time at the Eden Gardens, spectators were ejected, and the final moments of the game were played in a near-empty stadium watched by a "few officials, VIPs, journalists and police."

A term, "cricket diplomacy," has been coined to describe the use of the sport to bring about a thaw in relations between India and Pakistan. Despite the controversies dogging India's ill-starred tour of Pakistan in 1978, Pakistani President Zia ul-Haq said at a farewell dinner that the goodwill and friendship generated by the cricket matches should bring the two countries closer, even in politics.[129] A week earlier, India's foreign minister, Atal Behari Vajpayee, had insisted that the Indian cricket team had made a "significant contribution towards promoting goodwill and understanding between the people of India and Pakistan."[130] Nearly a decade later, in 1987, Zia watched an India–Pakistan match in Jaipur, using the slogan of cricket for peace to defuse tensions along the border.[131]

In 2004, India toured Pakistan for the first time in fourteen years, thanks to the astute diplomacy of Vajpayee, who was by then India's prime minister. At a reception for the Indian players before they left for Pakistan, Vajpayee put the series into perspective when he said: "*Khel hi nahin, dil bhi jitiye*" (Win not only matches, but hearts too).[132] The historic series and the complex emotions it inspired have been vividly chronicled by the cricket writer turned novelist Rahul Bhattacharya. Goodwill was in abundance during that series. This was especially true in the historic city of Lahore, where two Cricket Specials—train services to ferry cricket fans—between Delhi and Lahore carried more than 2,000 passengers across the border for the one-day match there. As a former diplomat and chairman of the Pakistan Cricket Board wrote about the tour: "20,000 Indian fans had gone back to India acting as Pakistan's ambassadors ... cricket has acted as a genuine bridge."[133] But when Pakistan capitulated in the third Test and lost the series, a distinguished Pakistani journalist wrote in the *Dawn* newspaper that it was Pakistan cricket's "blackest day."[134]

The next year, Pakistani President Pervez Musharraf was invited to India to watch a match. But after the terrorist attacks in Mumbai in 2008, cricketing ties were cut once again, confirming the role of the game as a barom-

Prime Minister Atal Behari Vajpayee with members of the Indian cricket team before its departure to Pakistan, 2004. On the first row extreme left is India's most famous cricketer, Sachin Tendulkar, and next to him is Sourav Ganguly, who was the captain during the Pakistan tour. The bat that Vajpayee is holding says, "*Khel Nahi, Dil Bhi Jeetiye*" (Win not only matches, but hearts too). Reprinted by permission of the Hindu Archives

eter of India–Pakistan relations. Even the IPL, which was touted as putting club over country, was not immune, with Pakistani players being shunned in player auctions after the Mumbai attack. India and Pakistan, however, played against each other at Mohali near Chandigarh in the semifinal of the 2011 World Cup, which was jointly hosted by India, Sri Lanka, and Bangladesh. The Pakistani prime minister was invited to the match and watched it in the company of the Indian prime minister, Manmohan Singh.

Obviously, cricket at the national level in the Indian, and indeed the South Asian, context is no longer two teams pitted against each other in a field. Television, nationalism, and marketing have made cricket *the* sport in India and all of South Asia. In the process, cricket and cricketers have had to bear multiple burdens that have taken the game very far from its Victorian origins. What is undeniable, however, is the popularity of cricket across the length and breadth of India. Neville Cardus wrote in a book published in 1930 about the ubiquity of cricket in England and the feelings it generated:

Has any true Englishman ever resisted the temptation, while travelling on the railway, to look through the carriage window whenever the train has been passing a cricket field? The train rushes round a curve just as the bowler is about to bowl, and never can we know what happened to the ball![135]

Some seventy-five years later, the same could be said for India. In the evocative words of Rahul Bhattacharya,

Leave the city, travel overland across the country, and like a flick book, cricket and children fall on the eye with their passing strokes and passing shouts. In the east in *lungis* and crocheted caps, they are playing upon rough-hewn paddy fields. In the arid Maharashtrian interior, they are baking with the red mud. Against the Himalayas, they are swinging their bats in a meadow, cheeks glowing, eyes keen, mouths animated.[136]

12

LIFE BEYOND CRICKET

IN 1986 AN IRATE READER WROTE IN A LETTER TO THE EDITOR in a national daily: "Unless cricket is banished from this country, the rest of the sports would not get any encouragement, people would not do honest work in their work places and youth would not get adequate exercise."[1] The writer of the letter was expressing a fairly common grievance, namely, the omnipresence of cricket in India, which had killed not only other sports but also Indians' athletic abilities. Of course, blaming cricket for India's poor showing in other sports is not logical. But it is undeniable that India's record in nearly every other sport, excluding its performance in hockey until the 1970s, has been mediocre. Several statistics bear this out, but three facts will probably suffice. First, India has won twenty-five medals (counting Norman Pritchard's two silvers) in the Olympic Games since 1900, of which eleven were won in hockey alone. Of the individual medals, only one was gold. Second, India has the lowest ratio of medals won to population among the competing countries. In the 2012 London Games, it won one medal per 207 million people, compared to one medal for every 15.5 million people in China.[2] Third, in football, by far the world's most popular sport, India was ranked an abysmal 171 of 207 countries in 2014. In fact, Simon Kuper and Stefan

Szymanski named India as the "worst soccer team on earth," taking into account population, gross domestic product (GDP), and football experience.[3]

Why India Does So Badly

By now it should be apparent that the glib explanation that Indians don't have a sports culture is not true. We must seek reasons for India's poor performance elsewhere. A country's GDP and per capita income do, of course, matter. As Kuper and Szymanski observed, The "world's poor people and poor countries are worse at sports than rich ones."[4] This theory seems applicable to India. According to a 2013 World Bank report, India accounted for a third of the world's poor—those living on less than US$1.25 a day—which amounted to more than 400 million people. But India's poverty does not tell the entire story. Perhaps the most empirically sound argument regarding India's underperformance was made by the economists Anirudh Krishna and Eric Haglund.[5] While they believe that a country's living standard and GDP do matter in determining a country's sports performance, they rightly ask why countries that are as poor as or even poorer than India and have a much smaller population win many more medals. Their answer: Despite having a huge population pool—currently at 1.2 billion, the second largest in the world—the "effective participating population" in sports in India is very small. They point to poor health, little education, and a lack of "physical connectedness" (information about and access to sports) as factors limiting the number of people who take part in sports.

The parlor game of predicting medal tallies for countries in the Olympics has now been elevated to a kind of science. The investment bank Goldman Sachs uses a measure that captures different aspects of countries' political, institutional, and economic reality in order to make predictions of medals.[6] Its predictions have proved to be reasonably accurate. In the 2012 London Games, for instance, Goldman Sachs predicted that that India would win five medals, including two golds. India actually won six (with a bronze in badminton won somewhat luckily, since the Indian player's opponent retired after being hurt during the bronze medal play-off), though it failed to win a gold.

Sometimes the handicaps of health and education associated with developing countries are overcome by a concerted effort by the state interested in national prestige. China is the foremost example of such strong governmental intervention, along with Cuba and North Korea, and the Soviet Union and East Germany when they still existed. China won its first gold only in the 1984 games but has since risen meteorically to win fifty-one gold medals in the Beijing Olympics, placing way ahead of its closest competitor, the United States. In the London Games, China did not win as many but still placed second behind the United States in the medals list.

China's sports prowess was tied to national glory beginning in the twentieth century and could plausibly be traced back to 1907 when the Chinese YMCA began a campaign linking physical education to national strength.[7] In a 1917 article, "A Study of Physical Culture," Mao Zedong wrote: "Physical culture occupies a place of first priority in our life."[8] Incidentally, around the same time, Vladimir Lenin declared in Russia, "The physical education of the rising generation is one of the necessary elements of the communist education of youth." Following the Communist revolution, in 1952 Mao offered the famous slogan—"Develop physical cultures and sports, strengthen the people's physiques"[9]—the same year in which a forty-one-member Chinese contingent arrived for the Helsinki Games, though too late to participate. It's little remembered that China's supremacy in table tennis was the outcome of a conscious decision to develop the sport once the International Table Tennis Federation in 1953 severed ties with Taiwan. In 1959, China's Rong Guotuan became the world champion, prompting Mao to call the victory a "spiritual nuclear weapon." In the 1980s and 1990s, China focused on its traditional strengths, like table tennis and badminton, but it was only in 2001, after Beijing was chosen to host the 2008 Olympic Games, that it began in earnest to chase medals. The Chinese government's Project 119, so named because it targeted 119 medals (now up to 122) in water sports and athletics, pumped in billions of dollars into its 3,000-plus academies to groom children into champions.[10] Thus, as two Chinese historians explained, "Throughout the 1980s, 1990s and 200s, the nation's morbid appetite for gold medals placed a heavy political burden upon Chinese athletes, whose mission was to improve China's international image and satisfy the people's expectations for national revival."[11] It is instructive, however, that China has not done too well in team sports, most notably football, which goes to show the limits of government intervention.

Not only the Communist countries, both present and former, have invested heavily in sports. Democracies like Australia, which have regularly punched above their weight in sports competitions, have also seen sports as a route to international prestige. According to Victor Cha, Australia has "effectively used sport to bolster its reputation and image."[12] After Australia performed poorly in the Montreal Olympics, the government created a national sports institute and pumped in money to boost the country's performance and raise its medal tally.

Yet another set of developing or poor countries has done well in the Olympics without government intervention. These are countries that typically do well in one sport in which they have developed a winning tradition, one that continues to produce champions. Ethiopia and Kenya, two of the world's poorest countries, have dominated long-distance running for several decades owing to geographical and physical reasons and a glittering legacy that inspires future generations to run their way out of poverty.[13] In addition, Jamaica has won a majority of its medals in track-and-field events, Turkey in wrestling, and Kazakhstan in weight lifting. The only sport in which India developed a similar dominance was hockey, but for the reasons detailed earlier, least of all the switch from natural to expensive artificial turf, it suffered a dramatic decline.

The Curse of Sports Administrators

To the generic factors we must add the ineptitude of India's sports administrators, a long list of whom have cornered various sports bodies in India and ruled over them as personal fiefdoms for years. The aversion of sportspersons, fans, and journalists to sports administrators has a long history in India. As early as 1956, a sports columnist passionately asked in the *Times of India*: "I wonder how long we have to wait before genuine devotees of sport decide to treat with some effective variety of insecticide those so-called governing bodies that suffer from the ravages of slugs, worms, petty dictators and other similar pests."[14] Milkha Singh, who had a long career in Punjab's sports department, insisted, "The all-pervading influence of politics on sports has to end."[15]

Although not too much should be read into the quality of India's sports administrators—those in the International Olympic Committee or the International Football Federation do not inspire much confidence, either—it is instructive that powerful politicians, many of whom have been accused of nepotism and corruption, are entrenched in a majority of India's sports bodies. In 2010, of India's thirty-five national sports federations, at least ten were headed by politicians.[16] The situation got so bad that both the president of the Indian Olympic Association (IOA), Suresh Kalmadi (who was also a sitting MP from the Congress Party), and the chief of the athletics federation spent time in prison on serious corruption charges related to the staging of the 2010 Commonwealth Games in New Delhi. There are others, such as K. P. S. Gill, a former police officer, who headed the Indian hockey federation for nearly fifteen years until 2008 and was locked in a legal battle with a rival organization over which one really represented Indian hockey. Some people, besides the politicians and bureaucrats themselves, believe that it not such a bad thing that former sportspersons have little to do with running sports, since they would be at sea in the politics of administration. A sports-loving editor of a national daily, Shekhar Gupta, belongs to that school and wrote that "it needs the enterprise, networking, ambition, entrepreneurship, and certainly the thick skin and greed of a politician, a businessman or even a bureaucrat in the Indian context to build, manage and then monetise a sport in India."[17]

India's short-lived minister of sports, Ajay Maken, thought otherwise. In 2011 he was instrumental in drafting a national sports development bill, some of whose provisions were that 25 percent of all the executive members on sports bodies would be sportspersons; the upper age limit would be seventy, with a maximum tenure of two terms or eight years for office bearers (exceptions would be made for the president of a federation, who could serve for twelve years); elections would have to be conducted transparently; and a sports *lokayukta* (or ombudsman) would be created to mediate disputes.[18] This legislation was not acceptable to the government, since several prominent politicians headed sports bodies and could not have met the provisions. (A revised sports bill was introduced again in 2013 but is yet to be passed by parliament.) In 2011, the sports ministry did, however, put in place a sports code that was expected to be followed by various sports federations, including the IOA. Among other things, the sports code limited the tenure of officers of the IOA and other national sports federations, and it designated these bodies as public entities answerable under the Right to Information Act.[19] This led to a peculiar situation in which the Indian government, the IOA, and the International Olympic Committee (IOC) were at odds with one another. This was due partly to a ruling in 2010 by the Delhi High Court, dragged into the controversy following a public interest litigation, which said that elections must abide by the government's new sports code. In end 2012, the IOC took the drastic step of suspending the IOA on the grounds that the election of its officers was tainted and had violated the IOC's charter, which forbids government interference. The ban was eventually lifted in February 2014, but it was an indicator of the various interests at stake in Indian sports and how they were damaging its cause.

The Power of Usha

The various factors conspiring against sports in India should have foreshadowed a gloomy present and future. On the contrary, the last decade or so have been one of the best periods for Indian sports outside cricket. Perhaps the best place to begin the story of non-cricket sports in India today is the 1982 Asian Games in Delhi. As I mentioned earlier, the Asiad coincided with the introduction of color television in India. India's performance in the Asian Games, however, did not really match the hype around the event. By 1982 China had already arrived as a sports power in Asia and had won a phenomenal sixty-one gold medals in the Delhi Asian Games. India won thirteen gold medals (and an overall tally of fifty-seven medals), which was two short of its total in the inaugural Asiad hosted in Delhi in 1951. At the conclusion of the games, *The Statesman*, while praising the organization and stadiums, wrote, "Questions will be asked whether the performance of the nation's sportsmen and women inside these arenas had matched those of the builders."[20] Although most of the Indian gold medalists, such as Charles Borromeo and M. D. Valsamma, are now only dimly remembered, a silver medalist at the games still is. That athlete was Pilavullakundi Thekeparampil Usha—or P. T. Usha, as she was popularly known—who won two silver medals in the 100- and 200-meter sprints. Usha, who grew up in the tiny village of Payyoli, some 25 miles from Calicut, in the southern state of Kerala, was a product of the state's unique position in India: the country's highest literacy rate, the best human development indices, and a passion for sports. Indeed, Kerala is touted as a "model" among Indian states by the Nobel Prize–winning economist Amartya Sen. For sports, too, as Robin Jeffrey observed, Kerala has "probably been India's pre-eminent sporting state, though it accounts for only 3.5 percent of the country's people."[21] Having been accepted by the Kerala government–sponsored sports school in Cannanore at the age of twelve, Usha had opportunities that most children in India would never have dreamed of. For Usha's father, the owner of a small shop, the Rs 250 monthly allowance at the sports school was a clincher, since he couldn't have afforded to pay her board and tuition.[22] Several other athletes from the state, including Asiad medal winners Shiny Abraham and Valsamma, benefited from the Kerala government scheme as well.[23] Indeed, the Kerala experience is a validation of the point made by Krishna and Haglund.

It was at the Cannanore school that Usha's athletic talent blossomed. From winning a string of medals at the national junior meet in 1978 to becoming the national 100-meter champion in 1980, Usha's rise was meteoric. Before Usha's silver medals, as well as her fellow Kerala athlete M. D. Valsamma's gold medal in the 400-meter hurdles in the 1982 Asiad, the presence of Indian women on the winner's podium had been all too rare. In the early years of the Asian Games, nearly all the women medal winners from India were Anglo-Indians like Christie Brown, Stephie D'Souza, and Elizabeth Davenport. The women's quartet, composed entirely of Anglo-Indians, won the 4 × 100-meter relay in the first Asiad in 1951. The first individual gold medal for an Indian woman in the Asian Games was not won until 1970, by Kamaljit Sandhu.

Usha single-handedly changed the situation. In the 1984 Los Angeles Olympics, she competed in the 400-meter hurdles, which for the first time was open to women. When Usha qualified for the finals of the event, she became the first Indian woman and only the fourth Indian to achieve this feat in the Olympics. In the finals, however, Usha lost the bronze by one-hundredth of a second—the closest any Indian athlete, man or woman, had ever come to winning a track-and-field event in the Olympics.[24] Subsequently, in the 1987 Asian Games in Seoul, Usha won the biggest-ever haul of medals by any Indian athlete when she picked up five gold medals and a silver.[25] Even though she might have missed a medal at the 1988 Seoul Olympics and was, along with her coach, even criticized for it,[26] Usha remains India's all-time greatest track-and-field athlete. Besides her natural talent, state patronage was an essential component of her success. After her home state of Kerala funded her initial foray into athletics, later the railways—which, as we saw in an earlier chapter, always was active in sports—employed her as a reservation clerk in

1982.[27] Usha's example could also be credited to some extent for the subsequent success of women athletes, particularly in the 2010 Commonwealth Games and the 2011 Asian Games.

Although India has not come close to winning an Olympic medal in track and field since Usha, it has won individual medals in several disciplines in the last two decades, beginning with Leander Paes—a Calcutta-born player who always managed to improve his performance by several notches when he represented India—who won a bronze medal in tennis in 1996. Astonishingly, this was India's first individual medal in the Olympics in the more than forty years since K. D. Jadhav's bronze in wrestling in 1952. Following Paes, Karnam Malleswari, from the south Indian state of Andhra Pradesh, won a bronze in women's weight lifting (2000) and an army officer, Rajyavardhan Rathore, a silver in shooting (2004) before shooter Abhinav Bindra in 2008 became the first Indian ever to win an individual Olympic gold medal. In the 2008 Beijing Games, Vijender Singh and Sushil Kumar each won a bronze, in boxing and wrestling, respectively, before India won its largest ever-tally of six medals—two silver and four bronze—in the 2012 London Games. Here India won medals in wrestling (Sushil Kumar and Yogeshwar Dutt), shooting (Vijay Kumar and Gagan Narang), boxing (Mary Kom), and badminton (Saina Nehwal).

India's performance in the London Games in terms of population, number of competitors sent, and high expectations, was ordinary. But placed in the context of India's Olympic record—in which, aside from the eleven medals in hockey, India had won only seven individual medals in all before the London Games (with three of them in the 2008 Beijing Games) in twenty outings—it was good. The incremental success of Indian sportspersons, particularly women, and several new initiatives has radically changed the country's sports landscape. It has built new sports centers and unlikely sports stars as well as renewed older traditions like wrestling. The glow of sports success has been reflected in Bollywood, the barometer of popular taste in India. Over the past few years, a string of films have had as their subject sports heroes not associated with cricket. *Chak de India* (2007), *Paan Singh Tomar* (2010), and *Bhaag Milkha Bhaag* (2013) are some of the films that have done well at the box office. Oddly enough, before *Lagaan*, few films based on cricket had tasted box office success. In recent times, however, a spate of films centered on cricket, including *Iqbal* (2005) and *Kai Po Che* (2013), have done reasonably well at the box office. Indeed, many more sports films are in the pipeline, with big-budget movies on Gama and Mohun Bagan's 1911 victory being planned.

The Uniqueness of Wrestling

Wrestling is perhaps the best place to begin an assessment of contemporary Indian sports. It is the only mainstream sport that has existed in India for several centuries without interruption. Traditional wrestling continues to flourish in *akharas* across north India as well as in *dangals* (wrestling tournaments). In 2011 when I visited the Chandgi Ram *akhara* in Old Delhi, named after the legendary wrestler who won a gold medal in the Asian Games and is now managed by his son, and the Bara Ganesh *akhara* in Banaras, one of the sites of Joseph Alter's pioneering study, it was obvious that wrestling is alive and well in India. *Dangals*—whose organization and political economy Alter has described in detail—also continue to be big draws in the villages of Uttar Pradesh, Haryana, Punjab, Madhya Pradesh, and Maharashtra, with the prize money sometimes rising to a substantial Rs 100,000 per bout.[28] Alter distinguishes between "ticket" *dangals*, in which organizers sell tickets and aim to make a profit, and "khula" *dangals*, which are free and open to everyone.[29] A body called the Indian Style Wrestling Association (as opposed to the Wrestling Federation of India, which is in charge of the wrestling in the Olympics and other international tournaments) nominally oversees the *dangals*.[30] What is noteworthy is the patronage of *dangals* by politicians. The former Uttar Pradesh chief minister and prominent national politician, Mulayam Singh Yadav, who was a *pehelwan* in his younger days, sponsors an annual *dangal* in his home constituency of Etawah. Other politicians, like the Chautalas of Haryana, underwrite *dangals* in their state. This shows the powerful hold that traditional wrestling has over wide swaths of northern and western India, prompting politicians to be associated with competitions. As P. Sainath said about wrestling in Maharashtra, "*Kushti* is located at the intersection of sports, politics, culture and economy in the rural regions of this state."[31]

Also finding pride of place are the religious symbols associated with wrestling. A shrine dedicated to Lord Hanuman is mandatory in most *akharas*; even the 2012 National Wrestling Championship in Gonda, Uttar Pradesh, was held with a giant cutout of a garlanded Hanuman in the background.[32] Most *akharas* have a strong Hindu element in both their symbols and their membership.

Wrestlers at the 2012 national wrestling championship in Gonda, Uttar Praddesh, with a cutout of Hanuman in the background. Photograph by Abhishek Madhukar. Printed by permission of Abhishek Madhukar

In his study of the *akharas* in Banaras, Alter found that all the wrestlers were Hindus, with 50 percent of them Yadavs, 20 percent Bhumihars, 15 percent Brahmins, and the rest divided among several lower castes.[33] Another scholar, Norbert Peabody, who studied *akharas* in Kota in the western state of Rajasthan, found that Hindu and Muslims trained in separate *akharas*.[34] Furthermore, the lower castes and the former untouchables, or Dalits, had their own *akharas*. This, of course, raises the question of the link between wrestling and Hindu nationalism. While Alter believes that the structure of *akharas* and the worldview of wrestlers are inimical to the sort of Hindu nationalism advocated by organizations like the Rashtriya Swayamsevak Sangh,[35] others, like Peabody, have documented the role of wrestlers in collective violence and riots.[36]

What has changed over time is the increasing coexistence in the traditional *akharas* of the brown earth with artificial mats, which is what international wrestling is conducted on, and modern weight-training equipment. This is a response to the success of Indian wrestlers and the demands of preparing for international tournaments. Sushil Kumar, India's wrestling superstar who has not only won two Olympic medals but has also been a world champion in his weight category, is a good example of the meeting of tradition and modernity. Born in Baprola, a small village on the outskirts of Delhi, Sushil began his training at the age of twelve in an *akhara* in Delhi run by the wrestling legend Satpal Singh, who himself won a gold medal in the 1982 Asian Games. Sushil initially trained in the mud pits of the *akhara* before switching to imported Olympic-standard mats. Since his Olympic success, Sushil has won endorsements—a rarity for non-cricket players—for several companies, including Mountain Dew, Eicher tractors, and the National Egg Coordination Committee.[37] Sociologist Shiv Visvanathan characterized Sushil's appeal as bridging tradition and modernity: "Boost [an energy drink] does not spell the secret of his success and Bournvita does not assure his future. He is as local as *desi* ghee but is quietly global."[38]

Sushil also is part of an age-old *guru-shishya* (master-disciple) tradition. While he learned the art of wrestling from Satpal (who, incidentally, later became his father-in-law), Satpal in turn learned his craft from another legend, Guru Hanuman, whose trainees have won several international medals. Indeed, Alter named Guru Hanuman the "best-known guru" of Indian wrestling, who taught his skills at the Birla Mill Vyayamshala in old Delhi, a unique example of an industrial house, the Birlas, sponsoring a traditional sport.[39] This tradition is now under threat at the highest levels of Indian wrestling, as India has increasingly turned to foreign coaches, mostly from the former Soviet Union, to train its wrestlers. Even though these coaches believe that the initial training of Indian wrestlers in *akharas* is an impediment to international success,[40] it is unlikely that the *akhara* tradition, with its historic and deep moorings, will disappear. At the same time, however, international norms and rules and their accoutrements—wrestling mats and modern weight-training equipment—are slowly changing the world of *kushti*. It also is true that in many urban *akharas*, the gym and weight-training equipment have a stronger attraction for young Indian males who want to build their physique rather than take the arduous path of learning how to wrestle.

The New Sports Landscape

Boxing in Bhiwani

Boxing, which, as we saw, has a much shorter history in India, is the other ring sport in which India has excelled in recent times. Bhiwani, a dusty town in the north Indian state of Haryana, some 75 miles from Delhi, is now the epicenter of Indian boxing. The transformation of this nondescript town into India's boxing capital had much to do with the Asian Games medalist Hawa Singh, who in the late 1980s established the Sports Authority of India (SAI) boxing center in Bhiwani. Although Hawa Singh can be credited with bringing boxing to Bhiwani, it was only after creating the Bhiwani Boxing Club—essentially a private enterprise begun by a former national coach, Jagdish Singh, but supported by the Haryana boxing association—that the sport really took off. Several of India's boxers who had been winning medals in international tournaments, including the Olympic bronze medalist and world champion Vijender Singh, got their initial training at the Bhiwani club. Despite the squabbling over whether the government-run SAI or the Bhiwani club should get the real credit, Bhiwani is, at present, home to as many as five boxing centers, including the SAI center, the Bhiwani club, and yet another academy run by Hawa Singh's son, where some one thousand boxers train.[41] Not surprisingly, a large majority of India's top boxers, including Vikas Krishan and Dinesh Kumar, are from Bhiwani. The advent of boxing has changed not only Bhiwani but also the lives of the boxers, none more so than Vijender, with his matinee-idol looks. He is undoubtedly the biggest star of Indian boxing, having signed several endorsements after his Olympic medal as well as a three-year contract with a sports management company. And in what was rare for a non-cricketer, he took part in reality shows, and there was even talk of a role in a Bollywood film. The high life also implicated him in a drug scandal in 2013.[42]

If Bhiwani is India's boxing capital, Haryana has become its sports factory. Indeed, in the 2010 Commonwealth Games, nearly half of India's medals were won by sportspersons from Haryana. There are several theories as to why this tiny north Indian state, which has only 2 percent of the country's population and a highly skewed gender ratio, is now the nursery of contact sports. One scholar offered two reasons for Haryana's success in reaping medals: The first is the volatile history of the region, which has faced invaders over the centuries and has developed a certain degree of aggressiveness; and the second is the peasant culture of the area, which values physical strength and perseverance.[43] We could add the sudden prosperity of Haryana's farmers, who have profited from the boom in land prices, owing to the state's proximity to Delhi, allowing the younger generation to focus on sports with-

out worrying too much about making a living. What also has contributed to
the sports renaissance is the state government's aggressive policy of funding sports. Medal-winning sportspersons are rewarded with substantial cash
awards, and the government has reserved 3 percent of the jobs in the police
for them. Consequently, many of Haryana's medal-winning sportspersons
are working for the state police. An economist's take on Haryana's success
is that it has built a sports infrastructure and given fiscal incentives directly
to individuals instead of pouring money into sports federations and public
training.[44]

The Rise of the Northeast

The other great, and inspiring, center of Indian sport is the isolated state
of Manipur, in the country's northeast, which for so long was better known
for its insurgent groups. One writer described Manipur's capital, Imphal,
as a "town so removed from the Indian growth story that aspiration is not
even visible on its streets."[45] Nonetheless, from boxing to archery to football,
Manipur has been regularly producing international-level athletes for the
past decade or so. Olympic bronze medalist and five-time world champion
boxer, Mangte Chungneijang "Mary" Kom, is perhaps the most recognizable
face from the state, with the rare honor of having a road named after her in
Imphal. The daughter of a landless laborer from Kangathei village and the
mother of twin sons when she won her Olympic medal in London—where
women's boxing made its Olympic debut—Mary's story contains a bit of the
magical.[46] Beginning with the National Women's Boxing Championship in
2001, Mary has won several national and international titles. The Special
Area Games center (a project of SAI) at Imphal and its legendary boxing
coach Ibomcha Singh were essential to Mary's success. She also credits two
other state-run organizations, the Youth Affairs and Sports Boxing Academy and the Manipur Amateur Boxing Association, with her and the other
Manipuri boxers' success, though she also decries the rivalry between these
two bodies and the SAI.[47] Like the male boxers of Haryana, Mary works for
the state police, having started as a subinspector with a monthly salary of
Rs 15,000.[48] Besides Mary, several other boxers from Manipur are now in
the upper echelons of amateur boxing. This state's boxing revolution, and indeed its sports revolution, can be traced to the boxer Dingko Singh, who won

Mary Kom (left) at the Asian Women's Boxing Championship in Guwahati, 2008. She was the subject of a biopic in 2014, with Bollywood star Priyanka Chopra playing Mary Kom. Reprinted by permission of the Hindu Archives

a gold in the 1998 Asian Games. Dingko, who is now with the Indian navy, is a role model for Manipur's rising boxers, such as Devendro Singh, Suranjoy Singh, and Nanao Singh.[49] Among the Manipuri women, Sarita Devi, who has always fought in Mary's shadow, is a former world champion and a five-time Asian champion,[50] and Sarjubala Devi is the new kid on the block, with a gold medal in 2011 in the first-ever youth world championship.

One early pre-monsoon morning in 2012 in Imphal, I was witness to the boxing fervor generated by Ibomcha Singh and his star disciples. In the sports complex, a few hundred boys and girls, aged between twelve and sixteen, were pounding away at punching bags or throwing jabs at one another under Ibomcha's watchful eyes. On the walls of the indoor auditorium, the words of the once-popular song eulogizing Muhammad Ali—"Float like a butterfly, sting like a bee"—inspired the young boxers, as did the roll call of greats, including Dingko and Mary, who once trained here. In the sprawling, if somewhat rundown, complex, other children were busy training in a whole range of sports, from weight lifting to the Chinese sport *wushu*. It's not difficult to fathom why Manipur has taken so enthusiastically to sport. In a state with few employment opportunities, sports are a passport out of poverty.

As a journalist put it, sports offer "a legitimacy few other endeavours can afford to in the stricken state."[51] And success in sports comes with secure jobs in the police and armed forces. Unlike Haryana, it has hardly any private sports clubs, although Mary Kom has now started her own boxing academy. The Manipur effect also has spread to other states in India's northeast, which is connected to the Indian mainland by a narrow stretch of land known as the "chicken's neck." One of India's best football players, Sikkim's Bhaichung Bhutia, ace boxers Shiva Thapa and Pwilao Basumatary from Assam, and archer Chekrovolu Swuro from Nagaland, are just a few of them. Manipur won football's Santosh Trophy in 2002, and Mizoram became the second northeastern state to win it in 2014. Sports have brought not only hope to a region that is home to numerous insurgencies but also the northeast closer to India in a way that military boots and government sops could not.

Guns and Arrows

Two other sports in which India has excelled in recent times can be traced to an earlier era. One is shooting, which is descended from the *shikars* organized by the maharajas and the colonial elite, and archery, which, of course, goes back much further. India's first shooter to excel in international competitions was a former maharaja, Karni Singh of Bikaner, a princely state known for its hunts during the colonial period. Singh was the seventeen-time national champion in clay pigeon and skeet shooting, and he also represented India at the Olympics five times between 1960 and 1980. Even though Karni Singh did not win an Olympic medal, he participated in the world shooting championship and the Asian Games and won India's first shooting medal in 1974. In what is perhaps a unique record, both Karni Singh and his fourteen-year-old daughter, Rajyashree Kumari, represented India at the Asian Shooting Championship in Tokyo in 1967.[52] The princely flag was kept flying as well by another former maharaja, Randhir Singh of Patiala (who also carried on his family tradition of sports administration with his long association with the Indian Olympic Association and International Olympic Committee), who competed and won medals in international tournaments.

As with other sports in independent India, the democratizing tendencies have affected shooting. India's first Olympic medal in shooting was won— again, not surprisingly—by an army officer, Rajyavardhan Rathore, in 2004.

This army connection was kept alive in the 2012 Olympics when Vijay Kumar won a silver medal, but it was left to a businessman's son from Chandigarh, Abhinav Bindra, to win India's one and only individual Olympic gold medal. The story of how Bindra took up and excelled in shooting is well documented in his autobiography, cowritten with journalist Rohit Brijnath. One of the most startling aspects of Bindra's journey to the gold medal was the lack of any kind of state support, which is amply illustrated by the title of a chapter in the book: "Mr Indian Official: Thanks for Nothing."[53] Bindra's was a sports quest mostly funded and supported by his family and the odd private sponsor. It also did not help that shooting is a sport with no big prize money or fans, but only "paper certificates and tin medals" and the Olympics as the "single moment" that defined shooters.[54] "I envy cricketers standing in the midst of Eden Gardens, surrounded by a collective of 100,000 fans, heaving like one worshipful beast. My name has never been chanted, it will never be," Bindra confessed. The relative obscurity of the sport did not, however, matter when Bindra ended up winning India's first (and only one to date) individual Olympic gold. It was testimony to the paucity of India's success in the Olympics that on his return to India, Bindra received more than 350,000 congratulatory telegrams (something that Indians still used in the Internet age until they were discontinued in 2013), and some cities named roads after him.[55]

Bindra and Rathore have had a ripple effect. When Bindra took part in his first nationals in the mid-1990s, he had 300 competitors, a number that by 2009 had jumped to around 3,000.[56] Similar democratizing tendencies can be found in other elite sports, such as golf, which is attracting a fair number of middle-class children in a country that still has very few golf courses. Perhaps the best advertisement for this trend is Jeev Milkha Singh, son of the legendary athlete Milkha Singh and his volleyball player wife, Nirmal Kaur, who shunned his parents' vocations and took up golf. In 2007 he became the first Indian to break into the top one hundred in world golf, inspiring several other Indians to excel in the sport.[57]

In archery, India hasn't yet won an Olympic medal, but Indian archers, especially women, have been doing well in international tournaments. One of the stars of Indian archery is Deepika Kumari, the daughter of an autorickshaw driver from the eastern state of Jharkhand. The state, which was carved out from Bihar in 2001, has always been famous for its hockey players, beginning with India's first captain in the Olympics Jaipal Singh and subsequently players like Michael Kindo, Sylvanus Dung Dung, and Ajit Lakra. Deepika's success is due less to state support than to the Tata Group's sponsorship, which has an inordinately large presence in mineral-rich Jharkhand. Initially spotted by talent scouts from a local archery academy, Kumari was accepted by the Tata Archery Academy at the age of eleven for a monthly stipend of Rs 500.[58] She hasn't looked back since, winning a World Cup gold medal in 2010 besides eighteen other medals in international events. She and other archers from the northeast, like Chekrovolu Swuro and Bombayla Devi, were ranked second in the world in 2012. The success of India's marginalized tribals in competitive archery is an inversion of the Ekalavya story from the Mahabharata. In fact, such is Kumari's star value that before the 2012 Olympics, there was a tug-of-war between the state-run Oil and Gas Natural Corporation (ONGC) and Tata Steel, two major sponsors of sports, over which of them would employ her. Eventually it was Tata Steel that hired her as a manager in its sports department.

The Resurgence of Badminton

Saina Nehwal's bronze medal in badminton in the London Games might have been fortuitous, since her Chinese opponent forfeited the medal play-off game after injuring herself. Badminton, however, is a sport that India has a long tradition to fall back on. Prakash Padukone's win in the 1980 All-England tournament, regarded as the unofficial world championship, renewed interest in the sport. Among the several fine badminton players in India in the 1980s and 1990s, including Syed Modi, who was shot dead in 1988, was Pullela Gopichand, who became the second Indian to win the All-England in 2001. The story of Gopichand, the son of an officer in an agricultural bank, is in some senses the familiar one of a talented sportsperson from a middle-class background battling the odds to excel in his chosen sport. Gopichand's first serious training began on the Fateh Maidan badminton courts in Hyderabad. Although he had access to courts and coaches, Gopichand's family struggled to pay for his passion, especially the cost of shuttlecocks.[59] Once he had won tournaments at the national level, however, Gopichand followed the usual route of taking jobs with companies that had a sports quota. His first job was at the Tata Iron and Steel Company (which he left within six months owing to the lack of strong practice partners), followed by a scholarship from the national air carrier, Air India, and finally a job at the Indian Oil Corporation. To attend international tournaments, however, Gopinath had to raise his own funds. His win at the All-England changed everything, and he was inundated with cash awards on his return to India. Unlike many sport stars, however, Gopichand has made a mark as a coach after retirement. His coaching academy in Gachibowli in Hyderabad has ensured that the southern city, famous for the Charminar monument and its *biryani*, has become the center for badminton in the same way as Bhiwani is for boxing. The Gopichand Badminton Academy has trained several of India's young talents, including Saina Nehwal, who came under Gopichand's wing at the age of thirteen when she moved from her hometown in Haryana to Hyderabad. Besides the Olympic bronze, Nehwal has won several top-ranked international tournaments and a gold at the 2010 Delhi Commonwealth Games. Ranked in the top five in world badminton in 2014, with only the Chinese shuttlers ahead of her, Nehwal is by far the most successful and richest woman athlete in India. She signed a Rs 400-million, three-year contract in 2012 with a sports management company—the same one that manages India's cricket captain Mahendra Singh Dhoni—making her the highest-paid Indian sportsperson outside the cricket players.

A Brief Note on Kabaddi

I noted in an earlier chapter that kabaddi is perhaps India's only indigenous sport that has won some international recognition. After it was included as a demonstration sport in the 1951 Delhi Asian Games, India took the lead in forming the Asian Amateur Kabaddi Federation in 1978, headed by the Maharashtra politician Sharad Pawar (who later headed the International Cricket Council, in addition to being a central minister on several occasions). Besides India, only two countries, Bangladesh and Nepal, were present at the federation's inauguration, though four others—Pakistan, Sri Lanka, Bhutan, and Malaysia—were invited but couldn't send their representatives.[60] In the 1982 Delhi Asian Games, kabaddi was once again a demonstration sport, which paved the way for its inclusion in the official program of the 1990 Asiad. The majority of the other countries that have backed kabaddi are from South Asia, with the exception of Japan. Since 1990, kabaddi has continued to be a part of the Asian Games program, with India having won the gold medal every time. Indeed at the 1990 Asiad, India's gold medal in kabaddi was the only one that it won in the competition, and the kabaddi team returned to a rousing reception in Delhi.[61] In the 2010 Asian Games, women's kabaddi was introduced, and again the gold medal was won by India. Although India has been dominant in international kabaddi, it has also developed a rivalry with Pakistan. In the 1993 South Asian Federation games in Dhaka, India suffered its first-ever loss to Pakistan, which was prematurely bemoaned as an end to "Indian supremacy."[62]

The popularity of kabaddi in India, however, remains moot. John Arlott observed that there are "thousands" of kabaddi clubs across India.[63] In the 1990s, the former kabaddi player and Arjuna Award winner, Shriram Bhavsar, claimed that Mumbai alone had one thousand kabaddi clubs. In fact, he believed that kabaddi was more popular than cricket or football.[64] While there is little doubt that kabaddi is popular, particularly in rural India, the claims of its overtaking cricket are not supported by any real evidence. In comparing kabaddi with cricket, Alter makes the valid point that while kabaddi's "popularity has been formalized, normalized and institutionalized," cricket in India has "not only been vernacularized but vulgarized to the extent that it is played 'against the rules' in much the way the authors who write about kabaddi imagine kabaddi to have been played by 'strong and healthy folk.'"[65]

Inspired by the IPL, kabaddi was, however, revolutionized in 2014 by two leagues—the the eight-city Pro Kabaddi League (PKL) and the World Kabaddi League. The PKL, promoted by the Mahindra Group, which has had a link with kabaddi for several years, and telecast by Star Sports, which also holds the rights to broadcast cricket in India, was an unexpected success, with a television audience of 435 million viewers in its inaugural year, compared with 560 million for the 2014 IPL.[66] The top players, which included several foreigners, were bought by franchises for as much as Rs 1 million. The names of the franchises, such as Patna Pirates and Bengaluru Bulls, and the ownership, which included several Bollywood stars, bore the imprint of the IPL. In the past few years under the initiative of the Punjab government, World Kabaddi Cups have also been organized in India, where a version of the sport—known as ring kabaddi—has been played.

The place of kabaddi in international competitions is, however, tenuous. The process of including any sport in the Asian Games or Olympics is complex, as shown in the decision by the International Olympic Committee in 2013 to remove wrestling, which was part of the ancient Olympic Games, from its list of twenty-five "core" sports.[67] Wrestling, however, subsequently made it back to the Olympic program after making certain changes in its rules.[68] The decision to drop any sport is apparently based on several criteria, including popularity. The political and arbitrary nature of these decisions was illustrated by Myanmar (Burma), host of the 2013 Southeast Asian Games, which attempted to include fourteen traditional martial arts in the roster of events and drop such mainstream sports as badminton and gymnastics. Again, the inclusion of the Chinese martial arts, *wushu*, in the Asian Games (incidentally, an event in which India won three medals in the 2010 Asian Games) beginning in 1990, and its bid for inclusion in the 2020 Olympics is a good example of a traditional sport being modernized and internationalized, with the additional benefit of being pushed by a global sports superpower. As Joseph Alter noted, there are interesting parallels as well between *wushu* and yoga, whose roots go back to ancient India but in recent times is being organized as a competitive sport.[69] The International Yoga Sports Federation was formed in 2003 and regularly holds national and international competitions.[70] The organization's website even states that one of its aims is to develop yoga as an Olympic sport.[71] There are many lessons here for kabaddi—especially the intensely political nature of internationalizing a sport as it aspires to become part of the Olympics—even as it faces the threat of being dropped from the Asian Games program.[72]

The IPL Effect

Besides kabaddi, the success of cricket's Indian Premier League (IPL) has spawned several similar professional leagues in other sports. Though none of them is anywhere close to the IPL in terms of visibility and money-making abilities the leagues are an indication of India's growing economy and expanding middle class.[73] Indeed, hardly any other countries have professional leagues in so many different sports. Hockey, which had been in decline for several years, was the first to adopt the concept. The Premier Hockey League, which preceded the IPL by three years, folded in 2008 only to be reincarnated in 2013 as the Hockey India League (HIL). At its inception, the HIL had five franchisees with names reminiscent of its cricket counterparts—

Delhi Waveriders, Mumbai Magicians, Punjab Warriors, Ranchi Rhinos, and Uttar Pradesh Wizards—and a player auction modeled on the IPL. Besides the top Indian players, several international stars made themselves available for the tournament. The top players were bought for as much as $70,000 and up, a first for hockey in any country, and the telecast rights were bought by Star Sports.[74] The semifinals and the final of the 2013 tournament, which were played in Ranchi, the capital of Jharkhand, were played before packed stands.

The other IPL-style tournaments haven't had as much financial success. The Indian Volley League was held for the first time in 2011, and the prize money was much less than in the HIL. The tournament budget for the volleyball league was a mere Rs 10.5 million and the total prize money was Rs 2.2 million.[75] The Indian Badminton League, with six city-based franchises, was launched in mid-2013. In the player auction, top players like Nehwal were sold for as much as $120,000, which a few years ago she said she "couldn't even dream about earning."[76] The International Premier Tennis League, floated by Indian tennis player Mahesh Bhupathi and involving several international tennis stars, was launched in 2014. At the time of this writing, plans also were afoot for an Indian boxing league and Indian wrestling league.

Despite the plethora of IPL-style tournaments, there are some holdouts. One notable example is the annual hockey tournament held in Coorg (now known as Kodava), long a nursery for Indian hockey and soldiers. It is said that as a child in Coorg, you "pick up [either] a gun or a hockey stick."[77] At least sixty players from Coorg, including M. P. Ganesh, B. P. Govinda, M. M. Somaya, and Arjun Halappa, have represented India over the years, and since 1997, Coorg has been the site of the Kodava Hockey Festival, an interfamily tournament in which some two hundred families from the region take part. A brainchild of Pandanda Kutappa, a former bank official, the tournament is hosted every year by a different family.

The Curious Case of Football

Football has always had its city-based leagues and national tournaments run by the football federation or sponsored by private companies. As late as 1997, a "semiprofessional" national league, to use the words of the then football federation president, was organized by the All-India Football Federation. The tournament was sponsored for the first two seasons by the multinational electronics company Philips, for approximately Rs 20 million, with a purse of Rs 3.5 million for the winner.[78] Among the twelve teams that competed in the first phase of the inaugural tournament were the historic Calcutta clubs, such as Mohun Bagan, East Bengal, and Mohammedan Sporting; teams from other parts of India like Salgaoncar, Mahindra United, and Kerala Police; and newer clubs such as the Churchill Brothers from Goa. The tournament did not have a smooth ride, though, with Philips pulling out after two years and Coca-Cola taking up the sponsorship for the third season. In 2002 the sponsor changed again, with the Tatas and later the Oil and Gas Natural Corporation (ONGC) funding the national league before it was renamed the I-League in 2007. It is instructive, however, that of the original twelve clubs in India's National Football League, four, including the first national league winner, JCT Phagwara, have closed over the last decade. All four were clubs owned by private or state-run companies. The demise of the older clubs has, however, been offset by the formation of new clubs, reflecting football's geographical spread. Of the eleven teams playing in the 2014/2015 I-League (now sponsored by the Hero Motocorp and known as the Hero I-League), two, Shillong Lajong and Royal Wahingdoh, were from northeast India.

Even when older corporate sponsors like JCT and Mahindras pulled out from sponsoring football clubs, newer sponsors stepped in. The best known of these was the United Breweries Group (UB Group), which sealed simultaneous sponsorship deals before the 1998/1999 season, with two Calcutta clubs and bitter rivals, Mohun Bagan and East Bengal. United Breweries bought a 50 percent stake in both clubs in a deal worth Rs 27.5 million.[79] Officially, the clubs were known as Kingfisher East Bengal and Mcdowell Mohun Bagan, after two brands owned by United Breweries, but the renaming caused much heartburn in Calcutta, with some of the 7,500-odd members of Mohun Bagan taking the club to court.[80] In 2000 UB did the unthinkable by buying the third big Calcutta club, Mohammedan Club, which meant that for a while the company owned the three oldest football clubs in India.[81] At the time, the UB Group also backed a short-lived, new, Kerala-based club called FC Kochin, the first fully professional football club in India, but it was disbanded in 2002. UB also sponsored a national tournament, the Federation Cup, whose origins date back to 1977. Yet another recent and prominent corporate investor in football was the Essel Group, the owners of the Zee television channel, which took over the Churchill Brothers in 2000 and initially sponsored the Mumbai Football Club when it was launched in 2007. Zee also held the rights to telecast the I-League in its early years. A new club, Bengaluru FC, founded in 2013 and owned by the Jindal Group, won the 2013/2014 I-League.

During this period, though, India's ranking in international football dropped precipitously, and since 2000 it has not been ranked in the world's top one hundred teams. This hasn't stopped international players from seeking their fortunes in India, however, even though none of them are top-bracket players in their own countries. One of the first international players (except for the few from Pakistan in the 1950s) to play in India was the Iranian international player Majid Basker, who joined East Bengal in 1980, followed by another of his countrymen, Jamshed Nassiri, who, after retiring, stayed on in India as a coach. One of the most popular foreign recruits of the 1980s and 1990s was Nigeria's Chima Okerie, who played for all three big Calcutta clubs—Mohun Bagan, East Bengal, and Mohammedan Sporting—and, in his time, was one of the biggest football stars in India. Basker and Okerie were also among the highest-paid footballers in India during their playing days. In the 1997 season, Mohun Bagan went to the extent of paying Okerie's taxes, which amounted to Rs 2 million, in addition to giving him a car and an apartment.[82] Since then, several international players encompassing the entire footballing world, from Brazil to Australia and several countries in between, have been recruited by Indian clubs and, in some cases, turned around the fortunes of their adopted club. Even some foreign tourists with football skills have been signed by a major club.[83] The influx of foreign players, though, has resulted in an inflation of players' salaries. In the late 1990s, the average salary of a player was around Rs 100,000, while superstars like Bhutia earned around Rs 2.5 million.[84] But by 2010, the average salary of a player in the I-League had risen to between Rs 2 million and Rs 4.5 million, with the highest salary being Rs 10 million.[85] This was, of course, a pittance compared with the salaries of international football stars in 2010, which were more than $10 million (at current rates, Rs 636 million) a year.

As in many countries with a poor international record, the local tournaments have suffered from low attendance. The exceptions are certain pockets of the country, such as West Bengal, Goa, and Kerala, where football clubs continue to have a mass following. For instance, in 1997 a match between

Mohun Bagan and East Bengal attracted an audience of 131,000 at the Salt Lake City stadium, considered by FIFA as among the highest-attended club games in the world.[86] In 2000, a Mohun Bagan–East Bengal match in Kolkata drew 80,000 people; a Salgaocar–Churchill Brothers game in Margao, Goa, the same year attracted 20,000 spectators; and a FC Kochin–Churchill Brothers match in Kochi, Kerala, drew an audience of 35,000. However, that same year in other parts of the country, such as Punjab, matches involving local teams like JCT were attended by only 5,000 people.[87] Games between Mohun Bagan and East Bengal continue to be crowd pleasers with 70,000 fans in attendance in 2014 for a match between the two clubs.[88] The matches also led to extreme passions, and even violence, off the pitch. In one of the worst incidents, sixteen people died on August 16, 1980, after rival supporters clashed in the Eden Garden stands during a match between the two teams, causing a stampede.

In the country as a whole, however, it is international football that commands a much larger fan base. This was apparent from the ever increasing amounts that that broadcasters were willing to pay to telecast the football World Cup. ESPN–Star Sports bought the rights for the 2010 tournament for $40 million, which was way above the $8 million paid in 2006 and the $3 million in 2002.[89] Not just the quadrennial World Cup attracted Indian viewers. Manchester United and Barcelona T-shirts are now commonplace on the streets of India's metros, and in 2013 the viewership for the English Premier League (EPL) stood at 155 million, three times the population of a midsized European country. European clubs therefore see India as a huge potential market. Manchester United has begun training sessions for youngsters at the Cooperage Stadium in Mumbai, and the considerable price tag of Rs 22,600 for a two-week session has not deterred participation.[90] Several other European clubs, including Liverpool and Inter Milan, have begun similar schemes to compensate for the absence of youth academies in India. The foreign football leagues, too, are eyeing the Indian market.

In 2014, like the kabaddi league, the eight-city Indian Super League (ISL), backed by business tycoon Mukesh Ambani's Reliance Industries and broadcaster Star India, churned Indian football. Several prominent cricketers, including Sachin Tendulkar and Sourav Ganguly, and top Bollywood filmstars bought stakes in the franchisees. Some 410 million people tuned in on television to watch the inaugural ISL, won by the Atletico de Kolkata, and there were good crowds in the stadium too. The average salaries of Indian players, at Rs 2.4 million for the three-month tournament, were also higher than what the footballers normally drew.[91] Only time will tell whether the explosion of academies, which cater primarily to children of middle-class and rich families, and ventures like the ISL will contribute to lifting the standard of football in India. But it's clear that the older tournaments, including the I-League, might find it difficult to survive and draw crowds in the wake of the ISL. Many of India's football clubs are in poor shape. The top three Kolkata clubs—East Bengal, Mohun Bagan and Mohammedan Sporting—are facing financial troubles and how they deal with the ISL and their common city rival Atletico remains to be seen.

As the football audience in India has become globalized, football as well is feeling the global impact of Indian capital. In the last decade, Indian corporate houses like the Tatas and Indian businessmen like Lakshmi Mittal, who is among the richest people in the world, have acquired major foreign companies. Some of this acquisition fever has spilled over to football. Accordingly, the Mittals bought a stake in the English Premier League team the Queens Park Rangers in 2007, and the Indian poultry chain, Venky's, owns the iconic Blackburn Rovers. Ironically, both teams have been doing poorly, raising questions about the seriousness of Indian business tycoons' investment in football.

Why Now?

The preceding description should have given readers at least an idea of the vibrancy of sports in India today. Although cricket continues to dwarf all other sports, if we don't use international performance as a yardstick, India is not the one-sport nation that it is often made out to be. India definitely has a sports culture, and various factors have led to its recent flowering. Obviously, India's economic growth over the past decade or so has had an effect. From a long period of what was known as the "Hindu rate of growth"— roughly 3 percent per year—India's economy grew at an impressive rate of around 8 percent from 2003 onward before tapering off after the 2008 economic downturn. This meant, using the argument of the economists Anirudh Krishna and Eric Haglund, a bigger "effective participating population" now in sports. This is apparent from the fact that many of India's medal winners in international meets are from small towns and villages, or "India B," as one commentator termed it.[92] This might not yet be a sports revolution, but more youngsters from rural India are now able to take part in sports and see them as a ticket out of poverty. The most encouraging aspect of this is the number of women who are now participating in sports and doing well.[93]

What also has made a difference is more state funding. While the government and sports officials are justifiably blamed for India's poor sporting performance, the Sports Authority of India, which was established in 1984 under the Ministry of Sport and Youth Affairs (which was known as the Department of Sports when it was instituted in 1982), has had an impact, though its efficacy is doubtful. The Indian government's budget for sports and youth affairs in 2013/2014 stood at over Rs 12 billion. This was up from a mere Rs 430 million in 1990/1991. The lion's share of the budget usually goes to the Sports Authority of India (SAI), which was allocated Rs 326 million in the 2013/2014 financial year. Of this, the SAI gave funds to various sports federations according to their priorities. For 2013/2014, the top five sports based on money allocated were boxing, hockey, wrestling, shooting, and badminton.[94] Not surprisingly, except for hockey, the other five sports were those in which India has had the most success in the recent past. Despite the budget increase, it is still minuscule compared with China's spending on sports. According to back-of-the-envelope calculations, China spent about $3 billion before the 2004 Olympic Games, which works out to roughly $50 million for each of the sixty-three medals that it won in those games.[95] There is, of course, good reason why India would not want to follow the Chinese model, which is driven by the hunger for international medals and is often draconian and oblivious to the young athletes' individual rights.

The two training hubs for sports at the highest level are the Netaji Subhas National Institute of Sports (NSNIS) in Patiala, where the former maharaja's palace grounds have been converted to a sports center, and the Army Sports Institute in Pune. The latter was established in 2001 and offers training in seven disciplines, including archery, athletics, boxing, and wrestling. While these might be the best that India has to offer, they are far from world class, as this description of the Patiala center from a profile of Mary Kom before the 2012 Olympics makes clear:

Beneath the order it [NSNIS] is still India, no country for athletes. Kom will return to shared accommodation in a hostel, where she will boil vegetables with fermented fish on her portable stove, because the mess food can leave her with indigestion. She will hand-wash her clothes, scrubbing the blood off her socks, as there is a single washing machine for an entire hostel of athletes. Two years ago, two female boxers, one a world-championship medalist, were asked to serve tea.[96]

Besides direct state funding, the state-run organizations continue to be heavily involved in sports in other ways. The role of the armed forces, the railways, the police, the State Bank of India, and other state-owned organizations in encouraging sports since preindependence times was described earlier. Many of them have a formal setup, such as the Railway Sports Promotion Board and the Services Sports Control Board, to recruit and train sportspersons. Other state-run entities are relatively more recent entrants. The Steel Authority of India Limited (SAIL) is now heavily into sports, opening six residential sports academies in its integrated townships located close to its steel plants and mines. The disciplines on which SAIL concentrates are hockey, football, athletics, and archery. Until 2012, the Oil and Gas Natural Corporation (ONGC) employed 171 sportspersons who had played for India, and fifteen of the eighty-one athletes who represented India in the 2012 London Olympics were ONGC employees. The ONGC's hockey team has won several national tournaments, and its football team plays in the elite I-League. In addition, the Petroleum Sports Promotion Board, made up of public-sector organizations in the petroleum sector, has fielded teams in national tournaments. It has a particularly good track record in badminton and table tennis. Finally, we must mention the state-run airlines, Air India and Indian Airlines (which merged in 2005), which have recruited several sportspersons and have been a hockey powerhouse for several years. In the 2012 Olympics, three Air India employees, including medal winner Gagan Narang, were part of the Indian contingent. These are but a few of the many public-sector organizations involved in sports.

As detailed in earlier chapters, quite a few private companies have provided jobs and varying amounts of training facilities to sportspersons. A new element in recent times, however, has been funds and expertise for sportspersons supplied by not-for-profit organizations, such as the Olympic Gold Quest (OCQ) and the Mittal Champions Trust (MCT). This is in keeping with the rise of private enterprises and initiative since India opened its economy in the early 1990s. Olympic Gold Quest was formed in 2000 by two former world champions—Prakash Padukone (badminton) and Geet Sethi (billiards)—with the intention of working with the sports federation to help Indian athletes win Olympic gold medals.[97] The OCQ received large contributions from corporates, including Rs 10 million from the Bajaj group of industries. In 2013 the OCQ was funding five disciplines: athletics, boxing, badminton, shooting, archery, and wrestling. The MCT was organized by the steel magnate Lakshmi Mittal, an expatriate Indian who is also one of Britain's richest people; its aims are similar to those of the OCQ, and it funds the same disciplines. As many as thirty of the eighty-one Indian participants at the London Games were funded by either the OCQ or the MCT, up from only five in the 2008 Beijing Olympics. The MCT, however, shut down in early 2014.[98] In fact, in both the 2008 and 2012 games, all the Olympic medalists received from the two nonprofit organizations significant support for training, equipment, and participation in tournaments abroad. An important reason for the organizations' impact has been their ability to bypass the government red tape that has so often prevented athletes from reaching their full potential.

Besides help for athletes, private companies, most notably the Tata Group, have sponsored sports academies. The Tata Football Academy, located in the company's headquarters in Jamshedpur, Jharkhand, is a pioneering initiative to train a few young football players aged fourteen and under in a setting where their sporting, educational and financial needs were taken care of. Since the academy opened in 1987, several of its graduates have played for India and prominent Indian football clubs. A decade later, in 1996, the Tatas founded an archery academy, which is now India's premier training institute in the sport. More recent corporate initiatives include the real estate company Ozonegroup's football academy in Bangalore, formed in association with the Royal Dutch Football Association. It is unique in targeting underprivileged children between the age of seven and thirteen. The Mahindras, who until recently had sponsored a successful football team, took the unusual route of partnering with America's National Basketball Association in 2010 to organize community-based leagues in three cities, including Mumbai. It has also joined with Scotland's Celtic Football Club in 2010 to run an interschool tournament in Mumbai involving thirty-two schools from five cities, with the best players training under Celtic coaches.

Along with the corporate initiatives, there has been a recent boom in coaching academies in various sports, some begun by well-known sportspersons like Pullela Gopichand (Gopichand Badminton Academy, Hyderabad), P. T. Usha (Usha School of Athletics, Kozhikode), Bhaichung Bhutia (Bhaichung Bhutia Football Schools, with centers in several New Delhi and Mumbai schools), and others by lesser-known personalities such as the former national archery champion Dinesh Bhil (Eklavya Archery Academy in the tribal heartland of Gujarat near Vadodara).

The influx of corporate funds has also helped the elite sports like polo, which once were largely dependent on princely or military patronage. In an essay in 1992, political scientist and avid Rajasthan-watcher Susanne Rudolph noted that Standard Chartered Bank was already one of the main sponsors of the Prince of Wales exhibition match at Jaipur, a stronghold of both polo and royalty. She also pointed out that some of the spectator boxes at the Jaipur polo grounds had been bought by jewelers like Kejriwal and Durlabji.[99] This "bourgeoisefication" of polo, as Rudolph termed it, has become more pronounced since. Two decades later, in 2012 at the British Polo Day in Jodhpur, another traditional center of polo, several luxury brands were sponsoring the event.[100] In fact, of the forty or so polo tournaments organized by the Indian Polo Association in different cities, it was estimated that twenty had received significant sponsorship.[101]

Final Word

The vibrant contemporary sports scene in India is an optimistic and, to my mind, the right note on which to end this brief and selective history of sports in India. I have been selective with regard to the sports that I chronicled, usually biased toward sports with a mass following. I have dwelled at some length on polo, which by its very nature is elite, because of its unusual history. A more important bias, however, has been toward recording the history and stories of sportspersons and clubs that have been successful. I have a practical reason. It is far easier to find material on successful sportspersons and clubs than on the journeymen. I could have written a completely different history of sports in India if I had considered those countless sportspersons who never wore Indian colors or those nondescript clubs that rarely were mentioned in the newspapers. Indeed, failure is as much at the heart of sports as success is. As a sports writer succinctly put it, "Sport is only about winning: sport is mainly about losing."[102] That is why stories of both an athlete battling economic and social odds to win a medal and the lowly lower-division football club narrowly losing to a much superior team have a universal appeal.

Above all is the element of play and competitiveness in sports that makes a sports event, whether it is played in a grand stadium or on a neighborhood street, so important to participants and spectators. Some people, of course, believe that organized sports are "too structured, too dependent on techniques and technology, too much under the influence of market forces to serve the basic function of play."[103] That is why I examined the social, economic, and political context of sports in India. I used sports to illustrate the anxieties and aspirations of Indian sportspersons as colonial subjects and independent citizens. I hope that this hasn't been entirely at the expense of the sheer joy of sports that makes it universal.

I have tried to understand and analyze the evolution of sports in India—from the epics to the present globalized times—and what it says about Indian society. The story of the evolution of sports in India is told through their encounter in successive stages with colonialism, nationalism, the state, and globalization. Along the way, I have touched on the question of India's obsession with cricket and its poor performance in international sports events. This book has presented the richness of sports in India and some of its remarkable characters in order to debunk the notion that India does not have a culture of sports. What India doesn't have, as history cruelly shows, is a culture of winning at the international level. That by itself is not so big an issue as it's sometimes is made out to be, or is it unique to India when medals can be won or lost by a hundredth of a second. The mantra of Pierre de Coubertin about competing and not necessarily winning might sound archaic in today's hypercompetitive world. But there's more to it than we might think. India's mostly failed love affair with sports provides as much insight into its society and culture as sports success does about other nations. There is something heartwarming and, indeed, heartbreaking to see twelve- or thirteen-year-olds in Imphal or Bhiwani or Shivaji Park practicing at the crack of dawn in the hope of making it big or, at the very least, becoming good enough to land a stable job. The lives of many of the cast of characters who are part of this story are often as heroic as they are tragic. In that sense, sports mirror life.

NOTES

Introduction

1. Horatio Smith, quoted in Kausik Bandyopadhyay, *Playing for Freedom: A Historic Sports Victory* (New Delhi: Standard Publishers, 2008), 24.

2. Ashwini Kumar, quoted in Mihir Bose, *The Magic of Indian Cricket: Cricket and Society in India* (Abingdon: Routledge, 2006), 45. After retiring from the police service, Kumar was India's representative at the International Olympic Committee (IOC) from 1973 to 2000 and vice president of the IOC from 1983 to 1987.

3. Kendall Blanchard, "The Anthropology of Sport," in *Handbook of Sports Studies*, ed. Jay Coakley and Eric Dunning (London: Sage, 2000), 145.

4. Johan Huizinga, *Homo Ludens: A Study in the Play-Element in Culture* (London: Routledge & Kegan Paul, 1980), 8.

5. Ibid., 11.

6. Roger Caillois, *Man, Play and Games* (New York: Free Press, 1961), 6.

7. Ibid., 14–16.

8. Norbert Elias and Eric Dunning, *Quest for Excitement: Sport and Leisure in the Civilizing Process* (Oxford: Blackwell, 1986), 23.

9. Allen Guttmann, *From Ritual to Record: The Nature of Modern Sports* (New York: Columbia University Press, 2004), 55.

10. Michael Mandelbaum, *The Meaning of Sports: Why Americans Watch Baseball, Football and Basketball, and What They See When They Do* (New York: Public Affairs, 2004), 4.

11. Derek Birley, *Sport and the Making of Britain* (Manchester: Manchester University Press, 1993), 1.

12. Sarvepalli Gopal, "The Spell of Cricket," in *The Collected Essays*, ed. Srinath Raghavan (New Delhi: Permanent Black, 2013), 409.

13. Sunil Khilnani, *The Idea of India* (London: Penguin, 1997), 5.

14. Elias and Dunning, *Quest for Excitement*, 39.

15. Ian McDonald, "India," in *Handbook of Sports Studies*, ed. Jay Coakley and Eric Dunning (London: Sage, 2000), 540.

16. Dipesh Chakrabarty, introduction to *Sport in South Asian Society*, ed. Boria Majumdar and J. A. Mangan (London: Routledge, 2005), 3.

17. Shehan Karunatilaka, *Chinaman: The Legend of Pradeep Mathew* (New Delhi: Random House, 2011), 337.

1. Down the Ages

1. Nigel Spivey, *The Ancient Olympics* (Oxford: Oxford University Press, 2004), 3.

2. Norbert Elias and Eric Dunning, *Quest for Excitement: Sport and Leisure in the Civilizing Process* (Oxford: Blackwell, 1986), 137.

3. *The Mahabharata*, trans. J. A. B. van Buitenen (Chicago: University of Chicago Press, 1973), 1:xxiii.

4. *The Mahabharata*, trans. John D. Smith (London: Penguin Books, 2009), 607.

5. van Buitenen, *The Mahabharata*, 267.

6. Ibid., 273.

7. Ibid., 278.

8. Ibid., 55.

9. Ibid., 56.

10. Ibid., 50.

11. Ibid., 70.

12. Ibid., 71.

13. Ibid.

14. *Ramayana*, Book I, Boyhood, trans. Robert P. Goldman (New York: New York University Press, 2005), 345.

15. van Buitenen, *The Mahabharata*, 353.

16. Ibid., 357.

17. Smith, *The Mahabharata*, 101.

18. Ibid., 550.

19. Ibid., 552.

20. Ibid., 554.

21. Ibid., 559.

22. *The Mahabharata of Vyasa*, trans. P. Lal (New Delhi: Vikas, 1980), 3.

23. S. H. Deshpande, *Physical Education in Ancient India* (Delhi: Bharatiya Vidya Prakashan, 1992), 6.

24. Ibid., 2.

25. A. L. Basham, *The Wonder That Was India: A Survey of the Culture of the Indian Sub-Continent Before the Coming of the Muslims* (New York: Grove Press, 1959), 208–9.

26. Namrata R. Ganneri, "Notes on *Vyayam*: A Vernacular Sports Journal in Western India," *The Newsletter*, no 69 (autumn 2014): 8.

27. D. C. Mujumdar, ed., *Encyclopedia of Indian Physical Culture* (Baroda: Good Companions, 1950), 1.

28. Deshpande, *Physical Education in Ancient India*, 46.

29. Ibid.

30. Ibid., 49.

31. Mujumdar, *Encyclopedia of Indian Physical Culture*, 9.

32. Deshpande, *Physical Education in Ancient India*, 4.

33. Ibid., 199–201.

34. Mujumdar, *Encyclopedia of Indian Physical Culture*, 11.

35. Deshpande, *Physical Education in Ancient India*, 205.

36. B. J. Sandesara and R. N. Mehta, eds., *Mallapurana* (Baroda: Oriental Institute, 1964), 21.

37. Ibid., 22.

38. Ibid., 24–25.

39. Veena Das, *Structure and Cognition: Aspects of Hindu Caste and Ritual* (Delhi: Oxford University Press, 1987), 81–82.

40. Mujumdar, *Encyclopedia of Indian Physical Culture*, 15.

41. Robert Sewell, *A Forgotten Empire: A Contribution to the History of India* (London: Swan Sonnenschein, 1900), 271.

42. Ibid., 378.

43. *The Akbar Nama of Abu-l-Fazl*, trans. H. Beveridge (Delhi: Low Price Publications, 1989), vol. 1, preface. In contrast, H. Blochmann, who translated Abul Fazl's *Ain-i-Akbari*, writes about Fazl's "love of truth and his correctness of information." Abul Fazl, *The A'in-i Akbari*, trans. H. Blochmann (Calcutta: Asiatic Society of Bengal, 1927), vii.

44. Deshpande, *Physical Education in Ancient India*, 201.

45. Blochmann, *The A'in-i Akbari*, 309.

46. Ibid., 309-10.

47. Ibid., 309.

48. Ibid., 310.

49. *The Baburnama: Memoirs of Babur, Prince and Emperor*, trans. Wheeler M. Thackston (Washington, D.C.: Smithsonian Institution, 1996), 416.

50. Beveridge, *The Akbar Nama*, 456.

51. Blochmann, *The A'in-i Akbari*, 292.

52. Elias and Dunning, *Quest for Excitement*, 24.

53. Ibid.

54. M. N. Pearson, "Recreation in Mughal India," *British Journal of Sports History* 1, no. 3 (1984): 335.

55. Ibid., 339.

56. Ibid., 343.

57. Seema Alavi, "Of Badshahs, White Sahibs and Black Natives," *The Hindu*, May 2, 1999.

2. Empire of Sport

1. Edward Arthur Henry Blunt, *The ICS: The Indian Civil Service* (London: Faber & Faber, 1937), 221.

2. Boria Majumdar, *Cricket in Colonial India, 1780-1947* (London: Routledge, 2008), 75.

3. Ibid., 76.

4. H. J. Moorhouse, *The Calcutta Cricket Club* (Calcutta, 1956).

5. Charles Allen, *Raj: A Scrapbook of British India, 1877-1947* (London: Andre Deutsch, 1977), 93.

6. Patrick McDevitt, "The King of Sports: Polo in Late Victorian and Edwardian India," *International Journal of the History of the Sport*, March 2003, 20.

7. Charles Allen, *Plain Tales from the Raj* (London: Andre Deutsch, 1975), 105.

8. Ibid., 99.

9. *The First Fifty Years: Bombay Gymkhana* (Bombay, 1964), 11.

10. Allen, *Plain Tales from the Raj*, 101.

11. Henry Yule and A. C. Burnell, *Hobson-Jobson: A Glossary of Colloquial Anglo-Indian Words and Phrases, and of Kindred Terms, Etymological, Historical, Geographical and Discursive* (London: Routledge & Kegan Paul, 1985), 407.

12. Ibid.

13. Blunt, *The ICS*, 221.

14. Ibid., 222.

15. Ibid., 223.

16. David Gilmour, *The Ruling Caste: Imperial Lives in the Victorian Raj* (New York: Farrar, Straus & Giroux, 2006), 271.

17. Blunt, *The ICS*, 225.

18. *Times of India*, October 29, 1886.

19. Allen, *Raj: A Scrapbook of British India*, 96.

20. Raaja Bhasin, *Simla: The Summer Capital of British India* (New Delhi: Rupa, 2011), 196.

21. Richard Cashman, *Patrons, Players and the Crowd* (Delhi: Orient Longman, 1981), 1.

22. Majumdar, *Cricket in Colonial India*, 79.

23. Rudyard Kipling, *Plain Tales from the Hills* (London: Macmillan, 1949), 215-17.

24. Allen, *Plain Tales from the Raj*, 156.

25. Tony Mason and Eliza Riedi, *Sport and the Military: The British Armed Forces 1880-1960* (Cambridge: Cambridge University Press, 2010), 33.

26. *Report of the Commissioners Appointed to Inquire Into the Sanitary State of the Army in India; with Precis of Evidence* (London: Eyre and Spottiswood for Her Majesty's Stationery Office, 1863), 343.

27. Ibid., 38.

28. Ibid., 8-9.

29. Frank Richards, *Old Soldier-Sahib* (London: Faber & Faber, 1945), 205.

30. Mason and Riedi, *Sport and the Military*, 21.

31. Richards, *Old Soldier-Sahib*, 297.

32. *Report of the Commissioners Appointed to Inquire Into the Sanitary State of the Army in India*, 332.

33. Allen, *Plain Tales from the Raj*, 109-110.

34. The collection of the National Army Museum in London. Available at http://www.nam.ac.uk/online-collection/detail.php?q=searchType%3Dsimple%26resultsDisplay%3Dlist%26simpleText%3Dindia%2Bfootball&pos=1&total=4&page=1&acc=1968-01-66-3 (accessed November 1, 2014).

35. Boria Majumdar, "When the Sepoys Batted: 1857 on the Playing Field," *Biblio*, March/April 2007, 36.

36. Ibid., 37.

37. Blunt, *The ICS*, 221

38. Yule and Burnell, *Hobson-Jobson*, 720.

39. James Johnstone, *My Experiences in Manipur and the Naga Hills* (London: S. Low Marston, 1896), 136.

40. Alban Wilson, *Sport and Service in Assam and Elsewhere* (Guwahati: Spectrum, 1981), 128.

41. Ibid., 128–29.
42. George John Younghusband, *Polo in India* (London: W. H. Allen, 1890), 2.
43. Ibid., 4.
44. McDevitt, "The King of Sports," 3.
45. Allen, *Plain Tales from the Raj*, 112.
46. Blunt, *The ICS*, 224.
47. Robert Baden-Powell, *Indian Memories* (London, 1915), 32.
48. Ibid., 35.
49. Mason and Riedi, *Sport and the Military*, 70.
50. Baden-Powell, *Indian Memories*, 20.
51. Ibid., 8.
52. *Letters on Polo in India, Written to a Beginner* by "A Lover of the Game" (Calcutta: Thacker Spink, 1918), 3.
53. Mason and Riedi, *Sport and the Military*, 62.
54. Ibid., 77.
55. Mahesh Rangarajan, *The Oxford Anthology of Indian Wildlife* (New Delhi: Oxford University Press, 1999), 196.
56. Gilmour, *The Ruling Caste*, 265.
57. Rangarajan, *The Oxford Anthology of Indian Wildlife*, 209.
58. Allen, *Plain Tales from the Raj*, 116.
59. Gilmour, *The Ruling Caste*, 268.
60. Allen, *Plain Tales from the Raj*, 111.
61. Baden-Powell, *Indian Memories*, 38.
62. Pran Neville, *Sahib's India* (New Delhi: Penguin, 2011), 142.
63. Ibid., 143.
64. Mason and Riedi, *Sport and the Military*, 57.
65. Blunt, *The ICS*, 226.
66. Allen, *Plain Tales from the Raj*, 113.
67. Mason and Riedi, *Sport and the Military*, 73.
68. Dennis Kincaid, *British Social Life in India, 1608–1937* (London: Routledge, 1973), 242.
69. Shapoorjee Sorabjee, *Chronicle of Cricket Among Parsees and the Struggle: European Polo Versus Native Cricket* (Bombay, 1897), 8.
70. Ibid., 11.
71. M. E. Pavri, *Parsi Cricket* (Bombay: J. B. Marzban, 1901), 43.
72. Arjun Appadurai, "Playing with Modernity: The Decolonization of Cricket," in his *Modernity at Large: Cultural Dimensions of Globalization* (Minneapolis: University of Minnesota Press, 1996), 92.

73. Charles Box, quoted in Charlie Connelly, ed., *Elk Stopped Play and Other Tales from Wisden's "Cricket Round the World"* (London: Bloomsbury, 2014), viii. The rest of the quotation goes like this: "The Italians are too fat for cricket, the French too thin, the Dutch too dumpy, the Belgians too bilious, the Flemish too flatulent, the East Indians too peppery, the Laplanders too bowlegged, the Swiss too sentimental, the Greeks too lazy, the Egyptians too long in the neck, and the Germans too short in the wind."

74. Sorabjee, *Chronicle of Cricket Among Parsees*, 19.

75. Ibid., 21.

76. Ramachandra Guha, *A Corner of a Foreign Field* (London: Picador, 2002), 22.

77. Ibid., 23–24.

78. Ibid., 27.

79. Mason and Riedi, *Sport and the Military*, 34.

80. Kausik Bandyopadhyay, *Playing for Freedom* (New Delhi: Standard Publishers, 2008), 30–31.

81. Kausik Bandyopadhyay, *Scoring off the Field: Football Culture in Bengal, 1911–80* (New Delhi: Routledge, 2011), 48–49.

82. Richards, *Old Soldier-Sahib*, 297.

83. Ibid., 295–96.

84. Sorabjee, *Chronicle of Cricket Among Parsees*, 32.

85. Guha, *A Corner of a Foreign Field*, 18.

86. Ibid., 35.

87. Ibid.

88. Ibid., 36.

3. White Man's Burden

1. Richard Cashman, *Patrons, Players and the Crowd* (Delhi: Orient Longman, 1981), 1.

2. Richard Holt, *Sport and the British: A Modern History* (Oxford: Clarendon Press, 1990), 203.

3. J. A. Mangan, *The Games Ethic and Imperialism* (London: Viking, 1986), 36.

4. Norbert Muller, ed., *Olympism: Selected Writings* (Lausanne: International Olympic Committee, 2000), 108.

5. Charles Allen and Sharada Dwivedi, *Lives of the Indian Princes* (London: Century Publishing, 1984), 120.

6. Mangan, *The Games Ethic*, 125.

7. Herbert Sherring, *The Mayo College, "the Eton of India": A Record of Twenty Years 1875–1895* (Calcutta: Thacker, Spink, 1887), 1–2.

8. Chester Macnaghten, *Common Thoughts on Serious Subjects Being Plain Words for Boys* (London: Unit Library, 1904), xvii–xviii.

9. Ibid., xxviii.

10. Ibid., 86.

11. H.H. Sir Bhavsinhji, comp., *Forty Years of the Rajkumar College 1870–1910* (London: Hazell, Watson & Viney, 1911), 158.

12. Macnaghten, *Common Thoughts*, 87.

13. Ibid., 88.

14. Ibid., 91.

15. Simon Wilde, *The Strange Genius of Ranjitsinhji* (London: Aarum Press, 2005), 11.

16. Dane K. Kennedy, *The Magic Mountains: Hill Stations and the British Raj* (Berkeley: University of California Press, 1996), 136, 142.

17. Mangan, *The Games Ethic*, 182.

18. Ibid., 183.

19. Cecil Earle Tyndale-Biscoe, *Tyndale-Biscoe of Kashmir: An Autobiography* (London: Seeley Service, 1951), 128.

20. David Goldblatt, *The Ball Is Round: A Global History of Football* (London: Penguin, 2007), 159, 127.

21. Ibid., 129.

22. C. E. Tyndale-Biscoe, *Kashmir in Sunlight and Shade* (London: Seeley Service, 1925), 277.

23. Tyndale-Biscoe, *Tyndale-Biscoe of Kashmir*, 131.

24. Susan Brownell, *Training the Body for China: Sports in the Moral Order of the People's Republic* (Chicago: University of Chicago Press, 1995), 40.

25. Ibid., 41.

26. Ibid., 42.

27. Tyndale-Biscoe, *Kashmir in Sunlight and Shade*, 280.

28. Tyndale-Biscoe, *Tyndale-Biscoe of Kashmir*, 142.

29. Ibid., 144.

30. J. A. Mangan, "Soccer as Moral Training: Missionary Intentions and Imperial Legacies," in *Soccer in South Asia: Empire, Nation, Diaspora*, ed. Paul Dimeo and James Mills (London: Frank Cass, 2001), 43.

31. James Mills, "Colonialism, Christians and Sport: The Catholic Church and Football in Goa, 1883–1951," *Football Studies* 5, no. 2 (2002): 23.

32. Ibid., 15.

33. Arjun Appadurai, "Playing with Modernity: The Decolonization of Cricket," in his *Modernity at Large: Cultural Dimensions of Globalization* (Minneapolis: University of Minnesota Press, 1996), 93.

34. Ramachandra Guha, *A Corner of a Foreign Field* (London: Picador, 2002), 55.

35. Ibid., 56.

36. Ibid., 76.

37. Lord Harris, *A Few Short Runs* (London: John Murray, 1921), 242.

38. Guha, *A Corner of a Foreign Field*, 73.

39. Harris, *A Few Short Runs*, 230.

40. Guha, *A Corner of a Foreign Field*, 73.

41. Harris, *A Few Short Runs*, 241–42.

42. Ramachandra Guha, *The States of Indian Cricket: Anecdotal Histories* (New Delhi: Permanent Black, 2005), 27.

43. R. P. Gupta, "His Master's Game," *Times of India*, September 20, 1987.

44. Ramachandra Guha, "A very good batsman but . . . ," *The Hindu*, May 14, 2000. On the occasion that Compton played for East Zone, play was interrupted by students, who were protesting an arrest of a nationalist leader, when he was on 98. The student leader, who obviously knew his cricket, said to Compton, "Mr. Compton, you are a very good batsman, but you must go." After the interruption, Compton duly got to his century.

45. See, for example, Sewell's reports in the *Times of India* on June 22 and July 20, 1936.

46. Mario Rodrigues, *Batting for the Empire: A Political Biography of Ranjitsinhji* (New Delhi: Penguin, 2003), 232.

47. Scyld Berry, *Cricket Wallah: With England in India and Sri Lanka, 1981* (London: Hodder & Stoughton, 1982), 124.

48. Guha, *A Corner of a Foreign Field*, 89.

49. Ibid., 132.

50. Ibid., 135.

51. *Lagaan* has been the subject of much scholarly discussion. See, for example, Nissim Mannathukkaren, "Subalterns, Cricket and the 'Nation,'" *Economic and Political Weekly*, December 8, 2001; Sudhavana Deshpande, "Subaltern Fantasies," *Economic and Political Weekly*, June 7, 2003; and Bruce Babington, *The Sport Film: Games People Play* (New York: Wallflower Press, 2014).

4. Players and Patrons

1. Letter dated January 17, 1928, from Sir Dorabji Tata to Count Bailet Latour, Olympic Studies Centre, Lausanne.

2. Charles Allen and Sharada Dwivedi, *Lives of the Indian Princes* (London: Century Publishing, 1984), 127.

3. Ibid., 110.

4. Ibid., 111.

5. Ibid., 113.

6. Ibid., 127.

7. Gayatri Devi of Jaipur and Santha Rama Rau, *A Princess Remembers: The Memoirs of the Maharani of Jaipur* (Philadelphia: Lippincott, 1976), 62.

8. Ibid., 63–66.

9. Barbara N. Ramusack, *The Indian Princes and Their States* (Cambridge: Cambridge University Press, 2004), 161.

10. V. A. S. Stow, *A Short History of Mayo College* (Ajmer: Fine Arts Printing, 1942), 12.

11. Herbert Sherring, *The Mayo College* (Calcutta: Thacker Spink, 1897), 225.

12. J. A. Mangan, *The Games Ethic and Imperialism* (London: Viking, 1986), 137.

13. Stow, *A Short History of Mayo College*, 16.

14. Sherring, *The Mayo College*, 227.

15. Ibid., 222.

16. Ibid., 230.

17. Stow, *A Short History of Mayo College*, 96.

18. Richard Cashman, *Patrons, Players and the Crowd* (Delhi: Orient Longman, 1981), 28.

19. Patrick McDevitt, "The King of Sports: Polo in Late Victorian and Edwardian India," *International Journal of the History of the Sport*, March 2003, 1.

20. Susanne Rudolph, Lloyd Rudolph, and Mohan Singh Kanota, *Reversing the Gaze: Amar Singh's Diary, a Colonial Subject's Narrative of Imperial India* (Delhi: Oxford University Press, 2011), 9.

21. Ibid., 10.

22. McDevitt, "The King of Sports," 16.

23. Gayatri Devi, *A Princess Remembers*, 92.

24. McDevitt, "The King of Sports," 4.

25. Cashman, *Patrons, Players and the Crowd*, 28.

26. *Times of India*, February 22, 1922.

27. Charles Allen, *Plain Tales from the Raj* (London: Andre Deutsch, 1975), 238.

28. Cashman, *Patrons, Players and the Crowd*, 47.

29. Charles A. Kincaid, *The Land of Ranji and Duleep* (London: Blackwood & Sons, 1931), 111–12.

30. Simon Wilde, *The Strange Genius of Ranjitsinhji* (London: Aarum Press, 2005), 172.

31. Satadru Sen, *Migrant Races: Empire, Identity and Ranjitsinhji* (Manchester: Manchester University Press, 2005), 21.

32. Wilde, *The Strange Genius of Ranjitsinhji*, 24.

33. Anthony de Mello, *Portrait of Indian Sport* (London: Macmillan, 1959), 16.

34. Mario Rodrigues, *Batting for the Empire: A Political Biography of Ranjitsinhji* (New Delhi: Penguin, 2003), 37–38.

35. Ibid., 229.

36. Ibid., 230.

37. Ibid., 231.

38. Ibid., 232.

39. Ibid., 233.

40. Ibid., 236.

41. Ibid., 239.

42. Ibid., 237.

43. Ibid., 42.

44. Ibid., 165.

45. Ibid., 203.

46. Cashman, *Patrons, Players and the Crowd*, 44.

47. Ibid., 31.

48. Khushwant Singh, "Exhausted Highness," *Outlook*, April 6, 1998. Bhupinder had a string of titles before his name, and by the end of his life, he was officially called Lieutenant General; His Highness; Farzand-i-khas; Daulat-i-Inglishia; Mansur-i-Zaman Amir-ul-Umra; Maharajadhiraj Raj Rajesh-war; Sir Maharaj-i-Rajgan; Sir Bhupinder Singh; Mahinder Bahadur GCSI, GCIE, GBE, ADC; and Maharaja of Patiala.

49. Cashman, *Patrons, Players and the Crowd*, 30.

50. Edward Docker, *History of Indian Cricket* (Delhi: Macmillan, 1976), 8.

51. Ibid., 17–18.

52. Ibid., 19.

53. Ibid., 65.

54. *The Times*, March 23, 1937.

55. Docker, *History of Indian Cricket*, 8.

56. Boria Majumdar, *Twenty-Two Yards to Freedom: A Social History of Indian Cricket* (New Delhi: Penguin, 2004), 36.

57. Ibid., 172–73.

58. Mihir Bose, *The Magic of Indian Cricket: Cricket and Society in India* (Abingdon: Routledge, 2006), 148.

59. Cashman, *Patrons, Players and the Crowd*, 41.

60. *Times of India*, September 14, 1931.

61. Majumdar, *Twenty-Two Yards to Freedom*, 44.

62. Ibid., 46.

63. Bose, *The Magic of Indian Cricket*, 153.

64. *Times of India*, June 22, 1936.

65. Ibid., June 23, 1936.

66. Docker, *History of Indian Cricket*, 121.

67. Cashman, *Patrons, Players and the Crowd*, 42.

5. The Empire Strikes Back

1. Mrinalini Sinha, *Colonial Masculinity: The "Manly Englishman" and the "Effeminate Bengali" in the Late Nineteenth Century* (Manchester: Manchester University Press, 1995), 21.

2. Thomas Macaulay, *Critical and Historical Essays* (London: Dent & Sons, 1961), 1:562.

3. G. W. Steevens, *In India* (London: William Blackwood and Sons, 1899), 75.

4. John Rosselli, "The Self-Image of Effeteness: Physical Education and Nationalism in Nineteenth-Century Bengal," *Past and Present* 86 (February 1980): 123.

5. Jogeshchandra Bagal, *Hindu Melar Itibritta* (Maitri, 1968), 102.

6. Indira Chowdhury, *The Frail Hero and Virile History: Gender and the Politics of Culture in Colonial Bengal* (Delhi: Oxford University Press, 1998), 22.

7. Sumit Sarkar, *The Swadeshi Movement in Bengal, 1903–1908* (New Delhi: People's Publishing House, 1973), 468.

8. Ibid., 469.

9. George Campbell, *Memoirs of My Indian Career* (London: Macmillan, 1893), 267.

10. Ibid., 273.

11. Rosselli, "The Self-Image of Effeteness," 138.

12. George F. Andrews, *Physical Education for Boys in the Secondary Schools of India* (New York: 1934), v.

13. Boria Majumdar and Kausik Bandyopadhyay, *Goalless: The Story of a Unique Footballing Nation* (New Delhi: Penguin, 2006), 14.

14. Sarkar, *The Swadeshi Movement in Bengal*, 470.

15. Nirad C. Chaudhuri, *The Autobiography of an Unknown India* (London: Macmillan, 1951), 246.

16. Amitava Chatterjee and Souvik Naha, "The Muscular Monk: Vivekananda, Sports and Physical Culture in Colonial Bengal," *Economic and Political Weekly*, March 15, 2014. The authors even dug up an incident in which Vivekananda tried his hand at golf and apparently scored a hole in one.

17. Swami Vivekananda, *The Collected Works of Swami Vivekananda* (Calcutta: Advaita Ashram), 3:242.

18. Chatterjee and Naha, "The Muscular Monk."

19. Kausik Bandyopadhyay, *Playing for Freedom: A Historic Sports Victory* (New Delhi: Standard Publishers, 2008), 42.

20. Mauricio Murad, "Soccer and Society in Brazil," *Panorama: Insights Into Asian and European Affairs* 1 (2014): 101. Also see Alex Bellos, *Futebol: The Brazilian Way of Life* (London: Bloomsbury, 2014), 29–33.

21. *Times of India,* June 9, 1920.

22. Ibid., April 2, 1911.

23. Bandyopadhyay, *Playing for Freedom,* 50–51.

24. Ibid., 52.

25. Ibid.

26. Rupak Saha, *Ekadashe Surjyoday* (Kolkata: Deep Prakashan, 2010), 19.

27. Ibid., 46.

28. *Times of India,* December 5, 1903.

29. Ibid., July 25, 1902.

30. Bandyopadhyay, *Playing for Freedom,* 40–41.

31. Hemendrakumar Ray, *Somoychitrakatha* (Calcutta: Talpata, 2014), 119.

32. *Amrita Bazar Patrika,* July 31, 1911. See also Saha, *Ekadashe Surjyoday.*

33. *The Englishman,* July 20, 1911.

34. Ibid., July 11, 1911.

35. *The Statesman,* July 20, 1911.

36. *The Englishman,* July 25, 1911.

37. *Times of India,* August 3, 1911.

38. Ibid.

39. *Amrita Bazar Patrika,* July 31, 1911.

40. Ibid.

41. Bandyopadhyay, *Playing for Freedom* , 59.

42. Ibid.

43. *Amrita Bazar Patrika,* July 31, 1911.

44. Ibid.

45. Partha Chatterjee, The Black Hole of Empire: History of a Global Practice of Power (Princeton, N.J.: Princeton University Press, 2011), 303.

46. Bandyopadhyay, *Playing for Freedom,* 70.

47. Ibid., 78.

48. Ibid., 76.

49. *The Englishman,* July 31, 1911.

50. Bandyopadhyay, *Playing for Freedom,* 87.

51. Ibid., 75–76.

52. Ibid., 113.

53. Ibid., 112.

54. *The Statesman*, August 2, 1911.

55. Rudrangshu Mukherjee, "Elegy on the Maidan," *The Telegraph*, June 20, 1998.

56. *The Statesman*, August 3, 1911.

57. Kausik Bandyopadhyay, *Scoring off the Field: Football Culture in Bengal, 1911–80* (New Delhi: Routledge, 2011), 93.

58. Achintya Kumar Sengupta, *Kallol Yug* (Calcutta: M. C. Sarkar & Sons, 1950), 66–67.

59. *Times of India*, August 9, 1940.

60. J. C. Maitra, *Indian Sports Flashback* (Bombay: Commercial Printing Press, 1965), 118.

61. Ibid., 118–19.

62. Tony Mason, "Football on the Maidan: Cultural Imperialism in Calcutta," in *The Cultural Bond: Sport, Empire, Society*, ed. J. A. Mangan (London: Frank Cass, 1992), 151.

63. *Times of India*, July 28, 1937.

64. Ibid., November 17, 1937.

65. Ibid., November 15, 1937.

66. Maitra, *Indian Sports Flashback*, 157.

67. Hiren Mukherjee, "Playing for Freedom," *The Statesman*, August 9, 1997.

68. Sengupta, *Kallol Yug*, 66.

69. *Amrita Bazar Patrika*, May 15, 1929.

70. Ibid., May 19, 1929.

71. R. P. Gupta, "His Master's Game," *Times of India*, September 20, 1987.

72. *Times of India*, August 28, 1931.

73. Ibid., August 31, 1931.

74. Ibid.

75. Ibid., August 12, 1940.

76. Ibid., November 18, 1937.

77. Ibid., July 8, 1936.

78. Ibid., July 10, 1936.

79. Chatterjee, *The Black Hole of Empire*, 292.

80. Ibid., 300.

81. Bandyopadhyay, *Scoring off the Field*, 217.

82. Sengupta, *Kallol Yug*, 72.

83. Bandyopadhyay, *Scoring off the Field*, 180.

84. Ibid., 178.

85. *Times of India*, April 22, 1936.

86. Kumar Mukherjee, *The Story of Football* (New Delhi: Ministry of Information and Broadcasting, 2002), 67.

87. Bandyopadhyay, *Scoring off the Field*, 184.

88. Ray, *Somoychitrakatha*, 120.

89. Sengupta, *Kallol Yug*, 66.

90. Ramachandra Guha, "The Socialism of Indian Football," in *An Anthropologist Among the Marxists and Other Essays* (New Delhi: Permanent Black, 2006), 266.

91. Bandyopadhyay, *Playing for Freedom*, 121.

6. Politics on the Maidan

1. C. L. R. James, *Beyond a Boundary* (London: Serpent's Tail, 1996), 49.

2. Ramachandra Guha, *A Corner of a Foreign Field* (London: Picador, 2002), 111.

3. Ibid., 113.

4. Ibid., 143.

5. Ibid., 184.

6. Ibid., 181–82.

7. Ibid., 182.

8. Ibid., 228.

9. J. C. Maitra, *Indian Sports Flashback* (Bombay: Commercial Printing Press, 1965), 30.

10. Ibid., 33.

11. Guha, *A Corner of a Foreign Field*, 251.

12. Ibid., 270.

13. *Times of India*, December 7, 1940.

14. Ibid., December 9, 1940.

15. Guha, *A Corner of a Foreign Field*, 275.

16. Boria Majumdar, *Twenty-Two Yards to Freedom: A Social History of Indian Cricket* (New Delhi: Penguin, 2004), 244.

17. Guha, *A Corner of a Foreign Field*, 276.

18. Majumdar, *Twenty-Two Yards to Freedom*, 244.

19. Guha, *A Corner of a Foreign Field*, 280.

20. Ibid., 283–84.

21. Ibid., 287.

22. Ibid., 289.

23. Ibid., 312.

24. Ibid., 307.

25. Ibid.

26. Majumdar, *Twenty-Two Yards to Freedom*, 230.

27. Guha, *A Corner of a Foreign Field*, 313.

28. Ibid., 314.

29. Guha, *A Corner of a Foreign Field*, 283–84.

30. Chimanlal Setalvad, "Communalism in Sport: Cricket and the Larger Issues," *Times of India*, November 20, 1941.

31. Majumdar, *Twenty-Two Yards to Freedom*, 260.

32. Suranjan Das, *Communal Riots in Bengal 1905-1947* (New Delhi: Oxford University Press, 1991), 1.

33. Joseph Alter, foreword to *Marrow of the Nation: A History of Sport and Physical Culture in Republican China*, by Andrew D. Morris (Berkeley: University of California Press, 2005), xvi.

34. *Star of India*, July 6, 1934.

35. *The Statesman*, July 6, 1934.

36. *Sydney Morning Herald*, September 12, 1936.

37. *Amrita Bazar Patrika*, July 6, 1934.

38. Partha Chatterjee, The Black Hole of Empire: History of a Global Practice of Power (Princeton, N.J.: Princeton University Press, 2011), 320.

39. *Times of India*, June 1, 1935.

40. Kausik Bandyopadhyay, *Scoring off the Field: Football Culture in Bengal, 1911-80* (New Delhi: Routledge, 2011), 114.

41. Kenneth Mcpherson, *The Muslim Microcosm: Calcutta, 1918 to 1935* (Wiesbaden: Franz Steiner Verlag, 1974), IV.

42. Bandyopadhyay, *Scoring off the Field*, 110.

43. *Times of India*, June 5, 1936.

44. *Amrita Bazar Patrika*, July 6, 1934.

45. *Scottish Daily Express*, August 29, 1936. Quoted in Bandyopadhyay, *Scoring off the Field*, 123. See also Boria Majumdar and Kausik Bandyopadhyay, *Goalless: The Story of a Unique Footballing Nation* (New Delhi: Viking, 2006), chap. 5.

46. Bandyopadhyay, *Scoring off The Field*, 124–25.

47. Chatterjee, *The Black Hole of Empire*, 321.

48. Bandyopadhyay, *Scoring off the Field*, 122.

49. *Amrita Bazar Patrika*, August 1, 1934.

50. Bandyopadhyay, *Scoring off the Field*, 119.

51. Ibid., 118.

52. Ibid., 119.

53. Ibid., 120.

54. *Times of India*, May 9, 1938.

55. Das, *Communal Riots in Bengal 1905-1947*, 170.

56. Bandyopadhyay, *Scoring off the Field*, 135.

57. Maitra, *Indian Sports Flashback*, 148.

58. *Amrita Bazar Patrika*, June 13, 1937.

59. *The Statesman*, June 13, 1937.

60. Maitra, *Indian Sports Flashback*, 146.

61. Ibid., 147.

62. *Star of India*, June 20, 1937.

63. *Times of India*, September 1, 1936.

64. Ibid., August 13, 1936.

65. Ibid., September 2, 1937.

66. *Bombay Chronicle*, September 1, 1937.

67. Ibid., September 3, 1937.

68. Guha, *A Corner of a Foreign Field*, 279.

69. Novy Kapadia, "Triumphs and Disasters: The Story of Indian Football, 1889–2000," in *Soccer in South Asia: Empire, Nation, Diaspora*, ed. Paul Dimeo and James H. Mills (London: Frank Cass, 2001), 19.

70. *Bombay Chronicle*, July 20, 1940.

71. M. K. Gandhi, *An Autobiography: The Story of My Experiments with Truth* (London: Jonathan Cape, 1966), 18.

72. Ibid.

73. Joseph S. Alter, "Gandhi Body, Gandhi's Truth: Nonviolence and the Biomoral Imperative of Public Health," *Journal of Asian Studies* 55, no. 2 (May 1996): 301-22.

74. M. K. Gandhi, *The Collected Works of Mahatma Gandhi, 1884-1948* (Delhi: Publications Division, Ministry of Information and Broadcasting, Government of India), 72:381.

75. Gandhi, *An Autobiography*, 13.

76. Mario Rodrigues, *Batting for the Empire: A Political Biography of Ranjitsinhji* (New Delhi: Penguin, 2003), 39.

77. Even though Scyld Berry writes that Gandhi studied in Rajkumar College, Ranji's alma mater, there is no evidence of that (Scyld Berry, *Cricket Wallah: With England in India, 1981-2* [London: Hodder & Stoughton, 1982], 38). In fact, Ramachandra Guha points out that admission to Rajkumar College was restricted to children of Rajput lineage and there was no question that Gandhi, who was a Bania by caste, would be admitted. Ramachandra Guha, *Gandhi Before India* (New Delhi: Penguin, 2013), 25.

78. Guha, *A Corner of a Foreign Field*, 148.

79. Jonathan Rice, ed., *Wisden on India: An Anthology* (New Delhi: Penguin, 2011), 306.

80. Gandhi, *The Collected Works of Mahatma Gandhi*, 53:238.

81. B. R. Nanda, *The Nehrus: Motilal and Jawaharlal* (New Delhi: Oxford University Press, 2008), 72.

82. Ibid., 95.

83. Mario Rodrigues, "When Bapu Kicked the Ball," *The Mint*, June 12, 2010.

84. *Times of India*, April 18, 1934.

85. Ibid., August 13, 1934.

86. M .K. Gandhi, *The Collected Works of Mahatma Gandhi*, Vol. 82: 9 February 1942–6 June 1942, 28.

7. The Early Olympics

1. Ian Buchanan, "Who was Norman Pritchard?" *Journal of Olympic History*, January 2000, 27–28.

2. Gulu Eziekel and K. Arumugam, *Great Indian Olympians* (New Delhi: Field Hockey Publications, 2012), 95.

3. Letter dated May 21, 1929, from Sir Dorabji Tata to Count Bailet Latour, Olympic Studies Centre, Lausanne.

4. Ibid.

5. Boria Majumdar and Nalin Mehta, *Olympics: The India Story* (New Delhi: HarperCollins, 2008), 17.

6. Letter dated April 1, 1924, from A. G. Noehren to Sir Dorabji Tata, Olympic Studies Centre, Lausanne.

7. Jonathan Kolatch, *Sports, Politics and Ideology in China* (New York: Jonathan David, 1972), 45.

8. Ibid., 69.

9. Letter dated February 21, 1927, from Sir Dorabji Tata to Count Bailet Latour, Olympic Studies Centre, Lausanne.

10. Letter dated June 16, 1927, from Sir Dorabji Tata to Count Bailet Latour, Olympic Studies Centre, Lausanne.

11. Letter dated January 7, 1928, by Sir Dorabji Tata to Count Bailet Latour, The Olympic Studies Centre, Lausanne.

12. Letter dated May 21, 1929, from Sir Dorabji Tata to Count Bailet Latour, Olympic Studies Centre, Lausanne.

13. Letter dated December 28, 1928, from Henry Gray to Count Bailet Latour, Olympic Studies Centre, Lausanne. Gray had earlier been in China from 1919 to 1927 as the national physical director there.

14. Anthony de Mello, *Portrait of Indian Sport* (London: Macmillan, 1959), 49.

15. *London Times*, March 24, 1938.

16. Dhyan Chand, *Goal! Autobiography of Hockey Wizard Dhyan Chand* (Madras: Sport and Pastime, 1959). Available at http://www.bharatiyahockey.org/granthalaya/goal/ (accessed November 1, 2014).

17. Ibid.

18. Geoff Watson, "Affirming Identities? An Analysis of Imperial Rhetoric and Orientalism in the Tours of Indian Hockey Teams to New Zealand in 1925, 1935 and 1938," *Sporting Traditions* 21, no. 2 (May 2005): 120.

19. Chand, *Goal!*

20. S. Muthiah, *The Spirit of Chepauk: The MCC Story* (Chennai: Eastwest Books, 1998), 371.

21. M. L. Kapur, *The Romance of Hockey* (Ambala Cantt: M. L. Kapur, 1968), 159.

22. Ibid., 210.

23. K. Arumugam, *Profiles of Indian Hockey Olympians* (New Delhi: Field Hockey Publications, 2012), 83–87.

24. Probhatkumar Mukherjee, "Railways, and Indians and Anglo-Indians," *Modern Review* 12, no. 3 (1917): 304.

25. Interview with Feroz Khan, *Journal of Olympic History* 12 (October 2004): 40.

26. Watson, "Affirming Identities?" 120.

27. Ibid., 126.

28. Ibid., 120.

29. Chand, *Goal!*

30. Watson, "Affirming Identities?" 124.

31. Ibid.

32. Ibid., 125.

33. P. Gupta, "Brief History of the Indian Hockey Federation," *Inter-Provincial Hockey Tournament, Official Programme, 1936* (Calcutta: N. Mukherjee, 1936), 35.

34. *Times of India*, February 20, 1928.

35. *Hindustan Times*, January 31, 1928

36. *Isis*, November 21, 1923, 17.

37. Chand, *Goal!*

38. Interview with Feroz Khan, 43.

39. Jaipal Singh, *Lo Bir Sendra*, ed. Rashmi Katyayan (Ranchi: Prabhat Khabar Publication, 2004), 37.

40. *Times of India*, May 12, 1928.

41. Ibid., March 1, 1928.

42. Ibid., May 16, 1928.

43. Ibid., May 30, 1928.

44. Interview with Feroz Khan, 43.

45. R. Sriman, "Was It Penniger or Jaipal?" *Times of India*, May 6, 1984.

46. Kapur, *The Romance of Hockey*, 41.

47. For a brief discussion of Jaipal Singh's sports and political career, see Ronojoy Sen, "Divided Loyalty: Jaipal Singh and His Many Journeys," *Sport in Society* 12, no. 6 (2009): 765–75.

48. *Times of India*, May 30, 1928.

49. Ibid., June 25, 1928

50. Chand, *Goal!* (1932).

51. *Times of India*, March 18, 1932.

52. Ibid., April 6, 1932.

53. Jaipal Singh, "Indian Hockey Federation: Need for Reform," *Times of India*, June 24, 1938.

54. M. K. Gandhi, *The Collected Works of Mahatma Gandhi, 1884–1948* (Delhi: Publications Division, Ministry of Information and Broadcasting, Government of India), vol. 53, 2 July 1931–12 October 1931, 238.

55. Chand, *Goal!* (1932).

56. Ibid.

57. Kapur, *The Romance of Hockey*, 38.

58. *West Australian*, April 30, 1935.

59. Chand, *Goal!* (1932).

60. *Times of India*, August 13, 1932.

61. Chand, *Goal!* (1932).

62. *Mirror*, April 27, 1935.

63. *Western Mail*, May 2, 1935.

64. *Canberra Times*, August 6, 1935.

65. *Sydney Morning Herald*, May 6, 1935.

66. *West Australian*, June 3, 1939.

67. Chand, *Goal!* (1936).

68. *The News*, May 2, 1935.

69. Chand, *Goal!* (1936).

70. M. N. Masood, *The World Hockey Champions 1936* (Delhi: Model Press, 1937). Available at http://www.bharatiyahockey.org/granthalaya/champions/ (accessed November 1, 2014).

71. Ibid.

72. Chand, *Goal!* (1936).

73. Masood, *The World Hockey Champions*.

74. Ibid.

75. Ibid.

76. For an account of the 1936 Olympic Games, see David Clay Large, *Nazi Games: The Olympics of 1936* (New York: Norton, 2007); and Christopher Hilton, *Hitler's Olympics: The 1936 Berlin Olympic Games* (London: History Press, 2008).

77. Masood, *The World Hockey Champions*.

78. Ibid.

79. *Times of India*, April 28, 1936.

80. Chand, *Goal!* (1936).

81. Masood, *The World Hockey Champions*.

82. *Times of India*, August 3, 1936.

83. Majumdar and Mehta, *Olympics*, 87.

84. *Times of India*, August 3, 1936.

85. Ibid., August 17, 1936.

86. *Daily Telegraph*, August 5, 1936.

87. *Times of India*, August 29, 1936

88. K. G. Jodh, *Amravati Cradles the Nationalist Movement* (Amravati: All-Indian Languages Literary Conference, 1983), 123.

89. Joseph Alter, "Kabaddi, a National Sport of India: The Internationalism of Nationalism and the Foreignness of Indianness," in *Games, Sports and Cultures*, ed. Noel Dyck (Oxford: Berg, 2000), 95.

90. Joseph Alter, "Indian Clubs and Colonialism: Hindu Masculinity and Muscular Christianity," *Comparative Studies in Society and History* 46, no. 3 (July 2004): 509.

91. Ibid., 502.

92. Ibid., 512.

93. Ibid., 524.

94. Jodh, *Amravati Cradles the Nationalist Movement*, 123.

95. *Times of India*, July 10, 1936.

96. Ibid.

97. Ibid., August 10, 1936.

98. Ibid., August 19, 1936.

99. Ibid., September 26, 1936.

100. Joseph Alter, "Physical Education, Sport and the Intersection and Articulation of 'Modernities': The Hanuman Vyayam Prasarak Mandal," *International Journal of the History of Sport* 24, no. 9 (September 2007): 1167–69.

101. Chand, *Goal!* (1936).

102. Chand, *Goal!* (champions, 1936 Olympics).

103. Frank Anthony, *Britain's Betrayal in India: The Story of the Anglo-Indian Community* (Bombay: Allied Publishers, 1969), 230, 231.

104. Megan S. Mills, "Community, Identity and Sport: Anglo-Indians in Colonial and Postcolonial India," in *Subaltern Sports: Politics and Sport in South Asia*, ed. James H. Mills (London: Anthem Press, 2005), 207.

105. Biswarup Sen, *Of the People: Essays on Indian Popular Culture* (New Delhi: Chronicle Books, 2006), 78.

106. *Daily News*, August 27, 1947.

107. Ashok Mitra, "A Death in London: The Distinct Flavour of Calcutta's Fading Colonial Phase," *Telegraph*, June 20, 2011.

8. Lords of the Ring

1. The Polish wrestler's name is also spelled Zbysco and Zybysko.

2. Joseph Alter, "Subaltern Bodies and Nationalist Physiques: Gama the Great and the Heroics of Indian Wrestling," *Body & Society* 6, no. 2 (2000): 51.

3. Joseph Alter, *The Wrestler's Body: Identity and Ideology in North India* (Berkeley: University of California Press, 1992), 75.

4. Joseph Alter, "Gama the World Champion: Wrestling and Physical Culture in Colonial India," *Iron Game History* 4, no. 2 (October 1995): 4.

5. Ibid., 5.

6. Ajay Basu, "Aap Bangali? Kabhi Nehi! (You Are a Bengali? Never!)," in *Smaranika* (Calcutta: Gobor Guha Gymnasium, 2003).

7. Alter, "Gama the World Champion," 5.

8. Graham Noble, "'The Lion of Punjab': Gama in England, 1910," in *Martial Arts in the Modern World*, ed. Thomas A. Green and Joseph R. Svinth (Westport, Conn.: Praeger, 2003), 98.

9. Alter, "Gama the World Champion," 5. Gama's trip to London is the subject of a short story, too. See Tania James, "Lion and Panther in London," *Aerogrammes: and Other Stories* (New Delhi: Random House, 2012), 3–21.

10. S. Muzumdar, *Strong Men Over the Years* (Lucknow: Oudh Printing Works, 1942), 30.

11. Anthony de Mello, *Portrait of Indian Sport* (London: Macmillan, 1959), 253.

12. "Speech by H.E. Mrs. Indira Gandhi," *Olympic Review* 186 (April 1983): 198.

13. Abhijit Gupta, "Cultures of the Body in Colonial Bengal: The Career of Gobor Guha," in *Sport, Literature, Society: Cultural Historical Studies*, ed. Alexis Tadie, J. A. Mangan, and Supriya Chaudhuri (London: Routledge, 2014), 46–47.

14. *The Western Champion and General Advertiser for the Central-Western Districts*, April 11, 1899.

15. Noble, however, says that neither was there any John Bull tournament nor did Gama's size cause any problem. See Noble, "'The Lion of Punjab': Gama in England, 1910," 98.

16. Noble, "'The Lion of Punjab,'" 99.

17. Alter, "Gama the World Champion," 5.

18. Noble, "'The Lion of Punjab,'" 100.

19. *London Times*, August 9, 1910.

20. *New York Times*, August 9, 2010.

21. Noble, "'The Lion of Punjab,'" 102.

22. *London Times*, September 12, 1910.

23. *Adhaesit pavimento anima mea* literally means "my soul is attached to dust."

24. *London Times*, September 12, 1910.

25. Noble, "'The Lion of Punjab,'" 106.

26. *London Times*, September 19, 1910.

27. Ibid., September 4, 1911.

28. Noble, "'The Lion of Punjab,'" 109.

29. Alter, "Gama the World Champion," 6.

30. *Hindustan Times*, January 27, 1928.

31. Ibid., January 30, 1928.

32. Ibid., January 31, 1928.

33. *The Tribune*, January 31, 1928.

34. Ibid., February 1, 1928.

35. Alter, "Subaltern Bodies and Nationalist Physiques," 58.

36. Ibid., 65.

37. *Times of India*, May 5, 1928.

38. Ibid., February 26, 1929.

39. Ibid., August 12, 1936.

40. Ibid., September 6, 1937.

41. Alter, "Subaltern Bodies," 62.

42. *Times of India*, July 21, 1949.

43. A .F. S. Talyarkhan, *On with the Game* (Bombay: Hind Kitabs, 1945), 31.

44. *Times of India*, May 25, 1960.

45. Ibid., May 25, 1960.

46. Allen Guttmann, *Games and Empires: Modern Sports and Cultural Imperialism* (New York: Columbia University Press, 1994), 141–45.

47. Sabyasachi Bhattacharya, *Rabindranath Tagore: An Interpretation* (New Delhi: Penguin, 2011), 66.

48. Abhijit Gupta, "Cultures of the Body in Colonial Bengal," 43.

49. Ajay Basu, "Aap Bangali? Kabhi Nehi!"

50. Abhijit Gupta, "Cultures of the Body in Colonial Bengal," 45.

51. Abhijit Gupta, "Lord of the Wrestling Rings," *The Telegraph*, July 4, 2010.

52. Hemendrakumar Ray, *Somoychitrakatha* (Calcutta: Talpata, 2014), 113.

53. *Hindustan Standard*, January 4, 1972.

54. Muzumdar, *Strong Men Over the Years*, 115.

55. Ray, *Somoychitrakatha*, 113.

56. *New York Times*, November 23, 1913.

57. *Evening World*, January 21, 1921.

58. *New York Tribune*, January 27, 1918.

59. Ibid., January 30, 1921.

60. Ibid., February 1, 1921.

61. *Ogden (Utah) Standard Examiner*, February 1, 1921.

62. *San Francisco Chronicle*, August 30, 1921.

63. Ibid., August 31, 1921.

64. Ibid., September 14, 1921.

65. Abhijit Gupta, "Cultures of the Body in Colonial Bengal," 50.

66. *Morning Tulsa (Okla.) Daily World*, March 10, 1922.

67. Ibid., April 5, 1922.

68. Ibid., March 30, 1922.

69. Ibid., October 28, 1921.

70. *New York Times*, March 15, 1922.

71. Champak Chatterji, "A Champion with Brains and Brawn," *The Statesman*, August 6, 1995.

72. *Morning Tulsa Daily World*, April 7, 1922.

73. *Ogden Standard-Examiner*, April 13, 1922.

74. Ibid., May 13, 1922.

75. Abhijit Gupta, "Cultures of the Body in Colonial Bengal," 52.

76. *Ogden Standard-Examiner*, December 10, 1932.

77. *Amrita Bazar Patrika*, January 3, 1929.

78. Ibid., January 6, 1929.

79. Ibid., January 22, 1929.

80. *Ananda Bazar Patrika*, January 21, 1929.

81. *Amrita Bazar Patrika*, January 22, 1929.

82. Ajay Basu, "Aap Bangali? Kabhi Nehi!"

83. Muzumdar, *Strong Men Over the Years*, 42–43.

84. Birendranath Ghosh, *Bangalir Bahubal* (Calcutta: Saratchandra Chakraborty & Sons, 1932), 34–39.

85. B. Basu, introduction to *Bharatiya Kushti O Tahar Shiksha* (Calcutta, 1934).

86. John Rosselli, "The Self-Image of Effeteness: Physical Education and Nationalism in Nineteenth-Century Bengal," *Past and Present* 86 (February 1980): 144.

87. Ghosh, *Bangalir Bahubal*, 44.

88. Shamya Dasgupta, "An Inheritance from the British," in *Sport in South Asian Society: Past and Present*, ed. Boria Majumdar and J. A. Mangan (Abingdon: Routledge, 2005), 97. See also Shamya Dasgupta, *Bhiwani Junction: The Untold Story of Boxing in India* (New Delhi: HarperCollins, 2012), chap. 4.

89. Dasgupta, "An Inheritance from the British," 97.

90. Ibid., 104.

91. Ibid., 105.

92. Ibid., 106.

93. Dasgupta, *Bhiwani Junction*, 58.

94. Alter, "Subaltern Bodies," 59.

95. *Amrita Bazar Patrika*, January 22, 1929.

96. Alter, *The Wrestler's Body*, 19.

97. Alter, "Kabaddi, A National Sport of India," 97.

98. *Times of India*, May 25, 1960.

9. Freedom Games

1. *Times of India*, July 21, 1948.

2. Ibid., July 24, 1948.

3. Ibid., July 26, 1948.

4. Ibid., August 2, 1948.

5. A. F. S. Talyarkhan, *On with the Game* (Bombay: Hind Kitabs, 1945), 8.

6. Dhyan Chand, *Goal! Autobiography of Hockey Wizard Dhyan Chand* (Madras: Sport and Pastime, 1959); available at http://www.bharatiyahockey.org/granthalaya/hattrick/ (accessed November 1, 2014).

7. Ibid.

8. *Times of India*, August 9, 1948.

9. Ibid.

10. Ibid., August 11, 1948.

11. Ibid.

12. Ibid.

13. Ibid., August 13, 1948.

14. Chand, *Goal*.

15. Ibid.

16. *Times of India*, July 6, 1936.

17. *The Mirror*, October 1, 1938.

18. *The Worker*, September 13, 1938.

19. Kumar Mukherjee, *The Story of Football* (New Delhi: Ministry of Information and Broadcasting, 2002), 132.

20. *Times of India*, September 14, 1998.

21. Manas Chakraborty, *Shatabdir Shera Sailen Manna* (Kolkata: Deep Prakashan, 2002), 43.

22. Melville de Mellow, *Reaching for Excellence: The Glory and Decay of Sports in India* (New Delhi: Kalyani Publishers, 1979), 48–49.

23. *The Economist*, March 17, 2012.

24. Chakraborty, *Shatabdir Shera Sailen Manna*, 48–49.

25. *Times of India*, May 10, 1950.

26. Ezekiel and Arumugam, *Great Indian Olympians*, 106.

27. *Courier-Mail*, November 13, 1947. For more on the tour, see Ian Simpson, "'Exotic, Mysterious Creatures' and 'Road Warriors': Australian Perceptions of Touring Indian Cricket Teams, 1947–2012," *South Asian History and Culture* 5, no. 1 (January 2014): 37–53.

28. Rahul Bhattacharya, *Pundits from Pakistan: On Tour with India* (New Delhi: Penguin, 2012), xiii.

29. *Courier-Mail*, November 13, 1947.

30. Jonathan Rice, ed., *Wisden on India: An Anthology* (New Delhi: Penguin, 2011), 88.

31. Jack Fingleton, "Indians in Australia," *Indian Cricket Almanac, 1947–48*, 3.

32. Jonathan Kolatch, *Sports, Politics and Ideology in China* (New York: Jonathan David, 1972), 68.

33. Ibid., 64.

34. Boria Majumdar and Nalin Mehta, *Olympics: The India Story* (New Delhi: HarperCollins, 2008), 154.

35. Anthony de Mello, *Portrait of Indian Sport* (London: Macmillan, 1959), 307.

36. Fan Hong, ed., *Sport, Nationalism and Orientalism: The Asian Games* (Abingdon: Routledge, 2009), 5.

37. De Mello, *Portrait of Indian Sport*, 307.

38. *Times of India*, March 2, 1951.

39. Hong, *Sport, Nationalism and Orientalism*, 4.

40. *Indian Express*, March 5, 1951.

41. *Times of India*, March 5, 1951.

42. Ibid., March 9, 1951.

43. Ibid., July 25, 1952.

44. Ibid., July 24, 1952.

45. Ezekiel and Arumugam, *Great Indian Olympians*, 113.

46. Faisal Shariff, "We Don't Celebrate the True Heroes of India." Available at http://www.rediff.com/sports/2000/sep/13jhadha.htm (accessed November 1, 2014).

47. Suvam Pal, "Legacies, Halcyon Days and Thereafter: A Brief History of Tennis," in *Sport in South Asian Society: Past and Present*, ed. Boria Majumdar and J. A. Mangan (London: Routledge, 2005), 121.

48. De Mello, *Portrait of Indian Sport*, 320.

49. *Sydney Morning Herald*, March 7, 1935.

50. De Mello, *Portrait of Indian Sport*, 315.

51. *Sarasota [Fla.] Herald-Tribune*, May 3, 1954.

52. *Miami News*, May 10, 1954.

53. *Times of India*, June 20, 1954.

54. Ibid., June 9, 1954.

55. Ibid., May 14, 1954.

56. Ibid., June 21, 1954.

57. Ibid., July 20, 1954.

58. *The Statesman*, April 20, 1955.

59. *Times of India*, December 4, 1956.

60. Chand, *Goal!*

61. *Times of India*, November 29, 1956.

62. Ibid., November 28, 1956.

63. Ibid., December 2, 1956.

64. Laurie Schwab, *The Socceroos and Their Opponents* (Melbourne: Newspress, 1979). Available at http://www.ozfootball.net/museum/index.php/en/archive/84-1956-olympics (accessed November 1, 2014).

65. Novy Kapadia, "Rahim, Amal Dutta, P. K. and Nayeem: The Coaches Who Shaped Indian Football," *Football Studies* 5, no. 2 (October 2002): 41.

66. Chakraborty, *Shatabdir Shera Sailen Manna*, 89.

67. For details, see Majumdar and Mehta, *Olympics: The India Story*, 168–73.

68. Kapadia, "Rahim, Amal Dutta, P. K. and Nayeem," 41.

69. Chuni Goswami, *Khelte Khelte* (Calcutta: Ananda Publishers, 1982), 19.

70. Majumdar and Mehta, *Olympics: The India Story*, 172.

71. Kapadia, "Rahim, Amal Dutta, P. K. and Nayeem," 42.

72. Majumdar and Mehta, *Olympics: The India Story*, 111.

73. *Times of India*, September 6, 1960.

74. Ibid., September 10, 1960.

75. Ibid., September 11, 1960.

76. Ibid.

77. Interview with Milkha Singh, *Indian Express*, March 28, 2013. The exact words by Ayub Khan to Milkha were: "*Tum daude nahi, udhey ho* (You did not run, you flew)." See Milkha Singh (with Sonia Sanwalka), *The Race of My Life* (New Delhi: HarperCollins, 2013), 83.

78. *The Statesman*, October 24, 1964.

79. Ibid.

80. Ibid., October 27, 1964.

81. Jal Pardivala, "Asia at the Olympic Games," *Olympic Review* 34 (July/August 1970): 414.

82. *The Statesman*, November 1, 1968.

83. Ibid., October 26, 1968.

84. Majumdar and Mehta, *Olympics: The India Story*, 114.

85. *The Statesman*, October 26, 1968.

86. Ibid.

87. Rice, Wisden *on India*, 90.

88. *Times of India*, July 21, 1948.

89. Ibid., February 11, 1952

90. Ramachandra Guha, *A Corner of a Foreign Field* (London: Picador, 2002), 370.

91. Ibid., 377.

92. Ibid., 375.

93. Rice, Wisden *on India*, 107.

94. Guha, *A Corner of a Foreign Field*, 388.

95. Ibid., 384.

96. Ibid., 386.

97. Rice, Wisden *on India*, 116.

98. Guha, *A Corner of a Foreign Field*, 331.

99. David McMahon, *Wills Book of Excellence: Tennis* (Calcutta: Orient Longman, 1985), 78.

100. *Times of India*, August 22, 1921.

101. *Advertiser*, May 14, 1923.

102. Shreya Chakravertty, "The Great Indian Grass Hoppers," *Sports Illustrated India*, June 2011, 72.

103. *Times of India*, June 29, 1960.

104. Ibid., July 6, 1961.

105. Peter Ustinov, "Ustinov on Tennis," *Sports Illustrated*, June 23, 1969. Available at http://sportsillustrated.cnn.com/vault/article/magazine/MAG1082539/index.htm (accessed November 1, 2014).

106. Interview with author, July 1, 2011.

107. *Times of India*, August 1, 1956.

108. Ibid., December 10, 1954.

109. *Singapore Free Press*, June 26, 1946.

110. *Times of India*, January 31, 1953.

111. Ibid., May 9, 1954.

112. Ibid., February 1, 1953.

113. Ibid., March 1, 1953.

114. Vir Sanghvi, "Dara Singh Was the First Superhero." Available at http://
virsanghvi.com/Article-Details.aspx?key=813 (accessed November 1, 2014).

115. *Australian Women's Weekly*, February 29, 1956.

116. *Strait Times*, March 13, 1949.

117. *Times of India*, February 26, 1953.

118. Ibid., March 15, 1953.

119. Ibid., May 24, 1953.

120. Ibid., April 25, 1961.

121. Ibid., May 30, 1962.

122. Ibid., January 15, 1961.

123. Ibid., April 25, 1961.

124. Ibid., May 30, 1968.

125. *The Hindu*, August 14, 1960.

126. *Times of India*, April 14, 1955.

127. Ibid., April 4, 1968.

128. Ibid., May 27, 1968.

129. Ibid., November 20, 1933.

130. P. Lal, "Free-for-All," *Times of India*, March 17, 1954.

131. *Times of India*, May 19, 1970.

132. Ibid., May 27, 1964.

133. Roland Barthes, *Mythologies* (New York: Hill & Wang, 2012), 3.

134. Ibid., 4.

135. Avijit Ghosh, "The Original 'Mard,'" *Times of India*, November 16, 2008.

136. Barthes, *Mythologies*, 8.

137. Sanghvi, "Dara Singh Was the First Superhero."

138. John Arlott, ed., *The Oxford Companion to Sports and Games* (Oxford: Oxford University Press, 1975), 554.

139. Joseph Alter, "Kabaddi, A National Sport of India," in *Sport in South Asian Society: Past and Present*, ed. Boria Majumdar and J. A. Mangan (London: Routledge,
2005), 89.

140. *Times of India*, November 29, 1911.

141. Arlott, *The Oxford Companion to Sports and Games*, 556.

142. *Times of India*, November 30, 1937.

143. Ibid., February 23, 1951.

144. Arlott, *The Oxford Companion to Sports and Games*, 556.

145. *Times of India*, December 27, 1963.

146. Alter, "Kabaddi, A National Sport of India," 97.

147. *Times of India*, February 10, 1964.

148. Ibid., February 5, 1959.

149. Ibid., June 18, 1962.

150. Ibid., March 12, 1962.

151. Ibid., March 16, 1962.

152. M. C. Chagla, "Sport and Government," *XVIII Olympiad Tokyo 1964*, official souvenir program, Indian Olympic Association, 1964, 33.

153. Ibid., 34.

154. Ibid.

155. *Times of India*, August 30, 1962.

156. Ibid., August 12, 1967.

157. Rice, Wisden *on India*, 110.

158. Ibid., 111.

159. Guha, *A Corner of a Foreign Field*, 336–37.

160. Ibid., 123.

10. Domestic Sports

1. Ramachandra Guha, *The States of Indian Cricket: Anecdotal Histories* (New Delhi: Permanent Black, 2005), 21.

2. Ibid., 153.

3. Advertisement in *H.H. The Maharaja of Patiala's Australian XI vs Sind XI: Official Programme & Score Sheets* (1935).

4. Richard Cashman, *Patrons, Players and the Crowd* (Delhi: Orient Longman, 1981), 44.

5. Guha, *The States of Indian Cricket*, 137.

6. *Indian Cricket Almanac for 1947-48*, 165–68.

7. Boria Majumdar, *Twenty-Two Yards to Freedom: A Social History of Indian Cricket* (New Delhi: Penguin, 2004), 100.

8. John Arlott, *Indian Summer* (London: Longmans, 1947), 11.

9. For an account of Bombay cricket, see Sandeep Bamzai, *Guts and Glory: The Bombay Cricket Story* (New Delhi: Rupa Publications, 2002).

10. James Astill, *The Great Tamasha: Cricket, Corruption and the Turbulent Rise of Modern India* (London: Bloomsbury, 2013), 171.

11. S. Anand, *Brahmans & Cricket: Lagaan's Millennial Purana and Other Myths* (Chennai: Navayana, 2007), 55.

12. Cashman, *Patron, Players and the Crowd*, 102–3.

13. Ajit Wadekar, *My Cricketing Years* (Delhi: Vikas Publishing, 1973), 6.

14. Guha, *The States of Indian Cricket*, 161.

15. Guha, "The Stars of Kathiawar Cricket," November 30, 2013. Available at espncricinfo.com (accessed November 1, 2014).

16. Cashman, *Patron, Players and the Crowd*, 82.

17. Guha, *The States of Indian Cricket*, 226.

18. Ibid., 50.

19. Ibid., 54.

20. Ibid., 61.

21. Ibid., 62.

22. Ibid., 134.

23. *Times of India*, October 21, 1952.

24. Biswarup Sen, *Of the People: Essays on Indian Popular Culture* (San Francisco: Chronicle Books, 2006), 91–93.

25. There is a substantial literature in Bengali on the Calcutta football clubs. The pioneering work is by Rakhal Bhattacharya, or "RB," as he was known. His essays were collected by sports writer Sibram Kumar in one volume: Sibram Kumar, ed., *RB Rachita Kolkatar Football* (Calcutta: Prabhabati Prakasani, 2002). See also Ashok Bhattacharya, *Footballer Teen Pradhan* (Calcutta: Gyanthirtha, 1972); Shantipriya Bandopadhyay, *Cluber Naam Mohun Bagan* (Calcutta: New Bengal Press, 1979); and Rupak Saha, *Itihashe East Bengal* (Calcutta: Deep Prakashan, 2000).

26. *Amrita Bazar Patrika*, June 11, 1951.

27. For an analysis of football in Bengali films, see Sharmistha Gooptu, "Celluloid Soccer: The Peculiarities of Soccer in Bengali Cinema," *International Journal of the History of Sport* 22, no. 4 (July 2005): 689–98.

28. *The Statesman*, October 6, 1947.

29. David Goldblatt, *The Ball Is Round: A Global History of Soccer* (London: Penguin, 2007), 70–74.

30. *Amrita Bazar Patrika*, July 8, 1949.

31. Ibid., June 21, 1951.

32. *The Statesman*, July 17, 1957.

33. *Times of India*, October 13, 1948.

34. Interview with Ahmed Khan, June 28, 2011.

35. Novy Kapadia, "Triumphs and Disasters: The Story of Indian Football, 1889–2000," *Soccer & Society* 2, no. 2 (2001): 19.

36. Kumar Mukherjee, *The Story of Football* (New Delhi: Ministry of Information and Broadcasting, 2002), 105.

37. James Mills, "Colonialism, Christians and Sport: The Catholic Church and Football in Goa, 1883–1951," *Football Studies* 5, no. 2 (2002): 21.

38. Gulu Ezekiel and K. Arumugam, *Great Indian Olympians* (New Delhi: Field Hockey Publications, 2004), 129.

39. *Times of India*, October 12, 1953.

40. *The Economist*, March 17, 2012.

41. *Times of India*, October 31, 1952.

42. Manas Chakraborty, *Shatabdir Shera Sailen Manna* (Kolkata: Deep Prakashan, 2002), 56.

43. *Times of India*, January 19, 1955.

44. Chuni Goswami, *Khelte Khelte* (Calcutta: Ananda Publishers, 1982), 70. Goswami also writes that there were rumors that the famous Bollywood actor Dilip Kumar had personally escorted Fakhri all the way from England. Fakhri subsequently played for a second-division team in England. When last heard of, Fakhri had apparently become a bus conductor in Britain, his career cut short by injury. Manas Chakraborty, *Shatabdir Shera Sailen Manna* (Kolkata: Deep Prakashan, 2002), 90–91.

45. Interview with Arumainayagam, June 29, 2011.

46. K. Datta, "Our Soccer Colossus," *Times of India*, February 7, 1971.

47. Rob Hughes, "The Memories Are Forever. The Medals? Salable," *International New York Times*, November 12, 2014. Hughes writes that several members of the England team, which won the 1966 World Cup, have either sold their medals or put them up for sale. Also see Arthur Hopcraft, *The Football Man: People and Passions in Soccer* (London: Aurum, 2006), 39–48.

48. Interview with Goswami, June 20, 2011.

49. *Times of India*, March 18, 1936.

50. Interview with Leslie Claudius, June 22, 2011.

51. Trevor Vanderputt, *Hockey's Odyssey* (London: Athena, 2003), 44.

52. Interview with Gurbux Singh, June 21, 2011.

53. Trevor Vanderputt, *Hockey's Odyssey* (Twickenham: Athena, 2003), 25.

54. *The Statesman*, May 9, 1957.

55. J. Clement Vaz, *Profiles of Eminent Goans: Past and Present* (New Delhi: Concept Publishing, 1997), 323–36. For Leo Pinto's career, see Pat Sarte, "Olympian Leo Pinto," *Illustrated Weekly of India*, September 12, 1971.

56. *The Statesman*, May 4, 1955.

57. Vaz, *Profiles of Eminent Goans*, 326.

58. Interview with Gurbux Singh, June 21, 2011.

59. *Times of India*, January 9, 1954.

60. Vanderputt, *Hockey's Odyssey*, 37.

61. Ibid., 56–57.

62. Anthony de Mello, *Portrait of Indian Sport* (London: Macmillan, 1959), 3.

63. Steve Rushin, "Reign on the Wane," *Sports Illustrated*, July 22, 1996.

64. *The Statesman*, April 29, 1956.

65. Avijit Ghosh, "Memories of Another Day," *The Pioneer*, October 3, 1995.

66. Boria Majumdar and Nalin Mehta, *Olympics: The India Story* (New Delhi: HarperCollins, 2008), 257.

67. Ezekiel and Arumugam, *Great Indian Olympians*, 118.

68. Milkha Singh, with Sonia Sanwalka, *The Race of My Life: An Autobiography* (New Delhi: Rupa Publications, 2013), 23.

69. Ibid., 26.

70. Cashman, *Patron, Players and the Crowd*, 54.

71. Ibid., 65.

72. Ibid., 73.

73. *The Guardian*, July 29, 2006.

74. Siddharth Saxena, 'Who Was This Man?' *Times of India*, Crest ed., March 3, 2012.

75. *London Times*, October 5, 1981.

76. Moti Nandy, *Striker* (Calcutta: Ananda Publishers, 1973); Moti Nandy, *Stopper* (Calcutta: Ananda Publishers, 1974). The two novellas have been translated into English: Moti Nandy, *Striker, Stopper*, trans. Arunava Sinha (New Delhi: Hachette, 2010). *Striker* was also made into a movie with the footballers Shyam Thapa and Subhash Bhowmick having bit roles.

77. Surajit Sengupta, *Back Centre* (Calcutta: Sunny Publishers, 1986), 96.

11. 1971 and After

1. The chorus for the song composed by Relator went: "It was Gavaskar / De real master / Just like a wall / We couldn't out Gavaskar at all, not at all."

2. Martin Williamson, "India's Day of Glory," August 31, 2011, available at espncricinfo.com (accessed November 1, 2014).

3. *London Times*, August 25, 1971.

4. Sunil Gavaskar, *Sunny Days* (New Delhi: Rupa Publications, 2011), 77. When it was first published in 1976, *Sunny Days* sold out in three days, and by 1978, an estimated 30,000 copies of the book had sold. See Richard Cashman, *Patrons,*

Players and the Crowd (Delhi: Orient Longman, 1981), 152. The current edition of the book is the eleventh.

5. *Times of India,* August 25, 1971.

6. Ibid., August 26, 1971.

7. *Hindustan Times,* August 25, 1971.

8. Ibid., September 14, 1971.

9. Ramachandra Guha, *The States of Indian Cricket: Anecdotal Histories* (New Delhi: Permanent Black, 2005), 181.

10. Partab Ramchand, "Thirty Years After His Debut, Gavaksar's Legacy Endures," March 6, 2001. Available at espncricinfo.com (accessed November 1, 2014).

11. Satadru Sen, "How Gavaskar Killed Indian Football," *Football Studies* 5, no. 2 (2002): 27–37.

12. Ibid., 29.

13. Biswarup Sen, *Of the People: Essays on Indian Popular Culture* (San Francisco: Chronicle Books, 2006), 69.

14. M. L. Kapur, *The Romance of Hockey* (Ambala Cantt: M. L. Kapur, 1968), 135–38.

15. Cashman, *Patrons, Players and the Crowd,* 141.

16. Kausik Bandyopadhyay, *Scoring off the Field: Football Culture in Bengal* (London: Routledge, 2011), 254.

17. Cashman, *Patrons, Players and the Crowd,* 142.

18. Ramachandra Guha, *India After Gandhi* (London: Harper Perennial, 2008), 739.

19. Scyld Berry, *Cricket Wallah: With England in India and Sri Lanka, 1981* (Boston: Houghton Mifflin, 1982), 127.

20. Guha, *The States of Indian Cricket,* 193. Also see Mukul Kesavan, *Men in White: A Book of Cricket* (New Delhi: Penguin, 2010), xii–xiii.

21. Cashman, *Patron, Players and the Crowd,* 142.

22. Vasant Raiji, *Cricket Memories* (Bombay: Ernest Publishing, 2010), 77.

23. Arjun Appadurai, *Modernity at Large: Cultural Dimensions of Globalization* (Minneapolis: University of Minnesota Press, 1996), 100.

24. Ibid., 102. Also see Sankaran Krishna, "When Cricket Crackled," February 6, 2014, espncricinfo.com (accessed November 1, 2014).

25. Cashman, *Patron, Players and the Crowd,* 144.

26. Ibid., 148.

27. Ramachandra Guha, *A Corner of a Foreign Field* (London: Picador, 2002), 436.

28. Sujit Mukherjee, *Autobiography of an Unknown Cricketer* (New Delhi: Ravi Dayal Publisher, 1996), 143.

29. Cashman, *Patron, Players and the Crowd,* 151.

30. For details of the magazine's history, see Clayton Murzello, "25 Years On, We Still Miss *Sportsweek*," *Mid-Day*, January 30, 2014. Sunil Gavaskar briefly edited the magazine for a year before it folded in 1989.

31. For a tribute to Pataudi's inspirational leadership of the magazine, see Mudar Patherya, "A Man of Opposites," September 22, 2011. Available at espncricinfo .com (accessed November 1, 2014)

32. Cashman, *Patron, Players and the Crowd*, 155–57.

33. Guha, *A Corner of a Foreign Field*, 439–40.

34. Mukul Kesavan, "A Republican Prince," September 23, 2011. Available at espn cricinfo.com (accessed November 1, 2014).

35. Mike Brearley, "I Never Recovered," in *Pataudi: Nawab of Cricket*, ed. Suresh Menon (New Delhi: HarperCollins, 2013), 20.

36. *Times of India*, June 28, 1974.

37. Gavaskar, *Sunny Days*, 161.

38. *Times of India*, July 23, 1974.

39. Ibid., November 21, 1974.

40. Suresh Menon, *Bishan: Portrait of a Cricketer* (New Delhi: Penguin, 2011), 93.

41. *Times of India*, November 20, 1974.

42. Ibid., November 4, 1978.

43. *The Statesman*, November 22, 1978

44. Cashman, *Patron, Players and the Crowd*, 119.

45. Ibid., 121.

46. *The Statesman*, January 1, 1967.

47. Souvik Naha, "Politics in the Sport Press: Interrogating Representations of the 'Battle of Eden Gardens,' Calcutta 1967," *Sport in Society* 16, no. 9 (2013): 1120. See also Cashman, *Patron, Players and the Crowd*, 124–25.

48. Berry, *Cricket Wallah*, 112.

49. Alam Srinivas and T. R. Vivek, *IPL an Inside Story: Cricket and Commerce* (New Delhi: Roli, 2009), 26.

50. *H.H. The Maharaja of Patiala's Australian XI vs Sind XI: Official Programme & Score Sheets* (1935).

51. Cashman, *Patron, Players and the Crowd*, 133.

52. Ibid., 132.

53. Gavaskar, *Sunny Days*, 82. See also V. Ramnarayan, *Third Man: Recollections from a Life in Cricket* (Chennai: Westland, 2014).

54. Siddarth Ravindran, "A Madras Classic," September 1, 2013. Available at espncricinfo.com (accessed November 1, 2014).

55. Sujit Mukherjee, *An Indian Century* (Hyderabad: Orient Longman, 2002), 183.

56. Mario Rodrigues, "The Corporates and the Game: Football in India and the Conflicts of the 1990s," in *Soccer in South Asia: Empire, Nation, Diaspora*, ed. Paul Dimeo and James Mills (Abingdon: Routledge, 2013), 124.

57. *Times of India*, April 18, 1973.

58. Ibid., May 4, 1973.

59. Cashman, *Patron, Players and the Crowd*, 139.

60. Shubangi Kulkarni, "The History of Indian Women's Cricket," September 8, 2000. Available at espncricinfo.com (accessed November 1, 2014).

61. Avijit Ghosh, "Women's Cricket Will Outlive All of Us," *The Pioneer*, December 11, 1994.

62. Ibid.

63. Abhishek Purohit, "It's an Insult for Women's Cricket to Be Treated This Way," January 29, 2013. Available at espncricinfo.com (accessed November 1, 2014).

64. Mukul Kesavan, "A Man's Game," April 1, 2007. Available at espncricinfo.com (accessed November 1, 2014).

65. Amol Karhadkar, "Women's Game Not Ideal but That's Reality—Chopra," February 6, 2013. Available at espncricinfo.com (accessed November 1, 2014).

66. *Hindustan Times*, March 16, 1975.

67. *The Statesman*, July 12, 1976

68. Ibid., August 4, 1976.

69. Ibid., July 29, 1976

70. Ibid., July 28, 1976.

71. Ibid., August 2, 1976.

72. David McMahon, *Wills Book of Excellence: Tennis* (New Delhi: Stosius, 1985), 81–82.

73. Boria Majumdar and Nalin Mehta, *Olympics: The India Story* (New Delhi: HarperCollins, 2008), 196–97.

74. Dina Vakil, "Television: The Impending Explosion," *Times of India*, July 23, 1972.

75. Ibid.

76. *The Statesman*, November 26, 1982.

77. Majumdar and Mehta, *Olympics*, 201.

78. *The Statesman*, November 20, 1982.

79. Guha, *India After Gandhi*, 736.

80. Shyam Balasubramanian and Vijay Santhanam, *The Business of Cricket: The Story of Sports Marketing in India* (New Delhi: HarperCollins, 2011), 74.

81. *Times of India*, December 5, 1982.

82. Shekhar Gupta, "Hockey Just Isn't Cricket," *Indian Express*, September 7, 2002.

83. Majumdar and Mehta, *Olympics*, 205.

84. Gideon Haigh, *Spheres of Influence: Writings on Cricket and Its Discontents* (London: Simon & Schuster, 2011), 4.

85. N. K. P. Salve, *The Story of the Reliance Cup* (New Delhi: Vikas Publishing, 1987), 118–19.

86. Haigh, *Spheres of Influence*, 6.

87. Ibid., 8–9.

88. Ibid., 7.

89. Rahul Bhatia, "Before the Flood," *The Caravan*, February 2012.

90. Ibid.

91. Appadurai, *Modernity at Large*, 101.

92. Salve, *The Story of the Reliance Cup*, 124–25.

93. Balasubramanian and Santhanam, *The Business of Cricket*, 17.

94. Bhatia, "Before the Flood."

95. Archna Shukla, "Why Everyone Wants a Slice of the BCCI Pie," *Indian Express*, September 4, 2011.

96. Tariq Engineer, "Star TV Bags Rights for Indian Cricket," April 2, 2012. Available at espncricinfo.com (accessed November 1, 2014).

97. Haigh, *Spheres of Influence*, 107.

98. Chris Smith, "Ms. Dhoni, Sachin Tendulkar Lead the World's Highest-Paid Cricketers," *Forbes*, July 26, 2012. Dhoni's earnings were, however, much lower than the world's highest-paid athletes, who in 2013 were led by golfer Tiger Woods, with $78.1 million. Dhoni was a respectable sixteenth on the list, with $31.5 million in earnings. See Kurt Badenhausen, "Tiger Is Back as the Top-Paid Sports Star," *Forbes*, June 5, 2013.

99. K. R. Guruprasad, *Going Places: India's Small-Town Cricket Heroes* (New Delhi: Penguin, 2011), 3–4.

100. Ibid., xxi.

101. James Astill, *The Great Tamasha: Cricket, Corruption, and the Turbulent Rise of Modern India* (London: Bloomsbury, 2013), 182.

102. Ibid., xxvi.

103. Siddharth Mongia and Amol Karhadkar, "The Mumbai That Made Tendulkar," November 13, 2013. Available at espncricinfo.com (accessed November 1, 2014).

104. Much has been written on Tendulkar. For his early days as a cricketer, see Vaibhav Purandare, *Sachin Tendulkar: A Definitive Biography* (New Delhi: Roli, 2011). For an anthology of writings on Tendulkar, see Espncricinfo, *Sachin*

Tendulkar: The Man Cricket Loved Back (New Delhi: Penguin, 2014). More recently, Tendulkar's autobiography has been published: Sachin Tendulkar, *Playing It My Way* (New Delhi: Hachette, 2014).

105. Berry, *Cricket Wallah*, 107.

106. One of the most trenchant critics of IPL is Ramachandra Guha. See, for example, Ramachandra Guha, "Smash-and-Grab Crony League," *The Hindu*, May 25, 2012. Others, such as celebrated cricket writer Peter Roebuck, were very positive about the IPL. See Peter Roebuck, "Four Thumbs Up," May 1, 2008. Available at espncricinfo.com (accessed November 1, 2014).

107. Haigh, *Spheres of Influence*, 29.

108. Samanth Subramanian, "The Confidence Man," *Caravan*, March 1, 2011. For an insight into Modi's methods and thinking, also see Astill, *The Great Tamasha*, chap. 7.

109. Srinivas and Vivek, *IPL an Inside Story*, 61.

110. Sharda Ugra and Tariq Engineer, "Part Cricket, Part Entertainment, Part Comfort Food," April 5, 2012. Available at espncricinfo.com (accessed November 1, 2014).

111. Krishna Gopalan, "Looks Good, but Could Be a Sticky Wicket," *Outlook Business*, April 13, 2013. The average television ratings for the IPL fell from a peak of 4.7 in 2008 to 3.6 in 2012.

112. Haigh, *Spheres of Influence*, 57.

113. Bose, *The Magic of Indian Cricket*, 86.

114. Srinivas and Vivek, *IPL an Inside Story*, 9.

115. Samir Chopra, *Brave New Pitch: The Evolution of Modern Cricket* (New Delhi: HarperCollins, 2012), 12.

116. Ramachandra Guha, "The Serpent in the Garden," June 1, 2013. Available at espncricinfo.com (accessed November 1, 2014).

117. Ashis Nandy, *The Tao of Cricket: On Games of Destiny and the Destiny of Games* (Oxford: Oxford University Press, 2001), 1.

118. Ibid., 21.

119. Guha, *The States of Indian Cricket*, 8.

120. Guha, *A Corner of a Foreign Field*, 340.

121. Nandy, *The Tao of Cricket*, 46.

122. Bose, *The Magic of Indian Cricket*, 86.

123. Nandy, *The Tao of Cricket*, 48.

124. Appadurai, *Modernity at Large*, 102. See Soumya Bhattacharya, *All That You Can't Leave Behind: Why We Can Never Do Without Cricket* (New Delhi: Penguin, 2011), 20.

125. Ibid., 111.

126. Ibid., 109.

127. Rahul Bhattacharya, *Pundits from Pakistan: On Tour with India, 2003–2004* (London: Picador, 2005), 169.

128. Mike Marqusee, "War Minus the Shooting," *The Guardian*, March 10, 2004.

129. *Times of India*, November 21, 1978.

130. *The Statesman*, November 14, 1978.

131. *Times of India*, February 23, 1987.

132. Bhattacharya, *Pundits from Pakistan*, 24.

133. Shahryar Khan, *Cricket: A Bridge for Peace* (Oxford: Oxford University Press, 2004), 187.

134. Bhattacharya, *Pundits from Pakistan*, 293.

135. Neville Cardus, *Cricket* (London: Longmans Green, 1930), 7.

136. Bhattacharya, *Pundits from Pakistan*, xi.

12. Life Beyond Cricket

1. Ashis Nandy, *The Tao of Cricket: On Games of Destiny and the Destiny of Games* (Oxford: Oxford University Press, 2001), 2.

2. Max Fisher, "Neither the Will nor the Cash: Why India Wins So Few Olympic Medals," *The Atlantic*, August 2012. Also see Margherita Stancati, "India's Medal Count Is Worse Than It Looks," *Wall Street Journal*, August 13, 2012.

3. Simon Kuper and Stefan Szymanski, *Soccernomics* (New York: Nation Books, 2010), 289.

4. Ibid., 256.

5. Anirudh Krishna and Eric Haglund, "Why Do Some Countries Win More Olympic Medals? Lessons for Social Mobility and Poverty Reduction," *Economic and Political Weekly*, July 12, 2008.

6. Goldman Sachs, *The Olympics and Economics 2012*. Available at http://www.goldmansachs.com/our-thinking/archive/archive-pdfs/olympics-and-economics.pdf (accessed November 1, 2014).

7. Susan Brownell, *Beijing Games: What the Olympics Means to China* (Lanham, Md.: Rowman & Littlefield, 2008), 19.

8. Jonathan Kolatch, *Sports, Politics and Ideology in China* (New York: Jonathan David, 1972), 80.

9. Susan Brownell, *Training the Body for China* (Chicago: University of Chicago Press, 1995), 56.

10. Hannah Beech, "Crazy for Gold," *Time*, June 30–July 7, 2009.

11. Lu Zhouxiang and Fan Hong, "Sport and Nationalism in China," *Panorama: Insights Into Asian and European Affairs* 1 (2014): 35.

12. Victor D. Cha, *Beyond the Final Score: The Politics of Sport in Asia* (New York: Columbia University Press, 2009), 48.

13. See Adharanand Finn, *Running with the Kenyans: Discovering the Secrets of the Fastest People on Earth* (New York: Ballantine Books, 2013); and Brook Larmer, "Fast Living," *Time*, June 30–July 7, 2009.

14. *Times of India*, July 15, 1956.

15. Milkha Singh, *The Race of My Life: An Autobiography* (New Delhi: Rupa Publications, 2013) 141.

16. Siddharth Saxena, "Spoilsports," *Times of India*, Crest ed., May 1, 2010.

17. Shekhar Gupta, "Athletes Can't Run," *Indian Express*, October 23, 2010.

18. Vinayak Padmadeo, "One Step Forward, Two Steps Back," *Indian Express*, September 4, 2011.

19. http://yas.nic.in/writereaddata/mainlinkFile/File918.pdf (accessed November 1, 2014).

20. *The Statesman*, December 5, 1982.

21. Robin Jeffrey, *Politics, Women and Well-Being: How Kerala Became "a Model"* (New Delhi: Oxford University Press, 2011), 225.

22. Lokesh Sharma, *Golden Girl: The Autobiography of P. T. Usha* (New Delhi: Penguin, 1987), 26.

23. Amarnath K. Menon, "Queens of the Field," *India Today*, August 16–31, 1981.

24. *Times of India*, August 10, 1984.

25. Amarnath K. Menon, "The Gold Rush," *India Today*, October 31, 1985.

26. Sreedhar Pillai, "Idol Bashing Time," *India Today*, December 15, 1988.

27. Sharma, *Golden Girl*, 60.

28. Leslie Xavier, "Dangal and the Dough," *Sports Illustrated India*, December 2012.

29. Joseph Alter, *The Wrestler's Body: Identity and Ideology in North India* (Berkeley: University of California Press, 1992), 183.

30. Jonathan Selvaraj and Vinayak Padmadeo, "Gladiators in the Mud," *Indian Express*, March 10, 2013.

31. P. Sainath, "Wrestling with the Rural Economy," *The Hindu*, October 30, 2013.

32. Leslie Xavier, "The Mat Looks Slippery," *Sports Illustrated India*, December 2012.

33. Alter, *The Wrestler's Body*, 46.

34. Norbert Peabody, "Disciplining the Body, Disciplining the Body-Politic: Physical Culture and Social Violence Among North Indian Wrestlers," *Comparative Studies in Society and History* 51, no. 2 (2009): 378.

35. Alter, *The Wrestler's Body*, 261–63.

36. Peabody, "Disciplining the Body, Disciplining the Body-Politic," 375.

37. Dipti Jain, "Sushil's Brand New Appeal," *Times of India, Crest* ed., August 25, 2012.

38. Shiv Visvanathan, "Desi Ghee and Quietly Global," *Times of India, Crest* ed., August 25, 2012.

39. Alter, *The Wrestler's Body*, 67.

40. Xavier, "The Mat Looks Slippery."

41. Shamya Dasgupta, *Bhiwani Junction: The Untold Story of Boxing in India* (Noida: HarperCollins India, 2012), 19.

42. Mihir Vasavda, "Raging Bull to Million Dollar Boy," *Indian Express*, March 24, 2013.

43. Bhupendra Yadav, "Why Haryana Is a Mine for Medals," *Times of India*, October 31, 2010.

44. Bibek Debroy, "Sporting Lessons," *Indian Express*, October 18, 2010.

45. Rahul Bhattacharya, "India's Shot at Gold," *Intelligent Life*, July/August 2012.

46. See M. C. Mary Kom, *Unbreakable: An Autobiography* (New Delhi: HarperCollins, 2013).

47. Ibid., 36–38.

48. Ibid., 71–72.

49. Dasgupta, *Bhiwani Junction*, 158.

50. Ibid., 174.

51. Siddharth Saxena, "Candles in the Wind," *Times of India, Crest* ed., November 27, 2010.

52. *Times of India*, July 12, 1967.

53. Abhinav Bindra, with Rohit Brijnath, *A Shot at History: My Obsessive Journey to Olympic Gold* (New Delhi: HarperCollins, 2011), 196.

54. Ibid., 9.

55. Ibid., 178.

56. Ibid., 203.

57. Rudraneil Sengupta, "Last Tee-Off," *The Mint*, December 1, 2010.

58. Shamik Chakrabarty, "The Girl with the Golden Arrow," *Indian Express*, May 13, 2012.

59. Sanjay Sharma and Shachi S. Sharma, *Pulella Gopi Chand: The World Beneath His Feet* (New Delhi: Rupa Publications, 2011), 32.

60. *Times of India*, May 25, 1978.

61. Ibid., October 4, 1990.

62. Ibid., December 26, 1993.

63. John Arlott, ed., *The Oxford Companion to World Sports and Games* (New York: Oxford University Press, 1975), 556.

64. Rhys F, "Big Dreams for Kabaddi," *Times of India*, September 3, 1997. See also Shivani Naik, "Kabaddi 2.0," *Indian Express*, March 23, 2014.

65. Joseph S. Alter, "Kabaddi, a National Sport of India: The Internationalism of Nationalism and the Foreignness of Indianness," in *Getting Into the Game: The Anthropology of Sport*, ed. Noel Dyke (Oxford: Berg, 2000), 100.

66. Nalin Mehta, "And We Played Cricket Too," *Times of India*, December 28, 2014.

67. *International Herald Tribune*, February 13, 2013.

68. Ibid., September 10, 2013.

69. Joseph Alter, foreword to *Marrow of the Nation: A History of Sport and Physical Culture in Republican China*, by Andrew D. Morris (Berkeley: University of California Press, 2004), xix–xx. For the evolution of *wushu*, see Morris, *Marrow of the Nation*, chap. 7.

70. Internationally known yoga guru Bikram Choudhury and his wife, Rajshree Choudhury, are proponents of yoga competitions. See Tamara Abraham, "That's Not Very Zen! The Rise of the Yoga Competition," *Daily Mail*, January 1, 2013.

71. http://i.yogasportsfederation.org/about-iysf/overview/ (accessed November 1, 2014).

72. *Hindustan Times*, November 15, 2010.

73. "Not Cricket," *The Economist*, May 3, 2012.

74. *Indian Express*, December 17, 2012.

75. Karthik Krishnaswamy, "Leagues of Their Own," *Indian Express*, June 17, 2011.

76. *Indian Express*, July 22, 2013.

77. Mihir Vasavda, "Wake Up, Smell Hockey," *Indian Express*, July 7, 2013.

78. *Times of India*, December 1, 1996.

79. Mario Rodrigues, "The Corporates and the Game: Football in India and the Conflicts of the 1990s," *Soccer and Society* 2, no. 2 (2001): 107–8.

80. Sumit Mitra, "Club in Confusion," *India Today*, May 13, 2002.

81. Rodrigues, "The Corporates and the Game," 108.

82. *Times of India*, June 1, 1997.

83. Ibid., August 22, 1999.

84. Rodrigues, "The Corporates and the Game," 110.

85. Stanislaus D'Souza, "On the Front Foot," *Times of India*, Crest ed., January 9, 2010.

86. Shamik Bag, "Bend It Like Ganguly," *MintAsia*, November 14–20, 2014.

87. Rodrigues, "The Corporates and the Game," 123.

88. Bag, "Bend It Like Ganguly."

89. Ishita Russell, "Here's the Kicker," *Mint*, January 13, 2010.

90. Kunal Majgaonkar, "International Khiladi," *Times of India, Crest* ed., April 21, 2012.

91. Mihir Vasavda, "Indian Players to Earn More Than Foreign Imports in Indian Super League," *Indian Express*, 21 August 21, 2014.

92. Rajdeep Sardesai, "A Level-Playing Field," *Hindustan Times*, October 22, 2010.

93. Rudraneil Sengupta, "Women on Top," *The Mint*, October 13, 2010.

94. Mihir Vasavda, "The Money Game," *Indian Express*, March 3, 2013.

95. Minxin Pei, "Where Winning Is Everything," *Indian Express*, August 9, 2012.

96. Bhattacharya, "India's Shot at Gold."

97. Shivani Naik, "The Golden Team," *Indian Express*, May 15, 2011.

98. *Indian Express*, March 12, 2014.

99. Susanne Hoeber Rudolph, "All the Raj in Jaipur," *Polo*, September 1992.

100. Cordelia Jenkins, "Horse Power," *The Mint*, January 30, 2012.

101. *Economic Times*, January 5, 2013.

102. Simon Barnes, *The Meaning of Sport* (London: Short Books, 2006), 359.

103. Nandy, *The Tao of Cricket*, 118.

INDEX

Page numbers in *italics* signify illustrations.